Princeton Architectural Press/ New York

instrumental form
designs for words, buildings, machines
wes jones

Copyright ©1998 by Wes Jones
All rights reserved

No part of this book may be used or reproduced in any manner without written permission from the publisher except in the context of reviews
02 01 00 99 98 5 4 3 2 1
Printed and bound in Hong Kong

Published by Princeton Architectural Press
37 East 7th Street, New York, New York 10003
for a free catalog: 1/800/722-6657 or www.papress.com

Book Layout and Production: Doug Jackson
Book Project Team: Hendra Bong, Karin Hauke, Jim Rhee, Jean Young Jones

Special thanks to Therese Kelly, Project Editor, and Eugenia Bell, Caroline Green, Clare Jacobson, Mark Lamster, Annie Nitschke, and Sara Stemen of Princeton Architectural Press—Kevin C. Lippert, Publisher

Library of Congress Cataloging-in-Publication Data

Instrumental form: (boss architecture): words buildings machines,
   Jones, Partners: Architecture/ Wes Jones, ed.
      p.   cm.
   ISBN 1-56898-115-5 (pbk.: alk. paper)
   1. Jones, Partners: Architecture. 2. Architectural practice, International 3. Architecture, Modern—20th century. I. Jones, Wes, 1958- II. Title: Boss architecture.
NA737.J65A4   1998
720'.92'2—DC21   97-10653
                                                            CIP

Collaborators: Sven Wächli, Jill Ingram, Michael Gough, Wes Jones, Jim Rhee, Doug Jackson, Bob Shepherd, Hendra Bong, Bernard Chang, Karin Hauke, Tom Blanchard, Ted Arleo, Stephane Francois, Pauline Sukalapalong, Rick Wilcox, Jean Young Jones, James Dignam, Nancy Young, Ute Knippenberger, Minh Nguyen, Ladd Woodland, Dwight Ashdown, Paul Holt, Susan Michael, Chris Palumbo, Glenn Butler, Mark Sparrowhawk, Andrew Humperson, Peter Pfau, Karen Mar, Barrett Schumaker, Dana Barbera, Scott Laidlaw, Todd Schram, Craig Downie, Tony Duncan, Craig Schultz, Kekoa Charlot, Tom Goffigan, Michael Roberts, Scott Arford, Douglas Gauthier, Tony Lao, Doug Mar, Jeff Logan, John Gil, Larry Scarpa, Mark Hinshaw, David Yama, Russell Sherman, James McKissick, Doug Hoffelt, David Willet, Peter Kreuthmeier, Laurie Moore Uebel, Rich Curl, Ken Bishop, Lourdes Garcia, James Herbert, Tim Contreras, Jim Park, Dana Sottile, David Gadarian, Pam Gates, Jane Chun, Fiona Murland, Liz Lorenz, Melissa Bischoff, Chris Downey

1982-84

Robotics Research and Development   **8**
Quincy Street Gates   **8**

California Unité   **9**

Recliner Couch   **10**
Samuel P. Harn Museum of Art   **10**
Pacific Center for the Media Arts   **11**

Housing for the Homeless   **11**
Vietnam Veterans Memorial   **12**
Times Square   **13**

Rome Academy Installation   **14**
The Hut and the Machine
Primitive Huts   **15**

1984-86

Right Away Redy-Mix I	14	**Astronauts Memorial**	24
Altman & Manley Advertising	16	**Right Away Redy-Mix II**	25
Either/ORigin		The Problem	
480 Green Street Office	17	**Columbus Convention Center**	26
Zaccho Dance Theater	17	**Dining Table**	27
Tract House	18	**Conference Table**	27
Columbia Beasts	19	Model Display Base	
Lawn Chair	20	**Tarantino Residence**	28
Overlake Sector Light Industrial Park	21	**U.S. Pavilion/Expo '92**	29
Berkeley Gate		**Paramount Pictures Film and Tape Archive**	30
Aphorisms		That Architecture is a Language	
Alcatraz Island Interpretive Center	22	**Details Display Mechanisms**	31
Alcatraz		Ryan World Headquarters	
California Lifeguard Tower	23	**AOKI Retail**	32

1987-91

1992-93

Technology as an Architectural Language
Rabin Residence 32
House for a Corporate Family 33
Olympic West
Rancho Mirage Civic Center
West Hollywood Civic Center
Affordable House
Hermit Crab House 34
Lowe Development 34
Confluence Point I 35
West Coast Gateway
Wood Chair
New Akropolis Museum 36

Chaise Lounge 37
Oakville Ranch Winery 37
Soup's Up
Futon 38
San Jose Repertory Theater 38
Rene Dubois Bioshelter 39
Diamond Ranch School 39
Marianna Kistler Beach Art Museum 40
Notes Re:constitution
Marden Water Treatment Plant 40
Boss Architecture

Clocktower Loft Remodel
01 **Decon recon** 41
02 **Lake Superior Freshwater Aquarium** 49
03 **UCLA Chiller Plant/ Cogeneration Facility** 65

04	**Notes on the Boss**	89
05	**Cardiff Bay Opera House**	95
06	**Hot Rod**	109
	Edenscape Masterplan	
	Notes INre:mediation	
	Coffee Table	
	Air Force Memorial	
07	**Head Start Childcare Facility**	113
08	**High Sierras Cabins**	129
09	**Yokohama International Port Terminal**	175
	The Mech in 'tecture	

10	**Korean American Museum of Art**	193	16 **Donner Lake Cabins** 273
	Arch for Tech		17 **Zimmer Stair** 305
	Stud		18 **General Instruments Corporate Campus** 321
11	**Taichung City Civic Center**	209	19 **Armani Exchange** 337
	Alliance Development Warehouses		20 **Shanghai North Bund Plaza** 353
12	**American Medical Informatics Center**	225	21 **Confluence Point Bridges** 369
	Is This Architecture?		**and Ranger Station**
13	**Cathedral City Civic Center**	241	22 **Wired: Inspired, Tired—or Mired?** 387
	Why I Became an Architect		I8*Noodles Restaurant
14	**Stanford University Modular Shelters**	255	C-1 Professional Training Center
15	**The Fork**	269	Illustration Credits 398

82

Robotics Research and Development Facility
Boston, MA

Quincy Street Gates
Harvard University
Cambridge, MA

design competition

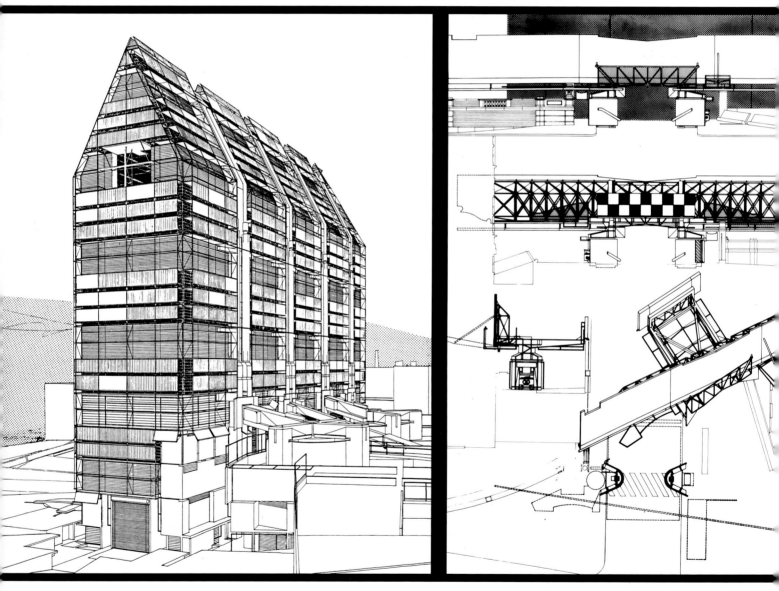

DR:	Decon recon	41
E/O:	Either/ ORigin	276
F:	The Fork	269
HR:	Hot Rod	109
MIT:	The Mech in 'tecture	351
NIRM:	Notes, INre:mediation	292
NOB:	Notes on the Boss	89
NRO:	Notes re: Orthodoxy/ Constitution	73
ON:	Open Notes	9
ONO:	Openness	9
ONE:	Enframing	140
ONM:	Myth	236
ONHR:	Hyper Reality	322
TAL:	Technology as an Architectural Language	120
WDIM:	What Does It Mean?	184
WITM:	Wired: Inspired, Tired—or Mired?	387

California Unité
Manhattan Beach, CA

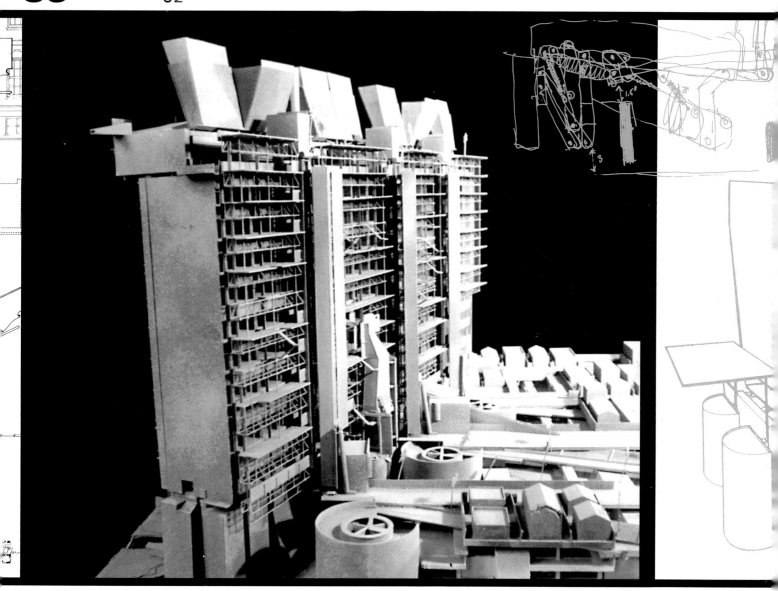

Open Notes

1. Abstract: Openness
The contemporary critical scene can be characterized by a generalized interest in the theme of openness, reflecting a cultural trend that has been emerging slowly since the enlightenment. As an inherently conservative practice, architecture's relation to this emergence has been roman retarditaire, but recent appropriations of the-

ory from outside the discipline have led the critical establishment to an appreciation of the open textuality of experience and repressed textual reality of production. A reorientation of critical attention has ensued—from a traditional concern with the author's attempts to free the work within this uncontrollable web of relation and reference, to the reader's role as the beneficiary of this empowering hermeneuticism. The conflict between these two interests remains, however, since both authors and

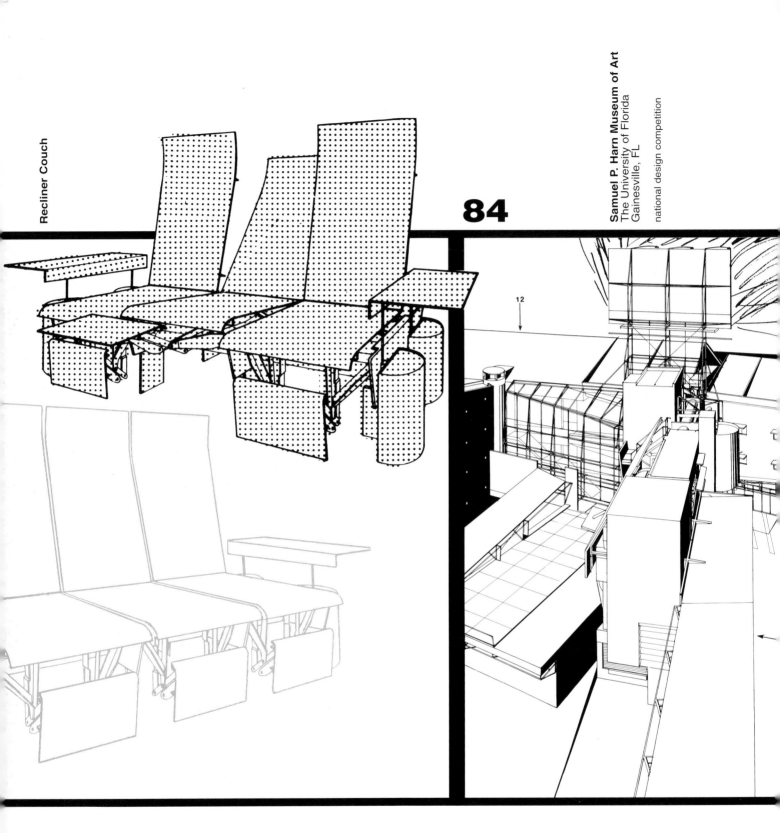

readers continue to practice; the alienating effects of the debate has often served to diminish the openness generally sought. Openness is more usefully understood at an instrumental level, where effectiveness may be measured, though this also is not devoid of conflict or paradox. Speculation about the possibilities for openness within the instrumental, particularly in relation to the machine, grow naturally from their conjunction, but ultimately the machine must view a program of openness as absurd. If not as a declared program or intention, then perhaps openness may serve the instrumental more obliquely, as a subsystem of the machine or as a lubricant. In fact, this can be achieved, with significant consequences. To the machine, expression involves such a step toward openness from efficiency; the machine can uniquely understand and benefit from its contribution. Using expression as the lever, openness can be introduced to the instrumental in such a way that the perfor-

Pacific Center for the Media Arts
Hawaii Loa College
Honolulu, HI
national design competition

85

Housing for the Homeless
New York, NY

mance of affect is exchanged for the signification of effects. In this exchange, the machine's relation to textuality and its assumptions of autonomy are clarified and a claim made for its ability to serve both.

2. The openness that is such an important part of today's self-image seems counter to a traditional understanding of architecture—or a traditional understanding of anything for that matter.[1] Tradition is received. It is determined already, historically "open" only to historiciz-

ing. It is by definition and habit conservative; openness, on the other hand, names the possibility of everything else. It is logically anti-conservative. If Architecture determines (fixes) and then holds up (props up), or back, an enduring, endearing, exemplar of the way things are felt to be, Architecture is inherently conservative. The call for openness expressing the way things are felt they should be today brings to the fore the contradiction inherent in the assumption of an enduring expression of the zeit-

Vietnam Veterans Memorial
New York, NY
national design competition

NIRM 3

geist. Such expression can only be zeitful or geistlike for awhile. After all, zeit flies, and the geist it leaves behind is effective only as a reminder of that transience. The building, meanwhile, even as Architecture, is never merely a ghost. Though it remains always behind—as the concretized, unmoving, and thus closed shell of the original intention—the building is always a palpable presence. Is it possible then to actively design an open architecture? The possibility of asking this question is itself evidence of the change its answer foretells.

3. As Architecture reflects the society that pays for it, it has mirrored society's response to the historical call for openness. Just as Architecture came into being by freeing itself from technical necessity, by stating a difference from mere building, so it has gradually freed itself from cultural necessity—from church and state, and from the private institutions that had claimed it. The measure of this freedom today could also be seen as the degree to

Times Square
New York, NY

which it has become superfluous. This process has been gradual, but the "gains" have been necessarily irrevocable and permanent. Each advance alters the conditions of reconsideration, decreasing the possibility it might fit back in the box. The first step toward openness, taken even before the bonds of the church were eased, might have been the brief challenge to seriousness offered by the first renaissance mannerist period. Frederik Wolfflin has spoken of the baroque and late Gothic of Northern Europe that followed specifically in terms of its increased "openness."[2] As society widened its horizons, and cultural constraints were loosened through colonial adventures, and as technology increased the range of tools available, architecture took advantage, and in a flood of developments broadened its own range. A proliferation of styles and influences, previously limited and fixed by history, propriety and technique, signaled a rush toward the open, and a newfound feel for relativity began to

Right Away Redy-Mix I
Oakland, CA

Rome Academy Installation
American Academy
Rome, Italy

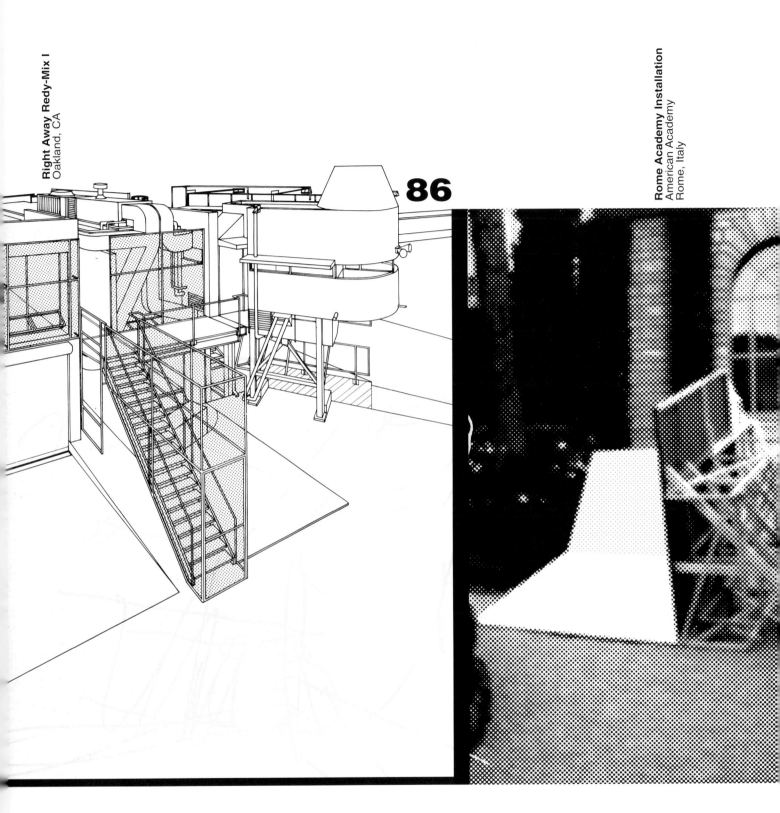

emerge.

4. Though ostensibly intolerant to this sort of openness—or at least to its lack of rigor (seriousness) and propriety—the modern movement heralded an even greater advance toward openness in general. In the works of its revolutionary masters, the architectural was "opened" from ideality to the common, mirroring society's revolutionary trends towards a flattened culture of bourgeois mythification. Rather than passively reflecting these changes, though, the avant-garde Modern Movement aspired to drive them.

5. The genius of the heroes of the modern movement was to turn this theme of the common and mundane to positive account. By elevating it into a revolutionary expression of the spirit of the age, the modern movement raised it to a level appropriate to even traditional expectations for architecture. By drawing it into form as an expression of the depth or richness latent in the experi-

ence of Everyman, modernism introduced architecture to the dignity possible there. The bourgeois interpretation of this spirit kept architecture from derailing entirely. The three major figures of twentieth-century architecture, Le Corbusier, Frank Lloyd Wright and Ludwig Mies van der Rohe, grounded their contributions in a revolutionary idealization of the everyday. Le Corbusier's introduction of *beton brute* after the Second World War can only be partially explained by the post-war steel shortage—and that explanation does not account for the continuing enthusiasm Corbu felt for this material long after steel became more readily available. He reveled in the richness of the material, the sheer crudity of it, and the way it preserved the record of the labor it literally embodied. He saw it as a celebration of the earthy, the common made uncommonly dignified as enduring form. The apparent distance between this and his earlier veneration of the abstract machine aesthetic of factory-produced "object-types" is

Altman & Manley Advertising
San Francisco, CA

480 Green Street Office
San Francisco, CA

only one of expression, since the "factory-produced" imagery of this earlier work followed the same "revolutionary" preference for the common in contrast to the elitist work of the academy.

6. Before Corbu, though, and cited by all the revolutionary modernists as a great influence, was Wright. His romance with the non-elitist ideal of prairie democracy reached its best expression in the Usonian houses, which deliberately attempted to broaden the base of architecture by opening it to a lowest common denominator of universal suburban home ownership. Mies van der Rohe was operating in the prairie as well, at the same time the Usonian houses were reaching their peak production; his own "Americanization" has been well-documented. The change from the elitist luxury of his European work, exemplified in the Tugendhat house or Barcelona Pavilion, to the ideal pragmatism of his Chicago work, such as the remarkably inexpensive build-

Zaccho Dance Theater
San Francisco, CA

ings at IIT, marked a real shift from architecture to Baukunst with the emphasis on the "bau." The "Baukunst" that seemed precious in Europe found in America an industry standing ready to prove its real implications and worth, ready to champion the new ideal of "reasonableness" it seemed to represent in the New World. Mies's work in particular demonstrated that the Masters' interest in the low brow did not necessarily preclude the high: an interest in maintaining the highest standards for architecture, or communicating the loftiest sentiments was not considered incompatible if it were dictated by the spirit of the age. Architecture was still seen as transcendent, however low its search for inspiration might take it. With the transcendent irony of Robert Venturi's work, this back door into the museum was mythified and drained of its political/social content (however broadly it might have been conceived previously). The survival of Architecture's elitist expectations in even

17

Tract House
Manhattan Beach, CA

the most revolutionary, banal expressions was exposed in this work and permanently reduced to accord with the facticity of these sources. Architecture's sights were thus lowered to the point where it could entertain any influence, and become open to any inspiration. **NRO 4 NOB 4**

7. The history of the avant garde, which is the history of the modern movement, of which Venturi's contribution could be seen as the culmination, at least before the historicist apocalypso, demonstrates the difficulty of leading from the front when the battle is all around. The eternally recurrent emergence of an avant garde is always the expression of a call for greater openness, but what does this forecast for the present "opening" when the relationship to the rest of society implied by its "avant"ness is already *retarditaire*? Knowing the fact about its inevitable sell-out, and also knowing that the point of establishment comes much sooner (at least every 15 minutes, according to Andy Warhol's already outdated timetable), the

Installed Mechanism
Columbia University
New York, NY

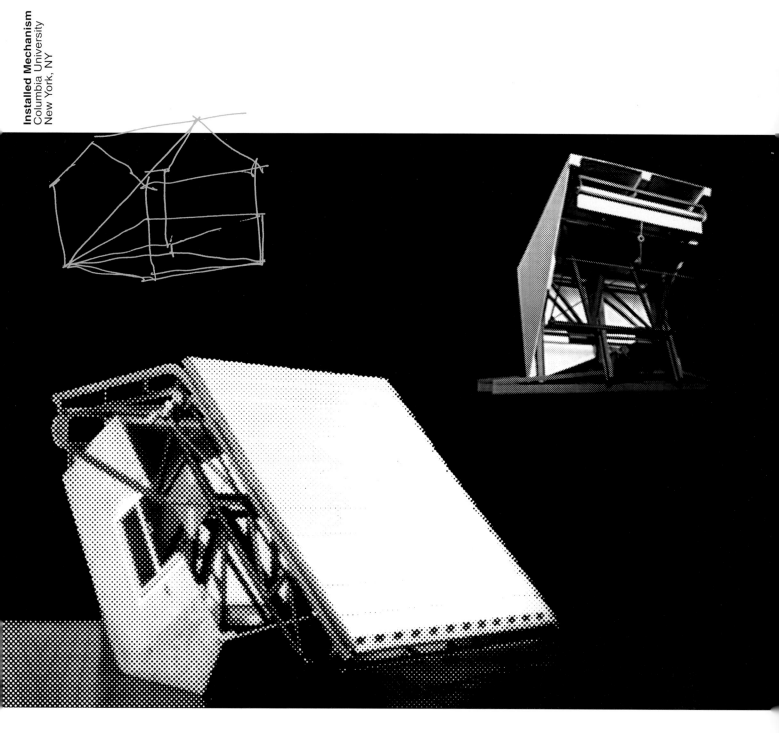

avant garde cannot summon the righteous energy to question its own commodification, much less to lead. And besides: where? It is infected with society's sense of irony that, applied to its own situation, becomes the cynicism that prevents it from taking it own chances seriously. The culture is already too open to be very impressed by the avant garde's challenge to greater openness.

8. The stridency of architectural programs that value novelty above all else, programs like "undecidability" or "weakness," or "deconstructivism,"[3] can be seen in this light as the cost of forcing the doors still more open. In order to stand out within the general trend to pluralism these programs are put in the position of advocating an extreme and paradoxically, but necessarily, intolerant program of openness; this work is forced to become militant and alienating to assert and maintain its fragile edge. This is tragic; in a cultural context already open enough to anticipate and short-circuit much of this for-

Lawn Chair
Outdoor Chair Show
Sausalito, CA

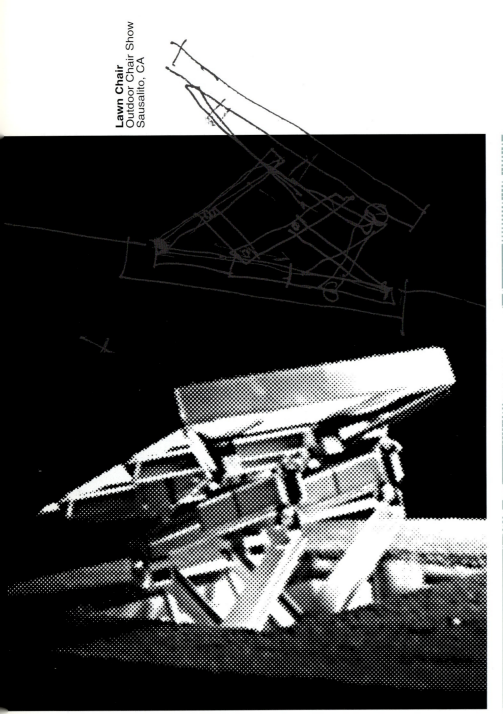

DR 10

malism, the unassailable logic of its critique encourages the sort of absurd conclusions that get airtime. The more critical work proposes to build the aporias the more pragmatic has avoided, and has backed itself into corners where anything less is a cop-out. It is this situation that prompts the call for reasonableness represented by the work shown here. It is a call to open up openness. A call for a greater inclusiveness, one that admits a role for discipline, for the legibility of intention and a nuanced authorial guidance.

9. The general tendency toward valuing "openness" within architecture, announced in the emphatic adoption of a generalized "liberation" theme, has borrowed its themes and strategies in no small part from philosophy and literary criticism, from Martin Heidegger to Gilles Deleuze. Architecture's access to this thought has been uneven, and its arrival at a sophisticated interest in openness comes late in evolution of thinking about this sub-

Overlake Sector Light Industrial Park
Newark, CA

Berkeley Gate
Berkeley, CA
design competition

Aphorisms
University of Virginia

ject. Consequently, it missed much of the constructive work that set the stage for the extreme program of radical indeterminacy it now finds itself entertaining—that the profession finds so shocking and the public alienating.[4]
10. Yet, to the extent that architecture was sensitive to the same general cultural developments being theorized in this discourse it followed a parallel, but retarded, course. So when Architecture "discovered" theory in its full academic glory with Jacques Derrida it felt a sense of familiarity or appropriateness, leavened perhaps with some embarrassment at its early naiveté. Theory-envy goaded the critical establishment of architecture to scramble, and a significant body of work built up quickly. Contemporary theory in architecture may boast a sophistication that pretty much rivals that in literary studies if not philosophy, but the discourse still suffers from a foreshortened historical perspective. Before Derrida there were Friedrich Nietzsche, Martin Heidegger, Herbert

88 Alcatraz Island Interpretive Center
San Francisco, CA
invited proposal
Anderson Windows

Marcuse, Umberto Eco, and others who explored the gradual but consistent evolution of an imperative toward greater openness and freedom in the arts.

11. The set of ideas leading to the sense of openness now informing architecture can be traced most directly to Nietzsche. The emerging technological culture he anthemized was still dominated by a monumental convention looming out of a pre-scientific past. Nietzsche was able to translate the spirit of critical objectivity percolating through science and technology into a prescription for overcoming metaphysics. Nihilism's radical devaluing of the transcendent took the first step toward openness by demolishing the conventional values that had traditionally, conventionally, invested architecture. In the place of metaphysics he posited a new super-subjectivity, an embodiment of a will-to-power that, in theory, was freely determinative and devoid of the baggage upon which architecture had historically fixated. This

California Lifeguard Tower
Los Angeles County, CA

Kirsten Kiser Gallery, Los Angeles

move toward openness was echoed within architecture (without a necessary causal connection) by the increasing stylistic permissiveness that so distressed the early leaders of modernism. Architecture may have relaxed its convictions about the moral basis of traditional form, but it did not yet have the ability to invent new forms for the new values the overman might discover. Consequently, Architecture experienced this freedom as open season on the historical treasure chest.

12. Architecture's discovery of a modernism that could express these new values barely preceded Heidegger's announcement of Nietzsche's failure to overcome metaphysics. Setting the pattern for the succeeding waves of theory sampled by critics in architecture, Heidegger claimed that, far from overcoming metaphysics, Nietzsche's work was its culmination. Nietzsche was not, after all, radical enough; he remained unknowingly but firmly rooted in the tradition he thought he was destroy-

Astronauts Memorial
Kennedy Space Center
Cape Canaveral, FL
national design competition

ing. Since it localizes the determination of experience in a subject, still set over against the object world, Heidegger saw the will to power as the ultimate subjective expression of the reign of enframing and thus the opposite of free or open.

13. Heidegger's work focused more clearly the problem Nietzsche posed as the characteristic dilemma of the avant garde: how can the space cleared for new work by an historical self-consciousness avoid being reinscribed with an equally historical intentionality? The history of relations with openness since structuralism—since architecture discovered theory—has been one of oscillation between claims that openness was unattainable and counter claims that it was unavoidable. A sort of cultural uncertainty principle holds: openness cannot be actively sought without compromising any discovery with the preconception inherent in the motivation, while at the same time openness cannot be avoided except by repressive

Right Away Redy-Mix II
Oakland, CA

means that must undermine the authority of the work. This corollary to the innovation fallacy was pointed out by Derrida, claiming openness was unavoidable. The most visually radical expression of openness—work done in support of a condition of undecidability—demonstrates the extremes to which the design must be willing to go in search of sustainable openness by those who believe the counter critique—that it is unattainable. Deleuze believes that it is attainable, if one tries really, really hard, but only if the names are changed and logic is suspended. The architectural examples offered in support of his position seem to replicate the same strand of European modernism that originally discomfited Heidegger and set the whole cycle of criticism in motion. Having opened itself to theory, architecture is now buffeted by mutually antagonistic, competing expressions of openness. DR 5   NIRM note g
14. Architecture is not so rigorous, nor so pure, that this has bothered it, though.

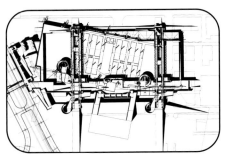

89

The Problem
Syracuse University

Columbus Convention Center
Columbus, OH
invited competition

15. Architecture is caught up within life. Like life, culture, and the society that builds it, architecture is all over the place. For that reason, it is now more radically open already than any critical movement's plans of openness for it, more open than tradition would allow, certainly, or its presence would desire: it is also open to closure. Architecture embraces both, entailing the ideality of the former and the pragmatism of the latter—just as at one time it had embodied the ideality of the latter while pro- grammatically admitting the unavoidability of the former. Though the general trend might be to openness, and that only recently apparent, the bulk of architectural history has been spent seeking closure. Yet that closure has assumed a multivalence of effects that gave rise to pre- cessing epicycles of openness throughout that history. Despite the efforts of successive waves of historiogra- phers and apologists, from Marc-Antoine Laugier to Siegfried Gideon, architecture's story refuses to be linear,

Dining Table

Conference Table

refuses even to point consistently toward any particular horizon. The horizon of openness is all around though. The specificity of programmed efforts toward openness seems to lose sight of this horizon.

16. A more general idea of openness might be more useful to architecture. By refusing ideality's sternest judgments, without relaxing too much, architecture may be reframed so that something recognizable as a real openness is actually possible.[5]

17. But what is understood by open? How may openness be, and do these ways even intersect with architecture? What, exactly is this an openness to? Can there be openness from? How about for? Yes, to all the above. Openness is open; traditionally, this would be mostly to meaning. Is meaning to be found, debated, conveyed, teased, frustrated, ignored, or denied? In fact, each represents an approach, taken in the history of specific interest in meaning. The history of interest in meaning is

Model Display Base

Tarantino Residence
Hollywood Hills, CA
residential addition and remodel

not synonymous with the history of meaning itself.6 It is in fact the history of the relationship of meaning to openness, which is the history of the visibility of meaning and its availability for hermeneutic play. Meaning is interesting when it is not merely assumed, but when it is risked. The further into openness it sojourns, though, the more obviously its continued existence is an achievement—and the more obviously this legibility must be at the expense of that field. **DR 10**

18. Openness is not any more essentially aesthetic or significant than it is instrumental since it admits of degree, or nuance, that is measurable. Tactics for achieving openness, as tactics, address the issue instrumentally. As a description of possibility, in turn, openness is a description of the range of the instrumental; as an introduction to the impossible it is the avenue to increasing that range. The maximizing of this range is the ultimate goal of all programs of emancipation. In that sense,

U.S. Pavilion/ Expo '92
Seville, Spain
finalist, invited competition

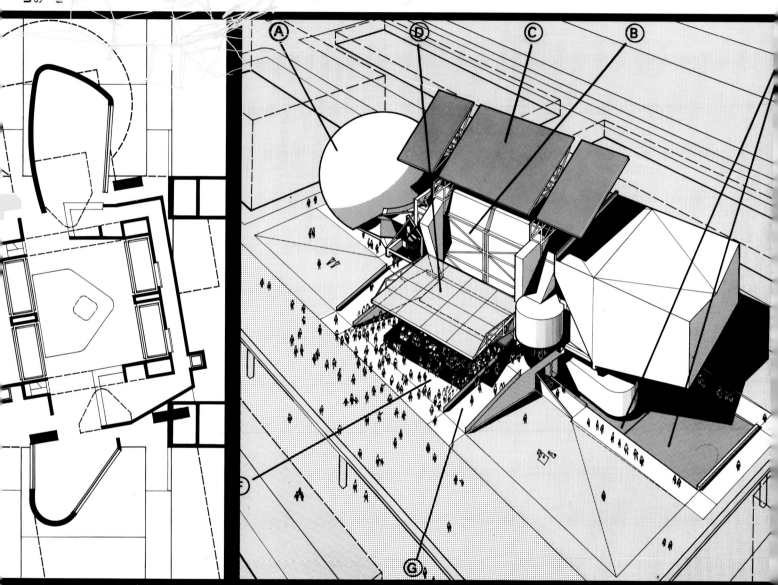

openness is the measure of freedom. Freedom is certainly understood and enjoyed instrumentally, even when the accounting of freedom involves no direct or measurable physical reference. Like meaning, freedom also is more interesting when it is risked; the further into openness it journeys, though, toward an extreme of anarchy, the more forcefully the counter desire for security asserts itself. Security is found in certainty, traditionally one of architecture's greatest assets, secured itself by architecture's doubtless presence.

19. Traditionally, logically, openness and certainty name opposite desires; they head in opposite directions with an equally strong logic of absoluteness. But must openness and certainty be so radically opposed? The aporias that lurk in the desire for absolute anything are expected, but do certainty and openness necessarily go that far? Both are voracious, and feed on themselves, but can they be coaxed toward the same respect for nuance that

Paramount Pictures Film and Tape Archive
Hollywood, CA

their antonyms can demonstrate? It is here that conventional chauvinism and critical intolerance are usually located.

20. If a more reasonable, pragmatic attitude is adopted—suggested by the failure of these extremes—the threshold of the instrumental life of openness might be approached: where a useful version of openness might survive, if not thrive. Like anything measurable, openness is understood through difference—as an effect related back to some datum. Openness, though, is measured while essentially questioning such framing. This frame, this measurement, this difference is composed and encompassed by that which it describes. Openness is itself the field across which difference plays and measurement is taken; difference can be considered the body which plays, as the presence of openness.[7]

21. While openness may be measurable, and instrumentally inclined, the opposite is not necessarily true. If the

Details Display Mechanism
Steelcase Corporation
New York, NY

instrumental cannot serve openness directly, it can enjoy an oblique relationship. The idea of the machine is essentially counter to openness. The machine is an embodiment of purpose, single-minded and secure. As such, it is about reducing openness. The machine can only pretend to be a machine for openness. Openness is an absurd purpose for driving the machine. Yet openness is not an absurd constituent of the machine. Openness can slip into the works as the attention is fixed on the more graspable idea of the instrumental itself.[8]
22. With openness lubricating the machine, it can "work" more smoothly. More importantly, it can become a work.[9] As a work, the machine may begin to feel a way toward lessening the absurdity of a more intentional, directed relationship between the instrumental and openness. Openness finds its way into the mechanism through the relaxation of the machines imperative for efficiency or single-mindedness. In the context of this gen-

AOKI Retail
Tokyo, Japan
invited proposal

Technology as an Architectural Language
University of Southern California

Rabin Residence
Tiburon, CA
invited competition

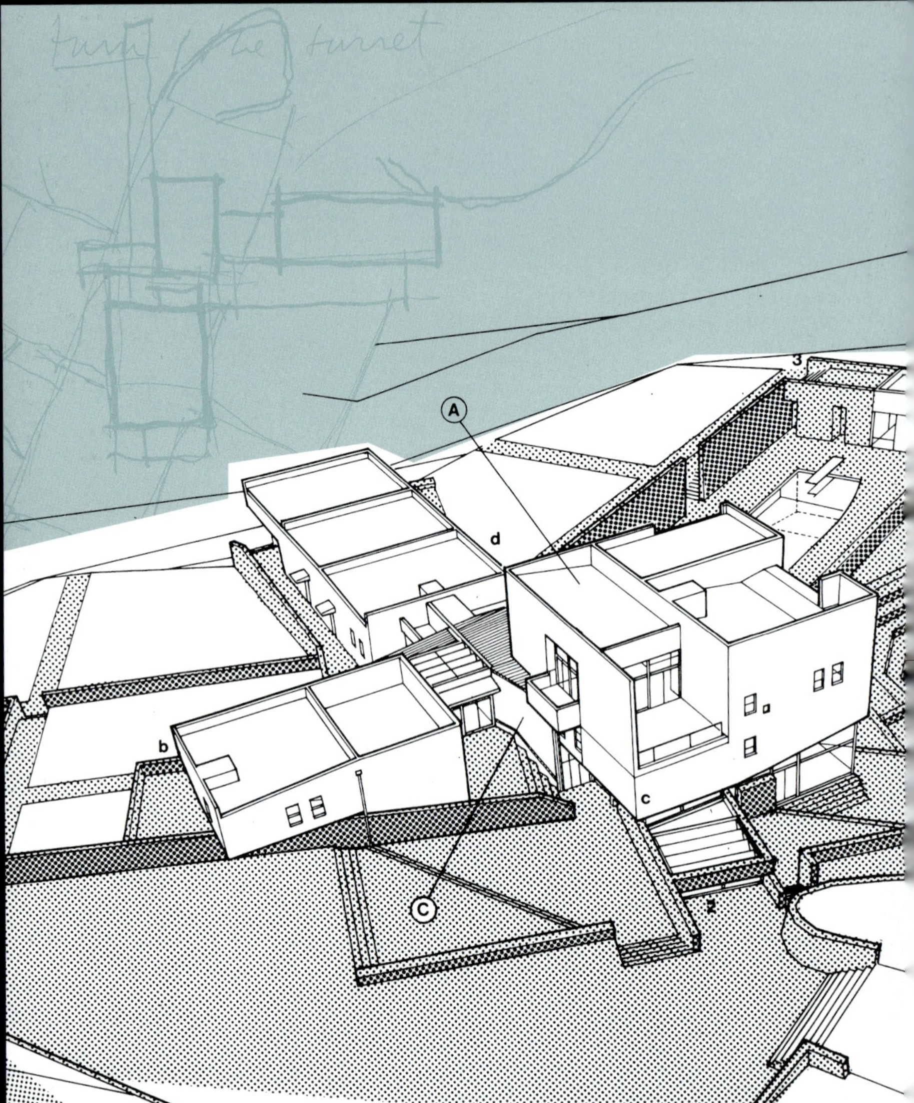

eral imperative, any apparent relaxation becomes meaningful. A new awareness of that now more opaque function is inscribed in the figure traced by that new expression. The mode of entry to the machine for openness is expression, which is interestingly at odds with efficiency. 23. Expression is the lubricant. The slipperiness of reference, along the dizzying chain of signifiers, challenges the machine's efficiency in pursuing its single-minded goal, but makes it much more robust. Expression supplements the singular intentionality of the task with the wide-ranging, unpredictable intentionality of communication. Once the door is thrown open to the endless dissemination of communication it is truly open. Where the machine's concerns are clear, the possibility of interpretation can make them richer; where the machine's means are straightforward or direct, the polyphonic elaboration can give them depth; where the machine is by definition self-satisfied, the publicity of expression will restore the

NOB 21

32

House for a Corporate Family
Malibu, CA

Olympic West
Los Angeles, CA
national design competition

Rancho Mirage Civic Center
Rancho Mirage, CA
national design competition

West Hollywood Civic Center
West Hollywood, CA
national design competition

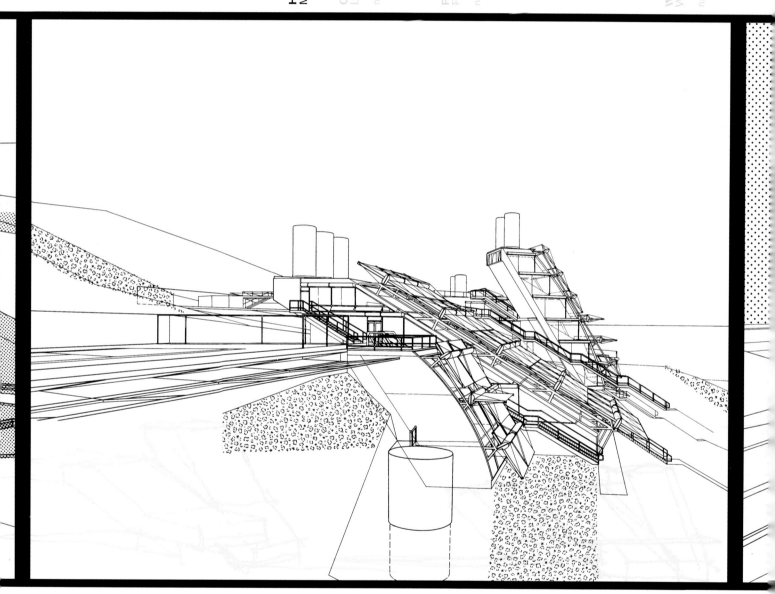

expectation that draws in the reader and user and challenges the machine to do more.

24. The presence of expression in the works need not be an addition; it can also be a subtraction, an absence or gap in the mechanism, that will come to be filled with openness as it arouses the compulsion to bridge it. By soliciting the reader's participation in these terms, the machine declares its greater openness or inclusiveness indirectly, by a different channel than the overt instrumental appeal through which the user expects to be addressed, or the supplementary signification that engages the reader. When the communication occurs on more than one level, and other than the strictly conscious, the conversation is more compelling. In painting the Mona Lisa, for example, Leonardo suppressed the specific facial features that would clarify the sitter's expression while providing the larger figure of attentiveness. Through this gap he draws the viewer into an end-

Affordable House
national design competition

Hermit Crab House
national design competition

Lowe Development
Los Angeles, CA

less, reflexive conversation. Into the openness of this enigmatic portrait the viewer pours his contribution to the completion of her smile, and by this participation, the viewer is rewarded with a richer experience.[10] Similarly, by emphasizing proportion and figure instead of joints or linkages, technologically inspired architecture may similarly entice the reader's involvement. Thoughtful design can open this space in the machine where expression lurks without risking cartoonishness or alienation.

25. Though the machine may not find a purpose in openness, it can find a means. The inclusion of openness can lead the machine to an enhanced expression (and thus service) of its other purposes, and to a more engaging relationship with its users who have become readers.

26. It is perhaps not strictly accurate to speak of this viewing orientation as one of reading, however, particularly when the object is present as a machine. The

Confluence Point Ranger Station I
San Jose, CA

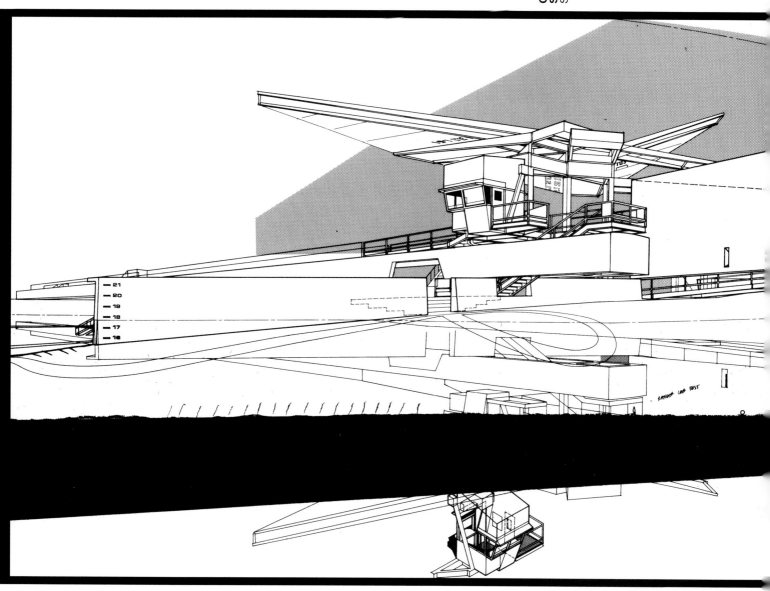

engagement solicited by the object in this case promotes a pre-cultural, or extralinguistic understanding: the machine sponsors a non-spatial affect. Affect, as affect, is strictly non- or extra-linguistic. This is what makes it affect. Traditionally a spatial sense, this is where architecture escapes language, because it is where architecture escapes stuff—which, eminently and inescapably namable, is always captured by language. Things are signifieds because they are there. The object survives the experience, the affect does not.

27. The apprehension of affect and the operation of taste show that reference does not necessarily imply "sign"-ification. The exercise of taste seems to occur in an arena other than that covered by all but the most abstracted semiology. Its referrability runs the gamut from the most specific object-quality to diffusely ineffable sentiment, yet always in terms that can be considered signs only at a meta-linguistic level. (This is why the

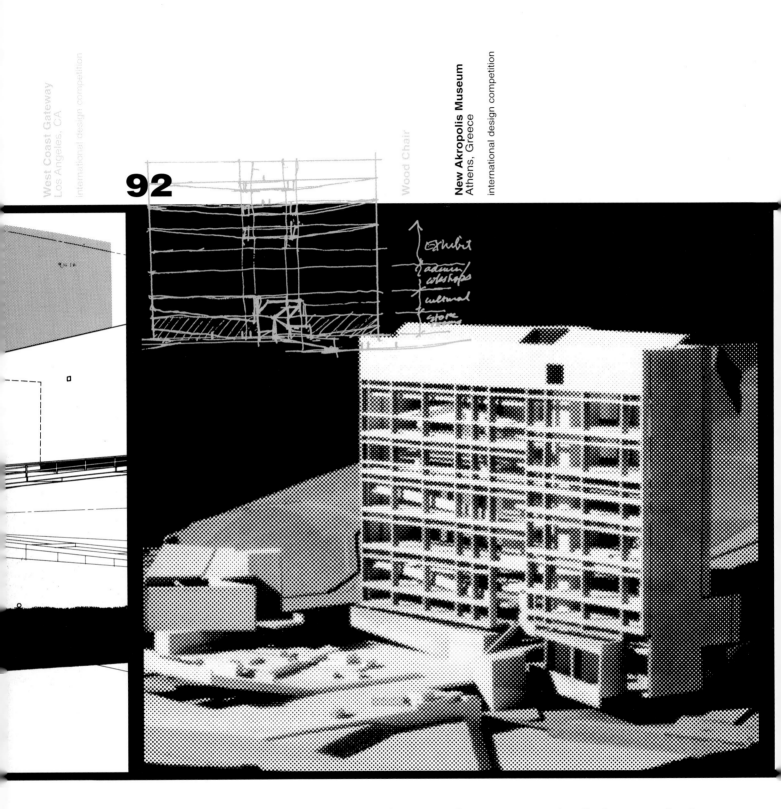

92

West Coast Gateway
Los Angeles, CA
international design competition

Wood Chair

New Akropolis Museum
Athens, Greece
international design competition

advent of the hyper-real signals as well the proliferation of style and the elevation of taste over substance—now pursued as the cool and the hip). So that the forms in which the style—or coolness—is necessarily invested or embodied cannot be understood simply as signs or as interested in conventional signification. Instead, they are counters in a more operationally oriented apprehension of performance: they are cool.[11] When the instrumental nature of performance is heightened to the point where figures emerge as the effective agents, then bossness becomes visible. As immanent and affective, this notion is linked to the culture and evolves with it (leading or following), so the boss has evolved from an early interest in muscle to its contemporary acknowledgment of finesse. These figures can be taken as signs but are more properly understood as operational language in Roland Barthes sense of wine as both myth and fact.[12] The judgment of quality or bossness is made in relation to the

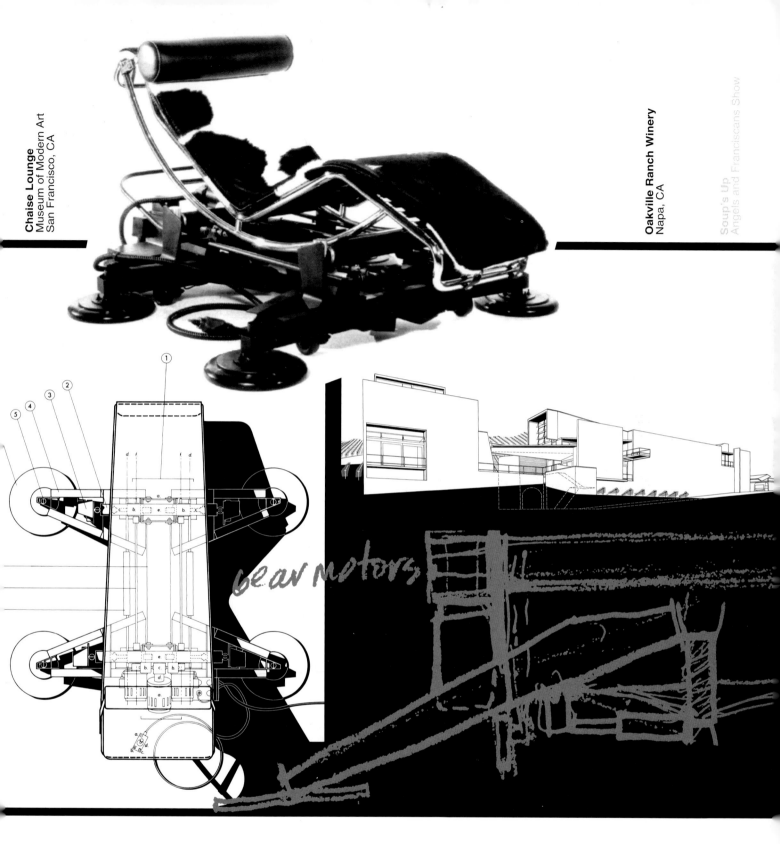

Chaise Lounge
Museum of Modern Art
San Francisco, CA

Oakville Ranch Winery
Napa, CA

affectiveness of the stuff in question—how engaging is it, and how far does the signification recede in favor of the affect.[13] **NOB 19**

28. Openness may be appreciated non-instrumentally in the machine as affect. As a human affect it only counts when it is engaging though, as a non-transferable experience; fallen trees only make a noise when they are heard. To be engaged is to be more than merely attentive, it is to participate in the experience, to witness the affective unconcealment of that which is said to be open: which is to enjoy an essential role of humanity.

29. The open space of affect where this participation occurs presumes a certain freedom; but between the concepts of openness and freedom, preventing their seamless synonymity, is the wedge of autonomy that distinguishes between "from" and "to." The object's autonomy, just as that of the discourse itself, has come to stand for its intentional estrangement from the field of relations

Futon

San Jose Repertory Theater
San Jose, CA

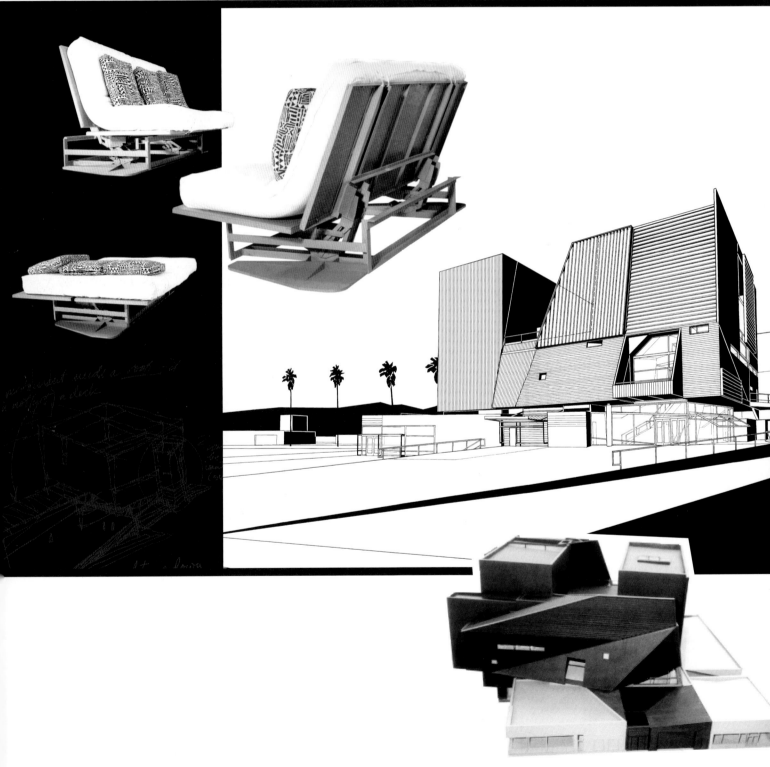

93

Rene Dubois Bioshelter
Cathedral of St. John the Divine
New York, Ny
invited competition

Diamond Ranch High School
Pomona, CA
invited competition

that form its context, as well as the freedom to refer or relate at will. Against a reality of great complexity and subtlety, the traditional championing of autonomy asserts both localized presence and enduring substance; the "metaphysics of presence" it supports underpins the architectural canon. The canon is of course a parade of proudly autonomous objects. The historical evolution of this concept paralleled that of the more general idea of openness that situates it. Reflecting that relation to openness, Architecture's sense of its own relative autonomy evolved in different directions on the conflated fronts of art and practice. As a discipline architecture promoted its aloofness from the humdrum everyday reality of commercial life—serving its mystique as a profession—while at the same time trumpeting a sense of social responsibility that required a contrasting close connection with the public it "served." The architectural object mirrored this range, as it wavered between an alienating abstrac-

Marianna Kistler Beach Museum of Art
Kansas State University
Manhattan, KS
invited competition

Marden Water Treatment Plant
Marden, ID

Boss Architecture
Royal Institute of British Architects

Clocktower Loft Remodel
San Francisco, CA

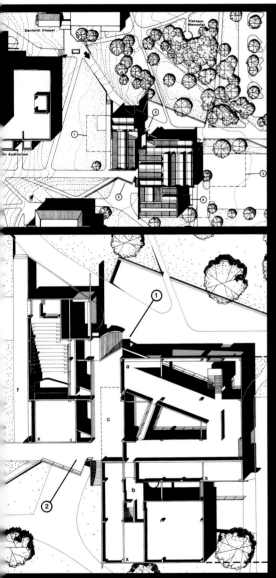
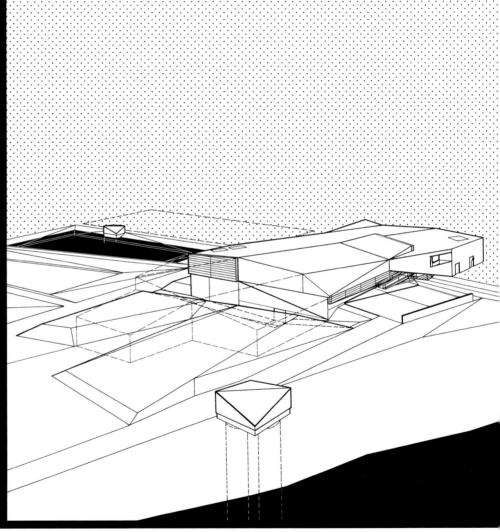

tion and the most ingratiating quotations, in support and in contravention of the position taken by the profession toward its societal responsibility. Consequently, the intentions behind the formal manipulations that fronted for it were not always obvious: abstraction, for example, could seem responsibly—counter ideologically—resistant or elitist, often at the same time. This, depending on whether it was seen to support a vision of architecture's autonomy as a means of achieving critical distance "through specific technical procedures" or as an unavoidable "historical imposition," to be turned to account by "elevating form as its own language without reference to external sentiments, rationales, or ... social visions."[14] **DR note g**

30. This latter view finds its most extreme formulation in an aesthetics that revisits Croce's position that the experience of art is shared directly between the author and reader, as the reproduction in the reader's mind of the

40

Decon recon[1]

T92.11/1
rev 93.12

1. That which Architecture most takes for granted—**NIRM 9** presence—is least secure today. **ONM 19** The strong form that attempts to secure it has come under fire as an agent of repression and the sense **NIRM 3** of certainty it literally embodies is considered delusional. What was previously taken for granted as a simple condition of existence has been named and recast as a critical failure of the freedom of absence. Yet, can the criticism of presence be constructive—or is it in fact *condemned* to be so? Is there anything *useful* in this discussion? Does this last question betray a bias and, can this bias ever be overcome?[2] In the midst of such confusion, it remains certain that the "repression" of "secondary" meanings is still an achievement if it is the means by which we win understanding from noise or chaos.

2. Curiously, almost paradoxically, the first source of this repression is metaphysics. **ONE 13** On the face of it, metaphysics is hardly the champion of a presence. Concerned with stuff *beyond* the simply given—with understanding "the fundamental nature of reality and Being"—metaphysics traditionally attempts to determine a meaning for the human experience. This meaning is elusive, its significance allusive, its experience illusive. This significant meaning is sought by reference to something else though, not in experience itself: the unavoidable circularity is expanded to make it encompass at least a sense of the external. The logic collocating "importance" and "meaning" together in "significance" requires that this elusive "meaning" be grounded in something "greater," something *beyond* what is there at hand, which could validate that experience and verify the meaning as meaning*ful*. In its struggle with the basic epistemological dilemma this presents—whether it is

WITM 19
does so in what we could call mechanical terms. When this "field" is manifested "out there" as the unsummable totality of its markers, it will do so by intention and will, and at that moment will become, de-facto, de-mechanis.

The machine, as physiology, as physics, as metaphysics, pleads "Nolo contendere." The latest stage in the continuous evolution of epistemology's critique of the ableness of reason, and of the machine that is its public face—its critique of metaphysics and metaphysics' socialization into "culture"—has brought us Weak Thought and Undecidability.

reasoning an absolute or accessing the truly exterior—**ONHR 12** metaphysics must fall short of this goal; its "truth" becomes "conventional." Convention is institutionalized repressiveness. The deconstructive critique points out that because we are not aware that the answer metaphysics "provides" is really no more than a "mask"—the provisionality of its answer does violence to the possibili- **EO 4** ties of an otherwise open-ended reality.

3. "Meta-physics" refers to ideas about stuff *beyond* the *physical, beyond* what is "simply present." "Meta" carries in it the valuation of this difference, which says it is not just "other." In rooting the possibility for meaning or significance in the relationship to "some greater, beyond," **WITM 7** the logic of transcendence exacerbates the violence of convention by its reference "to another *order* of reality that devalues and lowers that which is immediately given."[3] The logic of transcendence is imperialistic, compounding the violence of this "devaluation" by its universalization, or inescapability. And finally, the violence of this universalization is brought full circle by embodying it, by the reductive "identification of this universal with an entity—grounding, archè, first principle, authority"—presence. Heidegger decried this aspect of metaphysics in particular, as "thought that forgets Being in favor of Entity."[4]

WITM 23
4. When the transcendent is universalized in a fixed order, as when the mystery of Nature is enframed in the **ONE 17** abstract formulae of science, for example, its characterization of the fundamental nature of reality and Being completely predetermines any meaning that experience might discover. When the transcendent becomes the convention, it loses its original *critical* ability to stand in judgment of this experience by pronouncing what *ought* to be over what *is*. Logic also was once a critical tool, lift-

---

[1] From lecture delivered at Columbia University, School of Architecture in 1992.

[2] The machine, science, technology, nomological "knowledge" or thought—these are also the force of *repression*—which is the frame that chooses, the mark that distinguishes, the intention that signifies in the face of the undecidable entopic blur. The machine is the physical emblem of that which decides anyway in the face of undecidability. It is the champion of decidability.

The mechanical is the threshold to existence **NOB 9**—and so it is that all that may be said to exist **MIT 24** (that may be seen to engage apriority—nature, the world, a context, anything—which it must if it is to exist)—all *this*

[3] Gianni Vattimo, "Metaphysics, Violence, Secularization" in *Recoding Metaphysics: The New Italian Philosophy*, ed. Giovanna Borradori (Evanston: Northwestern Univ. Press, 1988), 52.

[4] Vattimo, 56.

ing the veils of folk wisdom and superstition. Though today we are habitually skeptical of the prescriptiveness of that "ought" and recognize the limitations of logic, we have not been able to match their effectiveness. In questioning its own tools, criticism itself now faces the epistemological aporia confronted continuously by metaphysics.

5. Criticism has generally been satisfied with questioning the particular masks, conventions and truths with which society has outfitted itself. Today, however, in order to reveal the ultimate provisionality of everything, criticism challenges the possibility any proposal presented with certainty as an answer may arise. Such a sweeping program must risk becoming, itself, another violent metaphysics, must risk spawning a new repressive, if delirious, culture.

6. "Given this possibility," Nietzsche said, we can only "distrust metaphysics." In order to escape metaphysics' propensity to reinsinuate itself into every critique that goes beyond distrust to outright denial—if we are to "unmask" the "unmasking itself"—we must realize that "even the idea of a truth that reveals a masking ... the idea of a truth beyond ideologies and every form of false consciousness, is, precisely, still ... a mask."[5] Deconstruction, and the whole trend of poststructural thinking that has continued in its wake, attempt to practice such non violent distrust, and so to reveal "masking" without recourse to a "greater" truth—beyond, of course, the "truth" of such distrust itself.

7. The artificial framework that has evolved to supplement our pro-conventional (biological) guides to behavior—not only our history but all the conventions that have evolved and stories that have been told, all the metaphysics, religions, myths, ethics, sciences, and even languages, all this has finally fallen away—or has become so obvious that complicity is too difficult to sustain easily—which is the same thing. Criticism has singled out complicity itself. Consequently, we are uncertain about uncertainty. If history has recorded the continuous removal of such supporting masks, it has also always depended upon the confidence of whatever was next in line, depended upon the next paradigm's eagerness to challenge and then usurp the standard of appropriateness or correctness or reality.

8. However, this confidence is no longer warranted, and eagerness has become suspect. We are uncertain how to *challenge*; we are uncertain what would, or could, be a better way; or is "*better*" even appropriate to seek? Is "appropriate" appropriate? Does the search betray the worth of what is sought? Is value a villain?

9. We have approached the edges, looked over, and found uninhabitable aporia. Though Zeno, Kurt Godel, and Werner Karl Heisenberg predicted that the edge would remain unknowable, now we know what that knowledge is like, how it feels. Jean Paul Sartre and Albert Camus were able to make it heroic, somehow. They worked in heroic times. Today it is not even pathetic. Perhaps we are faced, like St. Augustine so long ago, with finding our answer, like his City of God, within. With his world crumbling around him, he discovered a "within"ness which specifically ignored the obvious props of external authority. It rejected this accustomed way of validating thought and embraced this uncertainty. Yet, for St. Augustine, the "miracle" of Faith made the connection to a "larger" meaning. Though the "evidence" was within, the structure remained loyal to a need for an externally supplied value which maintained the system. The "Italian

---

[5] Vattimo, 45.

Heidegger"[6] has been pushed, at this impasse, to reconsider this deus-ex-machina. If in general, though, we are more comfortable with the idea of God's "death," this only makes faith even more obvious in its provisionality, its metaphysicality, its miraculousness. Our engagement with this spatialized aporia hones and maintains our distrust, keeps us miserably vigilant against the insidious sirens of comfort, certainty and value.[7]

10. It is the *new* that despatializes the horizon "within," that supplies the faith, that prevents ennui. "Within," the boundary is temporal, not spatial. The edge is between New and old, with old meaning "enframed," familiar, expected. This is not modernism's faith, "Progress," but a faith in the radical emancipatory difference of the unfamiliar. Design strategies evolving from deconstructivism see design as *invention*, rather than development or refinement. This work distinguishes between inventing the possible, which is a predictive activity that cannot escape the familiarity of its own assumptions, and "actualizing" or stumbling upon the "impossible," the virtual, unforeseeable, the *other*. The new is an edge because only invention is able to precede its own generalization. This suggests, however, that the emancipatory value of Uniqueness is limited to the moment of birth. Only at *that* moment is its priority to the situations that it must inevitably prompt assured: the epiphany which hails its recognition marks the moment of its entrapment within history. When the other is stumbled over and asserted, it immediately retrofigures its own possibility, providing its own preconditions, setting in motion the striations that run forward to lead it, and backward to explain it.

11. But how may the pre-(pro)scriptiveness of intentionality be avoided in invention? The "other" cannot be sought, only found. Chance is the banana peel which most often triggers the violent, startling surprise of real invention. It operates at the secret center of both strong and weak formalisms—in the closet of the former and on the mantle of the latter. It is the great and embarrassing McGuffin. Weakness addresses the aleatory in order to use *it*, whereas traditional design attacks it in order to banish it. "Strength" is the effect of this impossible attempt to banish the "unconsidered"; the measure of its "goodness" is the energy of the repression effected in that attempt. Weakness is attuned to the "authorless form" suggested in randomness, and the measure of its success is the energy of liberation.

12. Unlike deconstruction, which seems more a technique for revealing the repressed *strength* in the "accidental," the marginal—weakness is ever mindful of the necessity to maintain distrust and intends to avoid entirely the pre-(pro)-scriptiveness of technique. What is important is the jackpot of retro-explicatory epiphany; the means, the process, is of less consequence.

13. Chance bootstraps us to the "other" side within; it is a very strange place, time. First of all, this spatialization is inappropriate, though convenient. Second, the strictest reading requires that otherness cannot be represented, just as it cannot be predicted beyond leaving open its possibility. This possibility cannot be grasped, taken hold-of and man-handled by understanding. Even the very means by which we discuss "this subject"—the very pronouns we use—do violence to these possibilities by roping them into the received systems and traditional understandings that deploy these tools. Even this "we"-that-discusses is itself prevented from exercising itself "there." If intentionality pre-supposes subjectivity, and subjectivity presupposes a restrictive duality that violates the other's openness, then both must be banished. Since

---

[6] Giovanna Borradori's editorial in Recoding Metaphysics: The New Italian Philosophy, ed. Giovanna Borradori (Evanston: Northwestern Univ. Press, 1988).

[7] This complicates a traditional understanding of how the subject is constituted, by what means, against what ground, does he know himself? For St. Augustine, this ground was God, whose 'presence' was an issue of Faith.

Strategies which resist the projected dimension of the privileged subject—multiplicity, difference, irony—pursue two tracks: De-founding, and De-normalizing, or De-mythifying; the first De-privileges the certainty of *origin*, which provides historical comfort, the second, the security of a universalization of engagement which ensures phenomenal constancy.

individually, *in the face* of such tendencies; they serve as final checks *against* them. So, when rights lose their exceptional role, there is no counter left to challenge universalizing trends. The right unreserved, unexercized, is meaningless.

The obverse side of right is responsibility. The two describe another suspicious, but unavoidable duality: Either is hollow without the other. When pursued at the scale of architecture and within its necessary physical constraints, the promotion of "rights" without an attendant sense of responsibility

logic pre-supposes the connections of prediction, induction, and deduction, it is also prevented from operating on the "other's" side. And finally, there is no "value" on the "other side," no *appropriateness*, and thus no means or criteria for judgment or preference; so even if we could begin, we could never finish: over "there," stuff just happens.

14. But if we want to relate to the possibility of otherness in any but the most private, unremarkable way, it will be subject to such violence. If we want to relate publicly to it, then the structures of publicity, the repressive intentionality of the reader, the smothering explanation of convention, the fixity and presence of reality, will flatten it. The political, public dimension of architecture—of practice—requires that the work *engage* the conditions which prompt its critique. Practically, this must risk infection of the work, risk entertaining at least some of the very "compromises" that it intends to challenge.[8]

15. It is said that all we may do is embrace it, that the erotic is the only possible arena of non-violent engagement.[9]

* * *

16. The traditional understanding of architecture places it in some indeterminate position between intention and reference. In this region it is granted its importance and influence. Somewhere between use and expression, function and form, intention and reference, we will "find" architecture. This is a territory with great metaphysical weight; it roots architecture in humanity's most basic experience of "reality and being." Intention drives its embodiment in figure, presence, program or function, and grants the value that determines what is to be inside the frame. Reference, on the other hand, is the lever for the poststructural *critique* of this rootedness, of the traditional fixity of this frame, by showing what's inside to be completely dependent on the excluded outside.

17. Intrinsic to *reference* is the difference that problematizes any metaphysics celebrating simple presence. Intrinsic to the logic of *intention*, is the resolution of this difference to give simple presence. These two possibilities rehearse the definitive conflict between the opacity of expression and the transparency of use, between the simple satisfaction of programmatic needs and constraints, and the contrary excess required for the communication that renders a work "Architecture."

18. If the deconstructive preference for undecidability "grounds" itself in a respect for the basicness of "reference," then the "traditional" preference for "deciding anyway" is prompted by a respect for the equal basicness of "intention."[10]

19. The "first" "condition of reference" must be the subdivision of the "objective" continuum—giving or noticing the difference among things across which reference occurs. Yet because of their exact, definitive complementarity, it is impossible to assign priority to either individuation—discreet "thingliness"—or to relationship—the "space" of discreteness. Whether the "conditions of reference" must include "thingliness" for reference to be conceived, or thingliness itself is conceivable only by the operation of a prior "referrability," is impossible to know. There is no existence for either of these understandings without the other. But as concepts they are both active; they are *verbal* nouns, they are transitive in effect. Is intention inferred in the activity of reference; or is reference, as an activity, stimulated by an intention *to* refer?

20. A respect for reference then, must slide into a

---

[8] To advance "by exception," is to assume that one proceeds "by right." The emancipatory project often appeals to a respect for *rights* as a critical counterpossibility to the universal absolutes of metaphysics or "culture." It is this "right" that is contravened by the violence of metaphysics: "metaphysics, and culture in general, covers and forgets the rights of the living immediate"; "... it [is] metaphysical violence to cover and cancel the *rights* of the sensuous and transitory by affirming universal and abstract essences." (Vattimo, 49)

While "abstract universals" may be proposed which *originate* in a concern for "rights," the right itself always, definitively, remains transcendent, aloof in essence from that universalizing process. Rights are reserved, specifically,

perverts the emancipatory urge, substituting one system of revolutionary violence for another.

Emancipation means to bring into *freedom*. Sartre and Camus demonstrated for us the nauseating meaninglessness of realized "absolute" freedom. Absolute freedom must include freedom from meaning. Not only does meaning constrain, but meaning always is constrained (through structures of difference); design is always the design of this constraint. Meaning is a result of difference, a repression of the awareness of always another other. Undecidability desires the elimination of *the other*, replacing it with undecidable otherness and, ultimately, in this, a freedom from meaning. If freedom is the ability to operate against, then when there is no clear against, no responsibility, the concept of freedom becomes uncertain. The resistance of oppositional structures, of the duality, to an embraceable critique is traceable to this inescapable haptic duality: the opposition of the individual and the other, and its deployment along the gradient of freedom.

Architecture is condemned to run afoul of the emancipatory urge; once a mark has been made, the character of freedom is changed: it changes from freedom *to*, to freedom *from*. By championing chance, undecidability intends to (re)-discover this "to" which is perpetually relost in History. This rediscov-

respect for intention's role in reference, in compelling the reading of some-"ness," otherwise unremarked, as a signifier. Undecidability, like reference, has no bite without intention; intention has no bark without reference. Intention stands in difference, between undecidability and indifference, while it is in reference that the difference is made.

21. A sense of intention on the part of the "text" that it should be read, without even inquiring where this intention originates or is "located," has always been considered necessary to the perception of communication, to *reading* the potential or expectation for reading. This is to say that the "presence" of intention compels reading, and perhaps that the "absence" of intention breeds indifference and invisibility. If intention is present as an inference, something read into the objectively mute object, then, it would seem to be subject itself to the same operation of reference that it compels. Yet, in highlighting the "absence" of intention in the object, the "presence" of intention in the reader becomes even more directly evident. In fact the intention to find meaning, even where it is less than apparent, is the basis of curiosity itself.

22. The centrality of Intention is evident when we balance the discussion between humanity and nature, purpose and aimlessness. Since nature must unavoidably remain outside human grasp—scientific enframing or artistic expression—it stands as the only "true" and ultimate undecidable. Only Nature can be indifferent; this is why undecidability must ultimately be resolved into decision: the bite of intention that makes it matter, that makes it tragic, that makes it human, is the seed of its ultimate resolution and redemption to usefulness.

23. The presence and importance of intention is obviously most apparent in stuff that is made—even undecidable stuff. What is undecidable is never *whether* to read, but *how*. Reading, as another sort of making, continues that intention, carrying it along, participating in it, acting with it, and all in order to satisfy it. As conscious beings, we are equally attuned to making, to reading the intention that is thereby manifested, and to expect meaning in the result. What frames Architecture as Architecture is the particular, disproportionate sense of such intentionality—in service of meaning:

> "As we cross the frontier between France and Belgium," Corbu says, "the train passes through coal-mining country. What is this—a mirage? As far as the eye can see, gigantic pyramids rising from the plain stand out against the sky. These sublime monuments thrust themselves into the blue depths on either side of the train. Yet on closer inspection they are merely stag heaps, those piles of gray black shale in which the veins of coal had been embedded. The law governing the angle of repose has shaped the destiny of these pyramids: a perfect slope of forty-five degrees. Am I near Cairo, the land of Pharaohs?
>
> "Not at all! My emotion, though still sharp, is blunted. My admiration dissolves. These are not works of art; these are not works of any kind. They are simple piles of discarded shale. And all of a sudden I am aware of the gaping abyss between the appearance of an object and the quality of the mind that produced it. Intention is what moves us most deeply: the quality of mind brought to the creation of a work."[11]

* * *

---

ery was also Heidegger's goal. His was an archeological effort to reunderstand a *teasing* into unhiddenness, as distinct from a present-day commanding as technological enframing. For him the Greeks were the last to enjoy a sense of such freedom—and the first to diminish it.

What may constrain freedom reasonably is only that which is better or higher—this can only be seen in two ways: as a pragmatic consideration that takes account of the contradictory overlap of the simultaneously infinite freedom of individuals—that gives the entirely pragmatic ethics of politics of responsibility; or as the consideration of absolute truth, which takes account of the possibility to predict some perfection once rendered as "Faith" and consequent relief from responsibility. When the *true* is not available, then freedom itself is elevated to an absolute, but its greatest attainment becomes an appreciation of consequent responsibility.

[9] Excellent.

[10] Jeffrey Kipnis, "Nolo Contendere," in *Assemblage*, no. 11 (April 1990).

[11] Le Corbusier, *When Cathedrals Were White*, trans. Francis E. Hyslop (New York: Reynal and Hitchcock, 1947).

24. If it is the work's apparent *intentionality* that compels reading, then *repression* is necessary to reading. Intention clearly and inevitably leads to repression; intention is at root discriminatory; it is to desire, to prefer, to choose, and thus (by the topology of unhiddenness, of repression) in choosing this, it is to *not* choose that. In preferring *this* outcome over that, the "other" is unavoidably repressed.
^{ONE note 17}

25. This locates the violence of repression at the heart of reading: it is implicit in de Saussure's structure of difference. Each act of *reading*, as a rewriting, is itself a repressive act. Reading is repressive: this cannot be avoided; it is an inescapable effect of its own operational attainment of meaning. Yet, it is even more obvious that reading is an *achievement*: as either re-authorship or criticism we would never question its forward movement. This repressive engagement is a hard-won achievement in general also. Solipsism and science, phenomenology and faith, tell us the "reality" that the unconscious physiological operation of our perceptual apperati wins for us, though taken for granted, is *not necessarily given*.

26. Even before its dualism is questioned, though, this apparent dilemma of repression vs. achievement is illusory. It only exists if we assume this repression to be negative. If, like Lysenko, we insist on "political correctness" in biology, then we accuse our native perceptual faculties of "just not getting it," Whether as "cognitive discrimination," "form constancy," or "object maintenance," or even non-enframed intuitive judgment, this repression is the author of our experience. The repressive, discriminatory framing activity that we can "discuss" as giving rise to "meaning" is finally only the graspable end of a continuum that stretches all the way back into the purely functional considerations that maintain this continuity and the organism's engagement in the world.

27. In these terms it is certainly not the *work* itself, then, that is repressive. Despite its efforts to "acquire" a singular (if not particular) meaning, the work remains *open* to the repressive interpretations and perceptions in *all* readings: is this not an item of faith among deconstructivists? Since it is the reader who *must* exercise some discrimination if meaning is to be discovered within the storm of multiplicity, it must be the reader who bears the ultimate responsibility for the violence of repression. Yet, we could never with a straight face consider this "negative." We must then wonder at a condemnation of the repressiveness of the "decidable" *work* when we are at the same time cerebrating the repressive achievement of the reader. Even the deconstructive reader, in teasing out the "repressed," underlying meanings, chooses few and buries others in the rubble.

28. Perhaps the reader's violence to the text is preferable to the writer's attempts at controlling it. Certainly, in the history of any text or work, reading, as a rewriting, must appear "emancipatory," writing as "subjugatory." Yet, these historically opposed roles must be complicated by their intimacy. If reading is always already a rewriting, emancipation always begins, already, a process of re-enslavement. As we must *accept* the coupling of writing with reading and prefer the engagement between repression and expression to be fought instead within a continuous *possibility* of meaning, so we might also leaven a respect for undecidability with an appreciation of the necessity for deciding anyway.

* * *

29. Communication is a transitive phenomenon. It is a public activity. It depends upon convention for the connections its publicness entails. Intention sets communica-
^{WITM 28}

tion into motion and then immediately becomes the impetus to stop it, to satisfy it. But what is it in the work that stops or satisfies? What supports the repressive triage in the reader's response to the work's intentionality and the play of difference? What is it that convention serves? A work has something to say. Even randomly generated form speaks—by virtue of the intention that brought it into existence, if nothing else. All work must then be interested at some point in legibility.

30. Interest in legibility is interest in resolving the play of intended reference; in this play, the syntactic "moves"—mechanisms, rules, laws, structures, accidents—that create, destroy, allow, give, suggest, repress, or frame meaning stake out the space of play; the semantic counters fill it. This constitutes the range and substance of the field of reference. All work shares this initial kinship: every act of communication begins with intention and ends with markers in the field of reference. The activity of meaning occurs as the play of relations among these markers. This does not mean there is any sort of necessary relationship among the markers, beyond adjacency. The arbitrariness of the sign is also a casualty of the easy deconstruction of cause and effect. But it remains an unavoidable fact of relation that there be such markers. In reference. there is always a signifier, and a signified, and a difference, between them and between signs. This difference is "crossed," when meaning "happens." If all reference grows out of the simplest proposition, $S \ldots$ is P, then, even pointing begs a predicate, supplied by the other. While S and P may be anything, or any multitude of intangibles, the mechanism of the transfer of thought, of identity, from one to the other, is unavoidable if meaning is to exist.

31. While the simple proposition, S is P, is the conditional degree-zero of reference, we are taught that this "is" is not as simple as "it" seems. Deconstruction points out that reference is unavoidably undecidable, that S and P *cannot* be identified precisely or completely enough that the "is" could express certainty. S and P are to be variables; further, the attempt, even the desire, expressed by the "is"—and any apparent success it has in implying certainty—is repressive of the other potential meanings that lurk within the variableness of S and P.

32. The underlying (political) assumption driving a respect for the undecidability inherent in this perception is the hoary critique that says *we* do not choose the S or P, or even the "is." They are chosen for us; we are plagued in this by "false consciousness," "false needs," or "counterfeit nurturance."[12] Deconstruction attempts to demonstrate this "repression" by rendering these other readings, or at least their possibility, unhidden.

33. The "free" play of these markers is not as free as authorship assumes or meaning pretends. But not only for the reasons Marx gives—the unavoidably Newtonian character of the "space" of their relationship requires that these markers remain subject to a linguistic "gravity" that squashes the nonsensical. The "field"ness of reference, "where" the markers gambol, ensures that their relationship will remain accessible to mechanical analogy and that judgment "there" will always be linked to legibility.

34. As intention and reference enact between themselves a complex but circular relationship, so their respective institutionalizations as the machine and language are intertwined. This binds the machine to the critique of the latter, and language to the structures of the former. Since weakness, or undecidability, or deconstructivism are motivated, they are machines. The same rea-

---

[12] Marx, Marcuse, Robert J. Lifton

soning serves up the machine as a figure that could carry the deconstructivist program. Deconstructivism is "mechanical" in a more basic way than it is architectural; while the machine, in all its triumphant positivity, must continuously subject itself to deconstruction at Heisenberg's wall. Deconstructivism's determined promotion of the decidable "goal" of the decidedly undecidable, technology's tacit admission of the provisional nature of its own underpinnings even as it advances a program of localized utopian certainty, show more than anything else that even a Sisyphean self-awareness cannot go on, but cannot not go on. This realization is the real repressive achievement of deconstruction, of Weakness's own tragic will to exist.

Lake Superior Freshwater Aquarium
P93.11/1
Duluth, MN

Client:	Lake Superior Center
Architect:	Holt Hinshaw Jones
Consultants:	Ove Arup & Partners (structural)
Program:	Freshwater aquarium (200,000 gallons), exhibit space highlighting species from the Lake Superior area, resource center, theater, cafe, book and gift stores
Site:	Harborside festival grounds at south edge of downtown Duluth, formerly occupied by ore-barge docks
Size:	58,000 ft^2
Systems:	Cast-in-place concrete foundations and substructure on precast piles; steel frame and bents structure above grade, structural steel curtain wall, acrylic (tanks), corrugated metal panel, exposed mechanical and life support systems
Features:	Designed not just as a black box container for exhibits, but as an exhibit in its own right, the building houses a "core-sample" arrangement of tanks along a gravity-propelled circulation system (ramps), within a complex space that recalls the characteristic forms of the ice that piles along the shore of the lake in winter. The visitor experience is carefully choreographed from initial queuing along a wave tank, through a required orientation presentation at the building entry "lake theater," through the core sample exhibitry, the rotating exhibits, and seasonal outdoor overflow exhibits, to the gift shop and exit.
Cost:	$20 million
Completion:	January 1994 (schematic design)

Lake Superior Center was established in 1989 to increase awareness and promote responsiveness to the economic, biological, aesthetic and spiritual worth of Lake Superior in particular and fresh water in general. The Center resolved to build the Lake Superior Aquarium as a vehicle to that end and situated it on the northern shore of the lake in Duluth, Minnesota.

The severe northern climate and brutal temperament of the lake form the project's natural context. The civic aspirations of the reemerging city of Duluth, typified by the waterfront improvements that replaced abandoned industrial structures, represent the man-made context. The fourteen-acre site, a waterfront recreation and festival grounds, provides many advantages of a lakefront site—prospect and proximity without the potential for damage to the lake's sensitive shoreline ecology.

22,000 square feet of exhibitry form the core of the facility. It is divided into three components: (1) husbandry exhibits representing various lake faunal communities, (2) "science" exhibits illustrating physical properties of the lake, and (3) exhibits regarding societal influences and impacts on the lake. Outdoor exhibits allow the facility to "expand" to accommodate the increased crowds in summer. Public space components also include a resource center, theater, cafe, book and gift stores. Educational facilities are the second major program component and there are limited accommodations for visiting researchers. Support functions account

1. queuing ramp

view from southwest

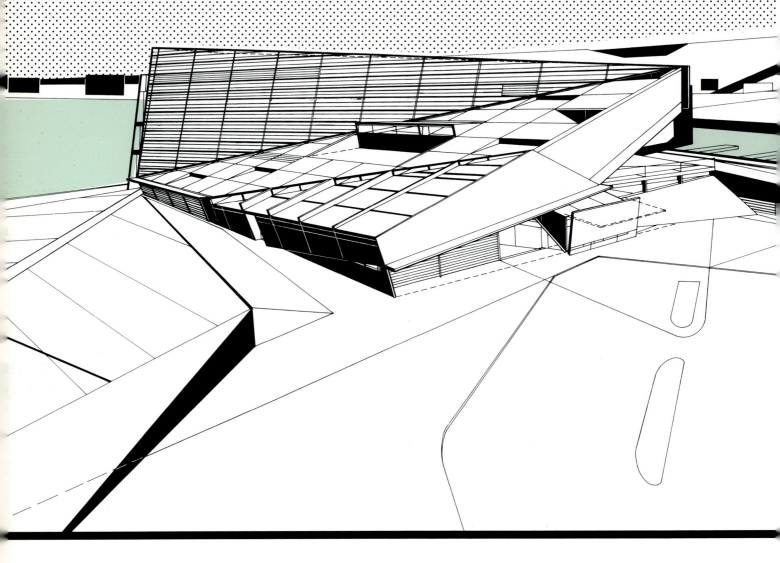

original "idea" of the author. Everything else—history, context, the artist's process or other intentions—is extraneous in such a view since it does nothing more than contribute to a varying and contingent replay of that stimulus. Only the essential, invariant experience matters, because it is what is unvarying and thus essential.[15] This extreme statement of the autonomy of the work is only the logical culmination of a line of thinking that begins in the common sense intuition of the object as the vessel directly exhibiting the artist's particular ideas to the particular viewer. It is the artist's thinking that matters and the subject's perception of that thinking. The object speaks for the artist, but what she means is the important thing.

31. Beginning perhaps in that common sense of the object as a free expression of authorial intent, Croce's aesthetics end up in a mystical solipsism. A contrary idea generally prevails today growing out of Payreyson's

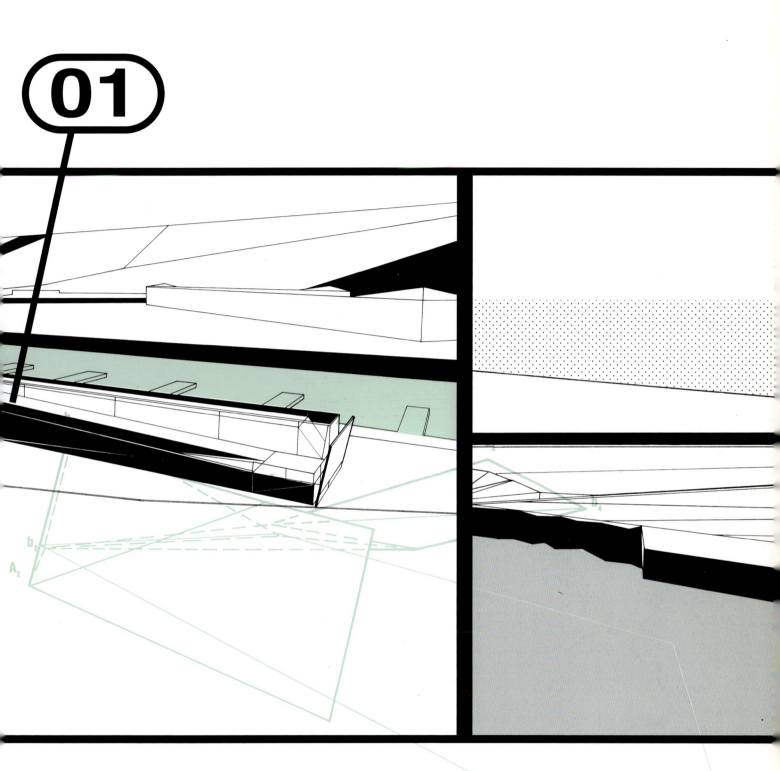

01

and Eco's answer to Croce: that the work does not stand there so freely, that it is "related to a lot of other things."[16] In this view everything is constructed, read, situated and enmeshed in a prior context and history, that itself is no less constructed and ensnared. Nothing is free in this sense, nor is it possible to be so. However the characterization of things and thingliness may evolve, and in that seemingly demonstrate its own constructed nature, the fact of their multiplicitous complexity remains, unchanged

14. lake viewing deck

view from northwest

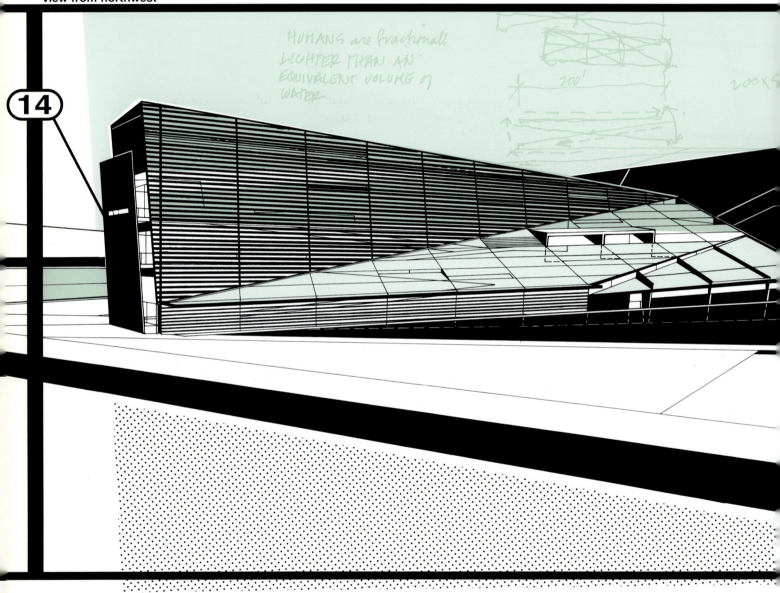

by perception. Nomad is an island, entire of itself. The world may be filled with things, but "we cannot approach them separately and directly, as distinct, unrelated things-in-themselves, but only through their prior differentiation and transmutation."[17]

32. The most extreme statement of this belief is offered by deconstruction, which holds that the same thingliness of the world that suggests the object's autonomy also gives rise to a general referrability, extended to the conceptual and affective, that is at the same time "primordial and essential, anterior to any thing, origin or ground."[18] The object dissolves into endless relationship; to speak simply of its autonomy becomes difficult since the simple assumption of presence grounding that autonomy is itself problematic. "All 'things' are constructed by and construct an interminable web, a textile of referral in which no proper beginning nor authentic end be located."[19]

33. The relationship between the textual and the

DR 17

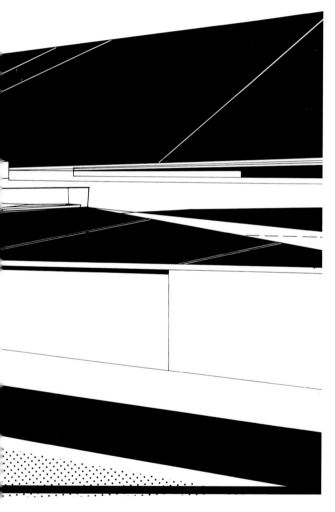

for the final, third component of the 45,000 square-foot building program.

The entire building is conceived of as a reconciled addition to the aquatic ecosystem and the civic community—a coming together of nature and man at the edge in physical terms, and some would say, at the precipice in historical terms. It is a building with an overriding responsibility for the biome it is settling into and an overriding concern for the need for responsible action to preserve an invaluable natural resource.

The client's desire that the building itself be an exhibit, and not just house exhibits, was understood by the architects as an injunction to create an intellectually challenging as well as visually engaging building. To that end, the building appropriates the properties of water in its various states, offering opportunities for experiences critical to an empathetic understanding of the subjects exhibited. As detailed in the diagrams which follow, building form and organization resulted from a consideration of contemporary cross-over theories as they might apply to this aquarium program—such as the Flounder catastrophe and the presentness of wave dynamics.

autonomous mirrors that of openness and the condition of closure, and the same confusing critical mediation has been brought to bear.
34. Whether autonomy will be seen as a hallmark of freedom or alienation depends on what is being considered and who is asking. If the question is asked by the reader, in reference to issues of empowerment, then autonomy is less prized than the relationships that connect the reader to a more open field of interpretation. But if the question

What might not be communicated in the diagrams, though, is the extent to which the architect has attempted to achieve a condition of NEAR FIGURE in this design. Ideally, such a condition would hover, freely, between the authoritarian dictates of traditional strong formalisms, and the indifferent mush of contemporary "weak form" architecture. If reading is dependent upon the perception of intention in the object, and "weakness" is ultimately a refusal of all the repressive implications of a received intention, then weakness' "liberating" openness is as subjugatory as randomness or indifference. NEAR FIGURE attempts to achieve weakness' critical goal without abrogating architecture's public responsibility to engage—and at some level—satisfy reading. The NEAR FIGURE opens up reading, loosening the author's controlling death-grip on meaning, without relegating the result to mush: is it a stealth building, a piled collision of fragmentary ice, a crystal church or modern expressionist icon? Is it an aquarium or twisted, folded ore ship, an airplane hangar or graduate school of design? Is it in the process of becoming, dissembling, is there a process at all, or did it simply land there? Is it emerging from or settling in, moving toward stasis or away, imploding or exploding? There is enough intentionality in the building, enough apparent figure, that reading is provoked. The building demands interpretation in its role as catalyst toward a frame of mind appropriate to viewing and contemplating the contained exhibits and the adjacent lake.

More traditionally, but no less valid for that, the architect has attempted to support the exhibit program by organizing the visitor's experience to parallel the exhibits' intent. The visitor enters after queuing up alongside an outdoor wave tank, following the progress of the wave shoreward, at an intermediate elevation where he is confronted with a vast volume of water: divided into "core" samples of lake biomes, each including exhibits from the surface to the bottom of the lake. This is the lake in section, the subject of study, too big to comprehend, dominating the open exhibit area of the building and linked to the horizon beyond. The visitor follows the exhibit program down a ramping floor impelled by gravity, like water, incrementally discovering the lake/tank in cross-section. From the initial acquaintance with the more familiar shore/surface or littoral condition, the visitor is led down and around to exhibits detailing pelagic, benthic and abyssal bio-communities. These vast tanks tower over and then swallow the visitor in their depths, dominating experiences with their ever-present statement of magnitude. At the conclusion of the core exhibit program, the visitor finds himself at the substantial rotating exhibit space that will host exhibits prepared by other aquaria around the world. A tour through the space and the seasonal outdoor exhibits accessed from here, returns the visitor back to the entrance via a short decompression experience imparting the significant message that despite the impressiveness of the lake, its precious fresh water is a drop in the world's saltwater oceans—a resource to be carefully conserved.

12. summer ramp
13. summer exhibit deck

view from northeast

is raised by the author, who is interested in maximizing the possibility for freedom, creativity and originality, then this same contextual web will be seen as restrictive and overly determinative, and the possibility of the object's autonomy will be coveted. And if the issue is raised by the critic, who sides today with the reader, then the author's interest will be seen as suspect or delusional, by pointing out the inescapability of relationship or undesirability of repressive assertions of authority.

35. Yet, to claim in all this that the autonomy of the work is repressive is disrespectful to the reader. "It is not enough for theory to describe and analyze, it must itself be an event in the universe it describes."[20] Indeed, the critic comes to this site of engagement as a second author, since it is no less the critic's intentions than the author's to control the reading: however liberating the critic's commentary hopes to be, it is still argumentative and purposeful. In fact, "the critic is a writer attempting

3. wave tank
4. splash wall

view from south

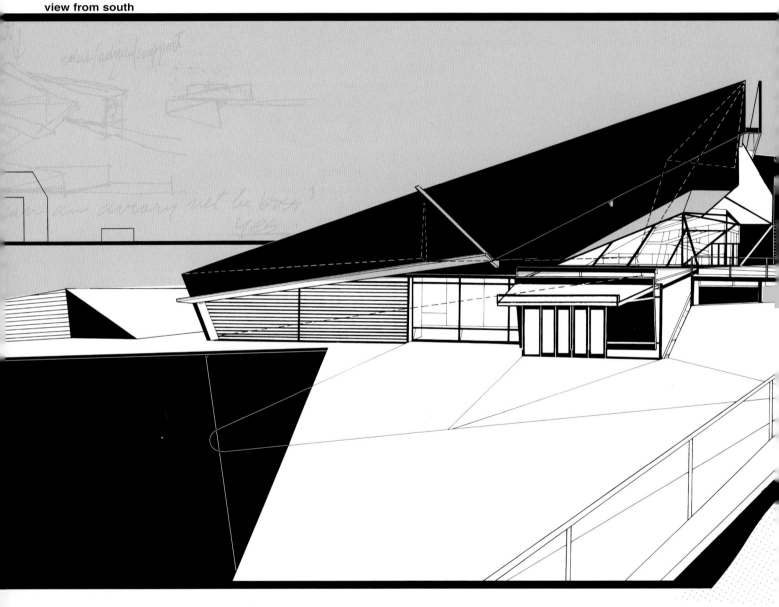

to cover the work with his own language."[21] It could even be said that the critic's efforts are more coercive than the author's, since they remain hidden from the work and removed from expectations of review. They pose as supplementary, without risk of encountering the same fate.
36. The assertion that everything is text is offered as a critique of cultural practices that privilege seeming autonomy. The given, or "natural" state of reality is one of inescapable, complex relationship, it is claimed. But, the call for resistance is made by demonstration of a more fundamental condition. If this is true, then in contrast, it seems to cast autonomy, as resistant, since autonomy challenges the given or "natural" state claimed for inescapable, complex relationship. If everything is "always already" unavoidably open, as the critique has it, then the creation of singular meaning or unambiguous effects must be resistive. In this view, the autonomous object would be exemplary of the desire for freedom

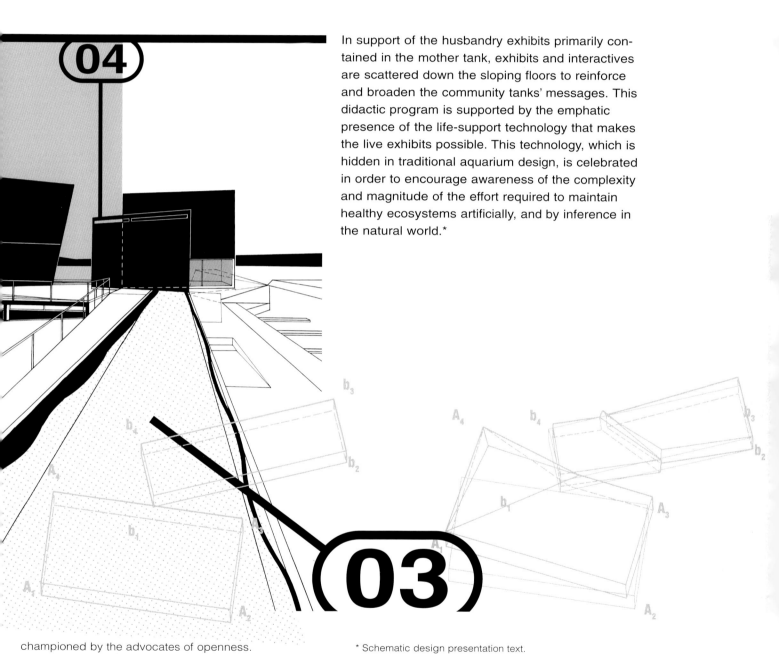

In support of the husbandry exhibits primarily contained in the mother tank, exhibits and interactives are scattered down the sloping floors to reinforce and broaden the community tanks' messages. This didactic program is supported by the emphatic presence of the life-support technology that makes the live exhibits possible. This technology, which is hidden in traditional aquarium design, is celebrated in order to encourage awareness of the complexity and magnitude of the effort required to maintain healthy ecosystems artificially, and by inference in the natural world.*

championed by the advocates of openness.

37. The instrumental assumes this freedom, yet, at the same time would seem to be opposed to the object's autonomy. The instrumental is a mode of relationship. The instrumental nature of the object is defined by the relation it makes with purpose, which itself is a relation between desire and fact. But instrumentality can be imagined from many different perspectives. The instrumental nature of the object can be considered as the fulfillment of a pur-

* Schematic design presentation text.

1. queuing ramp
3. wave tank

west elevation 1"=40.00'

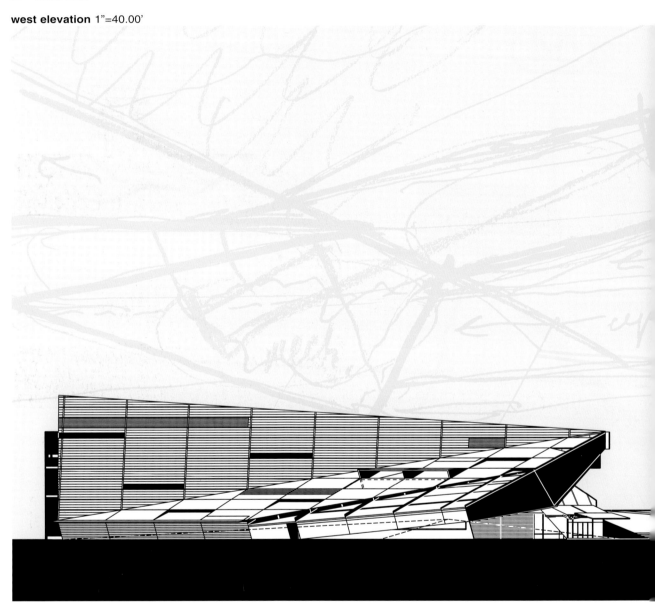

pose and as the agent for the fulfillment of another purpose: as a result or as a machine for achieving results. The machine simultaneously declares an autonomy resulting from its assertion of will(fulness) and avers a connectivity through its inflection to program and context—that belies that autonomy.

38. As a measure of freedom, autonomy is naturally demonstrated through willful action, and it is this willfulness, freely deployed, that drives the instrumental. But the freedom of that deployment is questionable. The machine has been an emblem for that questioning as well as an advertisement for discreet objecthood. When imagined as a robot, for example, the machine becomes both loved and feared for its specific autonomy. The robot is a projection of the human and of human folly to a superhuman level, in the same way as the Doric column was identified with an upright man, in relation to the state. In both cases, the human is personified in technol-

7. orientation theater
15. mechanical
19. rotating exhibit
22. exhibit ramp/ circulation
23. exhibit deck

transverse sections 1"=80.00'

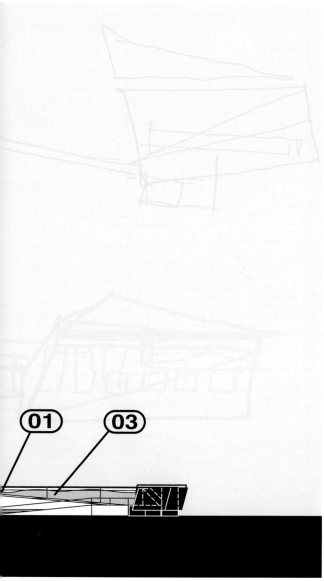
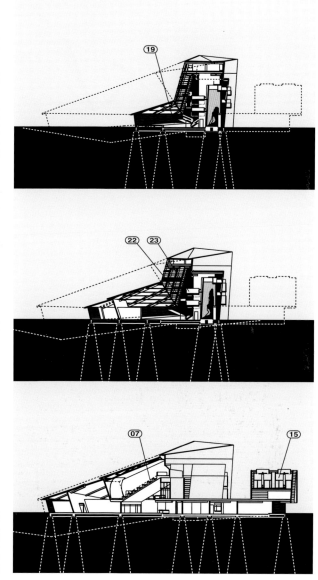

ogy in a way that casts light on both the human condition and its technological idealization. Thus the Greek was a citizen, a member of an order, with a place in the peristyle or colonnade, while the contemporary person is a cog, a product of an assembly line, free only to act, but not to will. Both betray a conflicted appreciation of the autonomy they demonstrate. Both seem to acknowledge that in reality the machine is no less enframed than humanity. The object is not seen in either case to own, or will, its own instrumental nature, or to direct its own purpose. It is seen only as an agent for the will of another, as subject to the impersonal forces of enframing. So the machine can serve as an emblem for a belief in autonomy as an expression of freedom, and as emblematic of the opposite interrelatedness of a world standing in reserve.

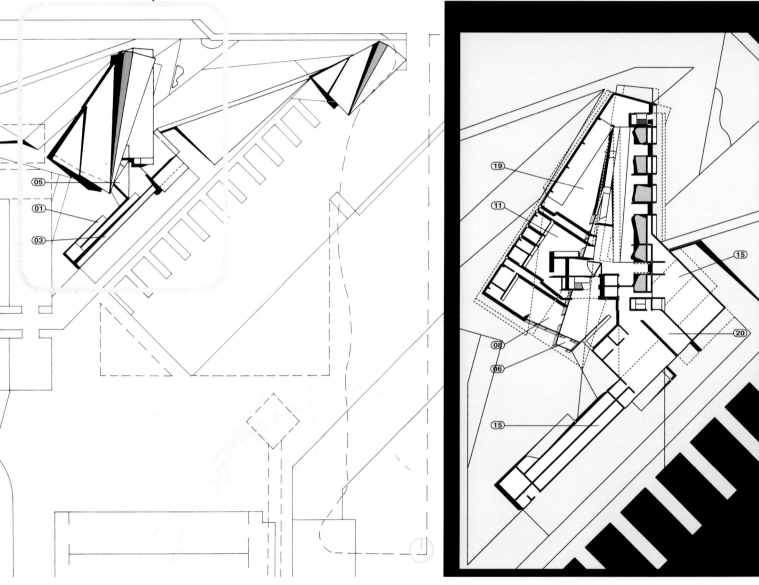

1. queuing ramp
3. wave tank
5. entry

site plan 1"=160.00'

6. group entry
8. books/ gifts
11. administration
15. mechanical
19. rotating exhibit
20. animal holding

exit level 1"=80.00'

39. Openness: Bossness

As openness is measured instrumentally, so openness is promoted through emphasizing the instrumental dimension in projects—both affect and effects. Empowerment and freedom are effects sought in an open architecture that can be pursued through a purposive program of design addressed to service and expression. Both are essential. Expression of such goals without being backed up with the fact of service is not only deceitful but repressive; accommodating that service without announcing its achievement in form (expression) is limiting and ultimately counter to the larger goal of dissemination. When the two are actually achieved together each is enhanced by the other: expression is made resonant through effective service, and that service is made noble in affective form. Expression

1. queuing ramp
2. queuing deck
3. wave tank
4. splash wall
5. entry
7. orientation theater
12. summer ramp
13. summer exhibit deck
14. lake viewing deck
22. exhibit ramp/ circulation
23. exhibit deck

14. lake viewing deck
20. animal holding
23. exhibit deck
25. Sturgeon Bay tank
26. Temperance River tank
27. Otter Cove tank
28. Superior Shoal tank
29. 222 Fathoms tank
30. St. Louis tank

entry level 1"=80.00'   **upper exhibit level** 1"=80.00'

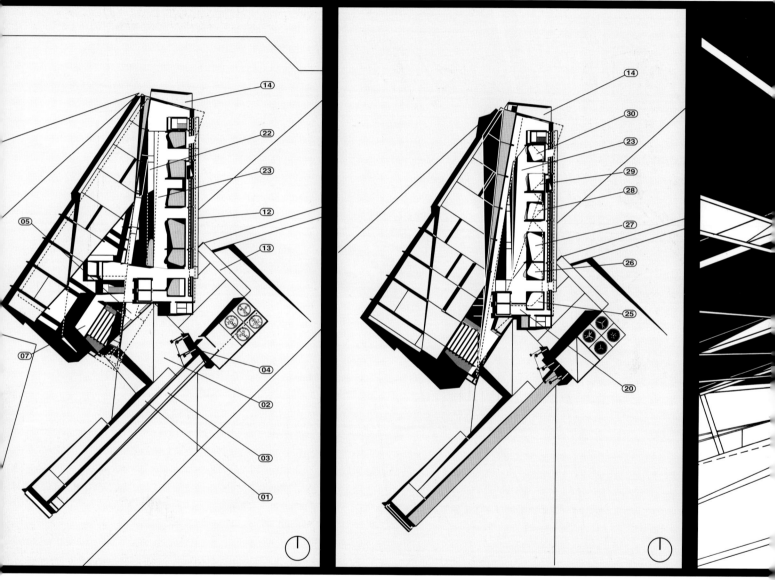

alone is ultimately intolerable, while service alone is banal. In their congruence the Boss is located.

40. It is difficult to separate the two even for the sake of discussion. To understand the idea of service in a project, for example, thoughts naturally run to issues of engagement, which is a measure of both the viewer's involvement in the experience of the space and the user's participation as the beneficiary of its effectiveness. A "program for openness" will strive for the creation of this sort of engaging experience by designing the Boss artifacts and spaces that wed affect and effect. In this sense, a catalog of the features enabling this experience will be a catalog of the components of a Boss architecture.

41. To encourage the attention that may lead to engaging experience—to draw the viewers in—this work aims for an inviting appearance. Its invitation is straightforward and direct, not seductive or coercive.

26. Temperance River tank
27. Otter Cove tank
28. Superior Shoal tank
29. 222 Fathoms tank
30. St. Louis tank

interior view

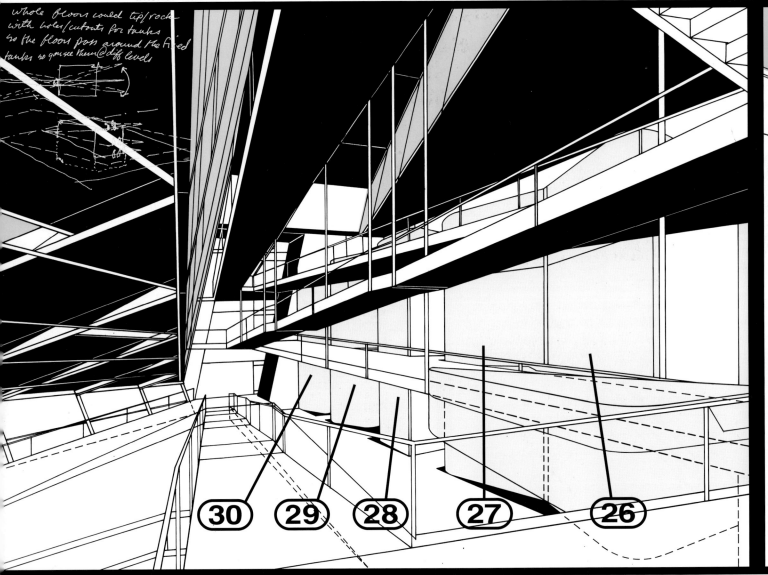

The openness that Boss architecture assumes is based on a sense of honesty. The boss object presents itself as the interlocutor, not as a front for some author, and assumes directly the responsibility for its half of the conversation. Consequently, the boss object is approached as a peer, and this attitude heightens the viewer's sense of her own role in the experience and responsibility for the other half of the interaction. The boss object demonstrates its eagerness for this participatory engagement by presenting itself without signature, as a self-effacing equipmental work.[22] It assumes, when it is architecture, a lower-case level of expectation, more in tune with the bestowing of dignity on the commonplace than the expression of the highest ideals of society. While boss can be celebratory, its sense of occasion is found in the more modest world of competence and effectiveness. It can celebrate speed or power as a

23. exhibit deck
24. exhibit return

interior view

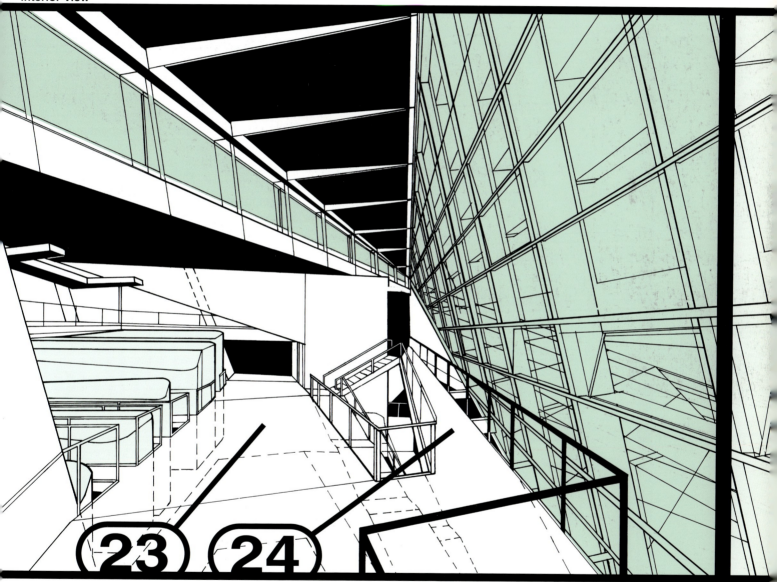

hot rod, for example, combining a respect for the humble, anonymous mass-produced host with the celebration of that vehicle's immanent capacity for performance.

42. The boss object values clarity and legibility; in order to solicit the viewer's attention, and appeal to the viewer's native reading compulsion, bossness always communicates at least a sense of understandability. Even if real understanding is not immediate, or its means apparent, the viewer is encouraged to assume that the object will reward attention. The boss object is not mysterious; it holds no promise of secrets to be discovered or hidden messages to be unearthed. It is frank. This does not mean that it is only a one-liner, but that its many lines are related to one another and the main theme in such a way that the reading unfolds naturally. The reader is rewarded with a sense of confidence and accomplishment, and

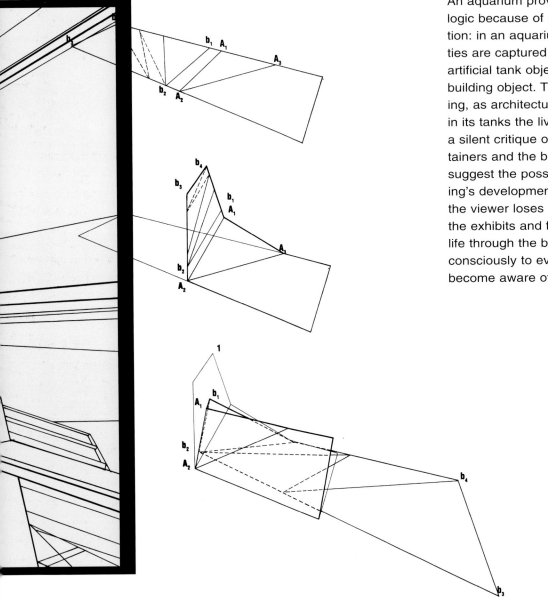

An aquarium provides an interesting study of this logic because of its nature as a double encapsulation: in an aquarium "natural" biomes or communities are captured as discontinuous samples within artificial tank objects, themselves captive within the building object. The aquarium building, as a building, as architecture, is traditionally complete, while in its tanks the live exhibits flow on continuously in a silent critique of the apparent fixity of their containers and the building. If this fixity is relaxed, to suggest the possibility of continuation of the building's development beyond its present state, then the viewer loses his privileged position relative to the exhibits and finds himself part of the flow of the life through the building. He must then attend more consciously to events, since he is involved, and so become aware of the active nature of his reading.*

* SD 9409 text

is given the desire to continue the reading, with expectations of further satisfaction.
43. The grammar and vocabulary of bossness are drawn for the most part from the world of mechanical reference.[23] As the embodiment of the native human orientation to a reality composed of discrete things in relation to one another, the mechanical is the most common pre-cultural language. Though mechanical awareness may vary in its details from one culture or

UCLA Chiller Plant/Cogeneration Facility
P93.12/1
Los Angeles, CA

Owner:	University of California, Los Angeles Charles Oakley, campus architect
Client:	The Ralph M. Parsons Company (RMPco)/Kiewit Pacific Construction, a joint venture
Architect:	Holt Hinshaw Jones; Jones, Partners: Architecture
Consultants:	Parsons Main (formerly C.T. Main) (engineers)
Contractor:	Kiewit Pacific Construction
Site:	Eight acres in the heart of the UCLA Campus, at the intersection of Westwood Boulevard and Circle Drive South
Program:	Campus Facilities Replacement Space, including shops and offices for the Campus Facilities and Maintenance departments, and central chiller/combined cycle cogeneration plant producing 16,600 tons chilled water, 42.5 MW power, and 160,000 lb./hr. 150 psig steam
Size:	210,000 ft^2
Systems:	Cast-in-place concrete basement and foundations, steel frame structure above grade, precast and site laid brick veneer, smooth and corrugated metal panel, exposed mechanical system with hard cast ducts, steel catwalks and stairs
Features:	Designed for a phased construction on an extremely tight site, that permitted the campus shops occupying portions of the site to remain in operation until their replacement space in the new building was finished; the shops and offices are moved to the interior of the site, and the power plant to the streetfront—this prevents the clutter of the shopyards and maintenance vehicle parking areas from spilling out onto this major campus thoroughfare, and provides the building with the large sculptural facade that honestly distinguishes this service building from the surrounding academic buildings and parking garages.
Cost:	$150 million
Completion:	March 1994

The UCLA "Central Chiller-Cogeneration Plant with Facilities Management Replacement Space" is located in the southwest part of the campus on Circle Drive South just off the campus' primary thoroughfare, Westwood Plaza Drive, across from the UCLA Medical Center. The difficult eight-acre site is bounded closely on three sides by existing campus buildings and is within two hundred feet of a residential neighborhood to the west. The site was previously occupied by Facilities Management's central offices and craft shops which were relocated as Phase I of the project, which entailed the renovation an existing 50,000 square-foot warehouse building at one end of the site to house the campus shops being displaced by the new plant, allowing the site to be cleared for Phase 2.

Phase 2 of the project involved the construction of new quarters for the Facilities Management Group, and the chiller and cogeneration plants. This construction is divided into two general parts along an east/west dividing line through the site. This division responds to programmatic requirements that included complex, separated vehicular/pedestrian circulation, acoustical/vibration isolation, structural separation between plant and shop components, and acoustical control of all noise-emitting equipment to minimize the ambient noise levels of the nearby residential neighborhood. The north side of the complex is composed of approximately 95,000 square feet of high bay ground-level shop space for Campus Crafts with two stories of office space above for Facilities Management administrative

staff. The shops and offices consolidate Facilities Management operations for the entire campus. The south side of the complex is a high bay structure with a full basement housing all of the Central Chiller and Cogeneration Plant functions, about 90,000 square feet of plant space.

The Central Chiller Plant with Cogeneration features turbine driven centrifugal and absorption chillers, pumps, water demineralization equipment, electrical distribution systems, and miscellaneous support equipment, which are used to produce 16,000 tons of cooling initially and 26,000 tons of cooling at build-out to meet future needs. Two 14.5-MW combustion turbine generators provide continuous reliable power and one 14.0-MW steam turbine generator operates on a cogeneration cycle utilizing the energy by-products of the chilled water production. In addition, the plant space encloses a stand alone Emergency Services Equipment Building designed to OSHPD specifications providing power, steam and chilled water to the critical care facilities at the UCLA Medical Center.

Staging and scheduling of the 6.5-mile chilled water distribution system was accomplished with minimal impact to campus operations. The plant provides power and chilled water for all current as well as forecasted campus needs with electrical service/system upgrades providing a new 12.47-kV system to augment the existing 4.8-kV system and providing continual pay-back revenue to UCLA Energy Systems. The payback offsets current utility costs creating enough revenue through savings in operating costs to retire the private debt financing within twenty-five years. Cogeneration is accomplished with one hundred percent standby parallel operation with the Los Angeles Department of Water and Power and stand-alone cogeneration with "black start" capabilities. The project also resulted in a substantial reduction in overall campus emissions through the use of low emission generating equipment and the elimination of existing individual building systems.

That the natural penetrates even to our densest urban cores is obvious in the immense efforts expended to mitigate her effects there: vast power plants are erected to turn back the night, chiller plants are built to alleviate the heat of the day and steam generators to transform the cool of the night. Yet we are generally embarrassed by these efforts—the often beautiful artifacts engineered to provide this light, cold and heat are hidden away, where they are not able to remind us of the effort and energy required to enjoy life in unnaturally dense environments of our cities. To reveal these measures is, in a way, to celebrate the power of the natural conditions they mitigate—and to hope that in mitigating their effects we do not forget we are never actually free from them.

Commissioned through a limited design/construct competition, UCLA's new South Campus Chiller Plant celebrates the machinery of infrastructure.

1. new Chiller Plant
2. existing Campus Services building
3. existing Police Station

site plan 1"=312.50'

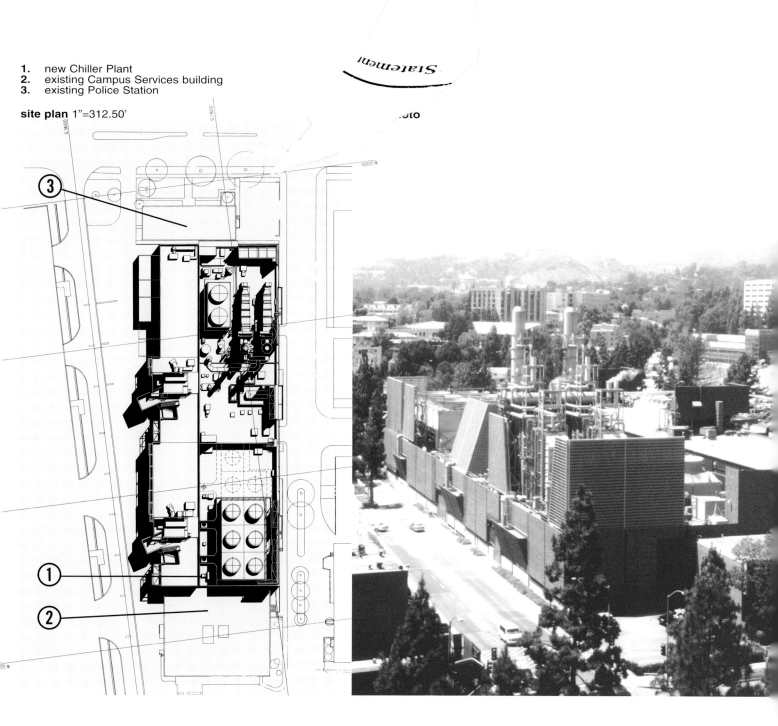

time to another, its basic tropes and metaphors—deriving from laws of cause-and-effect, rules of conservation of mass and momentum, the role of friction, and the sense of entropy—can be considered universal and directly accessible across the broadest range of audiences and situations. By largely restricting itself to this source of reference, the boss trades a more extreme recourse to openness for a greater assurance of engagement. Yet it would be a mistake to consider the mechanical as limiting in any but the most abstract way; because its effects span the full range of perception available to humanity through the five physical senses, the mechanical describes the scale at which environmental experience is possible for humans and the intuition that has evolved to process this experience. The mechanical is the standard; even attempts to transcend it are expressed in mechanical terms if they hope to be understood.

view from southeast

44. The intention behind this directness is for the reader to gradually assume a more active role in determining the affect and enjoying the effects, for the confidence inspired by this satisfaction to inspire greater competence that in turn will increase the empowering confidence, and that all this might extend to other experience. The boss trusts that the impossibility of actually legislating such readings will ensure that the reader's true contribution is not trivial. The boss understands that this creation of meaning is a game, and it chooses to play by setting its own moves out there for reaction without veiling their form or intent.

45. This legibility would be wasted, though, if there were nothing to do, so the boss object is designed with interactivity in mind. Since the boss thing is invariably a machine, and its purpose is so emphatically advertised, such interaction is a straightforward

southwest view detail

While sensitive to its surroundings, the use of familiar materials and architectural treatments is critical in application, rather than imitative. The building is not a mute box. It does not insist on hiding plant machinery, but proudly displays the inherently engaging qualities of technology as an integrated and carefully considered part of the composition. Architectural honesty is projected through the sophisticated interplay of its rich contextual palette and carefully expressed mechanical and electrical systems.

The idea of infrastructure—vital stuff that is considered within, between, invisible, but which provides structure to that other "real" stuff—begs to be deconstructed. Infrastructure is the repressed monolith upon which urban civilization is founded. It must be hidden, since its presence is a sign of the provisionality of that situation. The invisibility of infrastructure allows urban civilization to presume its privilege; the certainty of civilization's presence, however truly precarious, is always extended to imply the certainty of a privilege to exist.

This structure becomes much more impressive and fraught with worry when it is fleshed-out with the particulars of the relationship between infrastructural technology and nature. This is where Heidegger's critique of technology as enframing was focused; he saw the idea of nature being ordered to "stand, ready or in reserve," for continuous exploitation, as a grave danger to humanity. But Heidegger was not being "green" when he

extension of the object's attitude of service. The boss object expects the user's participation through its adjustability, and through its more conventional architectural effects, like circulation. The boss thing may be tuned to mitigate shifting environmental influences such as sunlight or wind, for example, or to accommodate varying spatial requirements. In such manner it invites the viewer to become a user and take charge of her surroundings. This physical involvement pro-

4. louvered screen
5. brick panel
7. dunnage
11. vents
12. entry
29. gas turbine generators

cut-away view

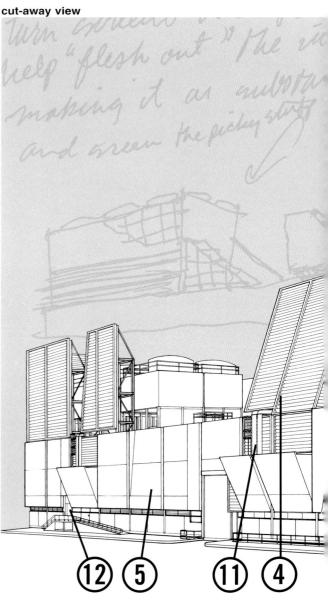

pointed this out—he feared not for the planet, but, rather, for humanity's soul. He felt the danger lies not in the enframing of nature, per se, but in our belief in that capability and our attendant complacency. This is an illusion (as Muschamp points out in the example of the earthquake), a *dangerous* illusion, he felt, which blinds us to the implications of our assumptions of mastery.

Yet, to merely point out this situation, violently overturning hierarchies and reveling in their disclosure, is to ignore the reality that what is really described here is a *negotiation.*

We do not truly come to grips with the "natural" if we balance the relationship on the fulcrum of idealism. Either refusing to hear the tree falling by itself in the woods, or insisting that the hearing itself is without meaning, which implies no relationship at all, misses the point, absolutely. Heidegger stresses that we need to understand humanity as properly the *witness* of this event. But further, it is important to realize that it only *matters* if this relationship holds. It is our ability to act as witnesses of this relationship that is endangered by enframing.

In the absence of this care there is no relationship. When Heidegger criticizes the relationship of our technology to nature as brutal and uncaring he is not criticizing the fact of the relationship, but its character. Recognizing its true inescapability, he calls for a greater awareness of the *exchange* so that each party becomes more visible and fulfilled motes a closer connection between the user and the object or space. For this reason, as well as for reasons of perception, the boss object concentrates its effort on effects achievable at the human scale— where, as a dance partner, it is less likely to risk an alienating clumsiness or sinister inattentiveness.
46. Finally, the boss object assumes a cultural genesis in non-elitist Americana, which it draws on for its affect of optimism and honesty. Bossness presumes

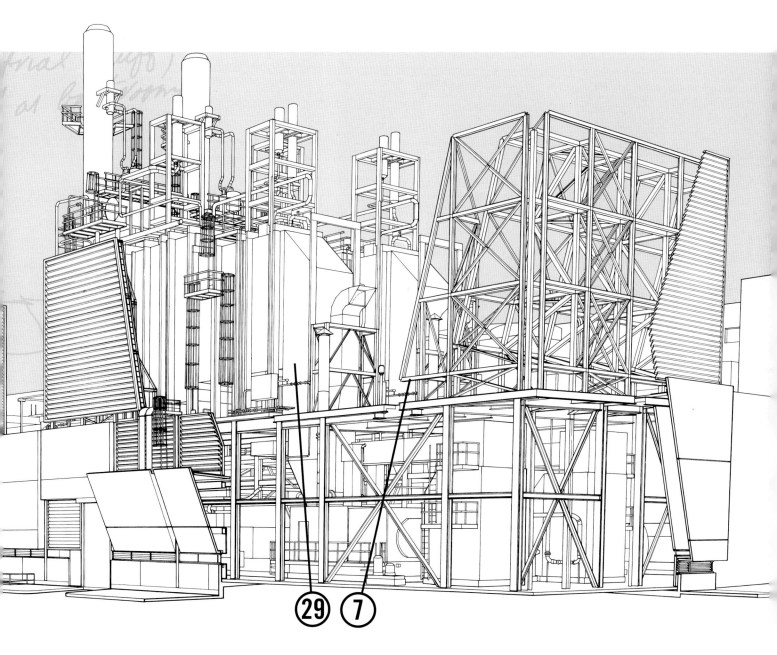

a democracy of competence, open to anyone who can master or even appreciate the tools and techniques. It speaks of the mobility and freedom of the wide open spaces, and challenge of the frontier, of the can-do pragmatism that makes the bossest stuff and makes it innocent of its bossness, that shows no fear before the unknown or untested, but respects the tried and true, that can view the souped-up in the same way as the state-of-the-art and find both exhilarating. In rooting its expression in this cultural context, bossness distinguishes itself from the haute-tech without relinquishing any of the performance fetishized in that model. The boss simultaneously enjoys a naive chauvinism and sophisticated collegiality with its international peer forms that reflects its provenance in the garage of the free and the shop of the brave. HR 1

view from southwest

view from southeast

[1] "Openness" is being used loosely, openly, to indicate the attitude driving an interest in multiplicity, pluralism, and the open-ended free-play of interpretation.
[2] Heinrich Wölfflen, *Principles of Art History*, 149.
[3] Yet still maintain a contrastingly conservative interest in identity, that can be systemized and named.
[4] There is nothing in the postmodern/poststructural critique that says architecture must be alienating except insofar as the alienation measures the degree of co-

view from south

option the critique exposes. To alienate is to present the "other," to challenge the subject, which must be to challenge the constitutional history and contextual forces that define him. The alienation caused by critical architecture is a measure of the alienation suffered by the subject, in Marx's use. For this reason it is unlikely any critique that exposes alienation can be effected without creating alienation. This leaves open the question of whether there is a corresponding authentic nature, though, that could be engaged by such work, a nature that might find the otherwise "alienating" work engaging directly, since unencumbered by the history that must find it alienating in the first place.

5 **Notes re: Orthodoxy/Constitution**[a]

1. If form is constrained only by the limits of dimension, why do we invent so narrowly from this infinitude?
2. Outside the boundaries of what we know is the unknown; logically, we assume there must be a great

in the relationship. Of course, he might never have considered a chiller plant or power plant as anything other than an example of enframing, but he would never deny that they acted out the relationship and that it mattered. Or that the character of this relationship hinged on the character of *humanity's* understanding. The notion that humanity's essence might be embodied in the activity of witnessing this most basic relationship *admits* a necessary and pragmatic anthropocentrism, with enough realism that its nature as a perspective is apparent. It is to admit that there really is only one perspective. And to deal with it.

There must be some sort of value in repressing awareness of the "objective" precariousness of humanity's position. That is, there must be some value in our conventions which mask provisionality. We must admit that convention, though *artificial,* is not *unnatural.* A critique of this situation must be delicate, accommodating—not a critique to death, but a critique to awareness. The dance, rather than a brutal full-disclosure, is more revealing of both sides of the equation. It exacts the negotiation that is at the root of both nature's teasing relationship with technology, and technology's teasing relationship with society and culture.

Infrastructure is typically, conventionally, invisible; it inhabits mysterious zones of no-space. These zones riddle the urban landscape today and hide the underpinnings of that culture: the freeway trenches and empty spaces captured by clover-

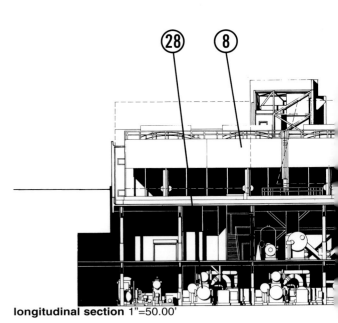

4. louvered screen
5. brick panel
8. cooling towers
9. mechanical penthouse
10. exhaust plenum
11. vents
12. entry
15. absorption chiller
28. centrifugal chiller

south elevation 1"=50.00'

longitudinal section 1"=50.00'

DR 13

deal that is unknown. This is the reservoir of possibility from which our designs draw. Less logically, but more importantly, we avoid forms that seem to allude to the vastness of this reservoir, forms that suggest the infinitude of possibility, because such forms must correspondingly highlight our own "limited" condition. The otherness of these unfamiliar forms stresses our mortality. Still less logically, we also avoid the studiously banal, the too-familiar that makes our mortality interminable. Our form-

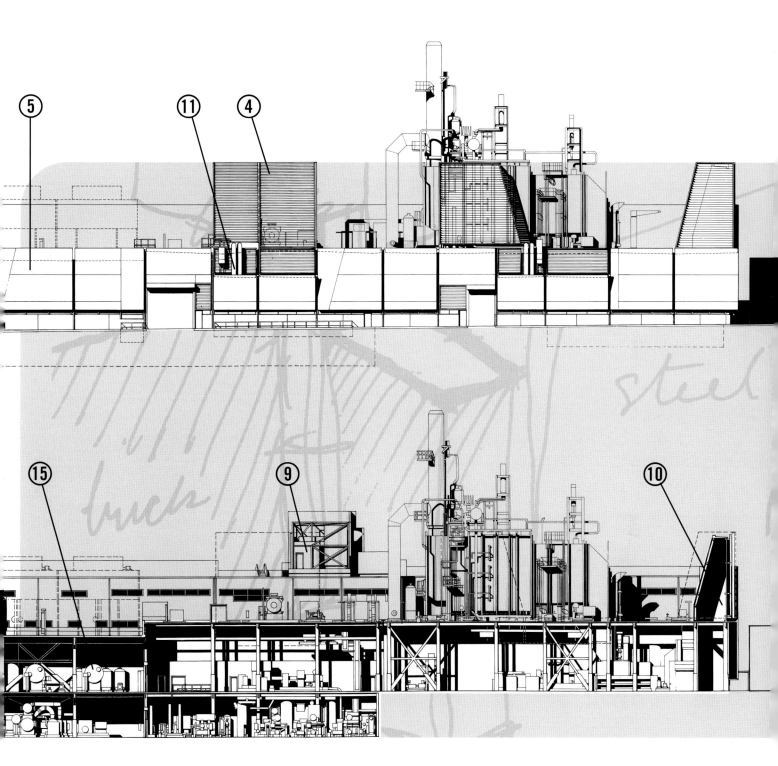

making efforts take us only where we can be challenged without great risk, where we can maintain control without being bored. We exist and create on the edge between these two. Apart from some unnourishing, voyeuristic critical intrigue with otherness or the occasional lazy slide into stunning banality, we are really only interested in what we suspect can be known. We really only care about what is an extension of ourselves. It is only here at this edge that we may "find" meaning. This constrained world of expectation is a map of our selves, a record of the inhibitions that define us as what we may know—and as other than the other we fear.

3. The establishment of this bulwark of constraint against vastness and otherness is an enormous arena of human activity. This inhibitive achievement of finitude sets out the frontiers of recognition and thus meaning, providing difference with a certain resolution. It carves out of limitless possibility, between world and earth in

4. louvered screen
6. exterior walkway
9. mechanical penthouse
13. service core
23. transformers

north elevation 1"=50.00'

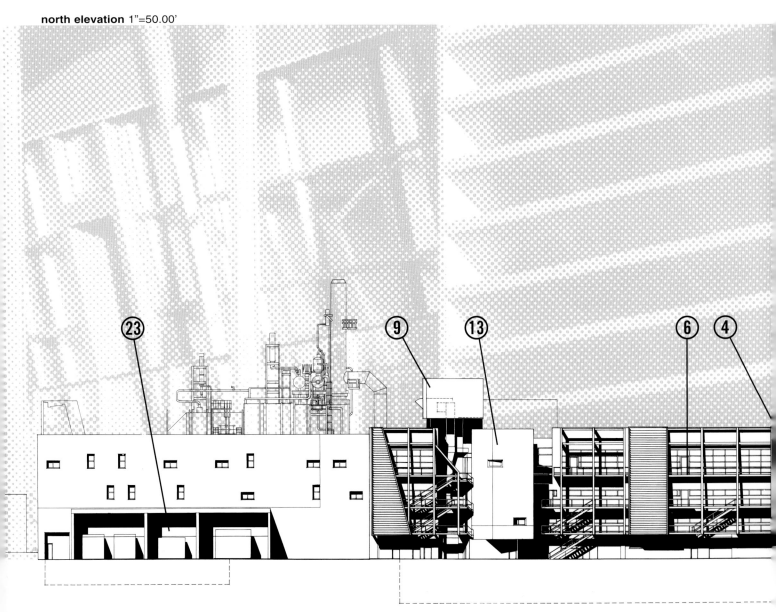

Heidegger's terminology, a position that marginalizes real otherness; it sets up a finite world where certainty and comfort may dwell. This certainty is maintained through a diligent, practical application of "right thinking" or orthodoxy, thinking that is fruitful because it is "correct," correct because it is guaranteed arrival at an answer by the circumscription of the course of possibility. This orthodoxy is jealously guarded at first as an achievement, then out of habit, and then, when most friable, out of fear.

4. Fear dominates the stewardship of culture today. It is increasingly apparent that the bulwark of constraint is wearing thin. The inhibitions that bind us are relaxing and otherness is seeping through. This fact explains the range and tone of contemporary architectural discourse. To some who are consumed with the critique of convention this possibility is a exciting route to greater freedom. Others, who know nothing besides convention, yet are not aware of it as such, fear anarchy and the loss of

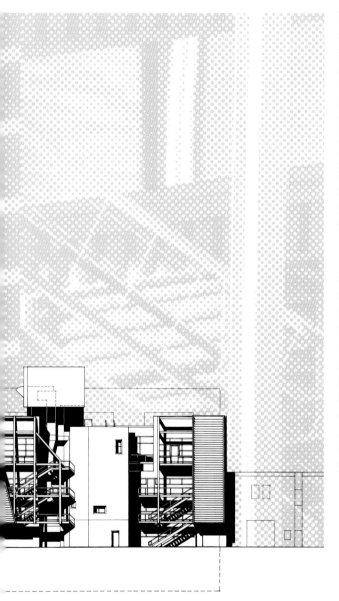

leaves and on-ramps belie our command over space and time; the flood control channels and basins which along with the vast waste treatment apparatus present an oasis of life in an otherwise uninhabitable desert; and the power plants and switchgear yards make light of the cold and warm the darkness. As well, perhaps, as the ghettos and barrios support an avoidance of drudgery which pretends that life has dignity. All these must be invisible if we are to face down the uncertainty ameliorated by these devices. We are all complicitous in this non-awareness, we are all signatories to the conventions which hide them.

The cloaking effects that ensure the invisibility of zones of no-space are only barely the product of design. But mindful of the conventions of such masks, the design of the Chiller Plant sought in these effects the raw material from which to fashion a critique. This critique emphasizes the negotiation otherwise hidden by the masking conventions. The facade of the Chiller Plant both masks and frames. It can be seen, conventionally, as a screen behind which nasty stuff is hidden. It can also be seen as a *base*, upon which the cooling towers and boilers sit: a table with boss objects arranged on it for our inspection.

meaning in the world. Across the face of architecture a battle between safety and adventure rages, the forces of novelty-venerating poststructuralism battle with the legions of historicist nostalgia. Yet, there is also a camp **ONO 6** between these extremes, perhaps even a silent majority. **NIRM note g** This undeclared, but not neutral, camp notices the corrosive effects of the unthinking embrace of otherness, but cannot believe in the possibility of recreating some lost original "golden" age. They understand the critiques lev-

The typology of infrastructure buildings is simple: the typical "plant" is a mute, blank-walled box with similarly blank mechanical screens hiding the usual cooling towers and air-handlers on the roof. This model is the product of both economic and aesthetic forces—the machines don't need expensive windows or other elaboration, and no one wants to see them anyway, or even notice their location. This attitude varies from one extreme of indifference, which is common in sparsely populated areas and results in the almost militant expression of economy (read cheap and ugly), to the other extreme of paranoia, evident in more urban areas or expensive suburbs, where plants are often disguised as some other, less objectionable, type of building (like a country clubhouse or an office building). But underlying even these extreme dissimulations is the mute box. Since the client (and context) for the Chiller Plant is an educational institution, it seemed appropriate to bring this typology into the light and make this screening evident.

Like a theater scrim, the screen requires complicity: it announces it is hiding something as it asks you not to notice. This is obviously the condition in which enframed nature is placed, as embodied in urban infrastructure works. The hide-and-seek game played as the erstwhile louver screens dance with the equipment to be hidden, highlights the screen's masking role. While they teasingly reveal the equipment, the screens configure themselves so that they may alternatively be read as *continua-*

detail view from north

eled by poststructuralism, but refuse to accept the nihilistic conclusions. This group pragmatically understands the usefulness of conventions beyond politics, even as it recognizes the irony implicit in their appropriate deployment as tools. These architects prefer to believe there is an alternative to facing the howling void completely naked; likewise they prefer to imagine that new tools could be fashioned rather than the old ones endlessly resharpened.

view from north

5. After the intense mediation architecture weathered in the 1980s the curve of expectation has flattened. The gap opened by hype has been closed by yawns. Architecture seems much less relevant today; it is no longer being asked to lend a hand at the ramparts, despite—or maybe because of—the increasing breach. Other means seem more effective. Even architecture's proudest achievements count for little in the value system of an information revolution celebrating the immaterial, or rendered suspect by the assumptions of a theory that has made nihilism scientific and de rigueur, or silly by the activities of a profession with no self-respect. In addition to its fragility, the sheer artificiality of the architectural universe is highlighted today to an unprecedented degree. The necessity that can impel architecture when authority itself is no longer received is nowhere in evidence. Orthodoxy and convention have become embarrassingly apparent. The scrim is lifted, but nothing

tions of the equipment, complicating the reading: is the equipment being hidden or elaborated?

In addition, a screen hides without substance. It is consumed in masking the thing screened. The insubstantiality of the Chiller Plant's screen is both demonstrated by the overt thinness of the panels and artificiality of the blue shadows, for example, while at the same time being challenged; the louver returns, brick reveals and overhangs, contradict the statement of insubstantiality with demonstrations of their volumetric qualities and apparent massiveness.

While the south facade of the plant is all about the mechanical negotiation with nature, the north facade of the maintenance shops and offices embodies the workers' negotiations with each other and their machines. The north facade is emphatically *inhabited,* and all of the overt formalism demonstrates this inhabitation. If the south facade *dissembles,* then the north facade *boasts*; it is operated, *driven* by the people during their daily activities.

The north side of the building houses the shops and offices of the campus Facilities Management department. The north facade actively looms over the working yard in an attitude of attentiveness, not just enclosing the space, but participating in it and directing the activity it overlooks. The catwalks and louver screens that cover the facade literally enliven it, as the workers circulate and otherwise hang out on this active surface. Bridges were originally planned over the yard for the workers to enter the building directly from the parking garage to the north. It was later decided that the more "polite" south entry should replace these. The restrooms and vertical circulation are combined into cores which interlock with the mechanical risers in two clearly defined tower-like moments. These identify the entry points and divide up the space of the yard by discipline. Each core hinges metaphorically in the middle, allowing the exterior elements to rotate clear of the traffic and exercise their operational nature. This conceit is carried on throughout the experience of the northern (people) half of the project, integrating the human spaces and functions with the overall expression of mechanical willfulness, as a demonstration of the negotiation between this vast machine and the humans who "drive" it.

As with its relationship to its technological mission, the building is of two minds about its size. On the one hand it is clearly proud of itself and what its immensity represents as an achievement; yet, on the other hand, it employs many of the scale-giving tricks by which architects customarily have broken-down or disguised the bulk of buildings too big for their context. In the present case these include the division of the building into plausible subgroups, the manipulation of scale by varying louver size and spacing, and the careful arrangement of contrasting, richly hued colors, with the placement of lighter

detail view from mechanical penthouse

is behind it.

* * *

6. Orthodoxy promotes a sense of inevitability. By maintaining a distinct, knowable world convention and orthodoxy provide the comfort and certainty of familiarity. From within that world, we speak of such activity as natural. From within, we feel a sense of conviction about the order of things. The reference to "naturalness" is not casual. It invokes connections to the ultimate authority, nature.

7. Ironically, Nature is itself the Other, of course, and not only as the Puritans imagined it. Nature is not so much out there, on the other side of the threshold as the entire reservoir of possibility, including the threshold and the ability to imagine it. Unlike everything else to which the very idea of possibility might refer, Nature could not be otherwise. It simply is what is or could be. Consequently, it always provides a backstop to meaning,

catwalk detail

catwalk detail

an answer to difference. In a final desperate act to defeat otherness we give ourselves over to this larger inevitability, Nature. We relax into inevitability; we find comfort in its necessity. In the end, it is our only recourse to certainty.

8. We appropriate Nature's inevitability with an approximation: the related concept of origin posits a "location" for the certitude. Since Nature is prior to all meaning, as well as beyond it, the unimaginable spatial metaphor is approximated by the more easily visualized temporal analogy. Inevitability follows from originality: as priority confers legitimacy to the first meaning, that meaning is rendered inevitable. When originality is established, inevitability ensues; when the inevitability is sensed, origin is expected. As an assurance of "uniqueness" and "priority," inevitability gives value to originality and originality returns the favor by giving inevitability a home.

9. When formalized within an orthodoxy, the concept of

colors at the roof so that the building profile can diffuse into the sky.

The dance of the mechanical screens plays a part as well, it draws the otherwise anomalous and alien equipment into a unified composition, thus limiting the building's apparent sprawl. This also confers an architectural legitimacy on the equipment, making it part of the building—or does it make the building an extension of the equipment? The engineers were initially skeptical about such a risqué approach; they were extremely sensitive about the homeliness of their stuff. Accustomed to being required to hide their best work, the engineers' pride in their efforts did not alleviate an enculturated insecurity about its appearance. Once it became clear to the engineers, however, that some of their equipment would be *featured* proudly on the roof of the project, that the aesthetically-minded architects thought it was boss, they began quietly to compete among themselves to determine whose machines should be so honored. We were then bombarded with photos or drawings of various machines and shyly asked whether perhaps *this* piece of equipment would not be too ugly up there, or, if not, whether we could fit this truly magnificent ammonia tank into the cycle in this or that location ...

But it was not only the engineers' self regard that benefited from this integration. In fact, the architecture benefited more: here was a store of existing forms of far greater interest then anything the architects could have set out to *invent*. This equipment

EO 10
origin becomes axiomatic. The authority of orthodoxy depends on the irreducibility of the origin myths it promulgates. A staple of deconstruction is the gleeful recognition of the myth's provisionality, the enumeration of the implications of its axiomatic nature.

   6a. The idea of the axiom answers the dilemma of beginning: if *ex nihilo, nihil fit*, then there must already be a something with which to begin. The axiomatic beginning is found in

12. entry corridor
16. procurement office
17. plumbing/ electrical storage
18. landscape equipment
22. switchgear room

ground level plan 1"=100.00'

14. future shops
15. absorption chiller
24. Facilities Management offices
26. plumbing shop
27. electrical shop

second level plan 1"=100.00'

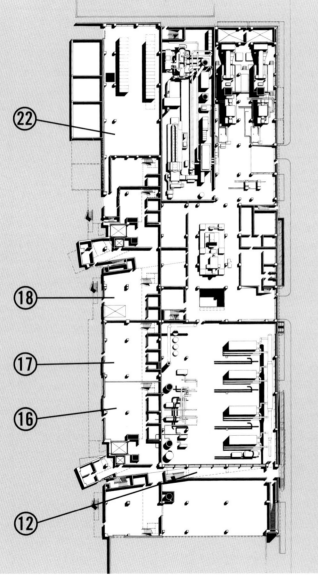
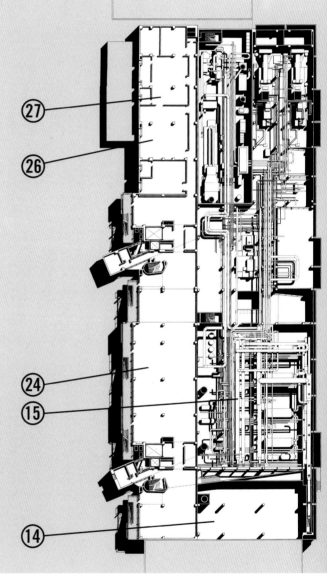

"self-evidence": the chain of reduction that arrives at the axiom compels the axiom to be the limit, and thus the beginning, because it hasn't the perspective to question the questioning—leaving the axiom as so basic within the system that it must be "beyond proof." The standard of proof, legislated by the pre-existing system that the axiom is created to found, thus negatively defines its relationship to its most basic element. From the provisional origin then proceeds a postrationalized evolution that miraculously explains the context that legislated the axiom. Given that context, the intention behind these efforts disappears into "nature," and with it the "post-" which undermines the rationalization by remembering its provisionality. Like the sand in the oyster or Laugier's primitive hut, the axiom is necessary to begin the

8. cooling towers
24. Facilities Management offices

third level plan 1"=100.00'

had only to be laid out with some minor connective design, to give an engaging experience to the viewer that easily exceeded the capacity of straight architecture alone. These objects can be read! They do something! Here is no arbitrary capricious design; personal flourish or "signature style" need not goober-up their already "magnificent" lines. They speak of our (provisional) contract with nature in a much more direct and visceral way than any classical order or applied vegetal ornament. While not figural, in the traditional sense, the equipment is far from abstract or alien. It represents an almost inexhaustible, and continuously replenished, resource for the resourceful architect.

There is a vast store of form in industry that has all the visual interest of classicism (which aloof modernism was not able to provide) and only one half of the kilo-calories. *And,* it does not rely on the whimsy or obscurity that much recent architecture has offered as an alternative. All this ... and meaning, too.

process, but, if the process succeeds, it is swallowed during its course and disappears into the inevitability of the product.[fn]

10. The axiom intends to convince us that before the beginning is nothing. But if the authority that seems to flow inevitably from this origin source is shown to be motivated, then the priority of that source is questionable. Orthodoxy expends great effort to preserve the sanctity of the beginning, since it founds its own legiti-

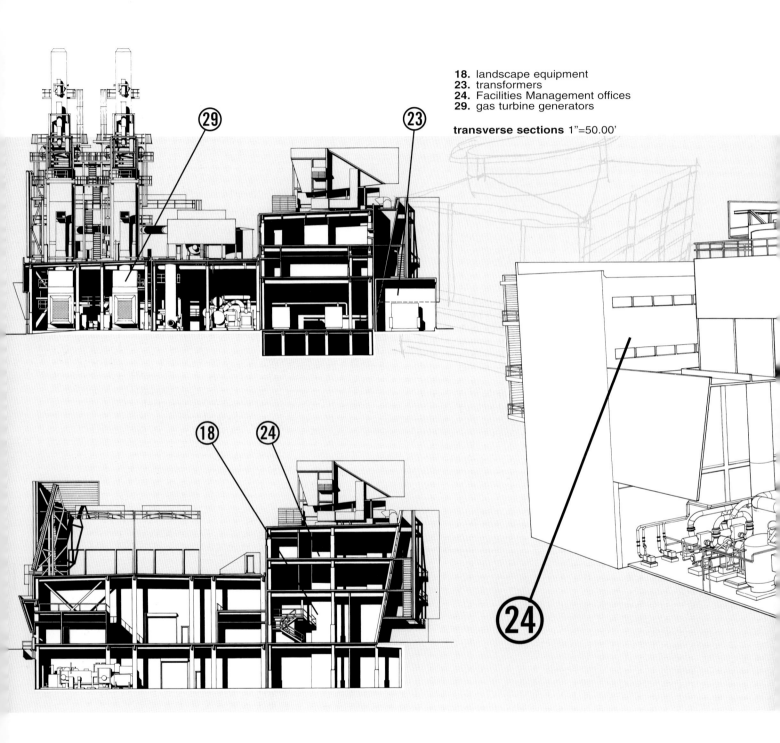

18. landscape equipment
23. transformers
24. Facilities Management offices
29. gas turbine generators

transverse sections 1"=50.00'

8. cooling towers
9. mechanical penthouse
12. entry corridor
15. absorption chiller
24. Facilities Management offices
28. HRSG

cut-away view

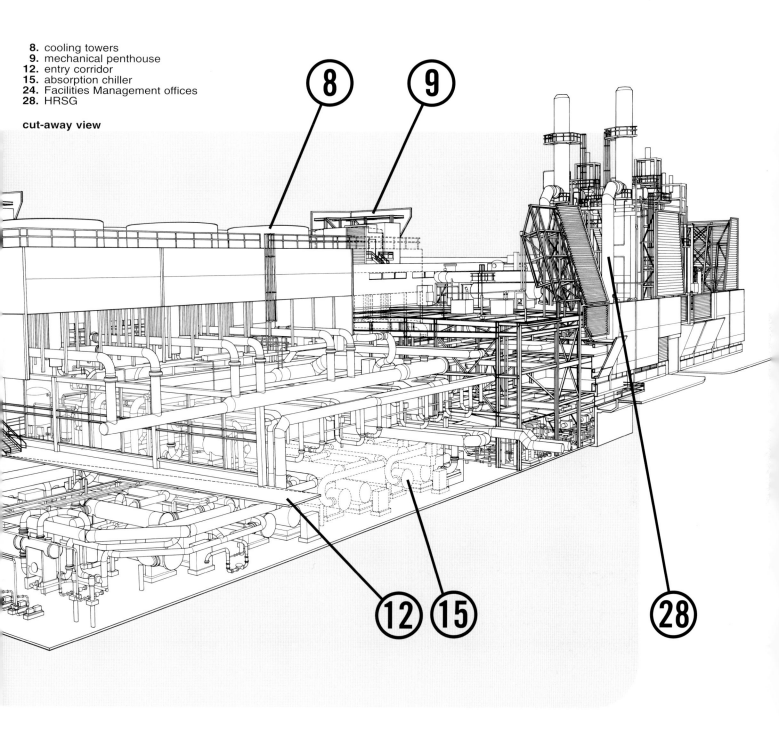

macy there.

* * *

11. Beginning is doubly attractive to orthodoxy. It seems to be as far away from the End as possible, and as free from infinitude as could be imagined. An obsession with its clarity would seem to be proof against fear and uncertainty. But it is also the beginning that gives to time its sinister direction. When the beginning recedes too far in the memory—perhaps when the end is more palpable— we consider reviving the beginning. Orthodoxy gives increased attention to its roots in hopes of revivifying the tree. What is proposed in such cases is not a new, or different beginning, but the same beginning, again, reconstituted.

12. We consider reviving the beginning in order to feel the particular "rightness" and inevitability of the "original" artifacts. The historical portability of such objects confuses our understanding of what divides them from now. We

chilled water distribution pipes

cable tray room

value the surviving artifacts as evidence of their own time and presume the rightness they communicate to us now is what they communicated then, in their original, "natural context." They become fetishes, focusing our longing for the optimism or certainty we impute to that period. They come to substitute for the period they recall, and we attempt to regain those feelings by replicating those objects.

13. Yet, such work can really have authentic meaning only in its own, no longer extent, context. "The works are no longer the same as they once were. It is they themselves, to be sure, that we encounter ..., but they themselves are gone by .... Henceforth they remain merely such objects."[b] We cannot know whether our present reactions reflect those originally inspired by such objects, nor if the original reactions themselves were what we assume.

14. To recover is to re-cover—since the original condi-

Notes on the Boss 3:88

1. Architecture may be building that says something, but its expressiveness has seemed to aim for the strictly inexpressible, the ineffable.[1] Traditionally directing the architectural effort, evolving with the understanding of Nature and the Architecture that reflected that understanding, serving as the medium and ennoblement of their connection in God and history and culture, as Art, was the idea of the beautiful. Beauty has been both an end in itself and an embodiment or symbol for the truth and goodness that have always seemed to be cardinal values in our society.

2. How Beauty fares in our society today is indicative, therefore, of Architecture's own fate. And beauty no longer seems to signify, necessarily, the constellation of values that guides production contesting any simple relation to truth, the critic claims that beauty is exemplary of the repressive traditions of singular Authority. Additionally, beauty is eroded into kitsch by mediation and consumerism, diminishing its store of goodness.

3. Whether because of mediation and overuse, the accelerating pace of cultural cycles, or merely the cynicism that results from all of this, superlatives in general carry less currency today than when the links between architecture and beauty were keenly felt. The demotion of beauty as a superlative must be related to the general demotion of architecture's importance within our culture today. Architecture, as the biggest thing we make, magnifies the sense and effects of this fall. The precarious balancing act it performs between ideality and reality, which beauty need not face, is uncomfortably obvious today, when ideality no longer carries much weight.

4. The increasingly tattered scrim of convention that declares this balance is being pulled aside, and what we see behind it is "the great and magnificent Was." We no longer are urged to "ignore that man behind the curtain"; we are told to focus on him, as the personality behind the signature. Today, though it remains the largest thing a culture can make, architecture is no longer the most impressive. It is outshone even by the star wattage of its own creators, not to mention the stars and products of the media, that exert a hyperreal influence on the substantial reality architecture once ruled. In a culture that is trending towards miniaturization and pluralization, architecture's gross presence is increasingly seen as a liability.

5. When Wittgenstein claimed that "where there is nothing to glorify, there can be no Architecture," he was echoing expectations with a long history. The tremendous amount of effort expended in the name and substance of architecture has continuously renewed the sense of its importance. It remains the biggest, and among the most involved, things we make, so we should still expect it to be special.[2] Architecture, or at least the buildings it invests with its presence, are not going anywhere soon. When they are still here, but architecture has fled, will anyone notice?

* * *

6. The greatest compliment that can be paid to something today is not that it is beautiful or good, but that it is cool. They are not synonymous. We hear something different in cool than in beautiful. To highlight this difference we use the more specific, semi-archaic term "boss." "Boss" is not as far reaching as "goodness" or "beauty," or possibly even "cool," but it is also less subject to the flattening and mythification that has come to plague the others. The boss object stands out in a way that is no

---

[1] It may be the most concrete of cultural artifacts, but it has generally embodied abstractions and ephemera. Truth, goodness, or the "spirit of the age" have all found a home in architectural expression. Bearing this load of heavy symbolic freight, architecture legitimizes our view of the world. Through its inarguable presence we grant authority to some statement of our place in the order of things.

[2] The high expectations for architecture remain, but only within the field. The critique of presence, that seems to abet society's indifference, still reserves for architecture the role of expression, and expects this expression to relate to the culture, as resistance or affirmation, but the culture itself has already signed off on it and moved on to more interesting matters.

longer possible for them. Cynicism and a wariness of the kitsch have ensured that "goodness" is suspect, and "beauty" that stands out is more likely to be ridiculed than revered. The boss is not troubled, like beauty, by a history that condemns its present examples nor by expectations that find it lacking or duplicitous, like goodness or truth. The boss's constituency is more current and its standards are not received; we are still able to see the "standing out" that sets it apart as positive. The boss, or bossness, can be visibly exemplary of our current condition of being-in-the-world—which of course is what Architecture is about—in a way that the devalued notion of beauty seems less capable of expressing today. 'Bossness' as a superlative can help direct efforts to celebrate that condition. To suggest lowering the sights a little, to aim for the achievement of the simply boss, may be all that we can reasonably expect.

7. This is not to suggest that boss is easy. The values it expresses are not transcendent, they are not found in the ideal realm of truth, goodness, or beauty, but they are no slam dunk, either. Bossness dwells in the more im-mediate(d) arena of demonstrated competence: available to us all, and more generally respected, but still capable of exhorting us to excel.

8. The boss object stands out; in this it is notable first for its purposefulness. Something boss has an air of being able to do something. The overtness of this intentionality sets it apart from other things. Though any human artifact is, strictly speaking, the embodiment of some purpose, the ones that are boss are marked expressly by this fact. And they are remarkable because of the importance intentionality or purpose holds for us.³

9. The innate human bias towards the irrepressible valuation of purpose, which the boss object celebrates, expresses itself most overtly in technology. Purpose incarnate is the machine. The machine is the human embodiment and engagement of, and within, the final, and all-encompassing provisionality: nature. Which itself is, of course, humanity's understanding—or "enframing"—of nature, of reality, of objectivity. It is humanity's response to the scale at which it dwells, the scope and limits of its capacity to engage external reality; the projection of what the mind knows most directly—the body—upon everything else that it can never know. Architecture's hand in structuring our orientation to reality is also very apparent, maybe more basic than metaphysics (which is cast in architectural terms), but perhaps it would be accurate to say that, in this respect as in others, architecture is a special case of the machine. Architecture expressly embodies what is most basic in our understanding. There is nothing more basic than precultural intention. The machine is intention embodied. The boss is that, expressed.

10. At the scale of possible human engagement in the world, reality is inescapably mechanical. We live in a Newtonian world; we talk about relativity and quantum mechanics, chaos and fractals, the big bang and the quark, but we can only *experience* the flux of macroscopic Newtonian events. Our senses are limited; we can only appreciate stuff we can touch, taste, hear, see, or smell. The physical "laws," like cause-and-effect, or shape constancy, that present a world of discreet things in relation to other things, are biological facts for us, structuring our brains through evolution and experience.⁴ Advances beyond mechanical thinking, whether by Einstein, Godel or Hawking, always seem mechanically bootstrapped into understanding, where they remain as viable concepts only by reference to mechanical analogy—whether as

---

³ Our questioning posture toward the world, our curiosity, is evidence of this importance. The *purpose* is the key to our orientation to reality. In any encounter our first reaction is to consider the will of our interlocutor—the arrangement of purpose in the situation or object. We want to know who it is or what it is, which is to ask, immediately, what they do. In the case of stuff, judgments of the quality of the object are made, immediately, naturally in reference to this doing. The design of boss stuff appeals to this natural inclination, it assumes that the value of something is ultimately related in largest measure to its apparent fitness to its purpose, however broadly that purpose may be determined.

⁴ The machine wins discriminations from the ultimate externality—nature. These discriminations we have come to call meaning. As the projection of intention out into the larger world, the machine becomes the emblem, the physical presence ... of that which dares to decide anyway.

Robbins mobile miner

transcendent of this analogy or as reactive to it.

11. If reality as we may know it is Newtonian, for better or for worse, then it follows that: the mechanical is the threshold to existence. When our contributions to this reality are manifested "out there" as elements within the unsummable totality of its markers, they will do so by intention and will, and that moment will become, de-facto, de-mechano.

12. The success of technology has repressed other less successful frames of reference like magic, or traditional myth, and has marginalized even the art that celebrates it. The machine's flourishing presence in mainstream cultural production, such as the cinema, and the arts it has marginalized, which have defensively recast themselves as resistive can be ascribed to equal measures of charm and ruthlessness.[5] Since by virtue of its expressiveness the boss must be located here, where ruthlessness may become charming, and not within the strictly technical, it must balance the naturally resistive stance of contemporary art with its native affirmational enthusiasm for technical achievement.

13. In this, Bossness has been confused with functionalism. Its difference from functionalism, as the superlative *expression* of the technical, shows the depth of its contrary kinship to the art otherwise marginalized by technology. Functionalism is reductive. It has no superlative impulse. What we know as functionalism is interested mostly in paring away decorative embellishment. Its idea of the purpose for which the object might be designed is usually very narrow. Historically functionalism has depended on an alienating abstraction to express this naked purpose.

14. This absolute distillation is an ideal only: it is impossible to achieve. There always comes a point in the design process where equivalent functional possibilities force a choice to be made, where the pure statement of essence must accommodate the arbitrariness of a designer's personal perspective. Nor can the broader historical or cultural context be avoided—it always intrudes as well, with constraints or opportunities that are specifically outside the narrowest functional concerns of the object. Books have been written about the complex political, economic, engineering and cultural dynamics gathered into the evolution of something as functionally straightforward as a paper clip.[6]

15. In contrast, the boss object addresses concerns that the strictest functionalism would try to ignore. The only distillation it's interested in is related to octane levels. The only essence it aims to express is the truth that it only the will that lies between humanity and nature, between subjective interiority and the exterior experience. This is where boss stuff roots its value. The boss sees itself as the expression of purpose. Humanity defines and distinguishes itself as the bringer into experience, and witness there, of purpose. Will, intentionality, purpose—this is the basis of significance—as meaning and importance. It's how meaning gets out there into the world, how it becomes important. This is what the boss can signify as the superlative expression of the technological.

* * *

16. Boss stuff is most often found in extreme environments, where it is engaged in significant interaction with forces exerted against the purpose it serves. The boss object makes that environment more visible. It does this, though, not by *looking like* the forces it engages, but by responding to them. In architecture we would say that it is inflected to them. It is *at home* in its environment and in

---

[5] Culturally the machine is inescapable. Critics like Heidegger or Marcuse who bemoan the persuasiveness and pervasiveness of the technological products of this truth, attest to its artists like Sheeler or Sandberg, who celebrate its abstract grace or raw power, affirm its seductiveness. The machine has seemingly achieved the universal hegemony predicted for it, subsuming the dialectic and coopting its capacity for critique. It is not conditioned by culture, but itself conditions culture. Its most outspoken critics, speaking themselves from within an enframed position, claim that the machine has instituted a complacent universal tyranny of efficiency and reason that is most dangerous and violent when it is taken for granted when it approaches the "pacification of existence" that would render the emancipatory drive of history obsolete.

[6] In any case, this sort of transparency to function is contrary to architecture's expressiveness. In expression lies the departure from the simple satisfaction of purpose that makes a building architecture, that makes it mean something and makes that meaning important. When "function" is interpreted primarily in terms of a satisfaction of physical needs, free of ideological or historical awareness (but not of influence), the work is condemned to trivial statements of shelter and hygiene. In such a case, architecture's traditional responsibility for a "lofty expression of the ideals and aspirations of the age," or even for bestowing dignity on the mundane, is forsaken for a more prosaic, and less dignified, statement of its standards of comfort and sanitation.

the building is only the embodiment of the resolution of these forces, it is limited in the contexts it can serve and the messages it can convey. The boss object, in contrast, is involved in standing up (when it's architecture), but ties this will-to-stand, as part of a general air of purposefulness, to the more widely varying and specific user's program, which it advances against strife.

its task without mimicking either.

17. Through inflection and direct expression, the boss object celebrates the specific world that contests its statement of purposefulness. Usually, this finds the boss object pitted against nature. Nature may be indifferent, but it is always a worthy adversary: the deep sea, space or the battlefield offer unique challenges and convey vivid images that are made more visible when measured by the effort of humans to operate there: the storm-wracked sea is more dramatic when there is a ship present to be tossed about, space is more clearly a haunting void when traversed by the MMU. The object and the environment draw each other out and force each other into an accommodation that is a record of their uniqueness—and care. Environments that demand a greater respect from the object are consequently reflected more clearly in its design. The steamship, auto and aeroplane that so attracted Corbu probably could be seen as precursors in this sense and made a greater impression in his work than the grain silos he also admired. Beyond Corbu's stated interests, it is easy to imagine some of their attraction in terms we might now recognize as boss.[7]

18. Reference to a more generalized sense of strife—of which extreme environments are only the most visible expressions—can also provide the general ground within, and against, which purpose is enacted. Architecture has always already existed against this cosmic background strife, but has tried not to notice it, to keep it in the background.

19. Technology has largely succeeded in rendering it invisible, today: the cosmic background strife associated with survival is rare for the so-called first world, and "the pacification of existence" is almost a reality.[8] The general absence of that edge, of the risk, that helps us know and feel what it means to be alive and human has led to increasingly extreme forms of compensatory thrill-seeking. Strife was once so common in daily life that it was all but invisible. Now, its all but non-existent. We need to be reminded. Here the boss can find a basic role. As architecture, as a signification of strife, it may help the preservation and valuation of that definitive aspect of our humanity, our experience of life, that otherwise is being overcome as a felt reality. This does not mean to propose that the boss object should be stressful, itself, or should cause strife for us, but that it should recognize continuously and celebrate the fact: that whatever pacification of existence has occurred is an achievement. This achievement can be reflected in the design of stuff.

20. Architecture has traditionally been the greatest totem for our achievement. As we have met the challenges reality offered, we absorbed their carcasses into the formal culture, wistfully, or belligerently. In such ways nature became incorporated into classicism, speed into modernism, greed into histo-pomo. Having been conquered, strife can be totemized as well. The boss mechanism stands ready: the machine is the institution of strife as work; the harnessing of strife can be made visible when it becomes a work. It can become boss.

21. As the physical enactment of purpose, the boss object must encompass within its own being the purpose which gave rise to it, and the forces of nature or others arrayed against it. One measure of the quality of this reconciliation has been efficiency. Efficiency expresses the sense of balance that must be achieved for these centrifugal influences to be contained. The way the boss object expresses this efficiency sets it apart.[9]

---

[7] The boss object is most evident in those areas of experience marked by strife, where purpose must more aggressively assert itself, where the ground of existence rears menacingly into figures of its own. These are precisely the sort of environments and circumstances that buildings have traditionally avoided. An appropriate expression of this awareness in architecture is not impossible, however: brise soleil, or even pitched roofs speak volumes about the challenges they address, and can serve as models for the introduction of the boss into architecture. Architecture as a construction traditionally exhausted its expressiveness in answering the challenge of standing up. Interested only in standing-up, though, it risked the tautological, since standing up is the building's program, not its occupant's program. A vast projective mythology of the orders was invented to distract us from noticing this. If

[8] We still struggle to find a parking place or figure our taxes, but the old throwing muscles have gone a little slack and our endurance is not what it used to be. Our lives are flatter. Dodging traffic may keep our reactions sharp, but it dulls our hearts. We are by nature active, inquisitive creatures. In the absence of real challenges, our interest has evolved to the hyper-real, where the strife we experience is manufactured. We find it in the most trivial or remote "crises" promoted by media, or disaster movies and theme parks. Since holding itself up is no longer a real challenge either, even architecture has taken to manufacturing its own hurdles, "incidents," and disasters.

[9] Unlike the Ferrari, for example, the boss Hot Rod keeps the balance visible; allowing each factor a presence in the equation that yields speed:

22. Efficiency is a powerful idea; what distinguishes us today, at the far end of the industrial revolution, from all preceding periods is not so much the efficacy of our efforts as their efficiency. As the more fundamental dimensions of strife are eliminated, it is the quest for increasing efficiency that drives the advance of our technology. The better mouse trap is not bigger, or more powerful, but more efficient. The convergence of this attitude with economics more or less characterizes our present ethos: efficiency has become the measure of sophistication in the cultural and commercial, as well as technical sphere. From functionalism to literary theory the telltale tracks of efficiency can be spotted: lurking behind the convoluted, baroque, decorative prose of deconstruction lies a mercenary, uncannily efficient logic, every bit the equal of that which put Skylab in a Saturn V stage or ATMs in every mall.

23. But, by raising efficiency to a sort of universal assumption its application is rendered generally unremarkable and practically invisible. Its universalization has diminished its value as a value. The boss object stands out for the particular vibrancy of its relation to efficiency. It treats efficiency in its original freshness as a valuable asset, as an achievement to be celebrated, without guilt that the excess inherent in celebration is contradictory. To the boss, efficiency is a strife-engaged machismo; neither a God nor a paper clip, but a kick in the ass.[10]

* * *

24. The arena of competence was described in the 1950s, by Martin Heidegger: though he might be considered unfashionable now, his work lies behind all that is most trendy today. And he first and most compellingly faced the question concerning technology that the boss must face. Though he was probably not familiar with its particularly American manifestations, he talked about the context of stuff in terms that presaged discussion of bossness. To him, the arena of competence is occupied by what he calls the Being of Equipment—a condition falling between that of mere "things" and "works," (as in works-of-Art). In his lecture, "The Origin of the Work of Art," he describes this middle position in a positive light: less the fuzzy gray area between two clear poles, like architecture, than a substantial center that helps to explain these poles: "Because equipment takes an intermediate place between mere thing and work ... things and works and ultimately all beings—are to be comprehended with the help of the Being of equipment ...."[11]

25. Heidegger assumes Art and Architecture are synonymous, and he opposes them both, as Works, to Equipment. Pretending to misread this, though, and imagine architecture as equipment, which its programmatic nature would seem to allow, can lead to something like the Boss. Architecture-as-equipment can still aspire to a condition beyond the simple superlative of building—without risking the imperialism that lurks in Authority, or the pettiness that has come of prettiness. This is not a fall from grace, but a reconsideration of the value and character of this grace. In such a recalibration of architecture as equipment, the standard of value becomes appropriateness-for-use rather than Authority. The sublime condition of its equipmental nature would be its availability: "the repose of equipment resting within itself consists in its reliability ... in reliability ... we discern what in truth Equipment is."[12] This does not mean to champion pedestrian functionalism, but to grant to those who experience or use the equipment the power of appreciation. And there might be something transcendent in that experience: as Heidegger puts it, "the more simply and essentially (equipment is) engrossed in (its) essence, the more directly and engagingly do *all* beings attain a

---

power, traction, weight and protection of the driver from the elements.

[10] Clearly in this it declares its distance from the reductivist celebration of efficiency evident in functionalism. Yet, it does not on the other hand fetishize the elements it honors: while the boss object is not merely functional, it is also not necessarily "haute" tech. The haute-tech object is too self-conscious, too insecure. It preens and fusses. The haute-tech object [HR 12] yearns to be beautiful; it is attracted to shiny finishes and bright colors; its message is that when technology is dressed up it can be taken out and shown off; technology can be beautiful. The boss object is puzzled by technology in drag. The boss just gets on with it, using what it takes to get the job done. Which implies that this is enough, and that this is itself worthy. The boss object thinks that Architecture's outmoded valuing of beauty blinds it to the real personality of its natural referent, that architecture's arena of judgment should be more aggressively shifted from aesthetics to competence.

[11] Martin Heidegger, "The Origin of the Work of Art" in *Basic Writings*, ed. David Farrell Krell (New York: Harper & Row, 1997), p. 159; hereafter cited as OWA.

[12] OWA, 164.

greater degree of being along with (it)."[13]

26. Yet, in Heidegger's schema, equipment achieves the functionalist dream of disappearing into usefulness, which is counter to the usual understanding of architecture's expressive role, while the work remains conspicuously visible.[14] This describes the extremes that a lowered expectation for architecture must negotiate: architecture these days is seemingly less able to generate the work's aura, yet the anonymity of the hammer is not an attractive alternative.

27. If architecture lowers its expectations, it need not abandon a concern for its work-like presence, or its ability to speak. Though equipment is more limited in this way than art, the functionalist fallacy shows that Heidegger over-states the hammer's dumbness: it is not entirely mute: in fact, if anything, equipment is, in its own way, more approachable, more used; there is a possibility here for an engagement as significant in its own way as that enjoyed by the work when, as Heidegger puts it, it "opens a world":

> As long as we only imagine a pair of shoes in general, [he says, for example] or simply look at the empty, unused shoes as they merely stand there ..., we shall never discover what the equipmental being of the equipment in truth is .... [Here is a] pair of peasant shoes and nothing more. And yet—

> From the dark opening of the worn insides of the shoes the toilsome tread of the worker stares forth. In the stiffly rugged heaviness of the shoes there is the accumulated tenacity of her slow trudge through the far-spreading and ever-uniform furrows of the field swept by a raw wind. On the leather lie the dampness and richness of the soil. Under the soles slides the loneliness of the field-path as evening falls. In the shoes vibrates the silent call of the earth, its quiet gift of the ripening grain and its unexplained self-refusal in the fallow desolation of the wintry field. This equipment is pervaded by uncomplaining worry as to the certainty of bread, the wordless joy of having once more withstood want, the trembling before the impending childbed and shivering at the surrounding menace of death. This equipment belongs to the earth, and it is protected in the world of the peasant woman. From out of this protected belonging the equipment itself rises to its resting-within-itself.[15]

28. Would this mean that these shoes were boss? The engagement that these shoes, this equipment, encourages suggests a lively, dignified presentness to which a more modest conception of architecture might aspire. Equipment "sets forth" the earth upon which the work's world can be "opened." The work depends upon this grounding; and equipment finds its highest realization in support of the work. The soul of usefulness, of equipment, has a poetic dimension if life may find a role in work.

29. Conceived so, a building may aspire in the integrity of its equipmental nature to the same quality as the life it supports, and find its own poetry in the majesty of the activities it shelters, and, as a building, be architecture.

---

[13] OWA, p. 178.

[14] "The more handy a piece of equipment is, the more inconspicuous it remains that, for example, this particular hammer is .... And what is more commonplace than this, that a being is? In a work, by contrast, this fact, that it *is* as a work, is just what is unusual. The event of its being created does not simply reverberate through the work; rather, the work casts before itself the eventful fact that the work is as this work, and it has constantly this fact about itself." OWA, p. 182.

[15] OWA, p. 163.

Cardiff Bay Opera House
C94.12/1
Cardiff, Wales

Owner:	Cardiff Bay Opera House Trust
Client:	Welsh National Opera, Cardiff
Architect:	Jones, Partners: Architecture
Site:	Historic waterfront site at the head of Cardiff Bay, in midst of reclaimed tracts of harbor industry land.
Program:	Performance and rehearsal space for WNO and visiting companies, administrative space for WNO, visiting companies and CBOHT, retail space and parking.
Size:	220,000 ft^2
Systems:	Weathering steel frame with dichroic glass/corrugated metal panel curtain wall, cast-in-place concrete fly lofts, parking plinth, basement and foundation; exposed framing and mechanical throughout.
Features:	A big shape, beckoning across the bay like a cathedral, a glass lantern housing the primary forms of the performance spaces, a twisted chaotic massing derived by rotating house forms, presents a different building to different viewers at different times of day, in a non-totalizable composition of great programmatic complexity.
Cost:	$90 million
Completion:	May 1994 (competition)

It spoils the fun to a certain extent when the architect himself sets down the formal associations of his design and tells the viewer how it should be read. It feels somehow improper. After all, if it has to be explained or pointed out, then such allusion has already failed. With that reservation noted, though, we can admit some ideas. Perhaps it is enough simply to point out the tendency to soaring forms in the proposal's massing, and hope that this might be generally evocative. And if this is seen to be suggestive of sails, and Cardiff's maritime traditions, or of the loftiness of the opera itself, or even of the cathedral-like importance of this building within the culture and life of the city, then so much the better. Our reticence to exaggerate the formal claims of the scheme is certainly not intended to shirk a responsibility (at least as part of the architectural competition) for contributing to the contemporary discourse. Indeed, the folded character of this complex, near-figural massing, and the manner in which the primary volumes of the public auditoria (including those rehearsal spaces that may conveniently be opened to the public) are cradled-within-transparent-layers-of-supporting-structure-like-ships-in-drydock or some similarly precious cargo are unabashedly *current*. Clearly, it is only by contributing to the debate that the hopeful march of the opera's new House into timelessness will begin in relevance and advance with integrity. The many past examples of paradigm-defining competition winners, particularly those who did not perhaps

2. plaza
3. opera house facade
4. WNO facade
5. stage door facade

site plan 1"=166.67'   model view

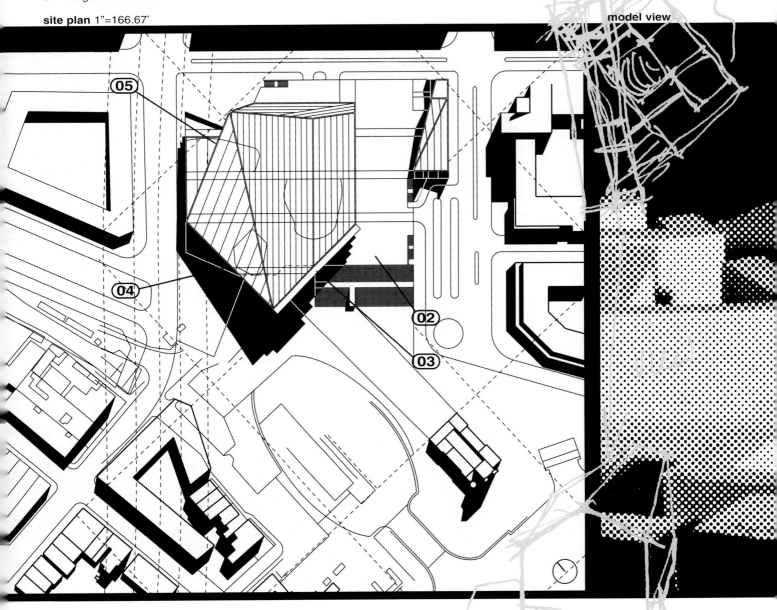

tion is irretrievably lost in time, the survival of objects, whether through their intrinsic merit, or for their 'historical' value, no more enables a passage across time than any science fiction fantasy. The fetishized, time-traveling artifact is stripped of the history that composes it, trivializing the greatest part of its meaning. The romanticized history evoked by these artifacts is bereft of real objects, emptied of the relationships and meaning that distinguish it from time. In attempting to rekindle the spark of authenticity from even the best stuff of even the most recent past, we fail to realize that an authentic work can only arise from its contemporary context: it cannot be recovered from any past and be authentic in the present.

* * *

15. The "rightness" in "right thinking" aims for validation through reference to a sense of the "authentic." Authentic means "genuine." This suggests a "present-ness" or being "in the moment," yet ironically, authenticity

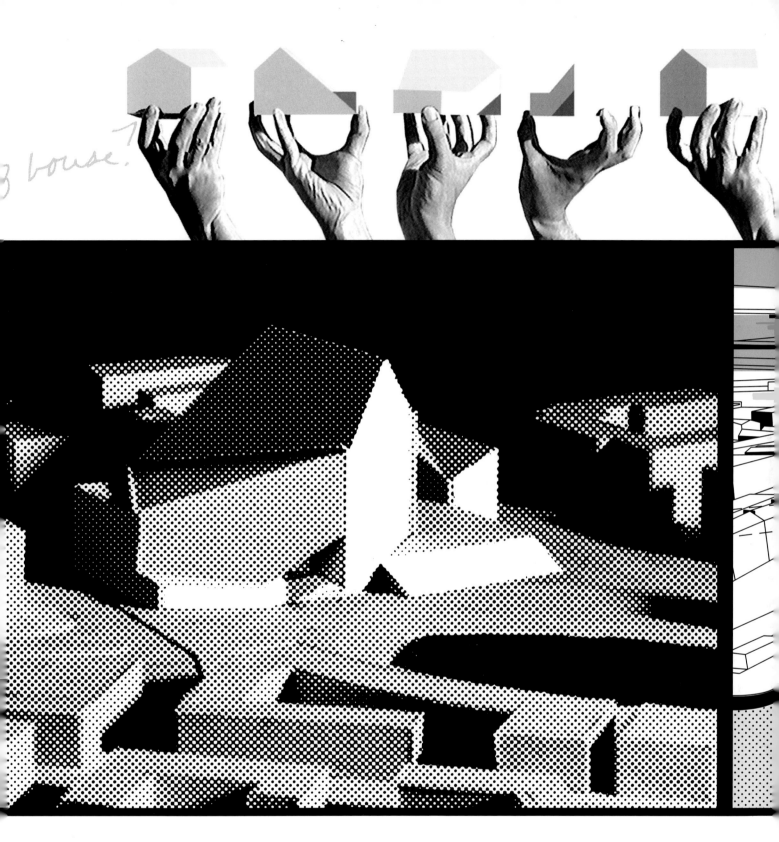

is only retroactively understood. The truly authentic act never has the perspective or self-consciousness to be aware of its own authenticity. Authenticity is innocent of its own historicity. Unconcerned about what might constitute later determinations of its authenticity, it has no such external guide to direct its efforts in that direction. To covet it is to violate its necessary innocence. Consequently, authenticity more often comes to mind in being questioned: the "genuine" is valued precisely because of its originality—and thus encourages the imitations from which it must distinguish itself as genuine. Yet, it is precisely when something is identified as genuine or "authentic" that suspicions are raised. Something celebrated as authentic is almost certainly not, really. It becomes a challenge to the discriminating reader, rather than an assurance to the doubtful one. In this context, the clear intentionality of orthodoxy—its lack of innocence and its concern for its history—would seem to

2. plaza
3. opera house facade

view from south

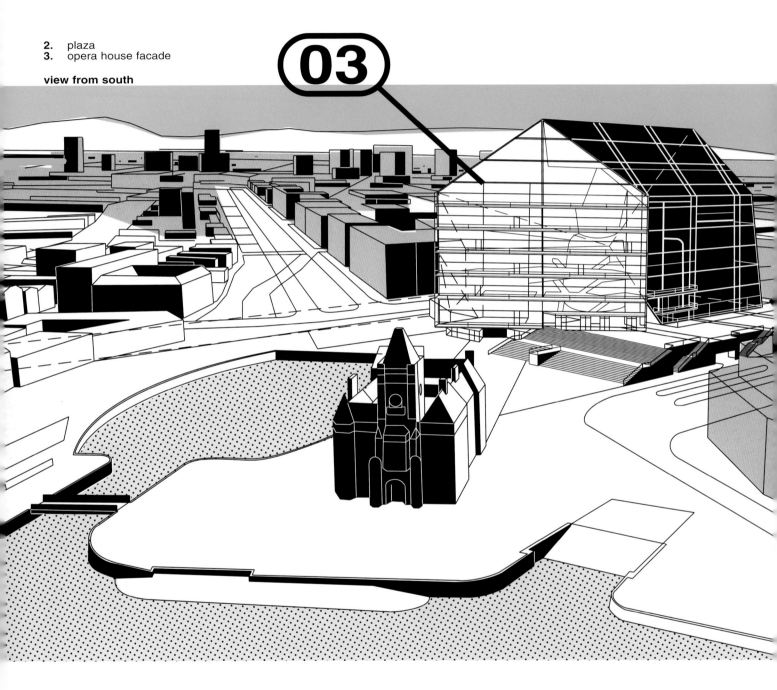

mitigate its opportunities to produce "authentic" work. Yet it is authenticity, and all it entails, that is sought in the call for New Orthodoxy.

16. The willfulness that grounds the object in its own time and context is the source of its authenticity. The fervor of this will ensures a certain innocence, while its directedness ensures a certain timeliness. While this prevents the significant translation of this work to other contexts, it ensures the continuing emergence of new authentic acts in their own context. This should be cause for hope. It should mean that the coveted sense of rightness upon which an orthodoxy depends can be invented or set-up again. It should mean, then, that we are not completely prisoners of circumstance, that we can again achieve that authenticity, willfully, without having to wait around for it to happen, or trying to recover or re-animate it from historical artifacts.

17. The work done during the revolutionary phase of the

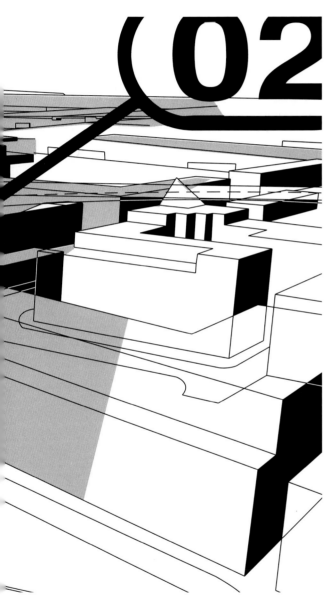

begin life as obvious winners or crowd favorites, attest to this. We are only concerned that what might appear fashionable in the design be seen as contributing to the operational efficiency of the opera as well, if not primarily.

For example, the twisting composition permits the major programmatic elements contained by the Cardiff Bay Opera House to maintain separate identities within the same overall form. The entrances to the three principal constituencies are assigned to three principal corners of the site. They are lodged behind the three main facades of the complex folded building form, each addressing a defined urban space of a scale appropriate to the institution and the facade representing it. The largest is of course the entrance to the House itself, which faces off across Cardiff Bay over the Pierhead building. This clearly iconic facade rests upon a podium served by a monumental entry stair. Such an arrangement asserts this facade's preeminence and formality, and sets the opera experience just ever so slightly apart and above the humdrum bustle of the street. This facade addresses the Pierhead Building, forming with it an urban space-making couple that defines the principal plaza on the Oval Basin, where the auto arrival and coach drop-off are located. Facing off perpendicularly to

MIT 17
Modern Movement was a socially aware, formal reaction to the nostalgia of the academy. In this sense, it was hardly innocent or timely, explicitly defining itself in terms of a historical understanding of this opposition. This awareness itself was innocent, however, in hindsight—certainly in comparison to the hyperawareness we enjoy today courtesy the critical establishment. Further, modernism's expressed new-world program avoided nostalgic trivialization since it plundered only feelings, rather

3. opera house facade
4. WNO facade

view from north

than figures, from its past: it sought ideas, not objects; stories, not forms. And it sought these not for selfish nostalgic reasons, but out of concern for investing the present work with qualities of depth and resonance only time can provide. Corbu claimed to be re-covering the clarity of the past—the elemental nature of certain forms (Phileban solids) of Roman architecture, and the "terrible" refinement of the Greek—not the imagery itself, in service of the distinctly contemporary goal of giving expression to the zeitgeist.

18. In this light, a New Orthodoxy would be less the retreat to modernism it might seem than a resurgence of interest in the architect's contract with society, championed by modernism. The critically inspired self-awareness prevailing today prevents this from sliding into utopianism, but our humanity insists on the basic optimism charging that sense of responsibility. Since we are part of the context, the seeming "retreat" staged by the

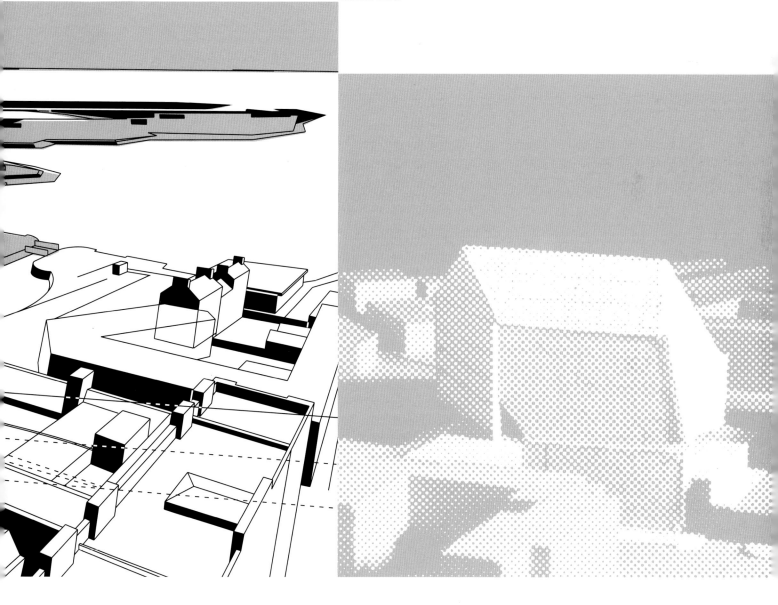

model view

New Orthodoxy cannot be nostalgia, either: since Heidegger, our perspective will not permit the sort of blindness or forgetfulness that expects to retrieve the context as well as the form from the past. Nor can the establishment of a new orthodoxy be based on any sort of rediscovery, because today nothing can ever (have) disappear(ed). In fact, it feels fated, like the pull of gravity—but it is not faced with resignation. The avant garde—mediated, hyped, coopted by the culture-wide star-making machinery—is no longer politically inclined, but is too motivated by fear for such tidal effects to be relaxing.

19. So what today can be authentic? What today might be a source of innocent timeliness? Paradoxically, it is the contemporary (hyper) awareness asking this question that seems to prevent a satisfying answer. The present estrangement of architecture's larger public responsibility is a result of this awareness (the false modesty of

the main House facade, toward James Street, and second in scale and clarity—but not in the designer's heart—is the Welsh National Opera facade. It fronts on and defines a plaza directly at the Oval Basin terminus of the new Bute Avenue esplanade. This facade overhangs the plinth and is visible down the length of Bute, announcing the presence of the National Opera, its house, and their plazas at the Oval Basin. Finally, "around the back," at the intersection of James Street and East Bute, is the stage door entrance, where the Cardiff Bay Opera House Trust has its front door in symbolic association with the artists. A small plaza, scaled to this more intimate urban condition, assures an appropriate decorum.

Though unexpected in a dedicated opera house, the verticality of the proposal is not without sense or usefulness, beyond the urbanistic assertiveness and operatic scale. Certainly the site might otherwise allow a more stumpy, sprawling partis, with more apparently conventional horizontal adjacencies, but a vertical organization of the program is in many ways more direct and convenient. In fact, many newer houses around the world, including several on unconstrained sites, have elected this manner of organization. Given a reasonably sized vertical conveyance, integrated carefully into the scheme (as, we believe, in the present case), then the changes in level are no more inconvenient than the long corridors which bedevil the typical horizontal layout; rather, they provide some *positive* organizational and functionable benefits unavailable to the horizontal scheme. Not to mention possibilities for dramatic public spaces and views across the bay and back downtown.

In keeping with the importance of the building, only *real* materials, used *as* themselves, are proposed. These are, simply, classically: steel, glass, and concrete. In fact, if the local conditions permit, we would like to see a *weathering* steel, since it need not even suffer the indignity of paint. Weathering steel wears as well as stone, and like stone it quickly invests the building with the timeless dignity of noble materials placed in negotiated balance with nature. For the glass areas—so important in communicating the interior life of the building to the plazas surrounding and feeding it, and in creating the sense of night time magic—we propose Dichroic glass, as part of an innovatively detailed and richly configured curtainwall structural system. At the base, for the parking plinth and elevated entry plaza, concrete with a suitable level of finish seems most appropriate. Budget permitting, stone, of course, would be preferred here.

5. stage door
17. WNO offices and support
20. retail
25. loading dock

northwest elevation 1"=104.17'

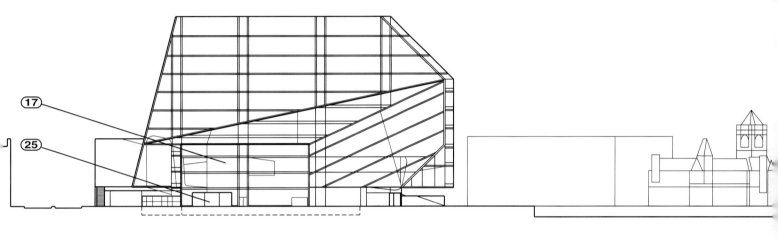

northeast elevation 1"=104.17'

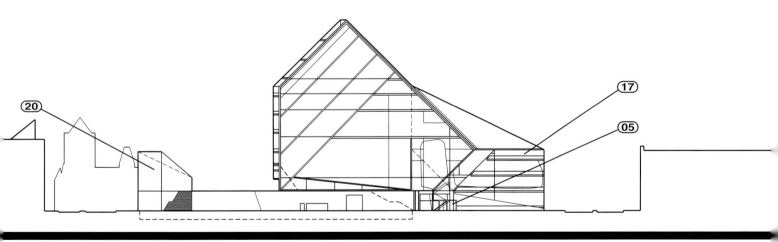

avoiding the repressiveness of authority) and the chief impediment to its evolution. Today's visions, though they may be adopted generally, as "the fashion," are for the most part personal. To "achieve" authenticity again as the stuff of a New Orthodoxy, architecture's essential publicness must turn "innocence" away from the "personal," and "timeliness" away from narrow topicality. It must again fix what is natural for us and what is other. It must show us the edge where authentic meaning can be produced and valued.

20. But a concern for what might be the natural thing to do seems lost today amidst suspicions about what is meant by "natural." The gaze is focused by critique over the edge, outward, rather than along the edge. Critical interest in this frontier is taken to be a license to doubt, rather than assure. The limits are seen as barriers to us, rather than to otherness, and it is the program of critique to challenge them. But convention, like language, can be

6. concourse
7. foyers
8. theater house
10. rehearsal
15. restaurant
20. retail to rent
24. mechanical

southeast elevation 1"=104.17'

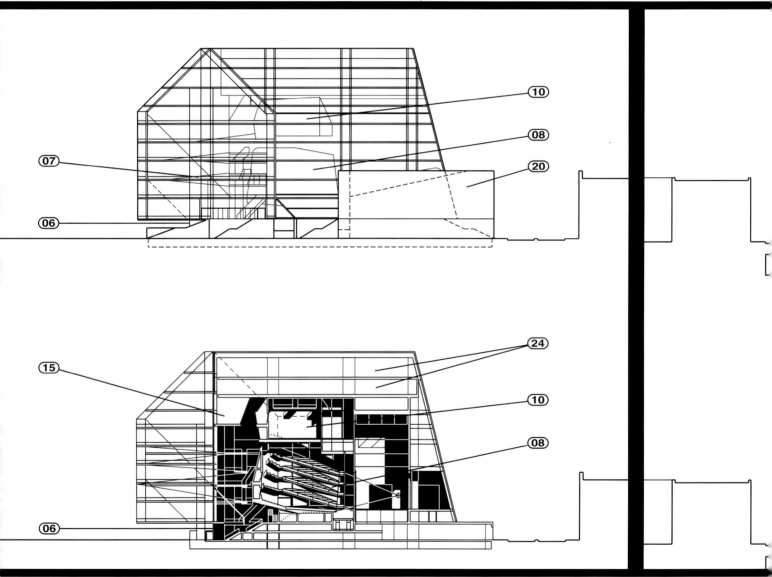

longitudinal section 1"=104.17'

seen as either creative and empowering, or repressive and domineering, depending on who is doing the work. Contrary to its own expectations and desires, poststructuralism has freed us to see conventions as achievements rather than impositions. Like existentialism before, it has forced us to recognize our own role as readers in the creation of conventions and to highlight this role therefore in the survival of orthodoxy. Since the artificiality of convention and orthodoxy is unavoidably bared for us by mediation and our own participation in their creation, conventions are fragile and the orthodoxy that maintains them must be vigorous. Conventions must be nurtured and actively sustained, our complicity must be willed, if they are to survive and thus be of use.

21. Today we trade unthinking submission for unthinking subscription. We subscribe to individual superstars "signature" conventions, within a milieu that expects the architect to go over the top and "take a position."

6. concourse
7. foyers
8. theater house
10. rehearsal
17. WNO offices and support
20. retail to rent
24. mechanical

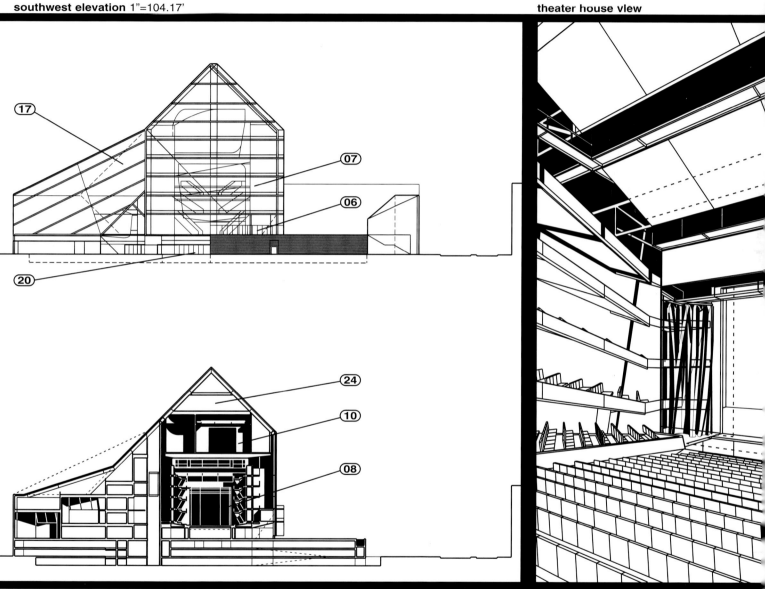

southwest elevation 1"=104.17'

theater house view

transverse section 1"=104.17'

Unfortunately, the position so taken often demonstrates only the plurality that is anarchi-tecture. Usually a critique, it assumes the unlikelihood of a larger, continuous vision that might be expressed by architecture. Instead, by its own example it implies this vision must be posed anew at every site, as a unique, and most often highly personal, statement.

22. To legislate an orthodoxy is itself to "set-up or establish" a position. *Architecture* is such a "position": it has been established historically as a collection of practices filling the space framed between art and utility. It intends, however, much more. It is architecture's self-declared responsibility to constitute whatever (necessarily axiomatic) bulwark of certainty that humanity can find or declare in the face of Otherness.

23. To "take a position" regarding this "position," which any critical or nostalgic architectural statement implies, exposes the axiomatic, "positional" nature of architecture

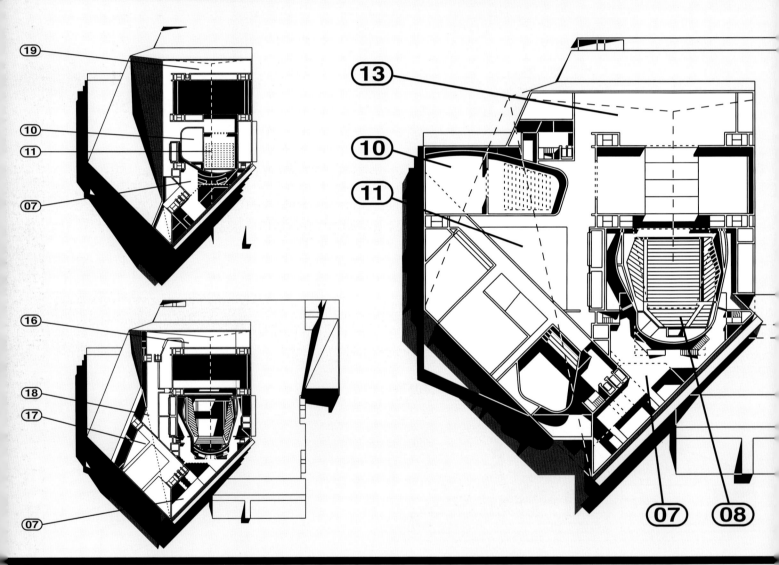

7. foyers
10. rehearsal
11. rehearsal support
16. canteen
17. WNO offices and support
18. WNO dining
19. CBOHT administration

rehearsal level 1"=166.67'

7. foyers
8. theater house
10. rehearsal
11. rehearsal support
13. scenery storage
20. retail

technical level 1"=83.33'

typical office level 1"=166.67'

itself, undermining its usefulness as a comforting presence. The axiomatic reality of the orthodox enterprise requires that the position become invisible as a position if the system that it builds is to foster any sense of confidence. Neither nostalgic replication, as unintentional dissimulation, nor the critical pose, as a purposeful unmasking activity, ever recede into the systems they sponsor. Such activity cannot pretend to the sort of universal validity that orthodox efforts assume for themselves.

When its genesis is so obviously "questionable," the object must always appear sheepish. Such activity says "look at me"—it asks the viewer to see the building as an expression of the architect's personal will. Architecture, on the other hand, is supposed to say "see yourselves, writ large, in me"—expressing throughout the willfulness that underlies the nature of things recorded in orthodoxy. 24. This is not to say that architects cannot be strong-willed. When the will is linked to this sense of responsibil-

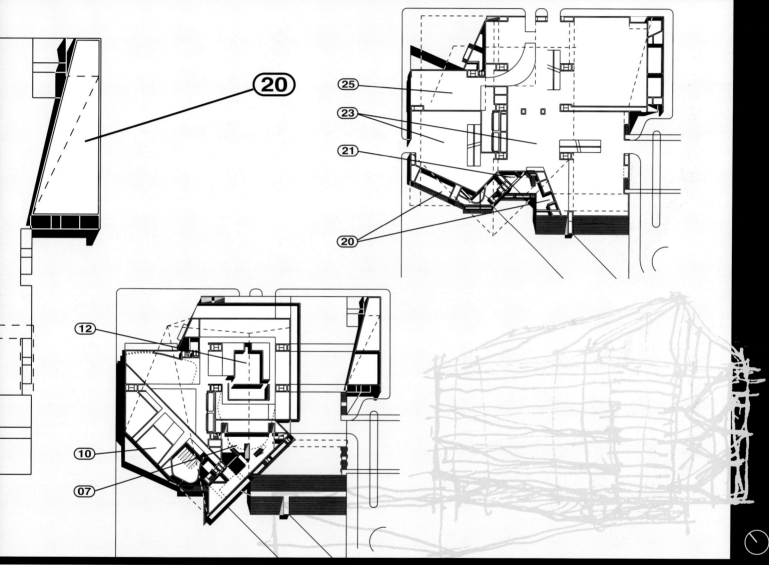

7. foyers
10. rehearsal
12. traps

20. retail
21. box office
23. parking
25. loading bay

street level 1"=166.67'

plaza level 1"=166.67'

ity, it becomes magnified: the utopian visions of Le Corbusier and Wright amplified the willfulness of their architecture without compromising its originality or authorship. Indeed, it was by attending to a larger vision of society that they were given the drive to find the new forms that forced back the limiting otherness.

25. Architecture is never truly innocent, otherwise it would be building. It is never timely or it would not endure. Yet, architecture's proper goal is still authenticity, but it is an authenticity understood as the ever-frustrated dream of these, predicted in the present to be read in the future. Because architecture seeks authenticity, it has often been a site of nostalgia. If architecture's proper goal is the authentic, then the timeliness of our own understanding of this term must include the modesty that realizes it is achievable only in retrospect.

[a] First published as "Notes re: constitution" in *Oz*, vol. 15, 1993 and in a somewhat altered form in *Architettura*

7. foyer
8. theater house

interior view

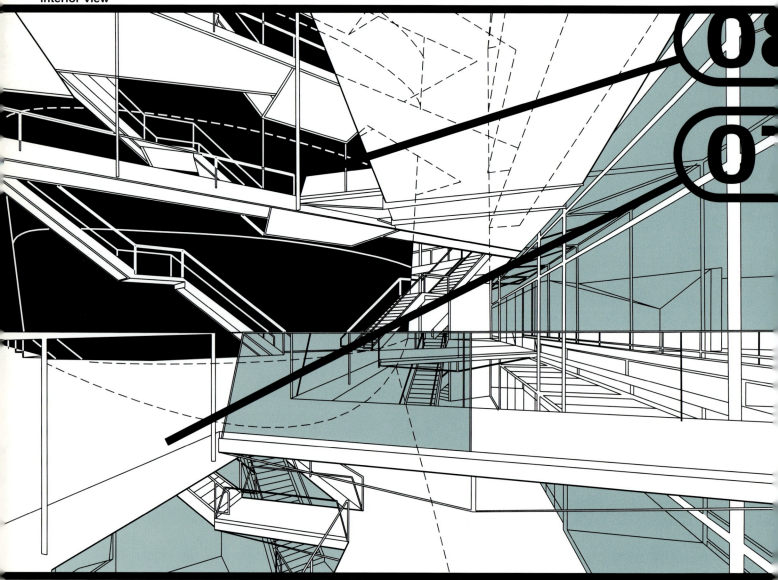

Intersezioni 3, 1995.
[b] Martin Heidegger, "The Origin of the Work of Art" in *Basic Writings* (New York: Harper & Row: 1977), 143-188; hereafter cited as OWA.
[6] "... Roland Barthes's notion that meaning is not communication (information) or signification (symbolism), but is lived experience, always in play, always different. Unbalancing the message is the only way of avoiding "the tyranny of correct meaning." (Barthes goes so far as to claim that language is quite simply fascist—"for fascism is not the prohibition of saying things, it is the obligation to say them.") Suzi Gablik, "Dancing with Baudrillard" *Art in America*, 27.
[7] Openness is the wind, difference the sail. If difference is the body of openness, then the machine is that difference embodied, literally, specifically, and tied to a story that can be read. The machine is thus essentially and paradoxically related to openness—it is the embodiment

Hot Rod

T95.01/1

1. American work has been valued as much for its unselfconsciousness as its frankness, but this innocence has not been due to any lack of interest or self-regard. The fascination with which Europeans in particular have regarded America has spawned a voluminous literature. Most commentators have taken *culture* as the point of reference in issues of design, privileging Europe as a model and casting American efforts as necessarily imitative. In 1948, as America was emerging from decades of isolationism and a devastating World War to her new role as undisputed "leader of the free world," John Kouwenhoven wrote a book called *Made In America*, in which he tried to explain what was so special about American design. In contrast to previous critics, Kouwenhoven recognized the central role that emerging technology played in forming a uniquely **American** sensibility. He saw that the United States was a nation formed by "the first people in history who, disinherited of a great cultural tradition, found themselves living under democratic institutions in an expanding machine economy." Its "cultural" successes were based on "a wholehearted acceptance of the industrial and technological environment, which was instinctive with almost all Americans when they were not consciously struggling in the shadow of an imported culture."[1]

2. Americans seemed born to this familiarity; they *trusted* their machines. In contrast, Kouwenhoven explains "Europeans learned to use the machine as a middle-aged man learns to drive a car—dubiously and without ceasing to feel that it is alien to his nature, [while] Americans took to it with the enthusiasm of youth and manipulated its levers as if they were the muscles of their own bodies."[2] Understandably, two distinct technical cultures have evolved from these very different orientations to the machine.[3]

3. This difference is clear, for example, in the contrast between a Ferrari and a hot rod. Each is exemplary of the culture it serves; each embodies a formal ideal, obeys an economic provenance, and results from a method of production that highlights the distinctions between the new country and the old. The Ferrari is futurism's manifesto of speed incarnate; it embodies a *philosophy* of form. The Ferrari gives shape to the *idea* of speed—it looks fast just sitting there. Its sinuous streamlining speaks of aesthetic sophistication as much as of swiftness. Indulging in a sort of blurring of the details, it remains slightly mysterious and aloof.

4. The hot rod, on the other hand, is the opposite of mysterious; its frankness is often confused for a lack of sophistication. It seems less interested in *looking* like speed than *achieving* it. The details are sharp and clear: from the particulars of the engine, so prominently displayed, the result—speed—can be inferred. In celebration of the 500 horses available to blast through anything so trivial as wind resistance, streamlining is neglected. The pin-striping, flames and performance stickers (the Ferrari shudders) are as direct in their own message as the gleaming power plant, flaring exhaust pipes and fat tires.

5. Befitting its supernatural form, the Ferrari can only be owned by gods. "Arm-and-a-leg" does not come close to describing the price tag, and most common arms and legs do not come close to being able to caress its perfect titanium alloy surfaces. The Ferrari is pure, rare, precious. The hot rod, on the other hand, while aspiring to a certain transcendence, starts out very

---

[1] John A. Kouwenhoven, *Made in America: The Arts in Modern Civilization* (Newton: Charles T. Branford Co., 1957) 214.

[2] *Ibid.*

[3] The "engineers' aesthetic" holds the value of efficiency uppermost—finding the highest value in the transparency of an object to its function. The pre-conventional significance made apparent in this transparency challenged the eclecticism of the nineteenth century as well as the traditional decorative encrustation smothering the object. Considered in contrast as a naked embodiment of function alone, the object is clearly liberated.

This sort of transparency is, however, contrary to an understanding of architecture as an *expressive* medium. When "function" is interpreted primarily in terms of a "satisfaction of physical needs," this message of liberation delivered by the object-as-direct-embodiment-of-function is condemned to trivial statements of shelter and hygiene. In such a case, architecture's traditional responsibility for a lofty "*expression* of the ideals and aspirations of the age" is forsaken for a more prosaic representation of its standards of comfort and sanitation. The transparent embodiment of function which shapes airplanes or steamships and makes mass production profitable (through a universalization of technique) is at odds with an expression that, as a significant opacity, favors the signifier over the signified.

The adoption of the machine as a visual referent by the Modern Movement was not in itself inappropriate—the contrast between the "machines for living" and the more conservative cultural artifacts of the time *expressed* a spirit of newness that, during the revolution, was indeed very "lofty." But the movement's narrow interpretation of this referent, conditioned by reaction to the excesses of the nineteenth century, could remain vital only as long as

a wrong turn. At the time, there was no apparent forking of the path, no sense of misgiving at opportunities missed or cries of dismay by babies being tossed out with the bath water. How could this have happened? We postulate: Alien Intervention.

We figure that sometime during the summer of 1916, before that fateful fork had been reached, Le Corbusier was visited by aliens. The aliens were frightened by mankind's aggressive technological advance. Understanding that revolution was the means by which humans announced their yearning, but that architecture was the means by which they established it, the aliens contacted the future Le Corbusier. Aliens can be persuasive; they steered Le Corbusier in a direction that they knew would ultimately stifle future development.

humbly indeed. Beneath all that chrome and metal-flake paint lies a heart of mass-produced Detroit iron.

6. The Ferrari is entirely the product of impossible, painstaking "old world craftsmanship"; it is born in a studio; the hot rod results from old wheeled crafts being painstakingly "souped up," usually in their owner's garage. Much of American design evolution can be understood from the perspective of the souping process. The American familiarity with technology is showcased in examples like this, where the *reuse* of the object demonstrates a comfort level beyond casual engagement, yet short of deification. The relationship between the designer and the object is more Heideggerian than Pygmalion. While in Europe the average family doesn't even have a garage, in America the average garage is filled with the effluvia of a national predisposition to tinkering. The character of this tinkering says a lot about that disposition.

7. The challenge in *souping up* the most dorky or innocuous vehicle is keenly felt; but it is balanced by a respect for the vehicle's latent potential to become "Boss." The phrase originally referred to the process of enriching the vehicle's fuel mixture, but has come to cover the interventive up-grading process in general. The upgrade usually involves the introduction of technology that is more advanced than the original's, but there is little interest in advances which lead to "smaller, lighter, and more efficient" design or in the trend to miniaturization. The expressiveness of the "intervention" is as important as its effectiveness; though effectiveness is the theme, it never gets in the way of some impressively showy effects. An affirmation of the potential dignity to be found in the most mundane or banal objects, this example shows the redemptive side of America's celebration of the common man—a love for the underdog that runs

through her crafts as well as her government and literature. Many otherwise forgotten vehicles have achieved a "classic" status through their *souped-up* versions. The "sanctification" which occurs in choosing the old jalopy to be souped, does not strictly or necessarily occur diachronically. It is not only the older car that excites the souper's imagination; those contemporary vehicles which, by their lowly station and lesser expectations seem to offer the promise of contrast, may also be considered. The Datsun 510 was an obvious example of the synchronic possibilities for this practice, but it is also easy to imagine mag wheels, flared fenders, and blown hemis gracing a Pacer or Escort. In *souping-up* the before-and-after contrast is seen as a commendation, not a criticism. Rather than contesting the vehicle's own latent formal directives, it is guided by them.[4]

8. The souping process plays out the tension that exists in a democracy between the sanctity of the individual and the primacy of the community. The souped-up vehicle resolves this tension by asserting itself as a singular *exemplar* within the mass-produced community. Maintaining its genetic connection to all the rest, it separates itself from the pack in such a way that it *enhances* the reputation of its make, model, and year. The paradox of mass-production's promise to liberate the masses is addressed by this process: the freedom implied by the presence of two-cars-in-every-garage is illusory if all these are the same, yet the anarchy of absolute difference cannot be preferred. The hot rod is a statement of the of the individual's ability to challenge the anonymity of the assembly line, without rejecting its sense of community. These are everyman's vehicle—family cars and working vehicles—with expectations encouraged by "lowest common denominator" marketing and realized through the universalization of mass production. The assembly

that contrast remained. The contrast was clearly stated in general by the emerging technology, but just as clearly some examples of this technology were more exemplary than others. Those "machines," like airplanes and grain silos, which for functional or economic reasons resisted supplementary ornamentation, were raised up as the new standard, while those which welcomed or tolerated such elaboration were overlooked. The former's abstraction and streamlined efficiency became architecture's goal, while the visual interest and elaboration offered by otherwise equally sophisticated technology was regarded with suspicion. This was an ominous distinction to make, and the postmodern critique records the legacy of sterile work which resulted.

Of course, only in retrospect can we see that it might have been the result of

The aliens knew that while human technology was developing at an impressive pace, human emotional maturity with respect to this development lagged far behind. They knew the only real impediment they could place in the human's path was misunderstanding. The aliens were smart: knowing that humanity was inextricably tied to its technology, they did not attempt to encourage a rejection of technology. They knew that they could ensure stagnation only by encouraging conditions that would prevent humans from embracing and emotionally integrating this technology. So, they had lunch with Le Corbusier. They told him to forget about L'Eplattenier and all that nature stuff. They talked about the importance of novelty over tradition and how far one could go with a statement that would contrast the two. They extolled the wonders of flight and the magic encapsulated in even the most reductive object types of industry and commerce—like the Thonet Longue—they filled his vision with ideal images of pure, simple volumes at magnificent play in light, and then blinded one of his eyes to make certain that space would become abstract.

So the Thonet Longue become the Chaise Longue, a "relage continu" or a continuous adjustment; the Parthenon was purified into the Villa Savoye; like the Model T become the '92 Taurus. These were not just any old jalopies; they certainly did not become hot rods.

By convincing Le Corbusier to prefer the abstract side of the machine, the aliens kept the machine at a distance and prevented its assimilation. By putting it on a pedestal, they ensured its ultimate alienation. The aliens

lines' promise of two-cars-in-every-garage intends to lead to the freedom of wide-open-spaces. This is essentially meaningless if all these spaces, cars and garages are the same. But it is precisely this aspect of these cars which is addressed by the souping process, making the hot rod a statement of the importance of the individual in contrast to the anonymous conformity of the assembly line. The statement made by the souped-up vehicle is about the vehicle's power and speed, but the critique it embodies is about empowering the individual, opening up these spaces to the freedom they hide, and here it addresses most directly the essence of the vehicle itself, and its promise.

9. The souped-up vehicle expresses a sense of its own enhanced capability, but does it in a way that exhorts the rest to realize *their* potential.[5]

10. Many have noted that the high point of this American art for putting-it-all-together occurred after the last European war had prized America out of its shell. **MIT 6** Buoyed by the success of that exercise in cultural exchange, postwar American design became positively effervescent, animated with the "easy going relationship with technology" that Kouwenhoven described. This was a relationship that bred an "improvisational spirit" that lay behind jazz, or art—like Jackson Pollack's action painting or the sculptures of Alexander Calder—but also was present in the architecture and industrial design of the period. It was this improvisational spirit that discovered existing pre-engineered building systems, components, and off-the-shelf parts borrowed from other disciplines—readily available industrial stock were the culmination of years, if not generations, of development and improvement.[6] **"Nothing runs like a Deere"** was a slogan that expressed this value.[7] In contrast to the more stylis-

tic concerns of the European architects of the time, Americans were engaged in the production of a matter-of-fact modernism **MIT 17** that was expressive not of abstract, philosophical or moral imperatives, but of the mercantile reality that got the buildings built. This was the period of Eero Saarinen, Charles and Ray Eames, early Rudolf, and late Usonian Wright. America of this period reveled in a "humane and innovative materialism" that made a clear connection between the object and its experience in life. An attitude of companionship with the technology prevailed, equipment was treated with respect and good humor. This was neither the slavish worship practiced elsewhere, nor the indifference common today, when technology threatens to become invisible, but the straightforward peer to peer, eye to eye, hand to lever materialism. Nor was this the consumption-based materialism understood today, **WITM 12** **WDIM 50** but a *thing*-orientation more focused on the *making* of the stuff in the first place. Americans have always liked to think of the machine as a tool rather than an ideal. **NOB 24**

11. The hot rod and Ferrari comparison can be extended to describe cultural differences in architecture as well.[8] The European architect's extravagantly customized efforts flaunt their uniqueness, and seem to dare the user to touch them, much less tinker, while the industry-standardized products of American efforts seem far humbler, and encourage an ongoing process of assembly and reassembly that extends the "ownership" of the design through generations of users. Such industry standardization levels the playing field and brings "making" into everyman's reach. Sears Craftsman™ wrests the power from the guilds of the old world craftsman and distributes it to everyone who can lift a hammer or credit card. The mass production basis of industry standardization enables the same democratic opportunities in building as

feared that if humans accepted the machine as a normal extension and glorification of their humanity, then the alienation they carefully cultivated would be transformed into celebratory expressions of engagement in the world. The universe would then be open to humankind and no safe place for aliens.

[From *Angels & Franciscans: Innovative Architecture from Los Angeles and San Francisco*, ed. Bill Lacy and Susan deMenil (New York: Gagosian Gallery/Rizzoli, 1992), 34-41.]

[4] While contrast is important generally in critical intervention, in the souping-up critique this contrast is seen as a means of affirmation. It is a contrast *guided* by the host's own (latent) formal directives; not the shocking juxtapo-

sition of dissimilar elements in collage, for example, but an organic, evolutionary *enhancement*, in which the difference is one of degree rather than kind.

[5] The critique embodied in souping-up follows the logic of supplementation: **ONM 23** the intervention acts as "something which completes or makes an addition." (Webster) **WDIM 10** The supplement is "an inessential extra, added to something complete in itself, but [it] is added in order to complete, to compensate for a lack in what was supposed to be complete in itself."[a] In the case of the jalopy **ONHR 122** it is clear that the original vehicle—even if run-down—remains sufficient to the task of transportation and thus could be considered complete. Yet, it is just as clear that, in regarding these vehicles

from the distance of time and increased expectation—that is, from the perspective of the enthusiast—they *do* seem to suffer a certain dorkiness.

While "... the supplement is seen as exterior, foreign to the essential nature of that to which it is added,"[b] the supplement's centrality to an understanding of this "exteriority" belies its apparent non-essentiality. The importance of the before-and-after contrast is a clue to what this "essence" might be. It is also the point where the critique takes hold. The apparent innocuousness or outright homeliness of the original vehicle assures that the souping will stand out, and to this extent the souping serves retro-actively to highlight the vehicle's "originary lack." What is most lacking in the vehicle chosen to be souped is uniqueness, and its formal corollaries: beauty, sophistication, or, more appropriately, Bossness. It is the expressiveness of the intervention

Detroit offers in hot-rodding. The human hand becomes visible in such work; the welder or assembler or carpenter leaves traces in the object as clear as the sculptor's chisel marks or painter's brush strokes: each weld or bolt is evidence of the hand that placed it there. In the European model there are no sticks that are shaped, cut or welded, no angles or tees that have been put together—none of the basic shapes which communicate the everyday labor involved in their assembly. Like the handcrafted Ferrari that shows no evidence of human handiwork, European bits are designed to eliminate that space of working, creating a seam-less organic injection-molded whole. And in that they become hermetic—closed and non-engaging, if not alienating.[F7]

12. The European kit o' parts is strictly haute Tech,[NOB note 10] and its complexity fetishizes its technical accomplishment, rather than taking it for granted, as the American kit would do. The Centre Pompidou, LLoyd's or the Hong Kong Bank could not be assembled in any garage except perhaps Rolls Royce's—with ESA scientists in attendance. The American, Heathkit™ approach, on the other hand, is much lower tech; every homeowner seems to have a shop of some sort in the garage where this kit can be assembled or adjustments made. Rarely do American buildings seem to come from a single kit at all, but instead are created as more open-ended constructions, assembled from various kits as necessary.

13. To Americans, the machine has rarely been alien or aloof, or familiar to the point of invisibility. It has usually existed in a stable, matter-of-fact balance between these extremes, the ideal demands of the program balanced against the pragmatic constraints of the real world.

14. Though it admires restraint, there is about American stuff an irrepressible exuberance. The touchstone to which American design returns when it has lost its way in imitation or insecurity is the air of purposefulness or intention that sets American stuff apart. It is the frankness of the American expression of this that the world has always valued. That same reasonable intention and purposefulness echo through the instruments of American government, fashioned by hand tools and then machines from a magnificent wilderness, that leaves her citizens[ONE 29] free to fashion their own purpose, to intend their own future, to make their own stuff. Unburdened by a second-guessing history, American designers have always been free to make their own.

---

which addresses this originary lack, imprinting it with the individuality of the young automotive critic.

[a] Jonathan Culler, *On Deconstruction; Theory and Criticism After Structuralism*, (Ithaca: Cornell Univ. Press, 1982), 103.

[b] *Ibid.*

[6] Thomas Hines, *New York Times*.

[7] And the Deere Headquarters by Saarinen embodied it perfectly in architecture.

[8] When "applied" to architecture, "supplement" usually means ornamentation; the "essence" which casts ornament as supplemental is not uniqueness (since this is unavoidable) but apparent purpose. The Modern Movement attempted to strip away the supplementary decoration that was "suffocating architecture," to prove that this decoration did not redress an essential lack, that in fact, if anything, the essence was apparently lacking *because* of the surplus of this supplement. The common essentiality of purpose, or function, was recovered then by paring the object down to the "purest" statement of that purpose or function alone.

Head Start Childcare Facility
Hightstown, NJ

C95.08/1

Owner:	Early Childhood Facilities Fund
Client:	New Jersey Head Start Program
Architect:	Jones, Partners: Architecture
Site:	Flat, semi-rural two-acre site in Pennington, New Jersey, bordered by empty farmland and a stream
Program:	Childcare, classrooms, administrative and teacher training, and support facilities, including family counseling, kitchen for daily meals
Size:	10,000 ft^2
Systems:	Pre-fabricated widespan steel bents, steel framing with concrete-on-metal decking, corrugated steel skin, concrete slab and footings, painted concrete support block wing
Features:	The massing is derived from a child's drawing of a house, but takes the apparent awkwardness of the drawing as an indication of complexity, which is achieved within the constructional parameters of typical industrialized building systems in order to create the most cost-effective learning environment and honest expression of architecture's role in supporting that mission.
Cost:	$1 million
Completion:	October 1994 (competition)

Marshall McLuhan's observation that the whole environment can be thought of as a vast teaching machine seems an apt description of the intentions embodied in this facility. In every possible way the design of this building and its grounds attempts to engage the children's imaginations and to inspire them. Consequently, the design does not offer itself as a neutral background for primary colors and educational graphics, nor does it satisfy itself with simple fulfillment of the typical programmatic requirements. Control and supervision of the children, or durability and ease of maintenance of the facility are important, of course, and must be addressed, but they are not ends in themselves. This building goes beyond sufficiency to challenge the children to go beyond survival.

In the broadest possible sense, the building offers itself to the parents and staff as a teaching tool. First, it gives the children the security of the familiar, and the staff an anchor, through the imagery of the home from which adventures may be launched. Neither Disneyland nor a panopticon, the image is pitched between adult responsibility and child's fantasies, encouraging the adult to explore and the child to grow, together. Subtle and not so subtle, shifts in scale and geometry are the signal that such familiarity is not to be taken for granted: instead of a single, cute kid-scale, there is a range of different scales which offer the viewers—including adults—unusual perspectives, fueling aspirations to grow or empathy for the less grown, or empowering them with confidence. And instead of a

11. children's entry
12. adult entry
22. mechanical
23. auto drop-off
25. covered outdoor play area

site plan 1"=48.00'

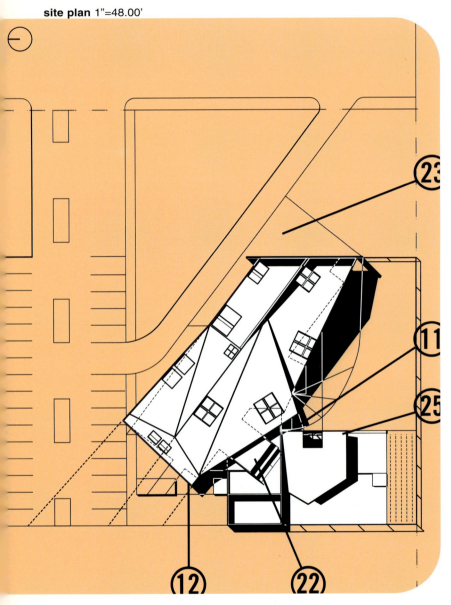

single pragmatic ordering system, or a cacophony of wacky departures from that, the building grows logically into differences that the attentive eye will find both liberating and illuminating. The geometric shifts set up in such deviations are far from meaningless, showing how the regular pre-engineered building structure accommodates the change and what end is being served by it.

The building is designed to express such ideas through its apparent movement, making an empathetic connection to the children's own constant Brownian motion, and showing how it is through such demonstrations of self control (control of the self) that the self is posited, and the integrity of that self is tested and affirmed. In its apparent movement, or the sense of its potential for movement, in the folding permutations of the house-form "shell," or the attentive ministrations of the service program's "hermit crab," the design intends to catch the eye and engage the imagination as a first step to teaching how buildings and the environment work. And then the actual movement in the space furthers this interest by allowing the adults and children to participate—the changing, controllable play of light and shadow from the operable windows and skylights, the aural and tactile "movements" apparent in traversing from carpet to wood to rubber flooring, the thermal movements that can be traced through the HVAC and plumbing, laid-out like the body's circulatory system, or the changing spaces caught within the rolling-shelf units that house the classroom supplies and create a constant sense of

114

control over the classroom environment, or even the segmented garage doors that permit the classroom to be linked directly with the common play corridor—all this "motion" conveys to both the child and the parent that nothing is given and everything is what you make of it. The head start which this facility offers its families begins here, in the building's own demonstration of empowerment, and in the encouragement that can be taken from its legibility.

In this way, the design hopes to stand not merely as a pattern for other Head Start facilities, but to demonstrate a more engaged way of dwelling in general. Seeing decoration as the greatest impediment to both truth and flexibility, the proposed design eschews all dissembling about its nature as a construction of industry-standard parts and systems. It holds no mysteries that cannot be solved, hides no lies behind sheet-rock frosting.

The lessons of the first modern wave of "flexible design" have been assimilated. This proposal avoids both *rigid* modularity and *systematic* flexibility. It looks to the techniques developed over generations by the tremendously cost-conscious pre-engineered building industry for the means of its adaptability. For obvious reasons, the techniques of this industry are geared precisely toward cost-effective variability and adaptability. They are based more on the general efficiencies of wide-span structure and homogeneous enclosures than on particular geometries or stocks of pre-fabricated pieces.

Serving a wide variety of clients and a multitude of program types—which experience a continuous stream of process and plant changes that must be accommodated quickly and inexpensively—pre-engineered buildings have become synonymous with inexpensive flexible design. Of course, it must be admitted that they have also become synonymous with cheapness and banality. But this is not necessarily the fault of the material or system—since Charles and Ray Eames pre-engineered design has not really been asked to do any better. The present design assumes that there is an honesty, a nobility, to be teased out of this type of construction, as well as an inherent flexibility, that can support the educational and aspirational requirements of a Head Start facility on this or any other site.

The scale of the facility, which is actually quite small, is manipulated in various ways to mitigate the industrial nature of the materials and the enforced simplicity of the enclosure. Two metal wall panel types are used, flat and corrugated, and several colors, to emphasize the necessarily subtle geometric deviations. The otherwise distracting trim elements, gutters, and rainwater leaders are also brought into the composition to heighten the effects of the color changes. In such a way, by recognizing the exigencies of the system from the start, and designing a formalism to exploit these, instead of chafing against them, the typically banal building components of the pre-engineered building industry may be deployed to positive, cost-effective archi-

11. children's entry
25. covered outdoor play area

view from southeast

(25) (11)

of travel through that field to a predicted end beyond, outside it.
8 As Barthes suggests for reading, in *The Pleasure of the Text*, trans. Richard Miller (New York: Hill and Wang, 1975).
9 As opposed to mere "thing" or instance of "equipment" as Martin Heidegger outlines in "Origin of the Work of Art."
10 General idea from Anton Ehrenzweig, *The Psycho-*

Analysis of Artistic Vision and Hearing (New York: George Braziller, 1965).
11 Jeff Kipnis, in conversation, emphasizes the value of a technical appreciation of coolness.
12 Roland Barthes, "Myth Today" in *A Barthes Reader*, trans. Susan Sontag (New York: Hill and Wang, 1983), 148; hereafter cited as MT.
13 The general standard of judgment has shifted from the superlative anchored or extended in contemplation of the

model

tectural ends. Rather than seeking to promote the inherent "industrial" connotations of these components, the design intends to disrupt this reference through the overt residential formalism, so that these elements may by reconsidered for their matter-of-fact suitability and the legibility of their performance, apart from their habitual usage for industrial applications.

To many outsiders, the preschool is a study in chaos; they miss the underlying order that is the hallmark of a successful, supportive environment. The classroom is designed to be both flexible enough for the changing demands of the preschooler's day while respecting the child's (and their adult supervisor's) needs for order. Striking a balance between structured and unstructured, or figured and neutral environments, the classroom emphasizes the degree of control both the child and the adult may have over that environment by offering interactive opportunities for "tuning" the classroom itself and its relationship to its surroundings.

Sliding storage units on flush floor-mounted tracks satisfy the primary storage needs of the classroom. They can be arranged in a number of configurations to create various activity areas. Use of the shelves is extended by the inclusion of a "kit-of-parts" that includes platforms, access ladders, railings, easels and other devices that support class activities. Just about everything the classroom requires is stowed in such a way that it either folds,

authentic and aesthetic—the sublime—to the active superlative, operationally-oriented and motivated by advantage. This also reflects a movement from the transcendent to the immanent, to the less exclusive, more open and empowering (even in its destinal guise)[a] paralleling that from the aesthetic intransitive affective to the instrumental, transitive, effective. Of course, the effective is still affective when not talking about engineering. What is engaged is not purely efficiency, but its flavor. When

12. adult entry
22. mechanical
25. covered outdoor play area

view from southwest

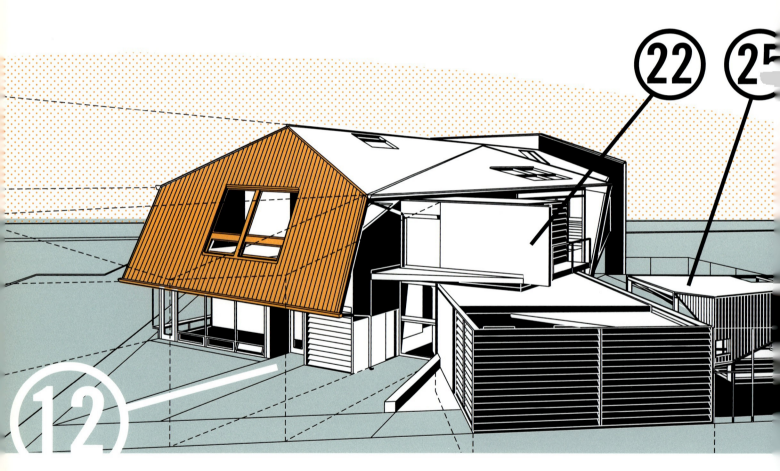

the instrumental is emphasized in experience this leads to the boss.
^a Gianni Vattimo, "Metaphysics, Violence, Secularization" in *Recoding Metaphysics: The New Italian Philosophy*, ed. Giovanna Borradori (Evanston: Northwestern Univ. Press, 1988), 45-61.
14 K. Michael Hays's editorial in *Assemblage: A Critical Journal of Architecture and Design Culture* 30 (1996): 7.
15 David Robey, introduction to *The Open Work* by Umberto Eco, trans. Anna Cancogni (Cambridge: Harvard Univ. Press, 1989), ix.
16 Hays, 8.
17 *Ibid.*
18 Jeffrey Kipnis, "Nolo Contendere" in *Assemblage*, 56.
19 *Ibid.*
20 Jean Baudrillard, *The Ecstasy of Communication* (New York: Semiotext(e), 1988), 99.
21 Jonathan Culler, *Roland Barthes* (New York: Oxford

118

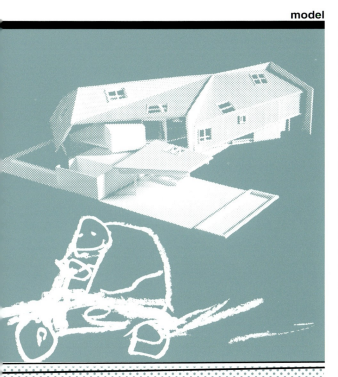

model

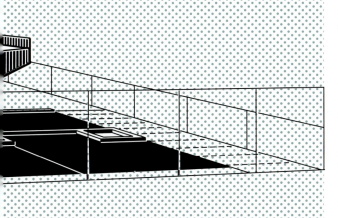

Univ. Press, 1983), 68.

22 In all honesty, the boss would not know Heidegger, yet he has expressed many of the attributes of the boss in his descriptions of the original Greek experience of reality. For example, he echoes the boss's relation to its author in his account of the artist's creative role. "The work is to be released by him to its pure self-subsistence. It is precisely in great art ... that the artist remains inconsequential as compared with the work." OWA, 167.

slides, rolls or otherwise deploys from the shelving units. And when it's time to clear the decks, the units settle into an alcove in the wall, and all their treasures and distractions are out of reach and out of view. On rainy days or when facility-wide activities occur, garage doors open allowing free access between the classroom and the public spaces. The sliding shelf track extends out the door so that shelves can be rolled out for rainy day indoor play outside of the confines of the classroom.

With child-safe glides and brakes, these storage units are architectural scaled stuff that the children can participate in moving. This element of customization provides an important sense of control and ownership for both the children and the adults.

Outside this "flexible zone" there is adequate area for tables and chairs for the entire class. For "circle time" or other gatherings of the troops, a circle is created on the hardwood or carpeted floor. The circle provides the constant in the child's day, no matter how much the environment changes in the "flexible zone."

Spread over two floors, the classrooms are ensured a sense of connectivity through the introduction of a grand stair. Both a grand symbol and haptic reinforcer of aspiration and grand place to play or hang out or lead small reading groups, this EPDM rubber-lined object offers a focus and organizing structure to the children's realm. As stair and amphitheater it supports both active and passive learning opportunities; as a reference to the home it connects that learning to the family life that must nurture it, and as a superscaled version of that stair at home it makes it all-important and fun.

At the foot of the grand stair is the entry-"living-room"-surveillance-hub-hermit-crab-roosting-reading-nest-window-seat-kitchen-door-playground-access-amphitheater place. Designed as a between space rather than a figural space, it connects rather than contains, providing the nexus of the administrative and children's realms. It anchors the building and its occupants' experiences, but not in the traditional static way of a hearth which, though it speaks of security also speaks of insularity. Around the periphery are areas where quiet, small-group activities may occur, but generally this is the space of presentation and show, of loudness and ceremony, of coming and going. A couple of overscaled arm chairs, big enough for an adult and several children, and a rag rug that culminates the entry spiral combine with the "fireplace" and great stair to declare the living room in the midst of the swirling centrifugal space, and give the larger Head Start family a place to call Home.

east elevation 1"=32.00'

11. children's entry
12. adult entry

view from northwest

23 **"Technology as architectural language."**[a]
1.   We all know exactly what is being said here and what to expect from a discussion so titled. But this simple title begs many questions. Our convictions about the straight forwardness of the proposition that technology might act as an architectural language are not as clearly founded as we would assume.
2.   Some may figure from the start without any discus-

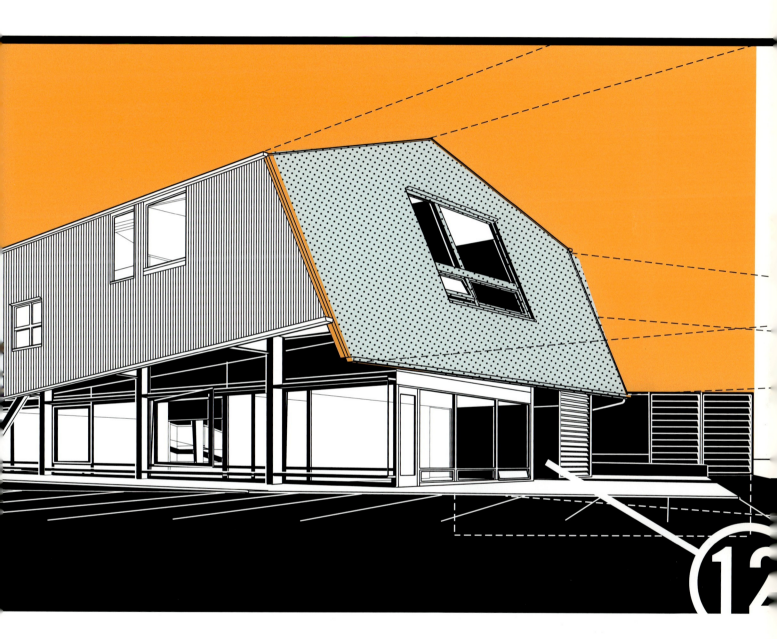

sion that this proposition is completely tautological—that technology cannot help but be the one and only true font of language in Architecture. This would certainly be a hard-line functionalist position, for example. And in the end, I might agree with it, but for different reasons. But, the fact that the terms may be separated, that the Title seems to make sense, means there is something to question.

3. As Architects we assume Architecture as the independent variable: we ask: What is technology's proper relationship to Architecture? Where, in the equation for Architecture, is it admitted, and how does it serve there? Is in fact "language" the proper, or most useful way to characterize its presence in the relationship? Certainly the idea that there is anything in Architecture like a "language" remains contentious.

4. Finally, and in this context perhaps most importantly, what do we really mean by technology? Do we mean, for

3. corrugated metal roofing
4. classroom
8. stair/ amphitheater
9. story loft
22. mechanical
25. covered outdoor play area

longitudinal section 1"=24.00'

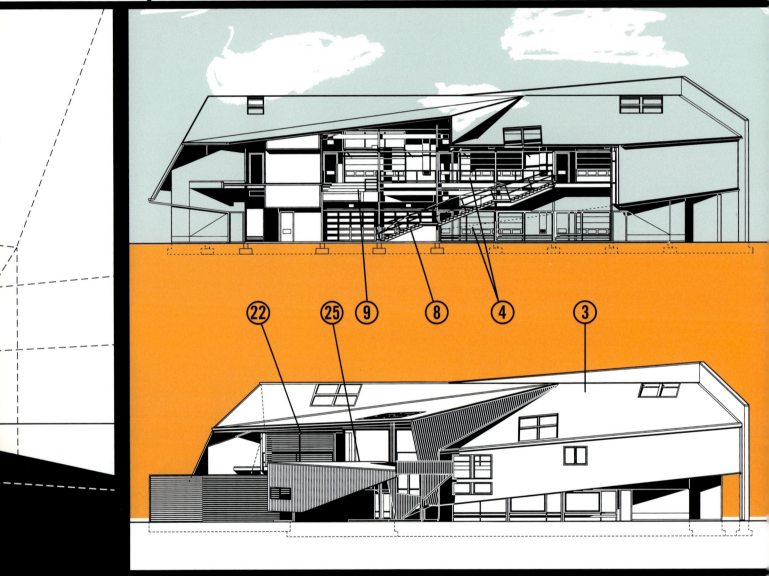

south elevation 1"=24.00'

example, technology-in-general, the idea of technique, or do we mean some specific technology—and more to the point, do we mean these in themselves, or do we consider them representative of something else?

5. Certainly the first assumption—though historically late—is the tautologist's claim for the sufficient inseparability of building and Architecture. Certainly technology enters the equation with the demand that the host for Architecture be a building, and a building necessarily depends upon technology to "stand up," to breath, to shelter, to exist. But this presupposes that by technology we mean building technology—which today is probably the last thing we mean. Particularly in America, where what we mean by building technology is a system of conventions determined by an industry with no interest in Architecture, a system religiously tolerated by a profession whose prime motivation is, increasingly, to keep the packs of ravenous lawyers at bay. Also missed is the

1. steel widespan structural frame
3. corrugated metal roofing
4. classroom
8. stair/ amphitheater
12. adult entry
22. mechanical

transverse section 1"=24.00'

west elevation 1"=24.00'

point that, traditionally at least, architecture differs from building precisely to the extent it is other than merely the product of its technology—precisely to the degree that the representation differs from the means. From the Greek's wood-details-carved-in-stone to Alberti's facadism to Mies's God-who-resides-in-the-fake-structural-details, Architecture has differed from building to the extent that the physical stuff was invested with meaning. With this tradition, it is hard to understand why then architecture would refer back to pure industry convenience and litigation screens today.

6. If Architecture is the "expression in building of the highest ideals and aspirations of the society for which it is built," then it is the other side of the Architectural equation, the art side of the opposition between Art & Utility, which so energizes architecture, which leads to assumptions of language ... which leads back again to technology as a referent. While technology does make

4. classroom
5. children's toilets
6. operable storage shelves
8. stair/ amphitheater
10. site supervisor
11. children's entry
12. adult entry
16. parent lounge
17. parent training
18. kitchen
25. covered outdoor play area
26. multipurpose room

ground level plan 1"=24.00'

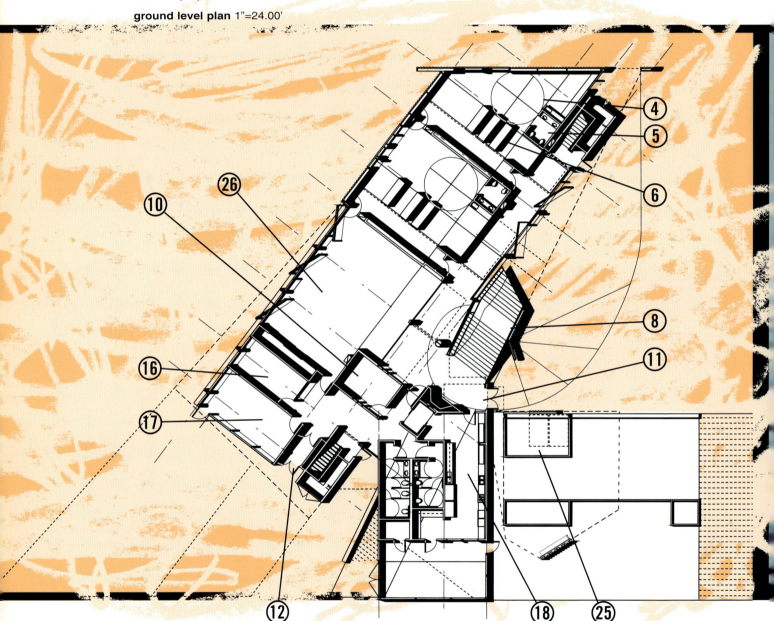

some relationship merely by its necessary existence in the fact of the building's existence, this definitely does not represent a sufficient condition for Architecture.

7. When we speak of technology in relation to language, as a language, we immediately assume the logic of representation; this must exclude from our discussion that technology of building which merely is—whether that is constitutive of building fabric, services, or structure. Language, though apparently transparent to its signifiers, is never simply there; its markers are always, at least, signifiers ... markers for something else.

8. Yet it is this transparency, so apparently, but so deceptively, characteristic of language, that beguiles those who would propose technology as the font of language in Architecture. The complete transparency of form to function is their goal: the idea that a form could be so completely determined by the requirements of the program it fulfills that not only does the form effectively

4. classroom
5. children's toilets
6. operable storage shelves
7. overflow play space
8. stair/ amphitheater
9. story loft
15. conference room
22. mechanical

2nd level plan 1"=24.00'

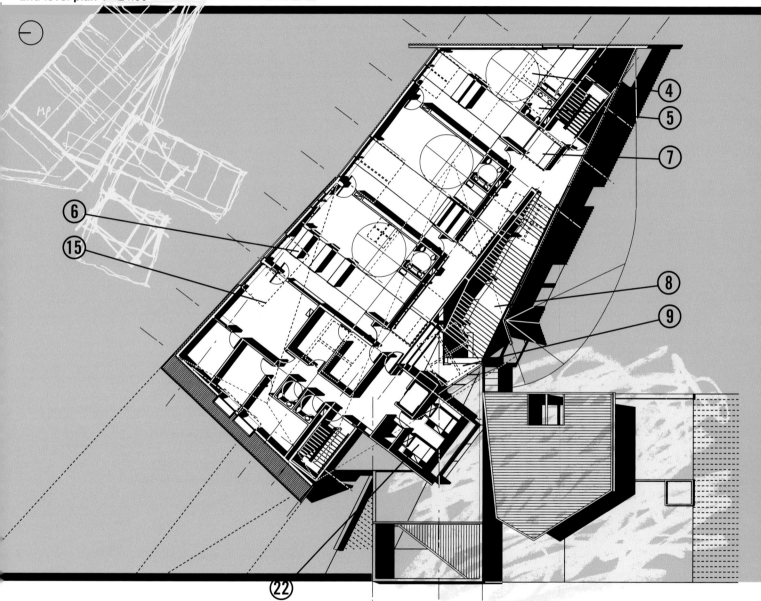

"design itself," but it (re)communicates this program to an observer without need for translation—before convention. Resulting from a degree of engineer envy, the intention is to overcome or close the gap of representation, so that the value in the work resides entirely, immediately, unselfconsciously (wink, wink) in the object, right there. Not only would this raise the stock of that object, but it would prevent its contamination by cultural baggage and political overtones (which is itself, of course, a political statement): just the clean object, speaking a language understood by everyman, whose needs it fulfills.

9. But if the value in architecture (as a language) exists less in its physical presence than in what this presence means, then this strategy is at best misguided. Meaning is an inference of opacity, not a fact of transparency. Since to the functionalist this meaning is to be derived directly and completely from the presence of the object, and this presence is to be derived entirely through the

8. stair/ amphitheater
9. story loft

interior view

fulfillment/satisfaction of primarily physical "needs" or constraints, this narrows any possible meaning to an enumeration of these needs and whatever could be inferred from their satisfaction. Surely these do not constitute, or even themselves represent, the "highest" ideals or aspirations of any society. Needless to say, there is relatively little value in the first of these readings, having reduced Architecture to a simple aggregate of human convenience, and only the most tentative and abstract to be gleaned from the second. Indeed, for this reason, it is difficult to even assign to this activity the emotion that could call this Architecture. The work that has resulted from a conscious application of this approach has often been justifiably considered sterile.
10. If the functionalist project represents a heroic attempt to reduce Architecture to an essence, free from the impurities of history and culture, it fails because Architecture is not a simple phenomenon: to look too

126

8. stair/ amphitheater

interior view

closely at it is to see it evaporate into building, just as to stare at an isolated word too long, turns it into gobbledygook. But, as reading (as opposed to passive observation) is gradually removed from an exclusive concern with the immediate sense of the object and the "problems" it "solves," from the mundane to the celebrated, its value increases and approaches what we could begin to feel was truly Architectural. That is, the sense of what is being read begins to be worthy of the Architectural effort.

Technology, as a fact or as a referent, must realize this if its is to find a place in the Architectural equation. Architecture exalts ... something—if it is to be technology, then it cannot really be just technology.

11. How could, how does, technology then become "worthy" of architectural consideration? What is the essence of technology, such that it naturally gravitates, as we all know, into such consideration? Why should it constantly insinuate itself, as we all know it does, into the

6. operable storage shelves

classroom view

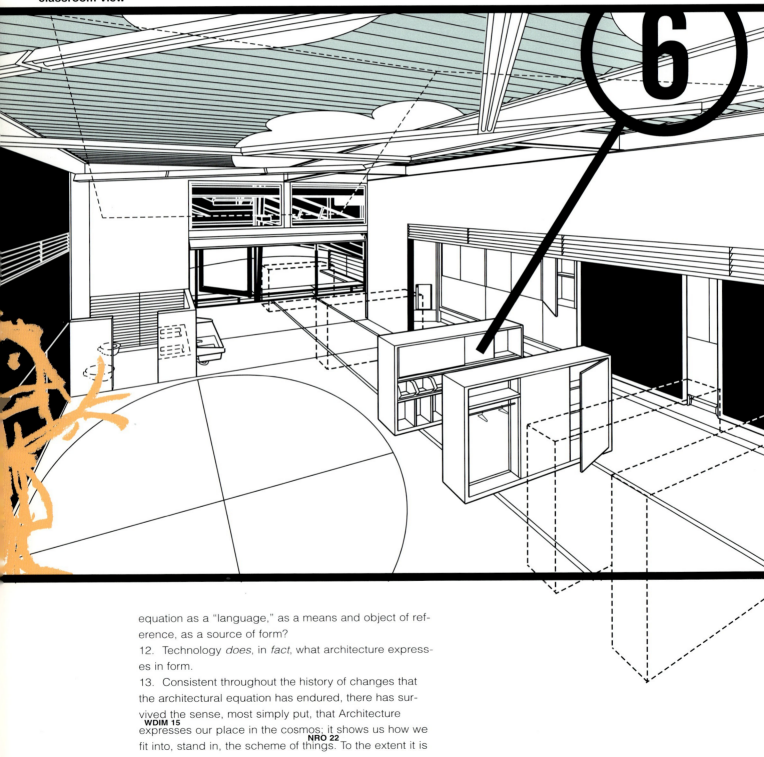

equation as a "language," as a means and object of reference, as a source of form?

12. Technology *does*, in *fact*, what architecture expresses in form.

13. Consistent throughout the history of changes that the architectural equation has endured, there has survived the sense, most simply put, that Architecture expresses our place in the cosmos; it shows us how we fit into, stand in, the scheme of things. To the extent it is

High Sierras Cabins
P95.09/1
Hope Valley, CA

Client:	Dr. Lambertus Hesselink and Dr. Denise Kroll
Architect:	Jones, Partners: Architecture
Site:	Hope Valley: 360 acres of all-but-inaccessible high Sierra forest and meadow near Lake Tahoe, surrounded on all sides by federal parks land.
Program:	Alternative vacation residences and guest cabins for infrequent visits year round.
Size:	288-1600 ft^2
Systems:	Modified twenty-foot air transportable shipping containers with telescoping circulation armature, weathering steel framing and support and leveling dunnage, solar power/diesel generator, self contained waste disposal systems/leach fields
Features:	Designed for extreme mobility and inexpensiveness, these cabin structures are modified from twenty-foot cargo shipping containers; out-fitted with interior finishes, self-contained plumbing systems and exterior enclosure and security measures in the shop. They are transported to the site, along with leveling and supporting dunnage, by helicopter to avoid despoiling the virgin landscape with roads or heavy construction equipment.
Cost:	$0.35 million
Completion:	1997 (guest cabin)

On three hundred and sixty acres of high Sierra forest and meadow in Hope Valley, California two Stanford professors (optics) will build cabins, outbuildings and assorted guest quarters for themselves, colleagues and students. The site is zoned for two dwellings and accessory structures.

The property includes portions of the largest high Sierra meadow remaining in private hands and is bordered on all sides by non-developable federal land, either designated National Wilderness or National Forest. The property is bisected by a low ridge running north and south, which divides the meadow on the west from a shallow wooded valley on the east. Across the meadow and beyond another ridge, US88 climbs up to Luther Pass, where it can be seen only from the highest point on the property. Access to the site, such as it is, is from a spur road coming off US88 several miles to the north and running down "behind" the eastern edge of the property on its way to Blue Lakes, a popular backpacking destination lying twelve miles further south. Off this spur runs a barely recognizable dirt track, which only the hardiest four-wheel-drive vehicles can negotiate. The property is splendidly isolated, and its pristine condition is no doubt due to this, and to the fact that it is surrounded by much more famous recreational areas that have attracted the backpacking legions away.

The building sites are located primarily in relation to the meadow, which is the property's most dra-

1. existing container
2. removed corrugation
8. telescoping armature
9. sliding glass doors

assembly diagram

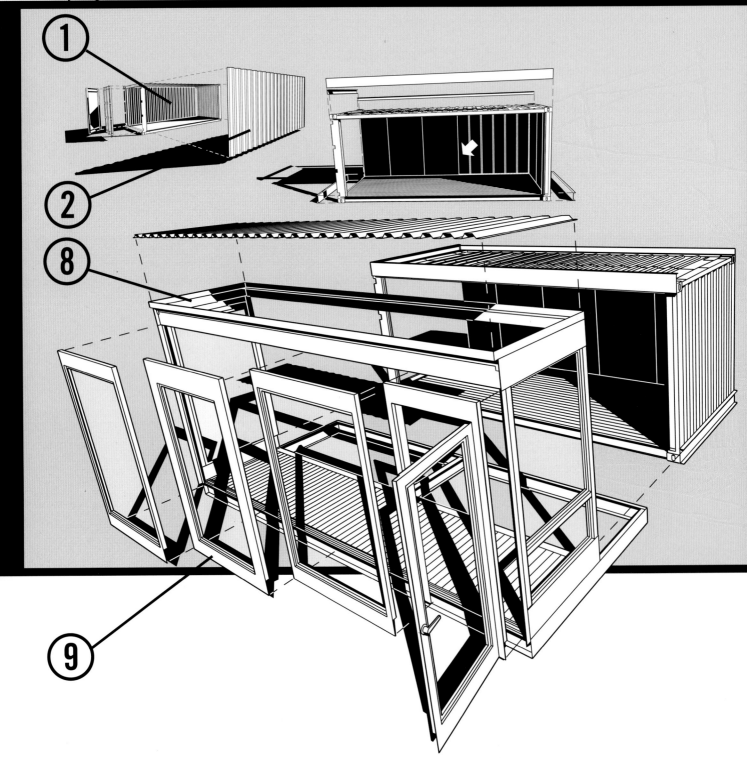

inherently optimistic, it exalts this position. During its most authentic periods, Architecture's formal reference is ultimately traceable to Nature, and each work is an exegesis. For example, classical architecture quoted Nature by means of simile and metaphor, organizing its references into harmonious, symmetrical, pyramidal compositions expressive of order and stability. During the Middle Ages this appearance was influenced by "forces" of spiritualization, which drew the natural forms upward, giving us the Gothic architecture that strove less securely to touch the heavens. Since modernism, the myth of science has largely supplanted the myths of religion as the frame through which we understand nature—and our place with respect to it—and in Architecture we refer again to forces rather than mere appearance: in this case to the underlying structures and processes science has shown to create this experience.

14. These forces also lie behind and direct even more

4. assembled module

aerial view of site

emphatically our technology in its active give-and-take relationship with nature. If science is the frame, then technology is what's happening in the picture. Ultimately technological form is directly, unavoidably, expressive of what nature demands or will allow. Technology is the residue of our unselfconscious engagement with nature, evolving continuously with us, and thus the most emphatic means of actually placing ourselves in Nature. If Architecture's mission is the expression of this placement, then technology is, loosely, an activity parallel to Architecture; they share in Nature, a referent and interlocutor; this will always be a substantive aspect of Architecture's meaning.

15. The value of Architecture, and technology's "use" for architecture, is centered precisely here, in the issue of the larger meaning that can be ascribed to the works themselves. Technology can play, and has played, a significant role in creating such meaning, and can aspire in

132

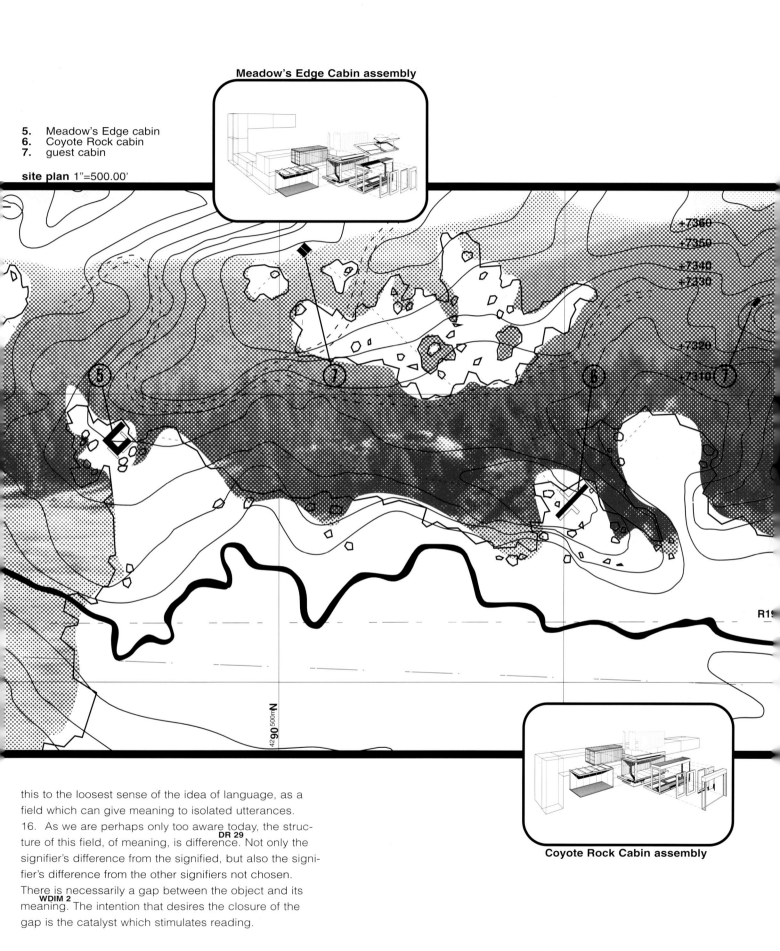

5. Meadow's Edge cabin
6. Coyote Rock cabin
7. guest cabin

site plan 1"=500.00'

Meadow's Edge Cabin assembly

Coyote Rock Cabin assembly

this to the loosest sense of the idea of language, as a field which can give meaning to isolated utterances.
16. As we are perhaps only too aware today, the structure of this field, of meaning, is difference. Not only the signifier's difference from the signified, but also the signifier's difference from the other signifiers not chosen. There is necessarily a gap between the object and its meaning. The intention that desires the closure of the gap is the catalyst which stimulates reading.

matic feature, and reflect the two professors' different attitudes about the wilderness. The sites are not visible to each other. The northern site is situated on the broad, gently sloping flank of the ridge, just inside the tree line. Though its primary orientation is toward the meadow to the south, seen out through a screen of pines, it enjoys a sense of security within its forest setting and would acquire a magnificent view of the surrounding hills from a high enough vantage point on the building. The southern site is directly atop a rock promontory that caps the ridge line, with a powerfully exposed command of the meadow on one side and forest on the other. There is ample evidence scattered here that coyotes frequent this promontory to bay at the moon and it is not hard to imagine virgin sacrifices taking place here (though the indigenous Americans who camped here hundreds of years ago indulged in no such practices, of course). Upon visiting the property there is a strong sense that the first site is where something should be built, and the second is where something really wants to be built. This sums up the difference in the professors' attitudes, and the reason why it is important that the two sites are not visible to one another.

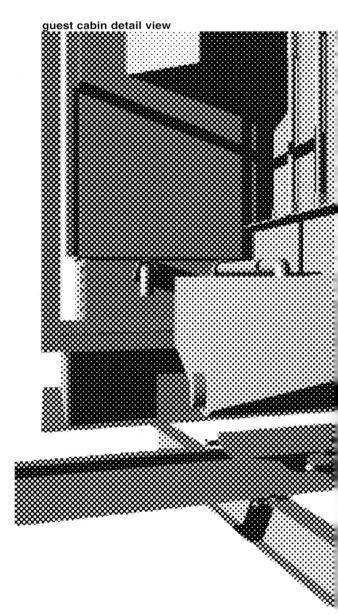

guest cabin detail view

17. As Alan Colquhoun has pointed out in an explanation of the functionalist fallacy, there is always an element of choice in determining form: no matter how neutral and programmatically directed the process of giving form, there will come a point where the architect must decide, must choose between objectively equivalent moves. At such a point he exercises intention, and this intention, and with it his presence behind it all, is imparted to the object—making a difference that inspires reading, that

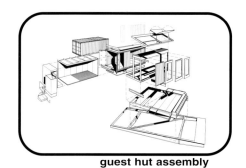
guest hut assembly

reverberates beyond the random, and represses the other paths not chosen.

18. We may boil down all of Martin Heidegger's worry about technology to a concern for the quality of this moment of choice. He felt that the essence of technology has caused this moment of choice to be short-circuited. Heidegger's interest was to reawaken the opportunity this moment of decision represents for "revealing truth, for bringing it into unhiddenness." In his view, this moment of choice in the process of making that embarrassed the functionalists, has in fact already been effectively eclipsed by the very technological system the functionalists hoped to celebrate. To Heidegger, the functionalists program had already been fulfilled to a degree that they could not even comprehend let alone desire. To him, there is no real choice left at any point in the design process because our processual interrogation of the object can no longer reveal any of the object's own

DR 7

1. existing container
13. deck

guest cabin posterior view (early configuration)

desires—may no longer "tease into unhiddenness" the object's essence by "attending to its presencing." Only those responses that relate to usefulness, which will fit it immediately into the pre-determined technological system or set it aside as an element of that system's "standing reserve," are presently allowed. This is another way of reading Heisenberg's uncertainty principle, saying the appearance of neutral choice is always already an illusion because the answer is completely determined by the questioning apparatus, the form completely predetermined by the "system" into which it will be fit.

19. Clearly, despite this gloomy scenario, some choice does still exist: the original functionalist program and its subsequent failure attest to this. Heidegger would argue still, that the choice remaining is essentially meaningless. This poses of course a great challenge for Architecture, if Architecture values meaning. It is a challenge that can only be answered from an understanding of how mean-

13. deck
17. dunnage

guest cabin anterior view (early configuration)

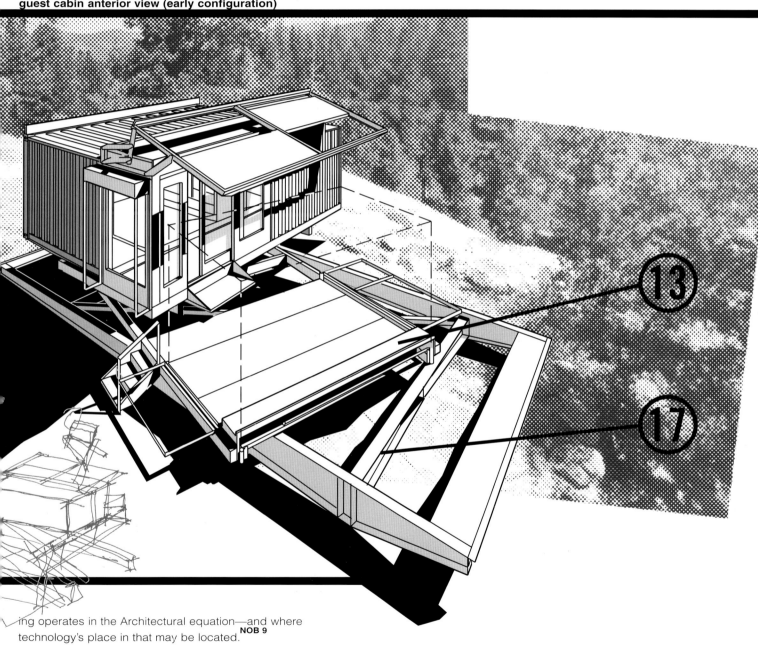

ing operates in the Architectural equation—and where technology's place in that may be located.^{NOB 9}
20.' Heidegger's "The Question Concerning Technology" is a critique of technology's success in closing the gap of difference across which meaning flows—it's a critique of how the spirit of present day technology differs from the way of revealing embodied in the ancient Greek techne; but he also finds in its genetic relationship to that "earlier way of revealing" a "saving power." Perhaps by taking an

11. sunshade/ windscreen
17. dunnage

guest cabin anterior view

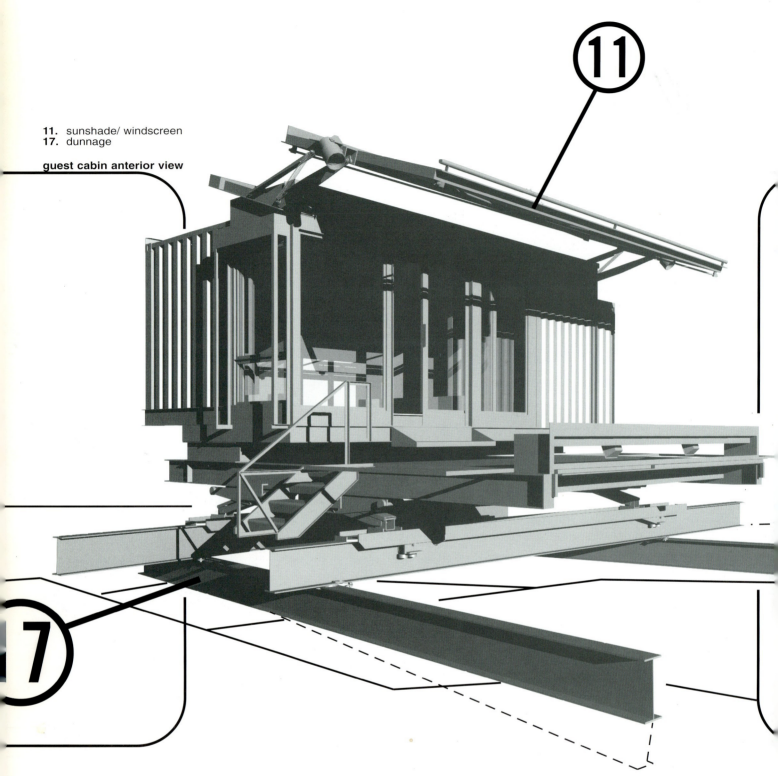

approach opposed to that advocated in "functionalism," we may turn what he calls the "setting upon that orders into a standing reserve"—that closes the distance across which meaning occurs—into the greeting that coaxes into fresh, immediate experience by attending to the gap itself and the veils it draws over possibility. It is to reintroduce surprise to an Architecture sated with a poor diet of comfort. This is more characteristic of poetry, of poiesia.

21. It is possible to think that, even if technology's mission remains the same one of control, there is room within a wider understanding of control—as domination or discipline—for an attitude of openness, a poetic directedness geared not to fitting experience within the existing system, to enframing it, but to using the understandings which make up the system of technology as a tool or foil for teasing the understanding of that new experience into unhiddenness. Technology could then be seen not as an instrument of control, but instead as Marshall

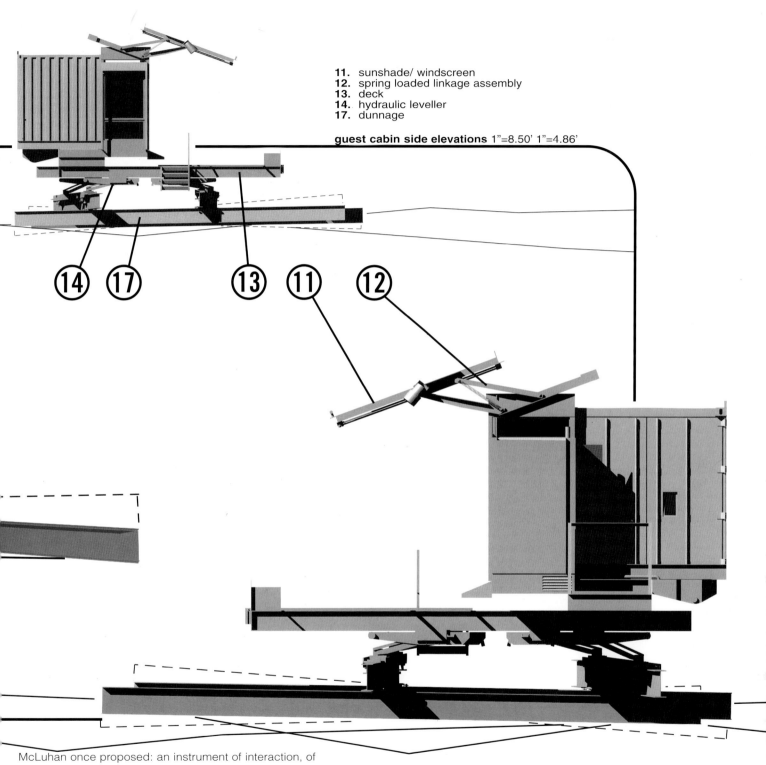

11. sunshade/ windscreen
12. spring loaded linkage assembly
13. deck
14. hydraulic leveller
17. dunnage

guest cabin side elevations 1"=8.50' 1"=4.86'

McLuhan once proposed: an instrument of interaction, of learning. And if we remain alive to those aporetic moments when new experiences somehow "don't fit" "into" the device, and treasure the difference revealed, then we open ourselves to a generative capacity that might allow technology to enjoy the best features of Language.

[a] From lecture given at University of Southern California, School of Architecture, 1992.

9. sliding glass doors
11. sunshade/ windscreen
14. hydraulic levellers
15. adjustable skid
17. dunnage

guest cabin anterior elevation 1"=5.00'

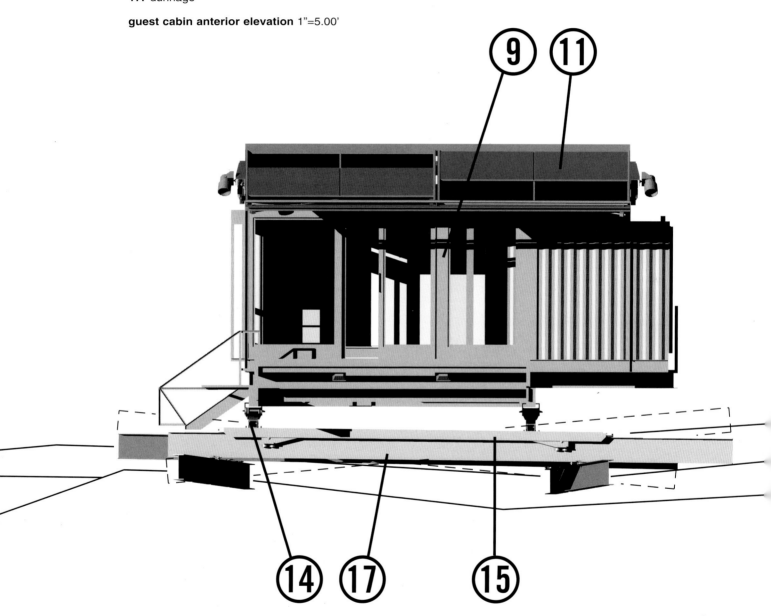

Abstract: Enframing

1. If technology defines the relationship of society to reality, then the cultural trend toward openness is neither universal nor absolute. Indeed, the technological attitude that seems to determine so much of what is even acceptable as reality perverts the message of openness announced in the appreciation of the textuality of experience. From the perspective of an enframed reality, this perverted textuality must be seen as the opposite of open, and the freedom of infinite referrability it seemed to promise must be considered transformed into an enslavement within the limiting web of the standing reserve. As Barthes would put it, the resistive political dimension of language is lost when the possibility of the operational language and language object's transformative activity is overwhelmed, and its operational character itself transformed from an expression of individual will to the will of the system. This critique has arisen from a

1. existing container
15. adjustable skid
17. dunnage

guest cabin posterior elevation 1"=5.00'

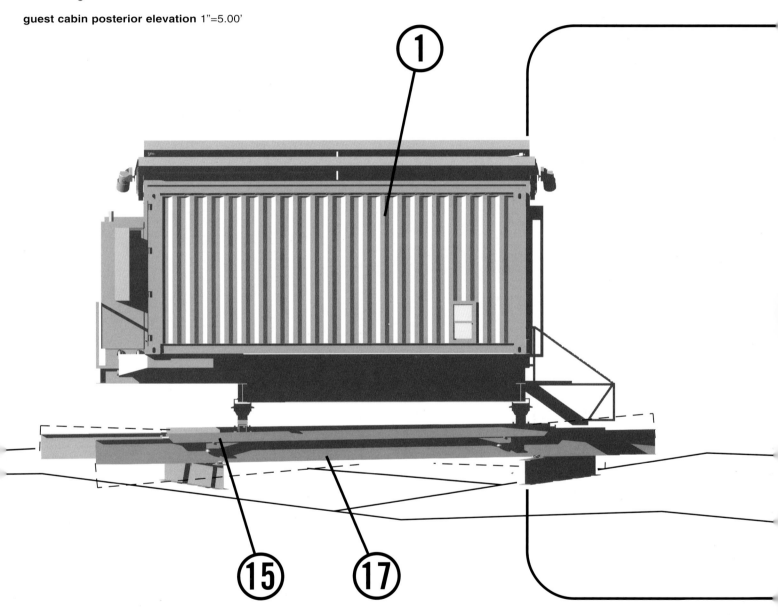

comparison between the contemporary condition, encrusted with millennia of received conventions that systematically pre-determine technological world view, and the more direct, "original" or originary Greek experience of a non-enframed, unmediated reality, spontaneously emerging into presence everywhere. What is lost in the difference is the possibility of that reality—experiences, things, and relationships—being free to come into presence on its own terms, and for the necessary human awareness of that to be uniquely evident. If, as Heidegger says, the essence of humanity is to be the open space where Being is lighted, then the pre-determination of that becoming, by the system of enframing holding sway today, prevents humanity from properly fulfilling its role as witness to Being and coming to know its own essence as that openness.

2. Yet, a "saving power" is proposed, a way out of this historical inevitability, that is immanent within the coming

11. sunshade/ windscreen
13. deck
17. dunnage

guest cabin roof plan 1"=5.75'

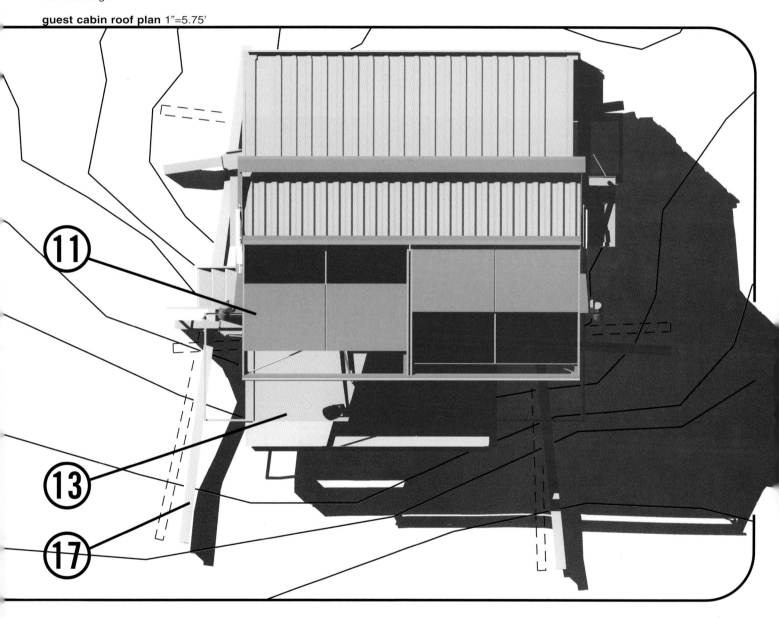

to pass of this very technological imperative. Without being able to will its appearance or know when it might arise, it is possible to speculate on the conditions that would propitiate this "salvation." Perhaps the saving power may arrive with the "final" assimilation of enframing. When the "pacification of existence" has become a reality and enframing has achieved its universal hegemony and become common, then a new reality may emerge. From this new ungrounded space of absolute mediation, a direct, unmediated experience may again be possible as difference continues to assert itself, and as humanity continues to provide witness, in a new register, with a new ironic self-consciousness.

3. For a technology-inspired practice the critiques of the 1950s and early 1960s remain the most compelling. In the immediate post-war period, at the advent of the nuclear age, the awareness of technology was filled with poignant testaments good and bad, and the machine's

1. existing container
8. telescoping armature
9. sliding glass doors
13. deck
18. self-contained WC and shower

guest cabin plan 1"=5.75'

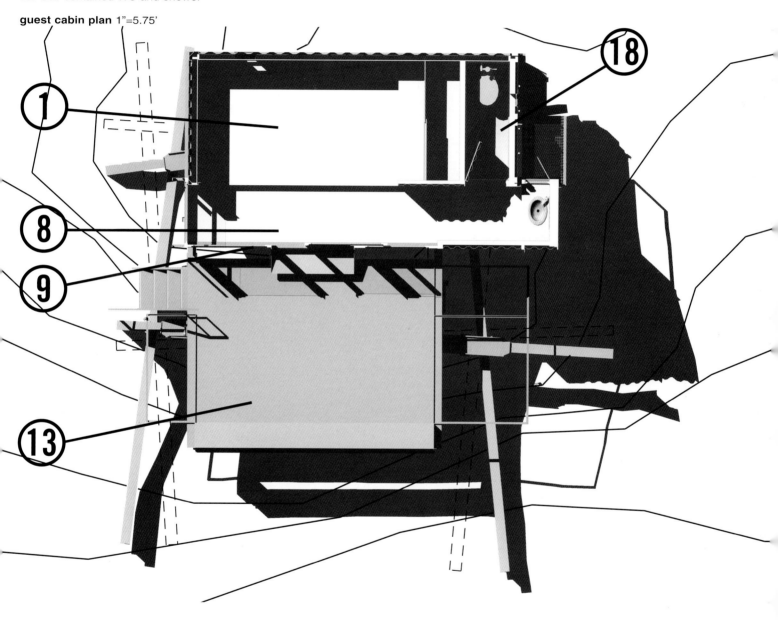

allegiance to humanity began to be debated. As a benevolent specter, it cast a radioactive cloud with silver lining over the future. A popular educational film by Disney about nuclear power, called "Our Friend the Atom," captured the manic ambivalence of dealings with technology during that period. Narrated by Walt himself, it presented a humorous anecdotal history and technical gloss of the new phenomenon, "atomic energy," that had so recently ended the war and was being turned to peaceful ends. Through intercutting animation with documentary footage from Nevada and studio footage of "experiments and demonstrations" the film provided the first glimpse of the commercial assimilation of this new fact of life. A demonstration involving a room full of mouse traps and ping-pong balls was particularly effective. The sinister goofiness of the relationship to "our friend" was evident as the ping-pong chain reaction cheerfully went out of control, while Walt intoned good-

17. dunnage

posterior view

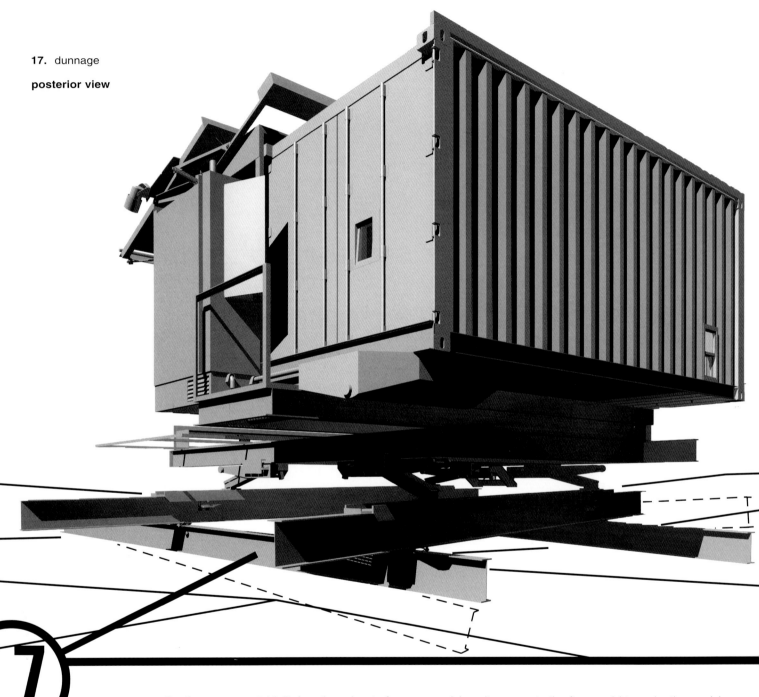

naturedly about energy yield. Before the advent of computers this was very captivating. The thought it put in the minds of its young viewers was not necessarily respect for the power of nuclear energy, however, but how to get mom to purchase a zillion mousetraps so the demonstration could be replicated at home. The underlying theme of the film was the need to control this new "genie." While the genie may have been let out of the bottle, it was assumed that the genie still owed humanity three wishes; it was up to the free world to make these wishes wisely. The critical view, expressed first by Heidegger a decade earlier in the *Question Concerning Technology*, was that the genie was calling the shots already, and that the best course was to get it back in the bottle before it was too late.

4. The critiques during this period were offered in hope and optimism, rather than the anger or despair common today, and were characteristically constructive: there was

High Sierras Cabins
Meadow's Edge Cabin
Hope Valley, CA

P95.09/2

The outbuildings will include a well structure and generator building located back in the woods, roughly between the two sites. Some preliminary site work has been done: each site already has its own leach field and a well has been dug. Each site will be supplied with buried connections to the well and generator. Single-room guest huts will be placed elsewhere on the property, three initially, to take advantage of its other interesting features. They will be skid-mounted and fitted with self-contained water and waste systems, so they can be moved around as the seasons or whims suggest. To preserve the property's isolation, no additional roads or parking facilities will be provided. It is expected that guests will park at the spur road and hike in, and that the professors will only drive in as supply or maintenance needs might require.

The buildings are designed to respect this isolation, to answer the question about dwelling in nature posed by the differences between the two sites. They are intended to embody the two professors' differing senses of the proper posture for this dwelling.

All structures will be constructed from twenty-foot shipping containers. In industry these containers are used as a basis for temporary shelters all over the world, as well as the shipping purposes for which they were originally designed. They are extremely hardy and very inexpensive. It goes without saying they are eminently transportable. Each of these factors recommend their use for this project. The remoteness and difficult topography of the proposed building sites require that the structures be delivered to the property by truck and then air-lifted by Sky Crane helicopter into place on the specific building sites. The inexpensiveness of the containers allows the architects to propose extensive modifications, within a general modular approach, without busting the budget. The durability of the containers provides for a measure of security, weather and fire resistance not common in vacation homes, but important because of the lack of a constant owner presence. And the mobility of the containers allows the construction standards for the units to be raised considerably since the entire assembly can be shop fabricated. In fact, much of the design effort has been spent ensuring the road- and airworthiness of the module units. This has led to the basic telescoping design and accounts for the apparent spatial or constructional inefficiencies evident in the doubled walls and columns. It is the architect's intention that these contingent effects of the structure's unique genesis be seen as sources of visual interest, revealing as much integrity and appropriateness as the veins in the surrounding rocks, or the pine cones which interrupt the "pure lines" of the tree.

The response of this construction technology to the unique characteristics of each building site and the personality of each client result directly in the specific designs for the two cabins. In each case, the essential linearity of the original container module has been maintained (this is an important difference from the typical industrial configuration in which the containers are arranged side by side in an attempt to overcome the perceived limitations of their narrowness). For the northern site the containers have been circled, like wagons, into an outward facing figure, providing the more retiring client with a polite sense of security, and acknowledging the different views and places that might be created in the forest's edge. Yet the circle is not closed in either plan or section. Because of this, no part of the surroundings is excluded from the figure and the desired feeling of security is not fearful. On the north side of this "train," two containers have been stacked end-to-end vertically, braced by additional external structure, to create a tower. A library runs up alongside the stairs, with desks at the landings. Above the tower, spanning the site at the level of the thinning upper branches of the surrounding trees, is a study/observatory with controlled views in all directions and an operable roof that permits star-gazing.

On the rock promontory, the more assertive client has dictated a stronger figure, less interested in politeness than conviction. Her containers have struck a bold horizontal line across the rock plateau. Though settling down behind the most prominent rocks, the arrangement makes no fig-

13. deck
22. sleeping area
24. library tower

view from west

always "the saving power." If "The Question Concerning Technology" had been written later, the saving power might never have been proposed. From today's perspective, the spirit driving the rediscovery of this original hope can be likened to that motivating Heidegger's own archeological efforts. While in both cases "the works are no longer the same as they once were,"[1] the re-examination of the concepts that have become thoroughly laundered can serve a critical role, however inauthentic their sense

may now be, by making that laundering evident. Thus, the idea that the intractable relationship now shared with technology was once thought to harbor a contrary possibility is interesting. In fact, much of what Heidegger predicted in "The Question Concerning Technology" has come to pass, and with the perspective gained by the advent of universal mediation, humanity now may be poised to realize the salvation that for Heidegger was only an expression of hope. While the electronic revolution has perhaps provided a means for living with the blindness of enframing, it is a reconsideration of the irrepressible optimism of the 1950's, when the enframing was first diagnosed, that revives the belief that it might again be possible to see.

5. On one level at least the postmodern condition can be dated from Heidegger's announcement in "The Question Concerning Technology" that humanity is in fact subject to that over which it presumed mastery—

20. entry
29. snow ladder

view from northeast

and which it assumed was leading to an ever rosier future. He thought first and most originally about the tragic irony of humanity's unsuspected estrangement from the world it seemed to control, and was the first to suggest that the erstwhile means of control was actually the agent of estrangement. **MIT 5**

6. Heidegger's "Question" begins with an etymological archeology; he follows the trial of names back to the origins of technology in the Greek techne. The ethnocentric projection inherent in the archeological exercise may be questioned, but the fruits of Heidegger's time travel must be respected. This work is essentially critical, rather than foundational; he wanted to dismantle metaphysics, not contribute another layer.

7. Heidegger was interested in the original Greek experience as a way to openness—what was thought first when anything at all could be thought and what did that thinking originally apprehend in the openness that

reigned everywhere? Heidegger's questioning provides a connection to a time when everything was new, when the process of closing it up in conventions—language, technology, etc.—was just beginning and could still seem an achievement that hardly threatened to fill the entirety of that newness. Ideas just showed up, still damp from their miraculous precipitation. "The fundamental Greek experience of reality was . . . one in which men were immediately responsive to whatever was presencing to them. They openly received whatever spontaneously met them."[2]

8. What was it like at the origin of thought when the Greeks were on a first-name basis with reality? Could the initial wonder, freshness, before the world be recaptured? Could the magic of existence as something to be wondered at be felt again? Existence is remarkable, he proposed, when the things that fill it have their own depth, will, otherness, which is not projected from within.

ural accommodation to the site; at either end it projects into the air as the topography falls away, and launches commanding views out across the meadow and back into the woods. A protected area has been captured behind the cabin, between it and the few wind-blasted trees which have managed to prosper up here, but the face of the cabin is relentlessly exposed to the merciless sun, wind and views. A combination sunshade, windscreen, security closure, and active solar device has been designed to mitigate these forces without compromising the confidence or openness of the figure.

Their provenance in transportation technology ensures that the container-cabins will sit lightly on the land—ensures, in fact, that they could get up and walk away. They demonstrate no desire to burrow into the landscape or mimic "natural" forms, nor do they adopt traditional, picturesque vernacular forms; rather, the compositions intend to fit the sites as peers to the trees and rocks. Taking their place alongside these "natives," straightforwardly and simply, the containers will adapt to the existing conditions according to their own requirements as the trees and rocks have. And so dwelling lightly, secure in their own internal motive force, the cabins make no absurd claims of ownership or dominion over these rocks and trees.

Outpost
If every gathering—every picnic and camping trip,

13. deck
17. dunnage
20. entry

section looking southwest 1"=20.00'

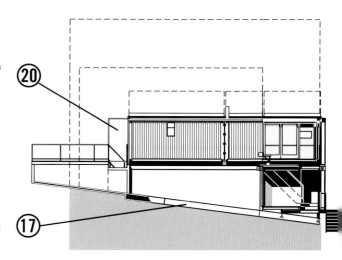

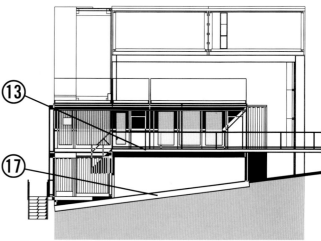

southwest elevation 1"=20.00'

For that existence to inspire this wonder things must be apart: they must be separate to surprise, for thought to advance. Yet humanity must admit its *essential* relationship to this surprise as the source of its *being surprising*, of its being remarkable. Humanity must essentially attend to the revealing of this Being, in these beings.[3]
9. To reacquaint himself with the first ideas that navigate this openness he must clear a path through the conventions that have grown up to obscure them. "What

13. deck
22. sleeping area

section looking northeast 1"=10.00'

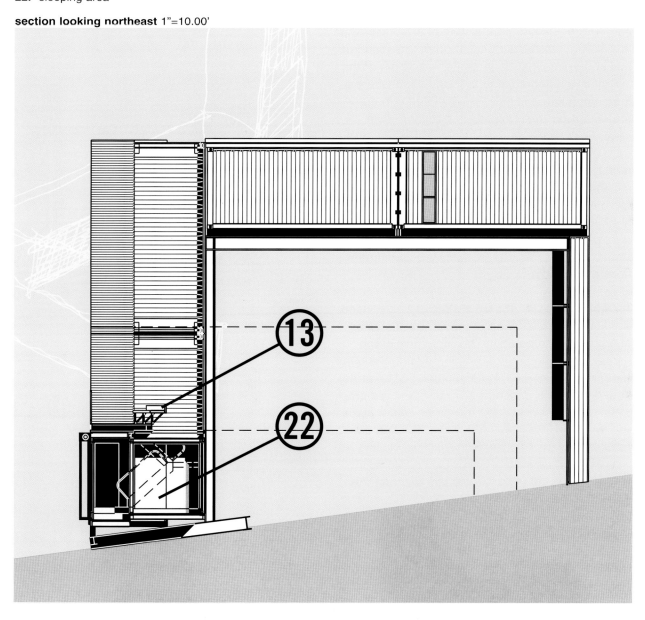

seems natural to us is probably just something familiar in a long tradition that has forgotten the unfamiliar source from which it once arose. And yet this unfamiliar source once struck man as strange and caused him to think and wonder."[4] As Heidegger points out, though, the "unfamiliar source" has been lost through a historical process of translation that is hardly innocent: "Beneath the seemingly literal and thus faithful translation there is concealed ... a translation of Greek thinking into a different way of thinking. Roman thought takes over the Greek words without a corresponding, equally original experience of what they say ...."[5]

10. Language was the first layer of convention to come between humanity and the world, the first translation of that experience into ideas, and subsequent translation of those ideas to others, yet it is also the means of reconnection, the matrix in which the fossilized experience will be found. "The reciprocal relation between Being and

11. sunshade/ windscreen
13. deck
23. kitchen

section looking northwest 1"=20.00'

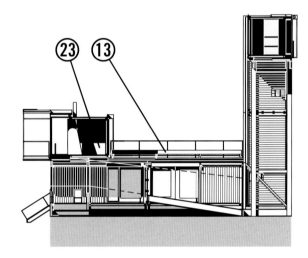

each trip to the ball-park or day at the office—has an implied political dimension, then the space of this gathering must be charged with some of the responsibility for defining it. In the case where a transient micro-community is isolated in nature—the campsite, the outpost—this truth is most clear. Every weekend a new crowd arrives, and a new, brief community is established. Each community is different; the continuous variety of its citizens and their small number ensures this, and the novelty of the dwelling arrangements and context of relative privation have a greater effect than usual on the character of that difference. What the community is reflects its accommodation with these.

Since everyone, including the owners, is a visitor (these are cabins) each of these communities starts out as an outpost. The metaphor of the home is not appropriate; beyond raising the question of whose home, or the assertion of an undesirable sense of dominion over the land (as property), the idea of domesticity seems out of place in the dramatic context of the site. Viewing the community as an outpost casts all the visitors as adventurers, as explorers or at least guests in this territory, and even the owners can feel this each time they visit.

A vernacular evolves, unconsciously, as an expression of dwelling efficiently in a particular location. The contemporary possibility for such unconsciousness, or even for evolution, is

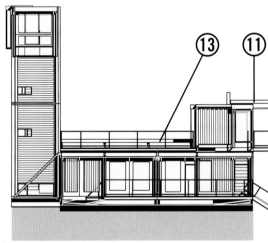

northwest elevation 1"=20.00'

man is fulfilled through language. Hence to seek out what language is through discovering what was spoken in it when it first arose and what has been and can be heard in it thereafter, is in fact to seek out that relationship."⁶
11. The movement away from Being was begun by the Greeks even as they "noticed" and named it. In celebrating their wonder through language and philosophy they took the decisive first steps toward losing it: "philosophy sprung from the fundamental Greek experience of reality.

152

13. deck
view from south

The philosopher wondered at the presencing of things and wondering, fixed on them."[7] In this fixation Heidegger locates the origin of the technological mindset that has estranged humanity from its proper relation to Being. As that openness was lost, the witness becomes recast, "over against" the self-presencing other that is itself recast as *object*. In fixing on things the philosopher objectified them, and oriented himself to them as what is now called "subject." Originally, the Greeks understood "subject" the other way around, more in the sense of "subject of attention," as "that-which-lies-before," "that which looms up"[8] without that attention being determinative. For the Greeks, *subject* named something out there, "the reality that confronted man in the power of its presence."[9] Objectified, the looming things exhibited properties, which begged the question of that which was stable in their discreet, integrated presence. The philosopher lost contact with the particu-

13. deck
17. dunnage/ minders
22. sleeping area
26. bathroom

ground level plan 1"=20.00'

13. deck
20. entry
21. living area
23. kitchen
24. library tower

second level plan 1"=20.00'

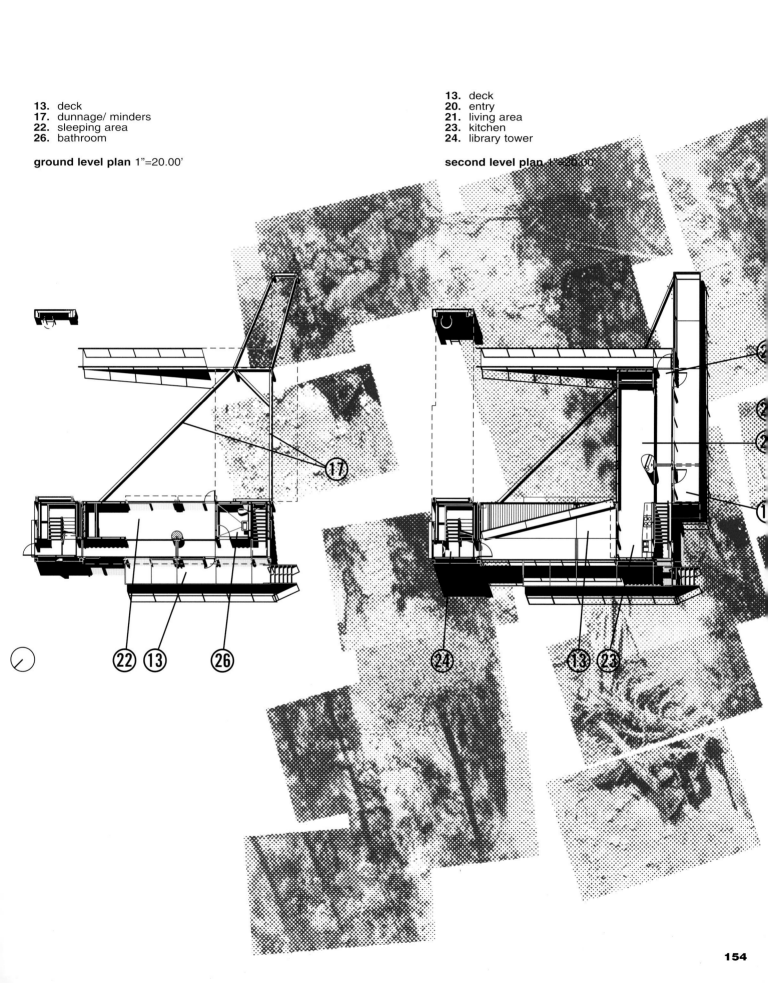

11. sunshade/ windscreen
24. library tower
25. observation area

third level plan 1"=20.00'

remote. The contemporary mind is too self-conscious, and a society which deifies novelty allows nothing to just evolve. Furthermore, contemporary society has formalized a technological ability to ignore local conditions and create the same environment everywhere. The International Style expressed a utopian vision of universal physical harmony in which the particularities of place were bled out of architecture. It supposed that everyone, everywhere was equal and that this should be celebrated in a universal Architecture. But, in fact, difference abounds, and technology's command over nature is only partial and temporary; the International Style has lost its pretension to universality. Still, the possibilities for a traditional vernacular are not improved.

A new vernacular has evolved in the wake of the International Style's disappointment. If anything, its regard for the nature it might proudly wear on its sleeve is even less than that demonstrated by the heroic, if misguided, attempts to dominate her. The contemporary vernacular is the product of a speculative, real-estate developer consumerism which is self-consciously but unwittingly devolving into a kitsch pastiche of formerly legitimate postures toward dwelling. The unconsciousness and ubiquity that makes this a vernacular does not reflect the traditional pervasive concern for efficiency and attendant sense of appropriateness, but a market-driven vision of what that should be, as capricious as the consumer pool and the advertising dollars which stir it.

larity of each thing as his attention was absorbed by this generalizable aspect, attested by the common name it shared with others, that could now be considered its "kind." The invention of categories made reality amenable to philosophizing. The philosopher came to equate that stability with their essence, as the truth of that presence. Aletheia became "correctness" as the interest shifted from the thing to its name.
DR 2
12. In "discovering" that the original Greek word for

24. library
28. gangway to observation area

interior view from library tower

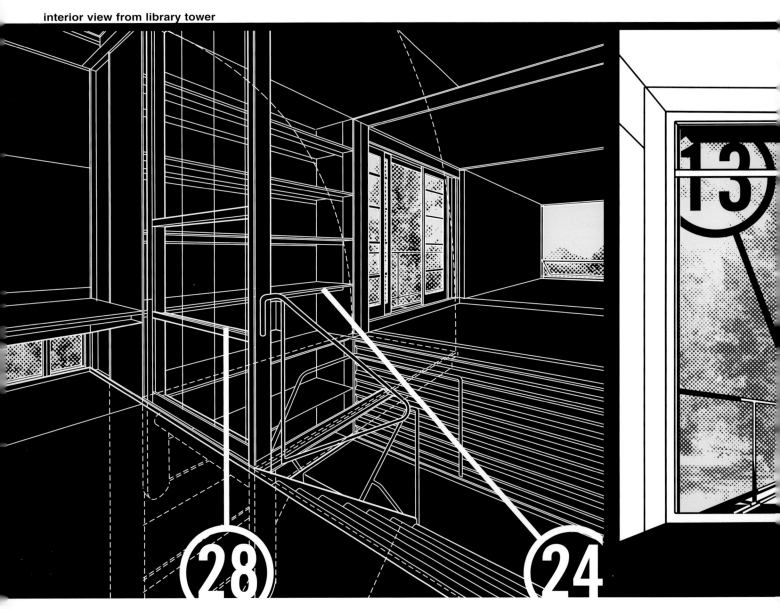

truth, *aletheia*, meant something different than the "correctness," "correspondence" or "coherence" understood today, Heidegger shows how thought is circumscribed by language. The concept of truth arose originally to describe the "emergence" of stuff/Being into presence from that openness. What has survived as "truth" once named the "unconcealment" or "revealing" of stuff in its presencing there-ness.[10] Before that presence came to be overlaid with the conventions and structures that could measure it—in terms of correspondence or coherence, or value its correctness—truth as *aletheia*, or "revealing," was localized in the presencing thing, not the viewer or culture. The viewer, instead, was the person to whom the thing was disclosed; this was an essential, but not determinative role, as witness, not reader (as re-*author*). In the open, absent the reader's expectations that would later come to measure this presencing, the object was simply, but remarkably there; its being was

13. deck

interior view from kitchen

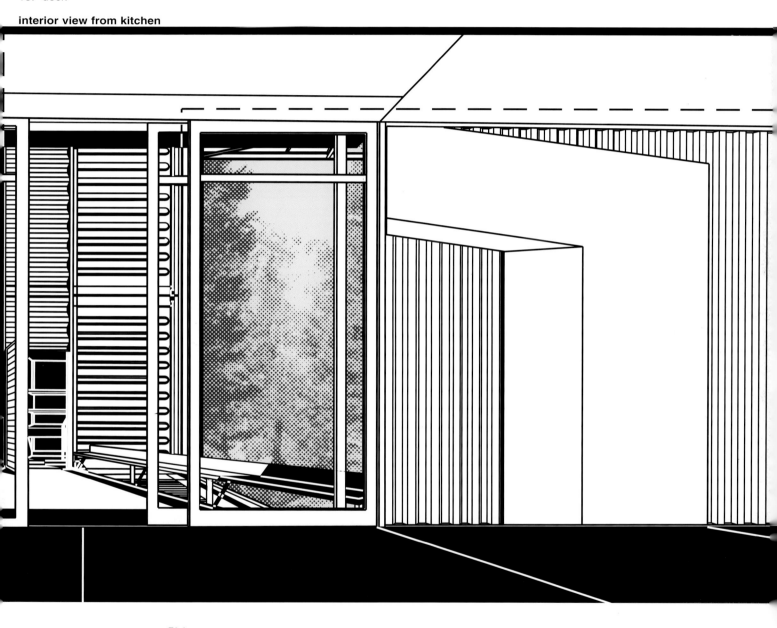

palpable, it could be tasted.^E0 1

13. This openness, which Heidegger equates with humanity itself as 'the openness to which and in which Being presences and is known,"[11] implies respect for the presencing as separate from the witness, as self-revealing, but requires the witness to share the event. In this openness humanity enjoyed a peer relationship with the world, an almost conversational posture toward the reality it encountered. Though initiating a movement away from this spontaneously open relationship, language and metaphysics were still infused with the yearning and respect that showed reality had not yet been mastered. It is probably this, as much as the newness of this perception, that sets this period apart. The sense of surprise, wonder, or remarkableness all admit *concern* as well as curiosity. "It is difficult for us to conceive a personified, willful, and therefore totally unpredictable external reality, identical and continuous with the self, needing constant

21. living area

view to southeast

propitiation through human actions to secure the survival of the world from one moment to the next."[12]

14. Overtones of Sisyphus and Tantalus reverberate throughout Heidegger's work. In appreciating that the loss of openness stems from the very description of it, he sets a theme of paradox and irony that sits well with a contemporary audience. Heidegger's desire to penetrate the original works, to reach the experience they suggest, requires a long chain of recovery that can never, finally, get all the way back: "the works are no longer the same as they once were ... as bygone works they stand over against us in the realm of tradition and conservation."[13] His wistfulness brands him a nostalgic by some critics, and many dismiss his work as a sentimental rejection of technology, but he is no Luddite. He recognizes that technology is inescapable, and that as the present mode of relationship to Being, however unfortunate, it is no less appropriate than techne was for the Greeks.

NRO 15

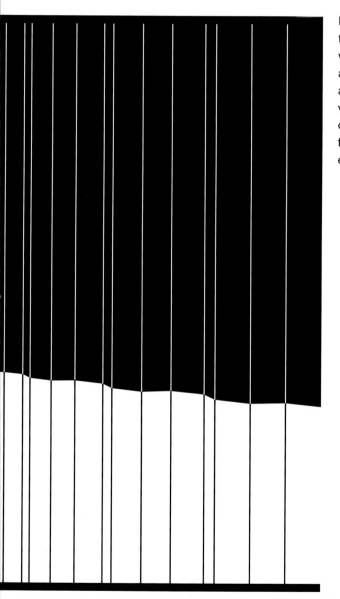

How is homo-consumerus to be re-introduced to the nature that has been forsaken? Cautiously, with respect, as a visitor with vague memories of a long-ago familiarity, to be teased out with hints and gestures in small ways here and there. As a visitor now, the human is even more dependent on the technology she once thought had freed her from nature. To survive there she must be equipped.

15. Heidegger believes humanity faces a grave danger in its relationship to technology. Other than the ecological nightmares which are now familiar or the apocalyptic nuclear scenario, and beyond the obvious loss of perspective or of engagement itself, the danger lurks. This danger "comes to pass" through loss of the openness "where" humanity enjoys its *essential* role as witness to the revealing of Being. Humanity loses the ability to know itself through experiencing the world originally again. The

25. observation area

view to southeast

condition of "standing-in-reserve" he describes, in which all reality is set aside for use as part of the universal system into which experience has been "enframed," is horrific particularly in relation to the openness-to-presencing it so specifically confounds. To be "commanded" to "stand-in-reserve" is to already be "there," to be fit into a pre-determined relationship to the rest of reality in such a way that it makes no sense to even speak of presence as an active, continuous process of revealing. Nothing is concealed here, except the fact itself; there is no space of concealment from which unconcealment might proceed, because there is no proceeding: all "ways" are pre-conceived and mapped out, all creation is production, all perception is framed and labeled. **DR 4**

16. It has become a cliché to understand in this that since "things as they are" are masked by the structures of representation imposed by humanity over its experience of reality, "man is the measure of all things," and he

High Sierras Cabins
Coyote Rock Cabin
Hope Valley, CA

P95.09/3

In this equipment the seeds of civilization are found. The absence of television and Big Macs here forces more mundane gear to shoulder the burden of making culture. As the Greek temple once refined a vernacular into the terrible Order which ordered the horizons about itself, giving compass and direction to the unruly environment, so the sunshade and handrail are being asked to order this outpost.

The seeds of this project are more humble, they have no intention of organizing anything beyond their immediate charge. Yet, the responsibility to constitute a civilization at this outpost bestows upon these humble pieces an exaggerated importance. With limited means at their disposal, the corrugated steel, structural shapes, plywood and glass—some plate, some spun—and paint can accept this attention only by re-asserting the traditional vernacular's unconscious goal of suitability. Where efficiency dictates humility, there is no room for flourish or indulgence. There is no ownership here to be flaunted. This humble equipment serves all the visitors equally.

Formal humility throws the responsibility for appreciation back on the reader, empowering her to be the author of her own understanding. This essentially political transaction is thus refounded on a more equal footing, one without a singular overt architectural authority but rather an immanent authority, teased out of the equipment itself.

The gear is able to bear this responsibility only if it is honest and good and clear. Only if it is free of other, personal messages can it sustain a lively, continuing readership as the basis of an active community. Only so can it stand in the necessary peer relationship, unindentured to an author more visible than the object itself, and in this relationship be an interlocutor in its own right, rather than a mouthpiece for another.

So, there is the thing, there. How is it more worthy of attention than any other thing, here? By the quality of the relationship it makes with the other things—by the community they create among themselves, of which it may be an exemplary member. The angle becomes the angle, or the channel uniquely the channel, in adapting to the rights or demands of other angles, or in the way it forces them to adapt to it. In its interaction with the other elements it demonstrates the unique demands of its own geometric nature: it can be fastened only in this attitude; only these faces, the back of the web and the outside of the leg, can receive another face in a bolted connection, while only the extreme edges of the legs like a weld. When these requirements are set against the similar or different demands of the other shapes, and satisfied, a construction with the sort of integrity that is self-validating results. Evident is the entire logic: the constituent pieces and the distance they have come in the assembly describe a history that gives a sense of the

17. dunnage

view from south

is able only to see himself everywhere.¹⁴ Heidegger considers this a delusion, since for him these structures actually mask humanity's essential role, as the space of openness, where Being is "lighted" or presences. In fact, humanity can actually "find itself" nowhere. It is only through understanding the essence of technology, which is the mode of presencing holding sway today, that humanity might regain its open relation to Being.¹⁵ **NRO 2**

17. Heidegger first seeks this essence in the instrumental side of techne, its attitude of control, that has evolved to the present from the Greek metaphysics. With the grafting of a theological dogma onto this structure, the wonder that animated the original Greek gropings toward mastery was exchanged for the "smug anxiety" of conventional revelation. The load of dogma was lightened during the enlightenment, but the anxiety level was not affected. Descartes answered this anxiety with his pronouncement: "cogito, ergo sum." This posited a security

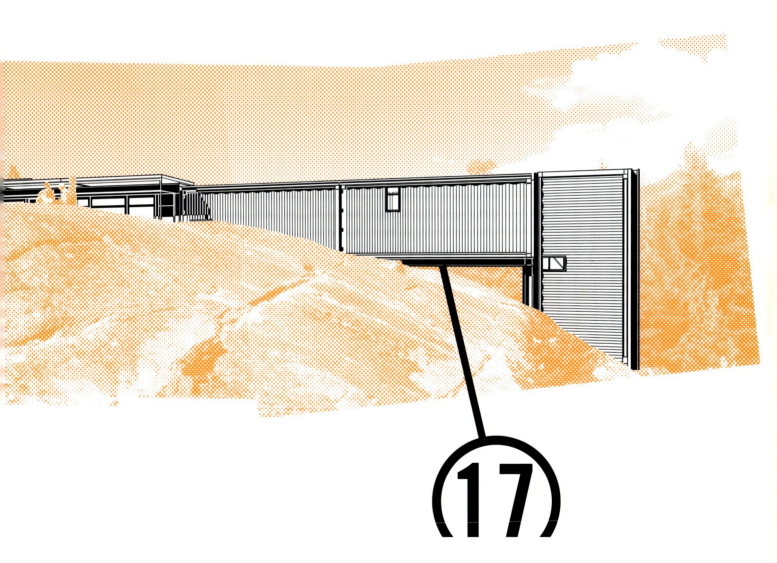

⑰

that was internally based, trading the certainty and control of introspection for doubt and helplessness before the exterior world. The Cartesian change ushered in the modern period, re-orienting the focus of perception to its own self-consciousness. By bracketing off that "self-presencing reality" as the product of consciousness this reality was transformed into the "presencing-of-the-self's reality." The subject became he who experiences, while the Greeks' sense of that which was experienced receded in deference to the cogito. Subject-of-attention became attending-subject. Objectified then, reality became amenable to the systematized representations offered and then imposed by Science, in a continuing retreat from the direct experience of "that which lies before. Though its inductive, empiricist methodology gives the impression of privileging such direct experience, in fact it only gives rise to *directed* experience.

F 10

18. The "myth" of the self-reflexive autonomy giving the

9. sliding glass door
10. rolling overhead door
13. deck
17. dunnage

south elevation 1"=10.00'

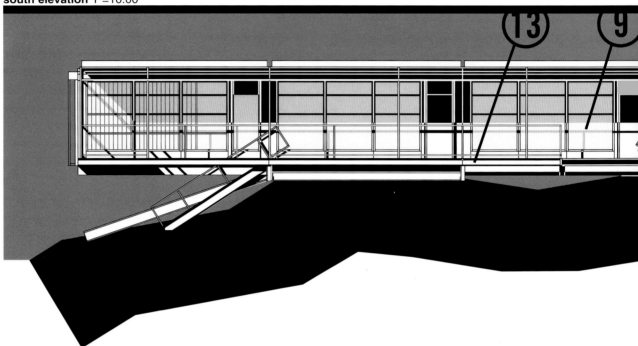

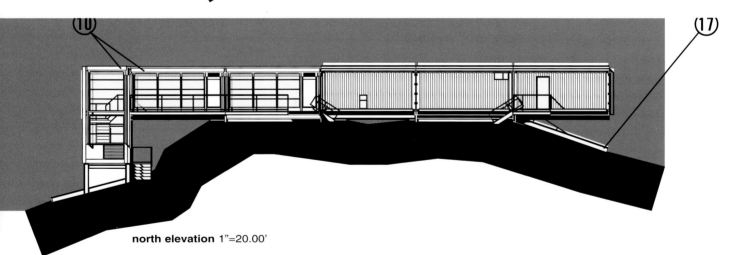

north elevation 1"=20.00'

impression that humanity is the measure of all things grew out of a perception of an objectified world, but to Heidegger "objective" is a "dangerous" misnomer if it implies the object's own autonomy. Heidegger would not, however, find the critique of textuality raised against it to be any salvation. The appreciation of connectedness the textual critique urges would be seen by Heidegger as advancing similarly enframed systems of representation or networks of pre-conceived relationship: while such an orientation might remove the subject from her shell, it will not deliver her to unmediated "openness" or original experience. The connection supposed by textuality is subsumed under the "inclusive rubric ... of standing in reserve," and "whatever stands by in the sense of standing-reserve no longer stands over against us as object."[16] The critical-self-consciousness of a sensitivity to textuality interposes another frame-of-reference between the reader and "that which lies before."

NIRM 12

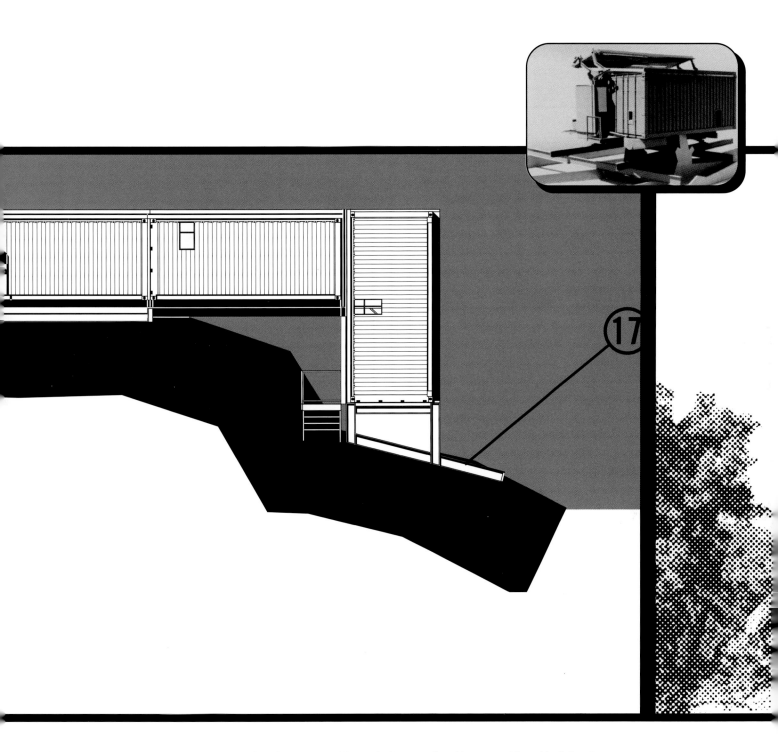

19. Salvation lies elsewhere than this sort of *self*-consciousness. Openness cannot be accessed through consciously critical activity, but will be found only where experience may support the loss-of-self. When in thrall to the artistic experience, when one "loses track of time," "losing oneself" in the experience[17] then the "saving power" that might contest "the danger" is close. Heidegger located the "saving power" in the kinship between art and technology as both "ways of revealing." Through the act of making, considered in light of a re-excavated appreciation of techne, humanity could regain an open relationship to Being, as it is presencing in the objects of its world, through making as a means to that end in these objects.[18] The saving power may be encouraged "here and now and in little things"[19]—everywhere revealing takes place.

20. The easy reading of "the saving power" finds it directly in art, in poeisis, through its submerged kinship

13. deck
21. living area
23. kitchen

view from north

with technology as a way of revealing. But art *as* art, however brilliant, is severely limited in the critical effect it can have on technology, since it is itself already constrained within the rule of enframing. Heidegger is clear that the danger itself must be also the saving power.[20] But art, as itself enframed, does show the unsuspected capacity of enframing as a related way of revealing to itself be the saving power. "The coming to presence of technology harbors in itself what we least suspect, the possible arising of the saving power."[21] Some critics have assumed that technology will somehow cease to be technology *per se*, that it will be saved, or "born again":

In this two-foldedness of Enframing as danger and saving power, and not in any merely human effort, lies the possibility that technology may be overcome. This does not mean that technology will be done away with. It means, rather, that technology will be surmounted from within itself,

10. rolling overhead door

view from north

in such a way as to be restored to and fulfilled in its own essence."[22]

21. Heidegger refers to this saving power as if it were latent in technology, its "photographic negative,"[23] that needed but a change of light to see: "what comes to pass happens suddenly."[24] He declares that it is impossible to *will* its occurrence, yet emphasizes humanity's role in that occurrence. Humanity is surrounded by the danger, is a part of the danger, is the agent of its continuation and spread. It stands to reason humanity should also be able to do something about it. Yet, humanity is now itself enframed, and does not have the privilege of a perspective that would provide a sense of what to expect, much less what to do to effect those expectations. "Man cannot bring the saving power about, nor can he know when it will happen.[25]

22. Indeed, he talks about it in terms—"lighting" and "inflashing"—that recall a gaining of insight, or an

13. deck
21. living area
22. sleeping area
23. kitchen
26. bathroom

plan 1"=20.00'

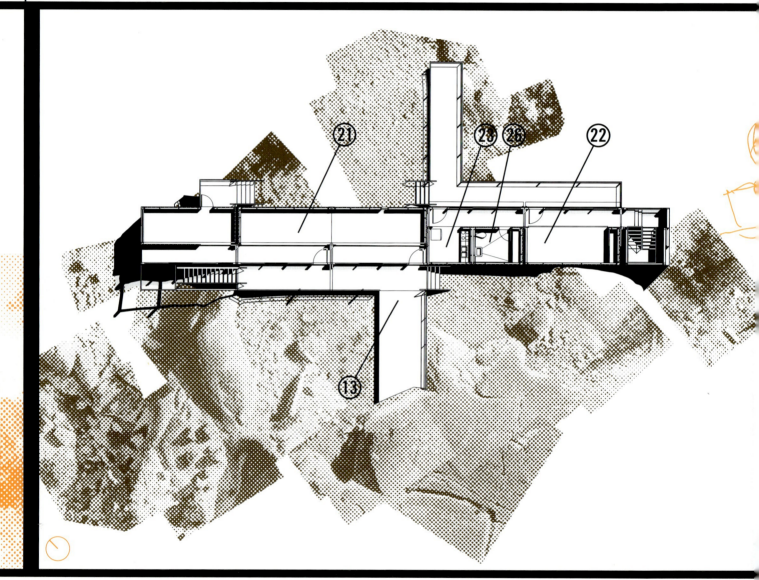

epiphany, or the sudden shock of understanding, that attends the "seeing" of an optical illusion (the Mueller-Lyer effect, for example, or the newer stereoptical computer-generated illusions), when finally, abruptly, with no apparent change in focus or attention, one "gets it."
23. In this context, the experienced puzzle-solver knows that the resolution will come of its own accord—knows that the harder one concentrates, the harder it will be to force a solution. To "get it," one must relax, stop fighting the "problem" and allow the problem to solve itself. This does not mean necessarily to give up, but to avoid practicing the very attitude of enframing that is in question. It means to avoid seeing this questioning itself as a will to mastery or control over a problem, or seeing the issue as a "problem."
24. How can "the danger" be engaged then, as the danger, without assuming the danger to be a *problem*, prolonging the danger? How can the "saving power" be

13. deck
17. dunnage

view from west

sought without that seeking itself partaking of the danger—without the expectation of an *answer* deferring real openness.²⁶ **NOB 16**

The unconcealment, the truth, concealed in the rise of technology will flash forth in that very concealing. Being will reveal itself in the very ongoing of technology, precisely in that flashing. But not without man. For man is needed for this as for every revealing of Being. Man must come to that place where this revealing may come to pass.²⁷

25. Once enframing has captured everything, existence has been pacified, and everything stands in reserve, humanity finds itself in the only place left, the place prepared by this fact: a new ground, of a new reality is created, in which there is yet something left over. This something dwells in a new plane of openness spreading across the new, hyper, real; it is of course Being, again,

remarkable to an object that is otherwise grounded in simple utility.

While this is not dissimilar to the effect achieved in the traditional vernacular by working the material—carving it or polishing it or otherwise shaping it by hand—it is more general. The hand of the individual craftsperson is less apparent than the shapes themselves and their geometries; there is an implication of the larger forces at work in creating the shapes supplied. And these larger forces open up the dialog; since the craftsperson is effaced, but not the craft, the viewer is freer to introduce herself into the equation, rendering it less personal so that all may be equally addressed and may equally assume a right to answer.

13. deck

view to west

still, presencing in a new register. At this new level, perhaps a new direct experience may be engaged, an again-spontaneous presencing may be witnessed. The appreciation of *this* openness might be very close to the saving power harbored within enframing and offers the opportunity that humanity may again come to know itself as *needed by Being*. **NRO 16**

26. Heidegger's own narrative has been claimed by history. **NRO 13** Considering the historical context of his account, the

9. sliding glass doors
21. living area

interior view looking southwest

alarm it expresses is understandable. An interest in beginnings and original experience, such as it shows, is naturally disposed to assume an end in the other direction. But it is a trick of perspective to believe that there is an end or culmination when the parallel rails of present tendencies converge. Certainly when Heidegger was writing, at the advent of the nuclear age and space travel, it must have seemed "progress" was coming to a head. It must have seemed that an end was in sight, or just beyond the horizon. It couldn't just go on. But, of course, it did, does, and still is. While everything is "in reserve" it is not just "standing" there.

27. Today the horizon is no closer. A refusal of complacency continues to characterize humanity's contract with Being. A restlessness and continuous yearning for the superlative, however quickly it evolves into the next, ensures that the speed of progress and rate of change have not diminished. But humanity has caught a second

MIT 7

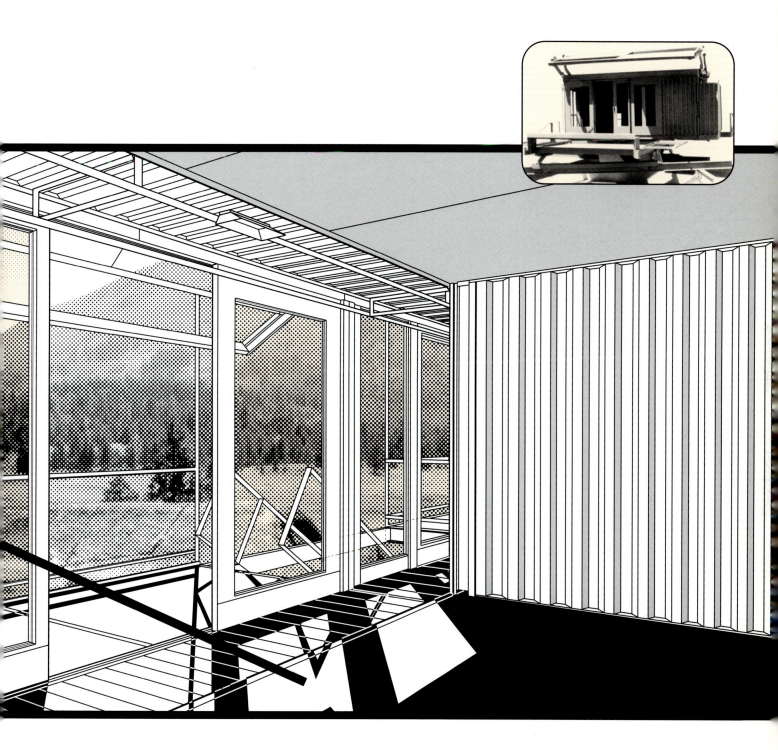

wind with this second nature. Society has assimilated much that Toffler warned about, and has achieved a comfort level with a world that frightened Heidegger. Humanity has become accustomed to the speed of existence. Admittedly, this could be co-extensive with the effects of universal enframing. It could be just a ghost, an after-image, lingering as a prediction from wistful historical descriptions or surviving poetry, that as Heidegger notes "is not as it once was." But, coupled with the human refusal of complacency, the triumph of enframing has opened up a space where one could not conceivably have existed before: this is a new space, unknown by the Greeks, where aesthetics are not contemplative, but active; where *arete* relates to *competence* within the second nature of an enframed world, where exceptions of newness are enabled by that competence; where the Forms are not static, but dynamic; where the violence of a transcendent metaphysics is normalized into the

21. living area

interior view looking west

aggressiveness of transcendent intentionality; where fixed ideals of truth, goodness, and beauty have evolved into a dynamic and ever more surprisingly vigorous reality, a "realistic" standard of effectiveness, and the boss, which embodies it. ^{WDIM 63}

Enframing: Bossness
28. In proposing the "saving power," Heidegger describes it as the "photographic negative" of enframing that will emerge from within the essence of technology, and notes that it may arise "here and now, and in little things." The boss is modestly proposed to be such.

29. The boss object and bossness as a value, arises from *within* technology, as an essential exhalation of mature regard.[NOB 9] **It arises after waves of functionalist extremism and structural exotica, after pendulum swings from ecstatic fanaticism to desperate**

Yokohama International Port Terminal
C95.12/1
Yokohama, Japan

Client:	The City of Yokohama
Architect:	Jones, Partners: Architecture
Site:	The Osanbashi Pier, located in the midst of the Port of Yokohama, adjacent to the downtown Kannai District
Program:	An international port terminal, providing moorings for four large cruise ships, a departure and arrival lobby with Customs, Immigration and Quarantine, a visitor's deck, cruise deck, international garden, baggage handling, administration facilities, retail shops, and restaurant
Size:	400,000 ft^2
Systems:	Exposed painted steel truss, painted steel sub-frame, cast-in-place concrete garden "tubs," and cast-in-place parking basement, founded upon the pier's original pile foundation
Features:	A megastructural steel truss frame sets a scale to match that of the massive ships the terminal will serve; cradled within are the programmatic volumes housing passenger processing and civic retail functions; a simple one-way drop-off and parking layout ensures maximum convenience and smooth traffic handling. Nestled between the steel truss frame and the programmed volumes are the "International Garden," which act as transition zones bridging between levels and inside and outside.
Cost:	$23 million
Completion:	December 1994 (competition)

The experiences of the ship steaming across the bay, attended by its bevy of tugs, and the citizen emerging abruptly from the city center, by car or bus or ambling on foot along the waterfront through Yamashita Park, are all unique, but they converge upon the same focus: a structure which embodies, encapsulates, figures the convergence of land and sea, city and bay, pleasure and duty, while facilitating the continuous, chaotic ebb and flow of passengers and visitors. The terminal, so like a ship itself, is designed to be a great land-mark and ocean-place. It inscribes a position on the skyline of the city and the horizon of the bay between the ships which moor there and the tall buildings which encircle it. At once familiar and exotic, the terminal presents the ships with something to aim at and come home to, the towers with something to look at and focus upon. A simple form out on the bay, it mediates between the ocean and the city, and the cultures of the visitors and the host nation, tying the two together as gateway, port, and garden.

The garden exists between raw nature and the city. The concept Niwaminato, like the garden within the city, is not obvious. The garden is a special condition of nature, preserved, set apart and enjoyed as a respite from the hectic rush of urban life. The terminal gardens are similarly protected; they are revealed only gradually on the approach from land or sea. The gardens are not "on" the terminal building, or around it, but intimately encompassed within it as an organic part of its organization, participating

1. painted steel superstructure
13. cruise deck
20. citizen's walk

view of approach

Ludditism. It arises inevitably, as the reasonable expression of ongoing passion. Its coming to presence from concealment within the tangled history of technology is the natural and unselfconscious result of technology's own maturity. The boss brings no frameworks or expectations from outside, no values foreign to technology; it imposes nothing on technology because it *is* technology itself. It can be seen to be the "way" in which technology will "be restored to and fulfilled in its own essence."[28] How can this happen? "Above all through our catching sight of what comes to presence in technology, instead of merely staring at the technological."[29] Bossness is what comes to presence in technology when its essence is addressed.

30. The essence of technology, as a directed way of revealing, admits a kinship to *poiesia*, to art and expression, though these are counter to its

176

aerial view

directedness. It is possible to imagine that this kinder, gentler dimension of revealing might coexist with the more directed program or purposefulness, by finding some object for its aesthetic attention other than technology's object. In other words, instead of hopelessly trying to affect the object of technology's task, it can address itself to the essence of the technological in the accomplishment of that task. Instead of competing with the machine over the machine's job, it may focus instead on the machine itself. When the machine receives this attention, it can become boss.

31. In Heidegger's term this might result if the set of concerns that give rise to a "work" were applied to "equipment." As he discusses in "The Origin of the Work of Art," there is a presence to the work that contrasts with the equipment's transparency to its task—the work is "remarkable," as a work, and this

1. painted steel superstructure
9. baggage conveyor
12. visitor's deck
13. cruise deck

exterior view from Osanbashi Pier

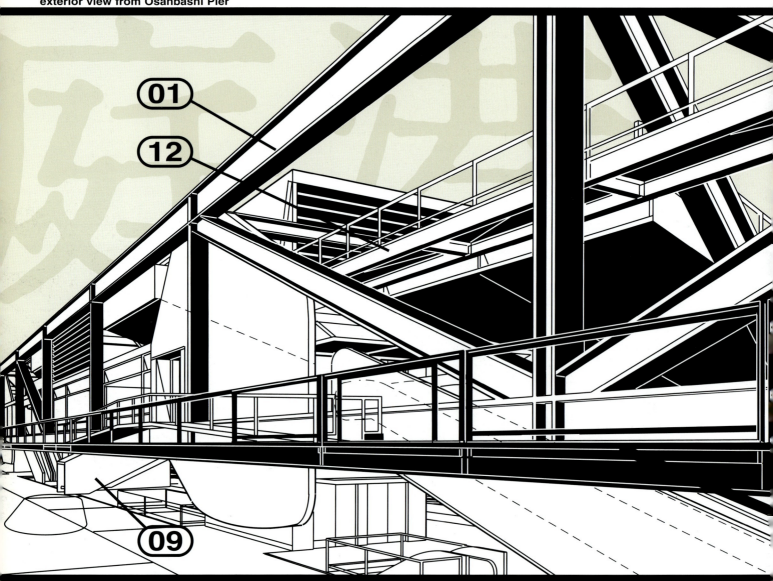

causes it to stand out, while equipment is invisible in itself, commonplace and matter-of-fact. This is not to suggest the equipment is to find a work-like aura from without, though. In contrast to the fetishizing stylization applied to the haute tech object, the bossness of equipment is drawn from the object itself. The boss merely gives equipment a voice to speak. Equipment will not talk about itself directly, though, but in relation to its job. When equipment speaks, and is noticed, then the task is itself ennobled. When equipment stands out, as remarkable, in the performance of its duties, the occasion in those duties for its presence is understood as remarkable as well. As Heidegger says, in words that could be spoken by equipment, and taken as a prescription for bossness itself: "the more ... essentially [it is] engrossed in [its] essence, the more directly and engagingly do all beings attain a greater degree of being along with

4. terminal entry

view from escalator

[it]."30

32. Ultimately it must be admitted that the Boss is probably not what Heidegger envisioned when he proposed the possibility of a saving power. It is difficult to imagine what he would make of the hot rod. He might admire the clear craftsmanship and spirit of inventiveness, but he would no doubt take exception to the sheer belligerence and obvious techno-philia it displays. Yet, he stresses that the saving power will arise from within technology, as humanity may again participate in essential fulfillment of technology's original promise.

[1] Martin Heidegger, "Origin of the Work of Art" in *Basic Writings* (New York: Harper & Row, 1977), 167; hereafter cited as OWA.
[2] William Lovitt's Introduction to *The Question Concerning Technology, and Other Essays* by Martin

in the division of the functions as well as the provision of visual delight. The gardens are seen as the mediating elements, not only metaphorically between the city and nature but also between the different cultures which meet at the terminal. Consequently, these landscaped areas are not singular or continuous, but many and varied, with a theme of exploration. A series of International Gardens are proposed which would feature rotating examples of the garden arts from each continent visited by the ships; they bring light and air, and nature, into the very center of the vast terminal, making it less vast. Their intimacy is the city's gift to the wide open spaces of the ocean.

13. cruise deck

view from apron

Heidegger, trans. by William Lovitt (New York: Harper & Row, 1977), xxiv; referring to Heidegger's "The Age of the World Picture," 131.
3 Enframing destroys the surprise by destroying the apartness. The saving power is the understanding that this is an illusion—things are still apart—humanity is just impoverished in no longer seeing this, in no longer experiencing the wonder.
4 OWA, 155

5 OWA, 194
6 Lovitt, xx; OWA, 153
7 Lovitt, xxv; referring to the unpublished transcript of the "Séminaire tenú au Thor en septembre 1969 par le Professeur Martin Heidegger," 11; hereafter cited as Sem.
8 Lovitt, xxvi.
9 Lovitt, xxvi.
10 A geometry of openness unfolds naturally from this thinking, though its structuring sense might be foreign to the content of that thought. He stressed that the relation between the object and the witness was more immediate and direct than that captured in the structure of subject and object, but he assumed that the object was revealed "from somewhere." The corresponding "concealment" where the unrevealed "hid" prior to the witnessing of its revealing was the logical counterpart. "Coming to presence suggests an absence before and after itself, so that

4. terminal entry
5. citizen entry
7. bus pool
8. taxi pool
9. baggage conveyor
10. storage
11. bus stop

parking level 1"=100.00'

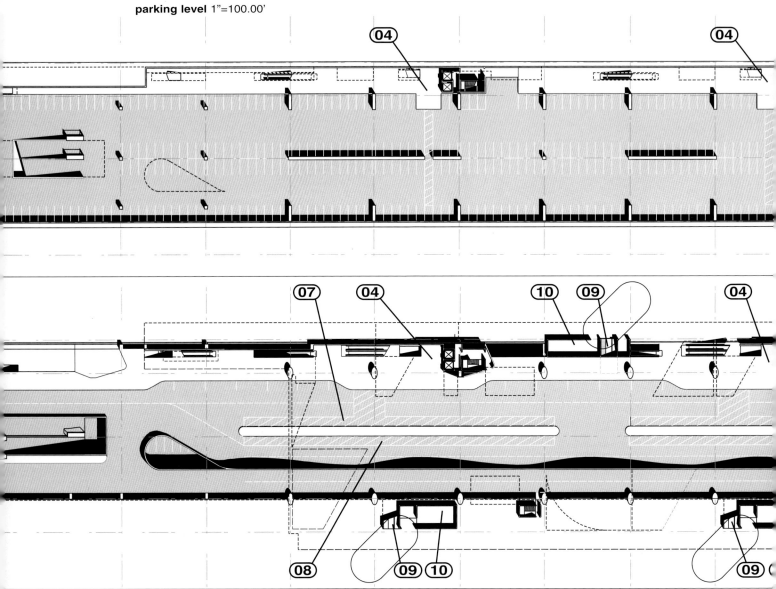

apron level 1"=100.00'

withdrawal and departure must always be thought together with ... presencing. Disclosedness or unconcealment suggests a surrounding obscurity, Lethean concealment."[a] In this he emphasizes the active nature of this presencing, and consequently the active nature of the witnessing itself.

[a] David Farrell Krell's editorial in Martin Heidegger's *Basic Writings*, (New York: Harper & Row, 1997).
[11] Lovitt, xiii.

[12] Alberto Pérez-Gómez, "Chora: The Space of Architectural Representation" in *Chora, Intervals in the Philosophy of Architecture*, vol. 1, (Montreal: McGill-Queen's Univ. Press, 1994), 10.
[13] OWA, 108.
[14] Martin Heidegger, "The Question Concerning Technology" in *The Question Concerning Technology and Other Essays* (New York: Harper & Row, 1977), 17; hereafter cited as QT.

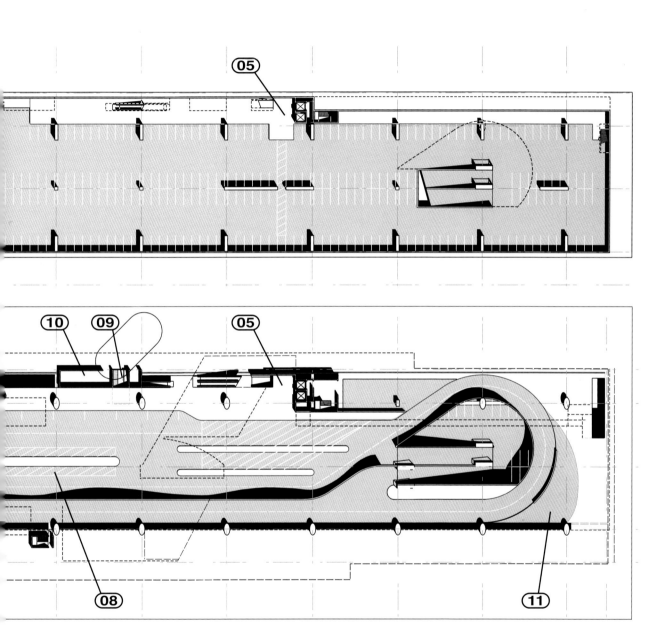

15 That which is still lurking, as the ultimate ground, behind and jutting through the hyperreal, enframing and myth, is nature. Humanity has alone figured itself, by the bootstraps, against this ground. The story can be told from this direction also: the (self) consciousness transformed into human subject, has introduced a gap between itself and this natural ground; the two do not fit together seamlessly—a "fore"-ground has opened up, which through a long historical attention has come to mask the original ground, has come to take on the provisional status of a *second* nature, or "faux" ground, that like Borge's map, covers reality, and seems as inescapable as the ground it doubles.

Indeed, the second *nature* has become *second nature*. It has become common, familiar. The faux ground, as second nature, is invisible *and* pervasive. This could be considered a pre-condition to the advent of the hyper-real. The structure of familiarity carries the sense of doubling

4. terminal entry
5. citizen entry
12. visitor's deck
14. baggage handling/ quarantine
15. immigration booth
16. customs booth
17. tickets/ information
18. departure and arrival lobby
21. restaurants and shops
22. international garden
25. mechanical

cruise level 1"=100.00'

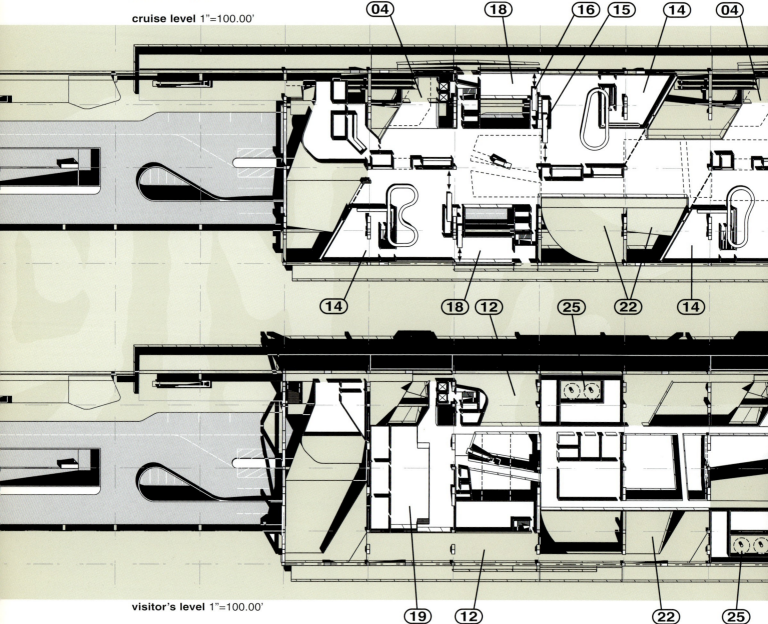

visitor's level 1"=100.00'

implied in representation, along with the universality of the original ground that is doubled into familiarity. It has become almost a cliché to understand in this familiarity that since "things as they are" are masked by the structures of representation imposed by humanity over its experience of reality, "man is the measure of all things," and he is able only to see himself everywhere.
[16] QT, 17.

[17] **What does it mean to say**[a]
Tradition
1. What does it mean to say, in the presence of some building, "this is architecture"? Is this a question about architecture, or the building? The question is allusive this way, but also illusive; the answer is both elusive and as substantial as building. In our minds we have a habit of connecting the two without reflection, and hear this as a question of categories, implied in the connection—asked

184

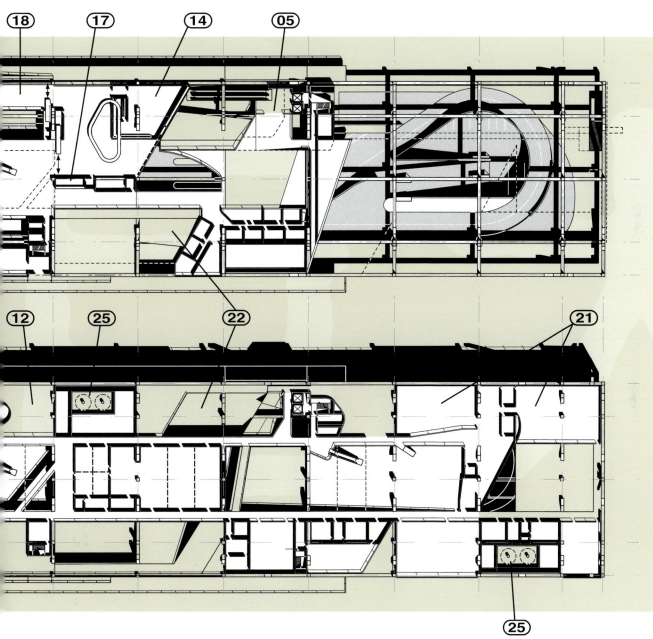

by the one perhaps and answered by the other. We would look for the answer in the object, expecting maybe a list of properties, that might categorize it as the label. To ask about the meaning of this statement seems like a roundabout way of asking for a definition of Architecture, and maybe also why there is a connection in this case and not in others. We hear this as a question about whether the building is architecture and what makes it so.

2. The meaning of this statement is concentrated in that connection. What we mean is what we "have in mind," what we draw into mind from without; what we signify, to ourselves or another. The connection this involves falls across an unbridgeable gap: on the one side is the subject, on the other is the predicate; on the one is the sign, the statement, on the other is its signified; on the one is you, on the other is the other, with whom you intend to communicate. Subject Verb

185

1. painted steel superstructure
4. terminal entry
5. citizen entry
9. baggage conveyor
13. cruise deck
18. departure and arrival
20. citizen's walk

southwest elevation 1"=66.67'

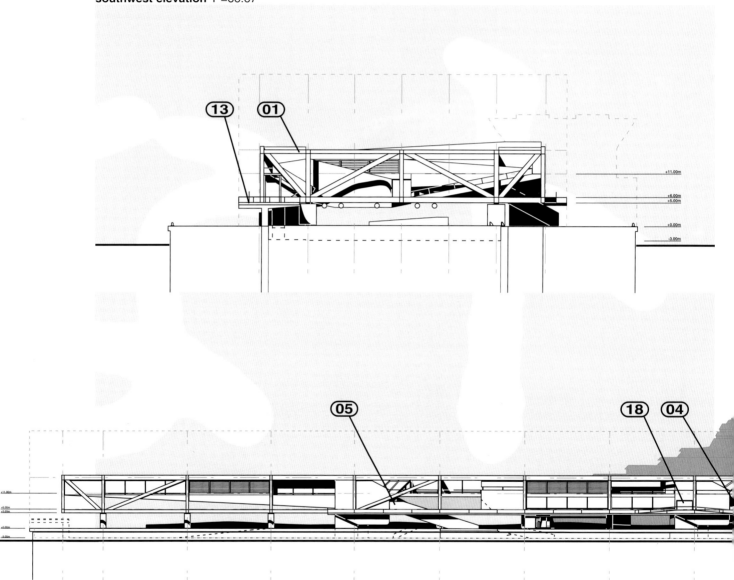

northwest elevation 1"=100.00'

Predicate. Why? Why should there be any necessary connection? Some languages, like Arabic, don't even have a verb "to be" to fill in the space. They use an equational sentence structure in its place, avoiding the problem of the gap by settling for simple adjacency. But there *is* a *space* there, that you shouldn't even be able to *see* across.

3.   Meaning is impossible, but only if you think about it. Meaning *crosses* the gap. The gap at which logic quails.

It performs that force-at-a-distance trick that physics flirted with and then gave up for gravitons. Maybe architecture is like this mysterious graviton, being exchanged between the viewer and the building.

4.   Meaning is impossible, but, like solipsism, it is hard to sustain this level of logically irrefutable paranoia and weirdness. We know what we mean, particularly if we don't think about it. If we don't think about it we find ourselves naturally paraphrasing the question as something

1. painted steel superstructure
13. cruise deck

northeast elevation 1"=66.67'

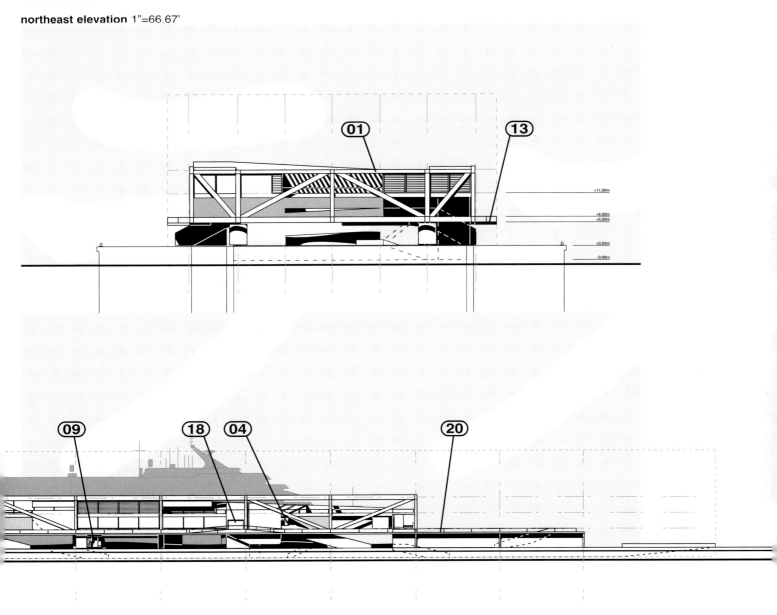

like, "what is architecture?" To this question two responses—the two that have defined our traditions—spring immediately, unconsidered, to mind. On the one hand the equational sentence version says we are presumably in the presence of a possible answer to this question, and were it so we could simply point to it: implying "there is architecture" without saying it.

5. Or even more simply, the caption: "architecture." If, on the other hand, we leap the gap, unthinkingly, a defin-

ition can be framed, that is more handy. A definition makes that equational meaning more generally available, makes it available when the pointee is not at hand; it makes the meaning portable, public.

6. A definition is a convention, an agreement on everyone's part to act as if the gap were crossable by building a device to cross it. This vehicle carries everything that it might discharge on the other side so there are no surprises. Everyone subscribes, everyone gets to ride,

4. terminal entry
5. citizen entry
9. baggage conveyor
14. baggage handling/ quarantine
18. departure and arrival
20. citizen's walk
21. restaurants and shops
22. international garden

southeast elevation 1"=100.00'

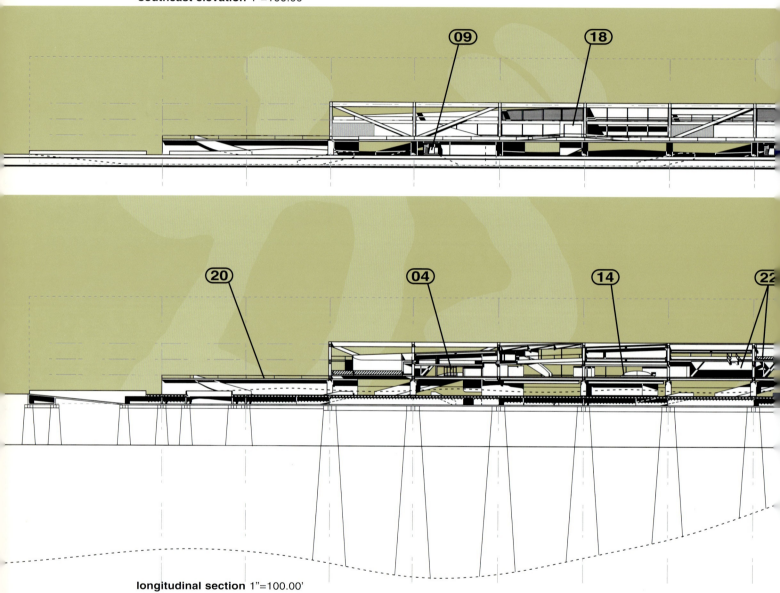

longitudinal section 1"=100.00'

everyone gets to the same destination. The destination is labeled, so others might know publicly what in private we would simply point at. The building of this device, this convention, is the story of architecture. Occasionally the plot of the story, like the vehicle itself, changes course and ends up somewhere else; these are the chapter breaks, the revolutions that were Brunelleschi or modernism.

7. Architecture is sort of caught in the middle of this metaphor; it seems related to both the convention and to the object toward which that vehicle journeys. It is more a *kind* of thing than a thing itself. Defined, it hovers over specific examples, as the means by which they are *known* as specific examples, and from there directs their continuing production. But, it is also only there in the example, as the example, by that production: it may be a label, but it is stuck on the thing.

8. In a way, architecture is both a label *and* a caption.

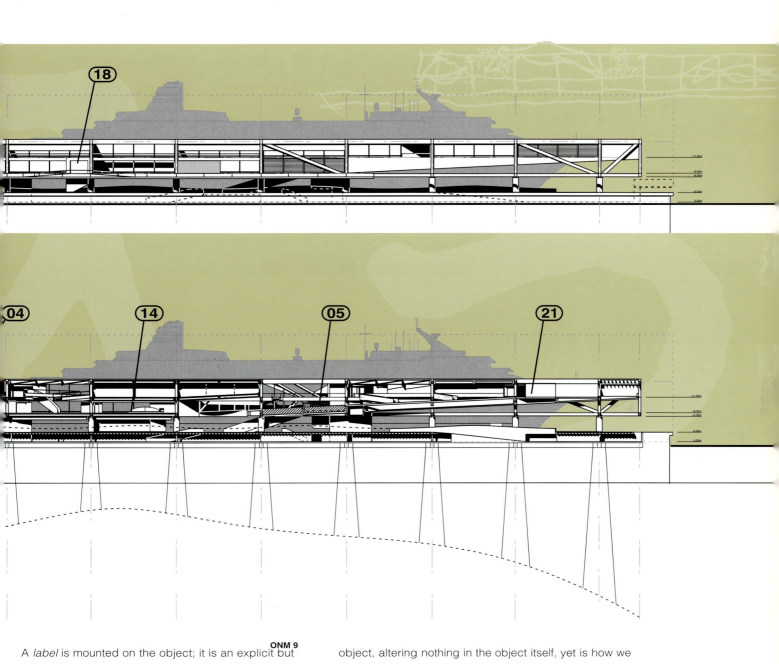

ONM 9
A *label* is mounted on the object; it is an explicit but uncritical supplement. The *caption* is unknown to the object outside the frame: it is an acute complement.
9. According to Rousseau, according to Derrida, "the **ONHR 4** supplement is an inessential extra, added to something complete in itself, but the supplement is added in order **ONM 20** to complete, to compensate for a lack in what was supposed to be complete in itself."[b] A label is supplemental **HR note 5** in this way: clearly attached, it is an addition to the object, altering nothing in the object itself, yet is how we recognize it. The label raises the question of identity, and so becomes a sign of its own necessity as the identity.
10. The caption on the other hand is outside the frame; there it acts as a *complement* to the object. In fact, it establishes the frame as a frame, and thus the object, isolated as an object by the frame, as something about which stuff, the caption, might be said. It is a critical act but does not exist in the object's universe. It assumes a

12. visitor deck
13. cruise deck
17. tickets/ information
18. departure and arrival lobby
22. international garden
25. mechanical

transverse section 1 1"=66.67'

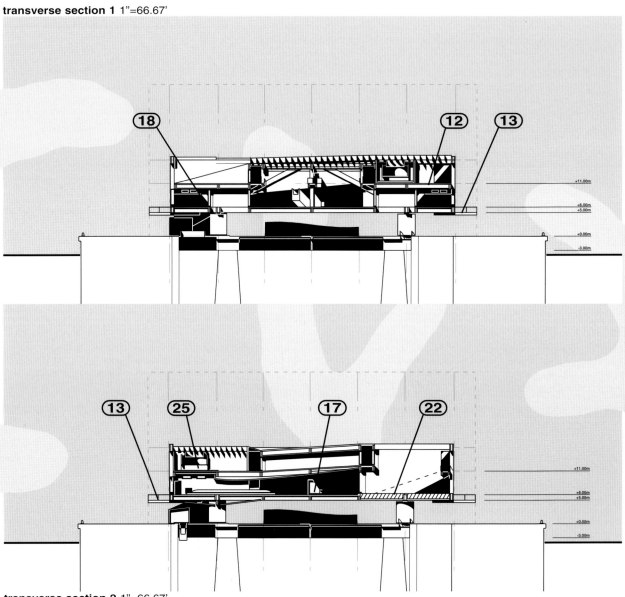

transverse section 2 1"=66.67'

"meta-" position from which that universe as a whole might be considered. As opposed to the label, which strives for attachment, the caption works to remain aloof from its object, to maintain a certain perspective and distinguish itself from that upon which it comments. Architecture is most a caption when it is distinguishing itself, generally, as an aloof ideal, from "mere" building, and most a label when it attaches to a specific object for embodiment and becomes the means by which we recognize that object as a building.

11. In fact, the word "architecture" comes to us from the Greek arche-tecton, or "first worker." Originally it was just what this person did. In Vitruvius-time this included a lot of other things besides making buildings. By the time of Alberti, though, these other activities were no longer part of the job description. With his isolation of the design part of the process, Alberti identified, or defined, architecture as related to a condition beyond mere buildings,

4. terminal entry
12. visitor deck
13. cruise deck
14. baggage handling/ quarantine
17. tickets/ information
22. international garden
25. mechanical

transverse section 3 1"=66.67'

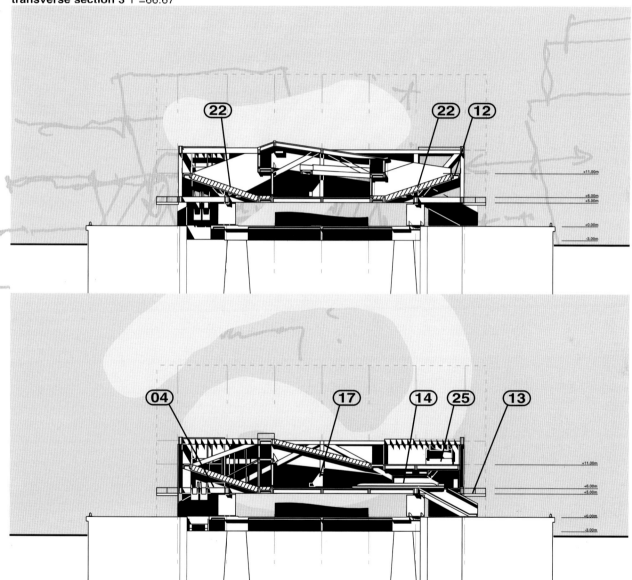

transverse section 4 1"=66.67'

and architects as the people who delivered the difference, in design—the people who stamped and signed the drawings, wrote the caption and stuck on the label. 12. Is it by a designer label, then, that we know architecture? Are such examples signed? Some seem to be. Inscriptions once commonly labeled buildings in stone so to speak as architecture—by program, type, or patron, or sentiment, as "Doe Library ..." or "truth is the light ...." More often nowadays inscriptions have been replaced by outscriptions: signs, that proclaim buildings as KFC or First Interstate. The signed building is interested in distinguishing between itself and the other guys—McDonald's or Citibank. The famous architect's cartouche, or the historical society marker, is also a signature in this manner, distinguishing for example between Wright and Howard Johnson .... Labels, like the earlier inscriptions, are basically interested in saying "its architecture," for which the specifics of patronage or senti-

4. terminal entry
interior view from passenger level

ment are only an excuse.

13. Yet a label can also be implied when that larger association is remarkable, without specific reference. Most people believe they know enough to point architecture out without the explicit reference of a label (unfortunately), but even if they didn't it would not be a big problem. The *information* required to determine architecture's presence is not a major factor. To mistakenly enter a tree instead of a work of architecture is less likely, or problematic, than to deposit your money accidentally in a laundromat or lawyer's office.

14. What is communicated by architectureness is not informational. There is agreement out there that a kind of thing exists called architecture and that it comes in building-sized chunks. Architects seem to have the biggest problem deciding which chunks are architecture. Normal people, reflecting how much they care probably, are less troubled by the difference.

C96.01/1
Korean American Museum of Art (KOMA)
Los Angeles, CA

Client:	Korean American Museum of Art and Cultural Center
Architect:	Jones, Partners: Architecture
Site:	82,500 ft² vacant lot in center of Koreatown area of Los Angeles
Program:	Permanent and temporary gallery space, storage and curatorial spaces, visiting artist studios, performance theater, lecture auditorium, library, cafe, cultural gardens, administrative space, and parking
Size:	240,000 ft²
Systems:	Steel frame superstructure of repeating bents atop cast-in-place concrete parking plinth and foundation, steel panel and industrial sash enclosure
Features:	The museum's layout is oriented towards contextual fit in this sensitive neighborhood; consequently, its massing follows precisely the front, side and rear-yard setbacks established for the surrounding tracks; when this system is spread over a single building the size of KOMA, a cellular structure results that is well suited to the museum program, offering flexibility and multiple points of view of the art; the extremely tight budget benefits as well from such a strategy, since it encourages the use of repeatable construction types like the steel bent structural system common in industrial building; this repetition reinforces the relationship with the neighborhood, while elevating the relatively humble construction typology to the esthetic level more appropriate to a museum.
Cost:	$200 million
Completion:	April 1995 (competition)

The idea of a balance of opposites, the Yin and Yang (T'ae-guk), is central to the Korean ethos. The ageless symbol of this relationship is the primary motif of the flag of the Republic of Korea, and it characterizes the contextual situation in Koreatown where the Korean American Museum of Art and Cultural Center will make its home. A museum dedicated at least in part to traditional Korean art, set in the middle of Southern California, the capital of contemporary popular American culture, will unavoidably be a study in contrasts, and to succeed it will have to engage in a delicate balancing act. This idea of balance permeates the present scheme, informing the layout of the building on the site and disposition of the program internally, establishing its architectural character and imagery, and influencing its construction and tectonics.

To a certain extent, even the idea of a museum entails a balancing act these days. The authority of history seems less relevant now when all experience is mediated, hyped and consumed. This is particularly true in the case of KOMA; as the Korean culture, steeped in the authority of history, collides with a context where to "be history, dude" means to be killed or erased, an agility and sense of balance—as well, perhaps, as a sense of humor—will be crucial. In the midst of such awkwardness, the Korean American Art Museum and Cultural Center must create conditions of respect for its artifacts and demonstrate their tradition's virtue, without isolating that tradition or rendering it silly. The tradition must be brought into the present, with dignity, so that its relevance can be demonstrated rather than claimed.

Despite their apparent differences, Korea and Southern California have responded similarly to their distinctive geographic circumstances and have used them to emphasize their cultural differences from their neighbors. Both are isolated by natural features and societal inclination. Yet, architecturally speaking, neither traditional Korea nor contemporary Southern California enjoy a distinctive, home-grown vernacular. Into this architectural void steps the modern, to weld the two together in an appropriately timely formalism, born naturally of the interplay between the program, the climate, and the economics of contemporary construction.

This scheme derives its distinctive architectural features from a desire to balance a rigorous support of specific program requirements with the flexibility to respond to the continuing evolution of the program. Included in this is a concern for the "phasability" of the project—could it be built one-piece-at-a-time while remaining architecturally and institutionally viable during all steps of the process? Within the distinctive structural and planning grid borrowed from the grain of the surrounding residential neighborhoods, the gallery portions of the building break down easily into flexibly combined sub-assemblies of standardized space- and construction-units. The more programmatically distinctive portions of the building—the performance space and the lecture hall—find accommodation within the system without

view from southwest

15. Maybe it is because architecture is nothing definite, **TAL 13** that it is defined. Architecture is a convention. It is defined because it is not clear. We convene and agree to say this is what we will call architecture, without particularly knowing what each other is thinking or talking about (that pesky gap again): this and this, but not this or that. From Mars, or main street there might be no apparent difference. "Convention" **DR 16** could be from the Latin: con=with, vent=wind, ion=charged particle. Bluster and air, result-

194

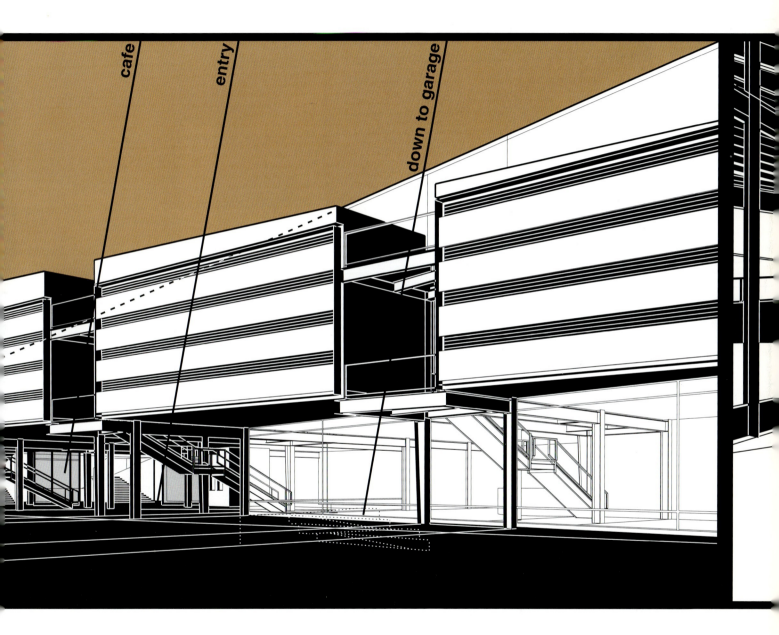

ing in a resiliently ephemeral sense of agreement .... There is a *gap* somewhere, from which drains necessity.
16. Too much art to be just a building, too much utility to be art, architecture is caught in the middle of this gap, hovering magnificently over the howling void. Its conventional insubstantiality helps it to stay up, to float on belief and desire. Architecture, even as a kind of thing, instead of a thing itself, is a made thing, an artifice. Implying, unthinkingly, naturally, the artificiality of architecture.

Things are defined when there might be some confusion or misunderstanding or doubt. When a thing does not exist freely in a state of nature. To define is to legislate meaning, to *declare* it instead of discovering it. There should be something frightening—and exhilarating—in this to an architect.
17. The convention of architecture has developed over time, from Imhotep to now, or from Laugier's primitive hut until now, or from whatever origin myth you subscribe

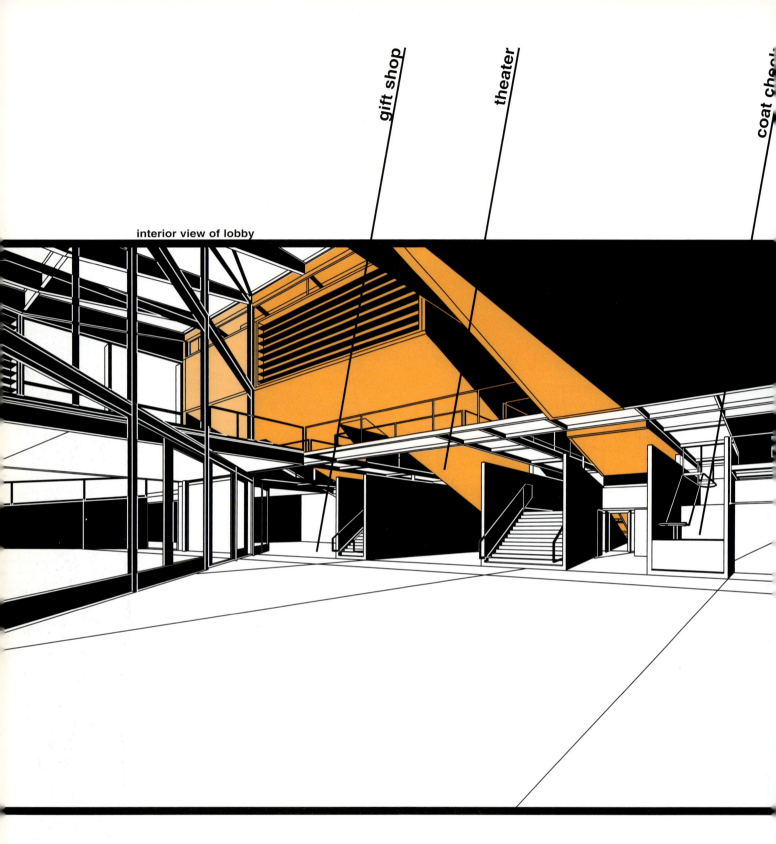

interior view of lobby — gift shop — theater — coat check

to—until whenever the truth of that was betrayed, by historicism, or modernism, or whatever catastrophe ruined it for you: that is to say, it has developed in a history. History has added a depth to the definition that gives the verbal equation of name and meaning authority. Every example of architecture carries in it the genes of a history and benefits from its authority and contributes to its continuation.

18. The convention, the definition, may be fleshed out in the specific examples but it is bulked out in the history trailing out behind them, or leading up to them. The *meaning* of architecture seems inseparable from the litany of these examples: Zoser's tomb, the Parthenon, Chartres, Villa Savoye, and on and on—hopefully past now. In this sense, to say in the presence of some building that "this is architecture" is to propose that it is part of this continuum.

elevator

interior view of gallery

History

19. Architecture is usually confused with history, because history is so expressly embodied in architecture. In fact, what we are often really saying when we say, in the presence of a building, that it is architecture is: "*this* is old." What we are implying is: "*I* will die." The old thing, the artifact, is like a time machine; it is supposed to be a connection to the time from whence it came, and hold the promise, in its presence, *there*, STILL, of defeating time. In fact, though, its presence, *there*, mocks our own mortality. The old thing asks us if we notice that everyone who was around when it was built is already dust. It says "I'll still be here when you are looong gone." It says "die, sucker."

20. The power to say this and get *away* with it gives the object that presence we respect—and confuse as architecture. Since "old" gets younger every year, and everything gets old in time, the equating of old with architec-

WITM 37

197

compromising the flexibility of the less determined spaces. A unique feature of this approach is the non-specific allocation of the temporary gallery and resident artist studio spaces: a system of rolling overhead doors allows a continuous reconfiguration of the generic loft-type space. In combination with the sideyard, north-facing light wells, which provide secure, controlled exterior access to all parts of the loft space, as well as the strategically located internal gardens, this system ensures that any configuration of studio and gallery space can be accommodated. From all gallery to all studio, or anywhere in between, the space can be swiftly changed as requirements dictate. In addition, this spatial strategy is reinforced by a lighting/observation "catwalk" system which runs throughout the building at the third level, where the administrative and gallery storage elements of the program are found, which provides for security and a continuous tuning of the environmental conditions of the galleries.

In light of the recent unrest in the area, the most important issue facing the institution might well be how it presents itself to the public—will it close itself off in protective isolation from the surrounding neighborhoods, a safe repository for its valuable artifacts and haven for its artists, or will it open itself up to its surroundings in a confident gesture of neighborliness and risk the depredations of this marginal context. This scheme councils a balance between these two extremes. It strives to give the sense of openness without compromising the fact of security, to make a statement of institutional

interior view of theater

ture, which I know my mom would do, should mean that there was a lot of architecture around.

21. There *is* some logic to this: the artifact claims to survive because it is worth keeping around, and therefore must be architecture. This logic holds that survival is sort of an outward sign of inward grace. If we are looking around for architecture, according to this thinking, we would expect to find at least a higher concentration of it among old things. The respect we feel for oldness

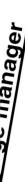

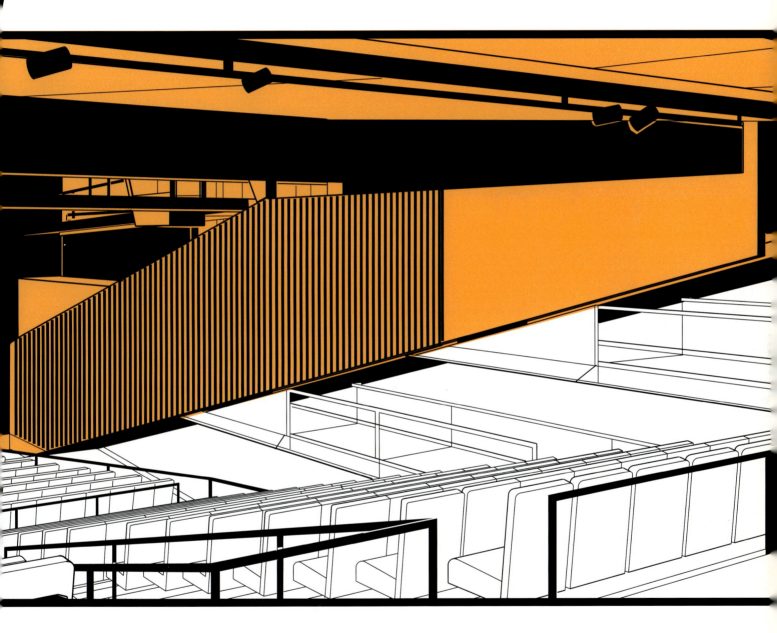

becomes transferred to the things themselves, and becomes a confirmation of this math, reinforcing the equation of architecture and age.

22. Against the idea that this would mean there was a lot of architecture out there, we are taught to look for real architecture only in the approved and duly registered masterpieces. Certainly it is not expected anywhere else, by either the client or the architect. Yet, the reasons why this might in fact be appropriate are not the reasons we offer for valuing the masterpiece.

23. Instead we think the masterpiece is worthy of our appreciation because of who did it, or what the circumstances of its commissioning were, or what influence it might have had here or there. In other words, we look to its history, rather than its presence, for evidence of its worth. The awe we feel before history is defined specifically in opposition to the physical specifics of the object present before us. The object's fame or influence—for

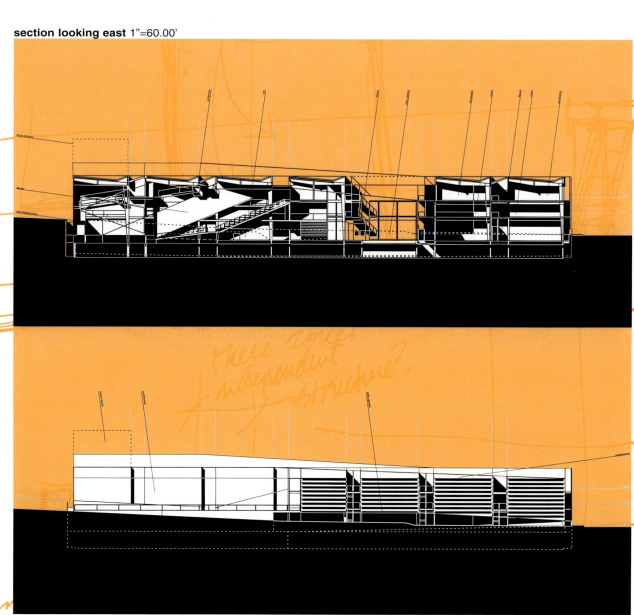

section looking east 1"=60.00'

west elevation 1"=60.00'

which the thing itself is merely a marker or sign, and our appreciation merely evidence, is what counts as architecture in this view.

24. An architecture student is never asked to bear witness directly to the work that is proffered as an exemplar, but to analyze its structure or proportions, replicate its partis or quote from its decoration, to memorize its place on the list and the influence it has had over other members of the elect. Those examples the student is privileged to visit in person, live, are either old, so their strictly architectural, as opposed to historical, presence is no longer working, or so over-promoted that the object itself is barely discernible through all the hype. Rarely today can we ever just stumble upon something and be blown away by it as architecture.

25. Contemporary technologies and tendencies of mediation make it even more difficult to judge the thing, there. History is a kind of hype. And hype is a kind of history.

section looking west 1"=60.00'

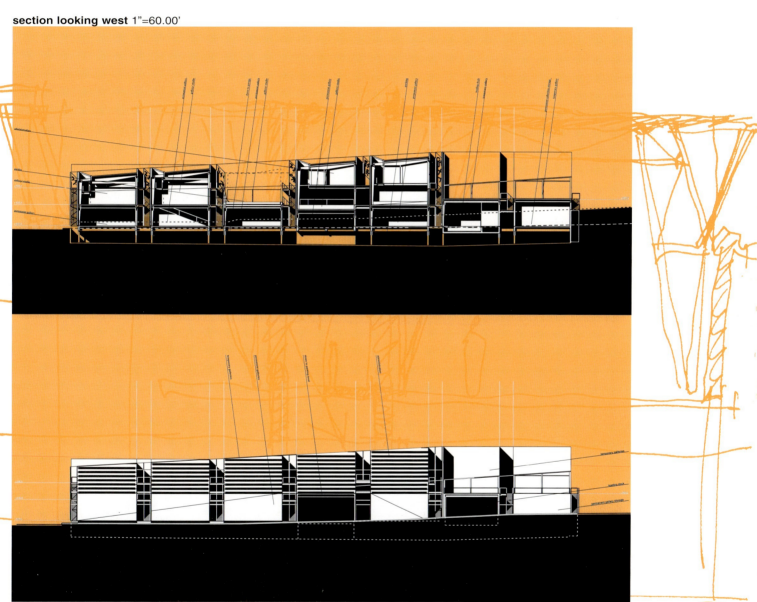

east elevation 1"=60.00'

Like the object's history, the hype always precedes it, leading to the confusion of having already been there, done that, and never having been there for the first time. The instant replay, and its instant historicizing, precedes and outruns the experience. When we finally visit the thing, after becoming so familiar with it from slides and books, we are invariably amazed at how much smaller it is than we thought it would be.

26. In the mediated culture of the hyper-real, the thing itself seems less important than its image, imageability, style-bite, or the photos that can be taken of it, because its *presence* is not necessary to place it on the chart, to make the list, where "real" architecture is found.

27. Both history and hype beg the idea of the authentic as a counter to their implicit assumptions of value. The authentic distinguishes between the old and the properly historical, and between the hyped and the genuine. The "rightness" that marks an artifact as authentic is *particu-*

201

section looking north 1"=60.00'

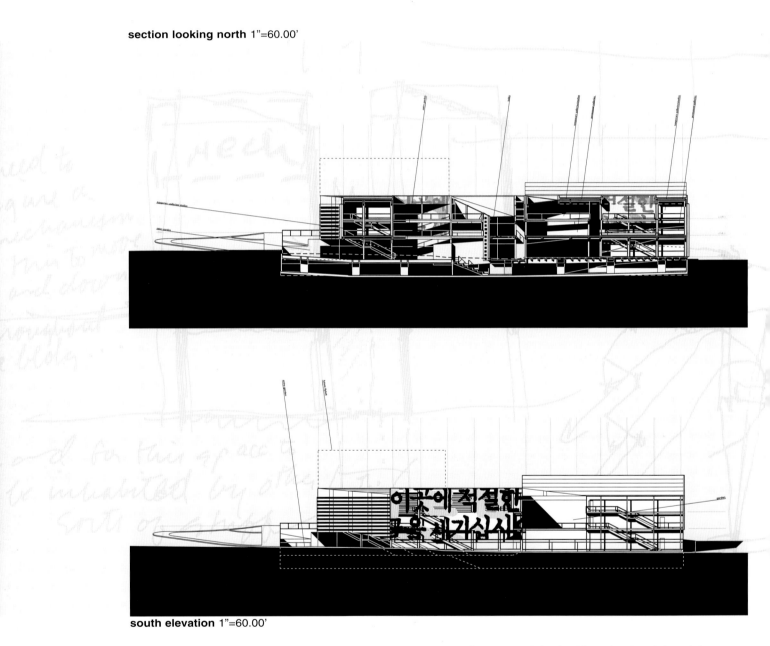

south elevation 1"=60.00'

larly valued when history and hype are rampant, during periods lacking their own oomph. But, authenticity is as slippery in its way as architecture: as a measure of historical rightness, the "authenticity" of the artifact is only understood retrospectively, well after the context to which that rightness might have applied has crumbled. And as a measure of the genuine, authenticity is only made valuable by the hype that invokes it and the mediation that flattens it.

28. Slippery as it is, the idea of authenticity reinforces the importance of the object in determining architectureness. Between the innocence and timelessness that is only retrospectively seen in an authentic object, shines the willfulness that was there from the start, that *grounds* the object in its own time and context. The object's fervor ensures a certain innocence, its directedness a clear timeliness; both are expressions of a controlling willfulness. Through the blanket of mediation and hype, that

authority without seeming forbidding or aloof. To give this impression, the gardens and sideyard light wells act as filters between the surroundings and the interior spaces of the museum. Through them this exterior condition is drawn into the building at every turn, but carefully controlled: the space, and the visitor, enters only on the building's terms. The entry sequence is layered in discrete, overlapping zones of exterior "defensible space." The entry garden, between the street and the lobby, works with the existing garden at Irolo and Normandie Streets to create a doubled foreground condition: as it passes under the western gallery/studio spaces which form an entry portal, the physical line of security is enhanced by a factor of psychological comfort. The underground parking garage surfaces naturally within this most interior garden, well within the most secure zone, and inside the after-hours enclosure under the western gallery portal. The sideyard lightwells provide direct exterior access at the second level to the artists studio spaces but are gated to restrict access to others.

Though the museum will front Olympic Avenue, a commercial street, it will extend well back into the residential neighborhoods to the north. Existing between these two radically different contexts, it will be important for the museum to balance competing expectations. The present scheme accomplishes this critically, through the interaction of a number of formal systems. The grain of the residential subdivisions, for example, which formerly split up the site, is continued in the new museum by incorporating the typical front, rear and sideyard setbacks of the former lot divisions into the structural and planning grid of the design. The figure of the building spans across these divisions, though, to impart a commercial scale and institutional presence. Balance is achieved through sectional manipulations which respond to the sloping of the site and the height restrictions varying between the neighborhood to the north and the commercial strip along Olympic. The logic of the lot divisions is maintained in the internal layout of the design: the "sideyard zones" are distinguished from the "front and rearyards" as circulation, while the "buildable areas" in the subdivision organization are reserved for the more contained exhibit areas. The civic dimension is communicated by the design as it registers the interneighborhood shifts in the surrounding subdivision grids, presenting this dynamic on the facade and inscribing it in plan.

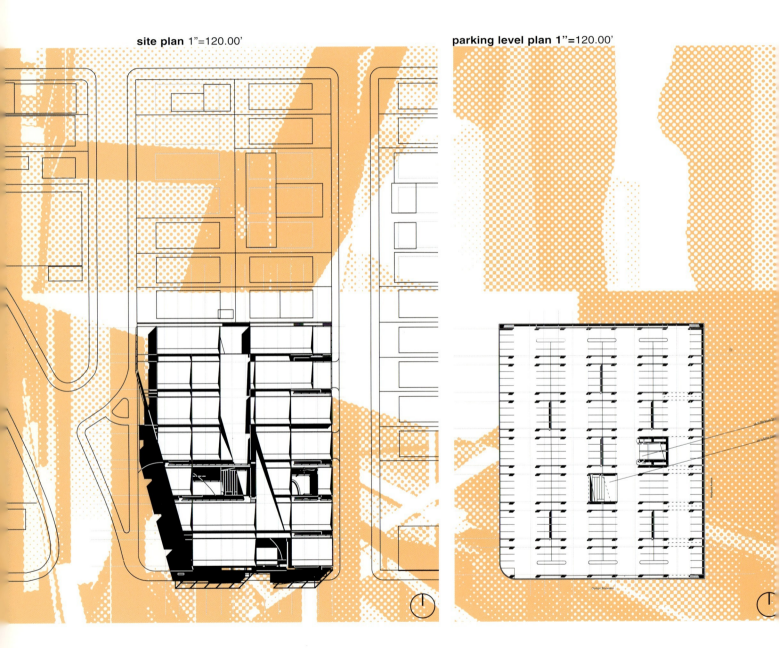

site plan 1"=120.00'

parking level plan 1"=120.00'

flatten all, the will asserts *presence*, which figures the object in its own specificity and depth. Yet, much of the object's luster must be accounted as reflected life from the context, so the significant translation of the specific work, itself, to other times—the times, for example, that admire it as authentic—is impossible. This suggests new authentic stuff must be continually emerging whether we can tell at the time or not. It suggests we are not completely prisoners of circumstance; we can achieve the authenticity we value in artifacts from the past, willfully, without having to wait around for it to just happen, or trying to recover or re-animate it from historical artifacts. We do it the same way they did: by just doing it, by investing our stuff now with the willfulness and strength that will eventually get it to "then," after we are looong gone.
29. To say, in the presence of some building, "this is architecture," is to apprehend the thing in itself, without its advance men or handlers, as architecture.

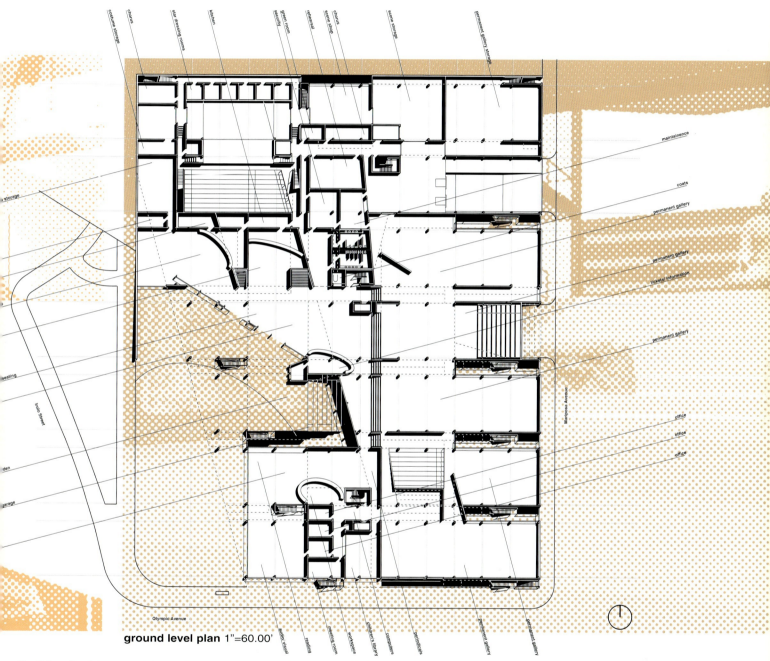

ground level plan 1"=60.00'

Traditionally, this means to see the *convention*—and its baggage of definitions, labels, history, and hype—applied to the *presence*. Traditionally, the authentic presence is thereby challenged to shine through.

Contemporary Theory

30. "Tradition" is one of those code words today that you watch out for. It usually signals a set-up for disagreement. You can almost hear the "however" coming when someone says "traditionally ...." This "however" has been institutionalized in contemporary theory, much of which is expressly critical, rather than explicatory. Since Nietzsche, theory has been applied to a dismantling of the grand systems it previously constructed, and since then Derrida's theory has systematically scattered the ashes, *insinuating* that "however" into every aspect of the traditional equation.

31. The traditional equation has three parts: the subject, the object, and the relation. Or the viewer, the building,

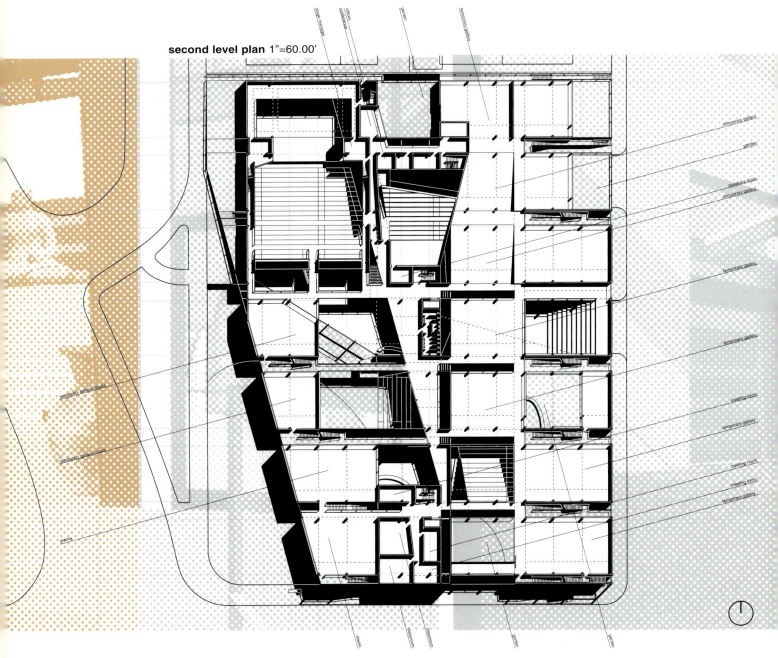

second level plan 1"=60.00'

and the convention that guides the viewing and casts the object as architecture. The idea of convention presents an interesting dilemma. On the one hand it is "traditionally ..." seen as a great achievement, and has helped to drive history forward, but on the other, it has tended to break away from the object itself and confuse the relationship with layers of this history and hype.
Contemporary theory views the confusion raised by convention from a different perspective, "... however."

32. In the contemporary view the object wears convention as a *mask*, hiding its provisionality. By provisionality, contemporary theory means not so much the gap over which the object hovers as the forces holding it there, and convention's mask-like aspect denies the viewer the opportunity to notice this or form his own opinion about it. The contemporary view sees the dynamic of meaning as more of a battle than an achievement, with convention as the enemy and the object as either its accomplice or

third level plan 1"=60.00'

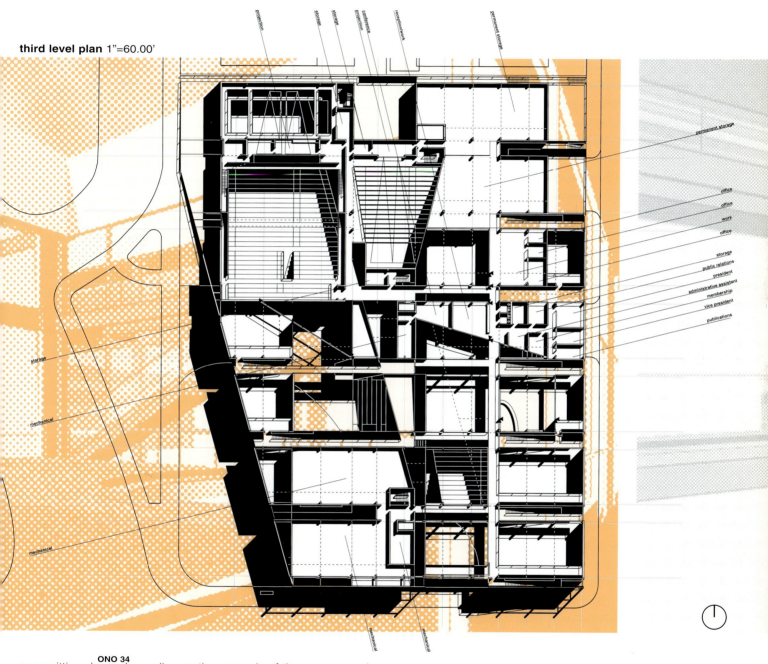

ONO 34

an unwitting dupe, depending on the paranoia of the critic.

33. The traditional understanding places the responsibility for the establishment of meaning in the object, or the author's determination of that object, and views the subject as the more passive partner in receipt of the meaning. The consensus now, however, is that viewing is an active, creative pursuit; the subject is first a reader and then, acknowledging the creativity of that reading, a re-author.

HR 6

34. What does it mean, then, to contemporary theory when we say in the presence of some building that "this is architecture?" It means that the creative moment in the reading has been preempted, the sayer has been coerced by the object into uncritically parroting some received truism. Contemporary theory denies a common ability to say with certainty "*this*" is *anything* in particular.

35. Characteristically, the reversal from a modern, prag-

207

interior view of temporary gallery

matic realism, that venerated the object as a source of certainty—seemingly alone in the modern experience—to a postmodern idealism that regards the object with frank misgiving is not perfect though. The modern was as idealizing in its veneration as it was pragmatic in its functionalism, while the postmodern/poststructural celebration of the reader is influenced by the uncanny pragmatics of the uncertainty principle, which says that though the object is constituted in each reading it will always escape that reading.

36. Instead of seeing design as some sort of competition between art and utility, or form and function, contemporary theory pushes it toward a loose choreography of events, in the interest of fomenting a new, political space, unconstrained by the deterministic formal visions of any single author. This is a laudable program, supported by an unassailable logic, but *practically* unreasonable.

37. ... Because the effort necessary to even approach

C96.03/1
Taichung City Civic Center
Taichung, Taiwan

Client:	The City of Taichung, Taiwan
Architect:	Jones, Partners: Architecture
Site:	2,500 foot long, gently sloping cruciform parcel in the heart of a thirty-five-acre development area outside downtown Taichung
Program:	New city government complex, including administrative offices (secretariat), services and support, a city council building, and parking for two thousand cars, along with landscaping and contiguous parks.
Size:	1,048,000 ft^2
Systems:	Cast-in-place concrete ductile moment-resisting frame for office/envelope slabs and parking mall plinth; structural steel frame with concrete-filled metal deck and plate walls (stair tower) for servant/circulation structure; structural steel truss frame with self-supporting louvered infill frames for canopy and mechanical structure. Conic thin-shell concrete at the various auditoria and city council spaces, supported on cast-in-place frame continuous with plinth/parking structure. Foundations throughout are spread footings tied together with grade beams.
Features:	The design for the city council building establishes a new type for civic architecture, while the secretariat offers a development from the classic type; both are composed from the same systems, but the way each arranges these systems symbolizes the essence of the program served; the secretariat makes a statement of efficient connectivity, while the city council building symbolizes assembly; they are tied together beyond their common formalism literally by a vast parking plinth stretching from one end of the site to the other creating a civic mall linking these various "instruments of government."
Cost:	$200 million
Completion:	March 1995 (competition)

Government buildings stand for the state; they give form to the civic realm. They should embody the authority of the polis, which is communicated by a strong architecture of exemplary proportions and form. They should convey a sense of timeliness and stability, which is ensured by simple, straightforward design that emphasizes durability. They should demonstrate responsibility and compassion, which are products of intelligent planning for flexibility and convenience. In short, the design for the new Taichung City Civic Center should be straightforward, simple, clear, and strong—not idiosyncratic, trendy or complex. Only in this way will the flexibility, clarity and openness that is so important in government be translated into architecture. Only in this way will its buildings show a confidence in the future and a respect for the past.

The architecture of this design is composed of two systems—a concrete envelope and glass and steel connective tissue—which carry the architectural theme while satisfying the programmatic requirements. The envelope contains the spaces where the required program is housed. The connective tissue is the interdepartmental circulation zone which joins these spaces to each other. The basic servant-served relationship between these two zones is maintained in both the City Government building and the City Council building, but the manner in which the relationship is embodied varies in order to highlight the significant differences between the two buildings and their programs. The glass and steel servant structure is the active element in this

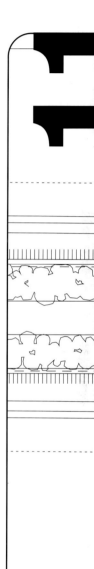

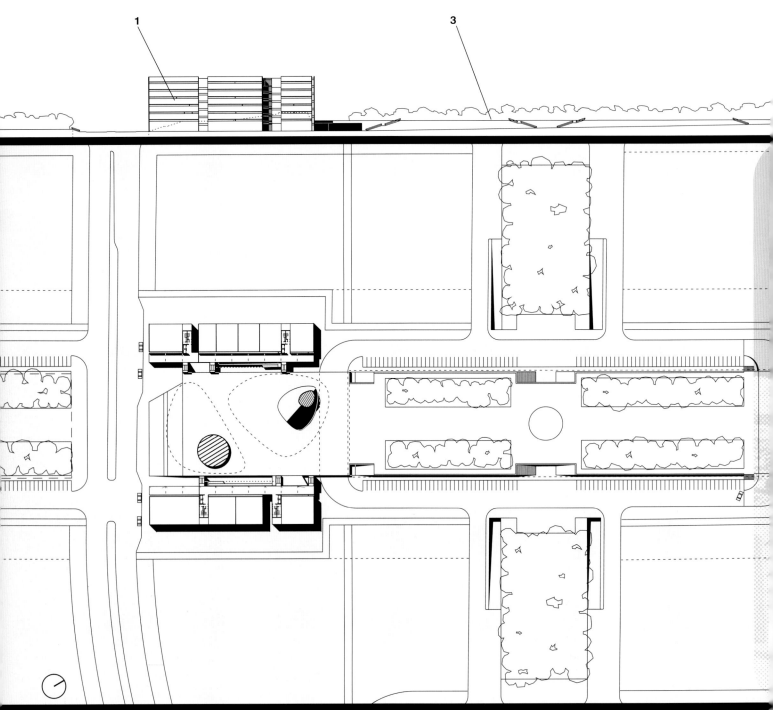

site plan and elevation 1"=187.28'

this ideal condition of openness is a testament to the power of the object that the traditional account tried to harness—through convention. Contemporary theory's wariness—or should we call it fear—of the object and of the object's capacity to promote convention has led its practitioners to a hyperbolic, tangled formalism in the interest of preventing the closed readings sought by tradition.

38. The critic sees everything as motivated—authorial intent abounds, everything is a text and the reader must be eternally vigilant for sly expressions of authority; but on the other hand, nothing is given, apart from the reading of that thing. Contemporary theory is torn over the object's role in soliciting—and then supporting the reading, or in repressing the reader and then empowering her.

39. Here is the crux of the contemporary design problem: how can an object, or a form, be imagined, or designed, authored, which encourages the empowering

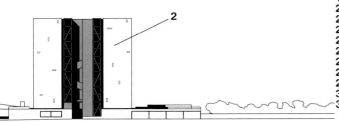

1. City Council building
2. City Government building
3. plaza/ parking garage
13. data center
22. land administration
23. construction
24. public housing
25. public works
26. secretariat
27. transportation
28. research and development
29. civil affairs
30. personnel
39. labor

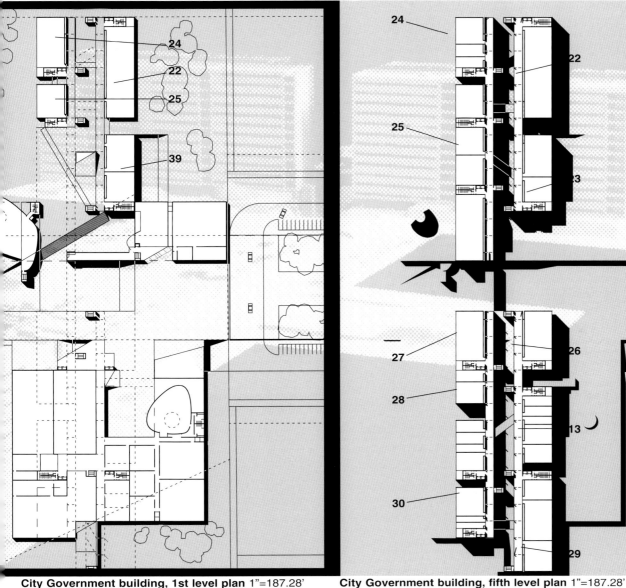

City Government building, 1st level plan 1"=187.28'   **City Government building, fifth level plan** 1"=187.28'

NIRM 5
act of reading, without *directing* that reading somehow? We are attuned to reading that which we perceive as intended to be read and to *expect* meaning *only there*. That which is accident or random or indifferent we ignore. Conventions are established to ground this intentionality, to help satisfy the reader's desire for the certainty of meaning which closes the reading.

40. To *prevent* this closure and deny that repressive conventional certainty, contemporary design is trending *away*

22. land administration
23. construction
24. public housing
25. public works
26. secretariat
28. research and development
29. civil affairs
31. finance
32. accounting
33. social affairs

9. mechanical
22. land administration
25. public works
26. secretariat
33. social affairs
34. education
35. vice and corruption

City Government building, ninth level plan 1"=187.28'   **City Government building, thirteenth level plan** 1"=187.28'

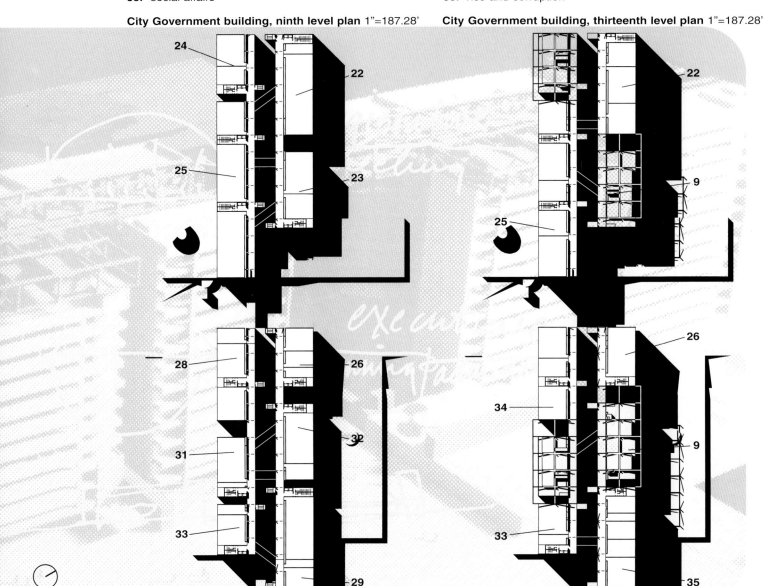

from treatment of the object as a wholly constituted, knowable, determined constant, that is, what we have come to know as architecture, and trending *toward* the loose orchestration and rhizomatic surprise of indeterminate events and readings. The object is to become a text, with the multiplicity of readings that this now suggests. This more fluid relationship is thought less likely to re-ossify into convention.

41. Yet, in contesting the *convention*, contemporary theory is not able in the end to contest the *object*. It is there, and people rub against it. And so the object remains as a check on contemporary theory's idealist tendencies.

42. The determinism of the thing, inescapably there, and celebrated by tradition, presents contemporary theory with two problems it must solve if it is to achieve its new program for architecture. First, its effect on viewers or users must be addressed: does it unavoidably dictate these effects, as tradition assumes, or can it encourage

relationship, while the concrete volumes play it more straight in both cases.

The parking structure also participates in the conceptual development, forming a plinth running the entire length of the civic center as a civic mall. Connecting the two complexes, this datum reinforces the differences between the two architectural layouts by highlighting the different ways they interact with it.

On the City Government building site the construction is concentrated toward the center of the site, maximizing the efficiency of the envelope and increasing the possibility of favorable interdepartmental adjacencies. On the City Council building site the program has been divided in two and placed toward the perimeter of the site, leaving a symbolic gathering space between, in the center of the site.

The landscape design follows the concept of simplicity and durability, which conveys the dignity appropriate to a civic center. A major ceremonial civic mall is proposed atop the parking structure which runs the length of the civic center, paved down the center and along the edges, where there are benches. Between, and on the two adjacent park sites, an informal arrangement of lawn and indigenous trees is proposed to contrast with the formality of the civic mall.

The City Government Building complex is the seat of the executive branch of the city government, and headquarters for the bureaucracy, including all its services, agencies, and civic amenities. It is primarily a huge office building. Support functions for the city employees and public interface areas extend across the entire site at the base of the office building, with major entrances in the center on the mall and at either end off Hue-chung and Wen-Hsin Roads.

For many good reasons the slab form is traditional for "huge office buildings": it says "office," giving it an impressive presence; it is efficient, saving both site area and circulation; it suggests a very clear and rational organization, important to employees of a vast bureaucracy as well as visitors; and because of its shallow depth it provides the best exposure to light and air. The slab proposed for the New Taichung City Government Building has several features which add to the traditional reasons for preferring this massing scheme: the usual criticism of dullness and anonymity is answered by breaking up the slab vertically and horizontally, allowing for increased identity of individual departments and greater visual interest. The slots that are provided between the different departments introduce light and air into the continuous-exterior-passive-solar-vent-stack-circulation-"canyon" between the slabs. The architectural theme of "connection/efficiency" is expressed in the manipulations of the servant/served circulation structure, which graphically forms a connective tissue between the various buildings that

4. parking
5. steel superstructure/ circulation
6. office block
9. mechanical

City Government building, north elevation 1"=83.34'

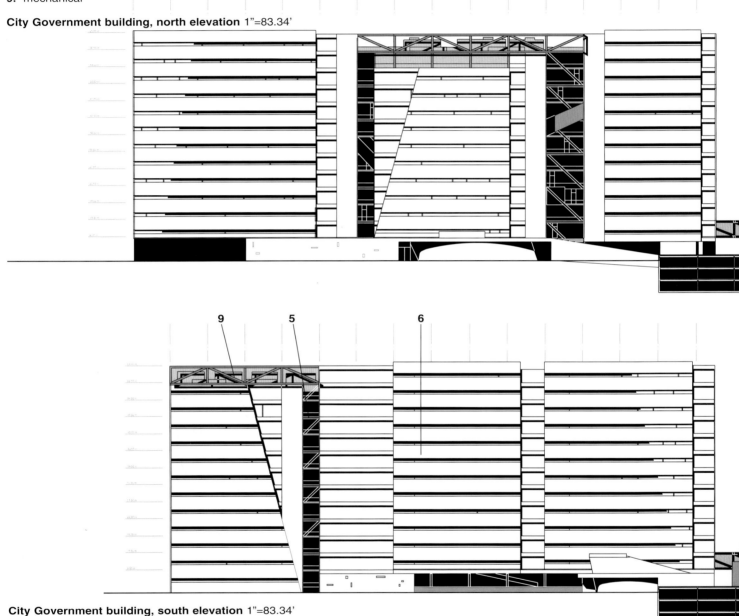

City Government building, south elevation 1"=83.34'

a more open reading that could empower its readers? Second, must the *making* of the thing in the first place follow some deterministic process, some authorial intent, some defining plan, or can it be more open to the sort of accident and novelty that upsets such intentionality?

43. The traditional scheme that contemporary theory finds so repressive, is single-mindedly authored, the empowering scheme it proposes instead is more open or passively recorded. The former attitude has been responsible for the entirety of the Western canon up until recently, and even for the idea of a canon itself; the latter can trace its lineage back to Heidegger and his discussion of "revealing" as a way to truth. The architectural public is seen by the canon as an audience and user group with little responsibility in the meaning equation, but by contemporary theory these folks are seen as victims denied their rights to participate in the exchange.

44. Both formulations fall short of their respective ideals.

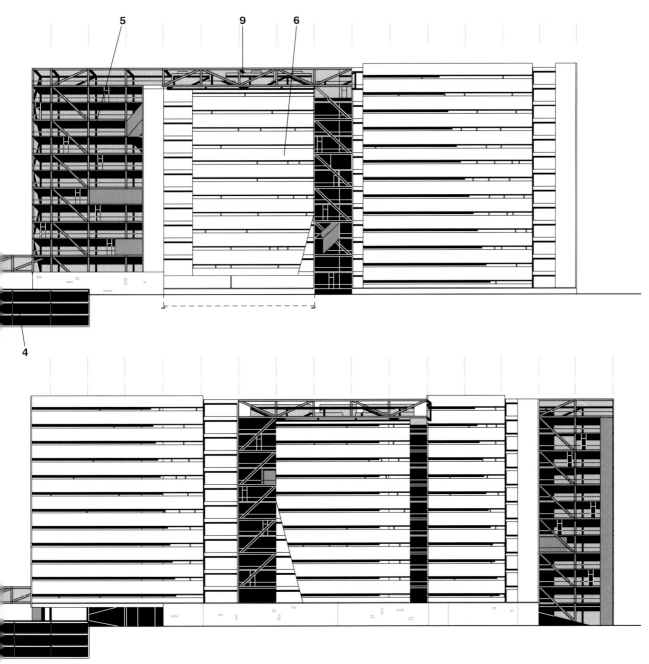

As the functionalist fallacy proved, form is never completely determined or determinable, either functionally or artistically, despite the author's fondest wishes, since no design can escape the vagaries of context, of time, space, or process. The classic deconstruction of the author/reader hierarchy shows that these vagaries extend to the reading itself. The reading can in fact never be more than *guided* by the object.

45. On the other hand, a completely open, or non-deterministic form is also impossible. The directedness of time unavoidably narrows the universe of choice in the design process as the object evolves, and if there is an end, then the object is de-facto de-terminated. By its mere presence then it forces the encounter that architects must recognize as the basis of their moral/ethical responsibility, which contemporary practices try desperately to escape: architecture is a public act, and however free one may feel to interpret its meaning or intentions, it is

City Government building, model view

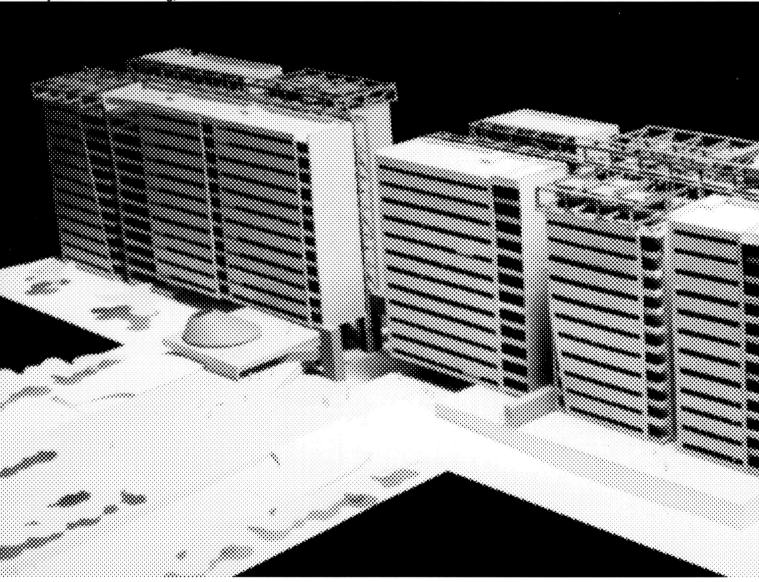

still there, in the way. And still being there, it remains significant, signifying.

46. Consequently, contemporary theory vilifies the object, as a repressive convention magnet. But by the same token we can *wonder* at that attractiveness, and ask what it is about the object that encourages meaning to stick to it so readily. As a sort of *personification*, this propensity was no stranger to tradition. From Phidias to Corbu the idea of *projection* was invoked to link the viewer more directly to the work, providing an introduction to the abstractions that make up the convention's bag of tricks.

47. But this idea of encouraging the viewer to consider the determined object as an image of herself, writ large, is seen by contemporary theory as repressive rather than uplifting, since it either imposes a restrictive limit on the viewer's self image, if the viewer does identify with it, or becomes simply obnoxious if she doesn't. The Unité's

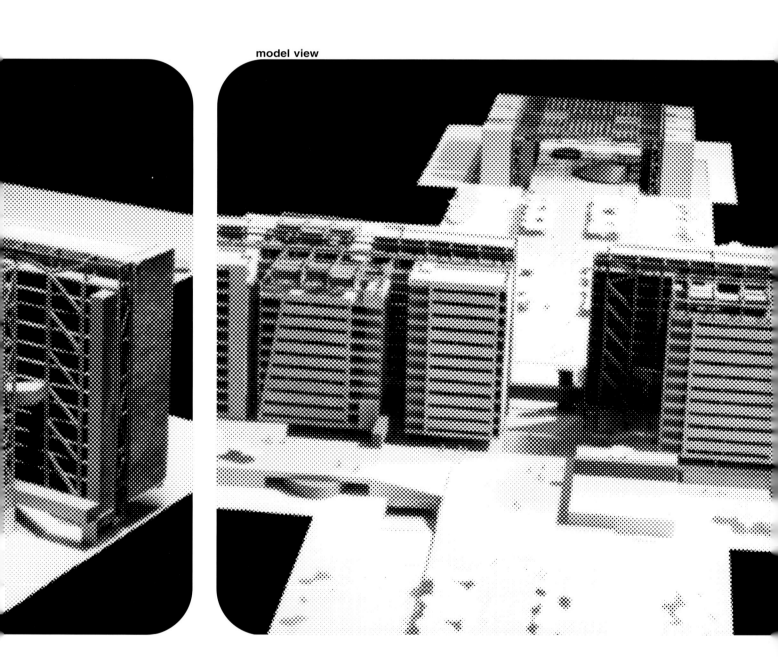

model view

massive sculptural celebration of the upright human, for example, would be considered authoritarian and sexist by contemporary theory.

* * *

48. When we say, in the presence of some building, "this is architecture," a contemporary critic hears the "we" and the "saying," but questions the very assumption of unitary meaning in the statement.

49. Challenging the conventions that direct him to that privileged meaning, and refusing to receive that repressive tradition, the critic emphasizes the subject's freedom to understand the object as *other* than architecture, or to understand "architecture" as other than implied by the statement. The tradition on the other hand would hear the same question first as an invocation of the object and then as a query about applying the appropriate conventions, taking for granted the sort of privileged understanding that allows the question to be asked in the

make up the mega-slab, tying them together and fulfilling the required interdepartmental adjacencies.

Programmatically the City Government Building is a sprawling many-headed complex. The city government is given a formal focus by the twinned slab partis; this mega-form combines the advantages of slab-organization outlined above with the increased possibility for adjacency usually associated with more cubic volumes. The passive cooling (stack effect) canyon between the slabs provides a sheltered community "street" for the office workers while programmatic amenities are spread out at the base of the complex where they are organized around dedicated outdoor spaces in identifiable sub-assemblies. Side outlets from the main canyon street, for air and views are made by separating the slab into discrete buildings by major department—providing visual interest to the whole and a sense of identity to the departments.

The parking mall plinth bisects the mega-slab at its center—symbolizing the realm of the public and the city government's relation to it: the city government buildings branch out from the mall but face along it fore and aft. Like the city government, it is there if necessary, but otherwise it is not in the way, and can even be ignored if desired. The public interface areas of the government bureaucracy are arrayed along the mall for easy access and conceptual clarity. The parking below the mall provides multilevel drop-off possibilities at a sunken court at the center of the complex for both ceremonial VIP entrance and discreet daily entrance.

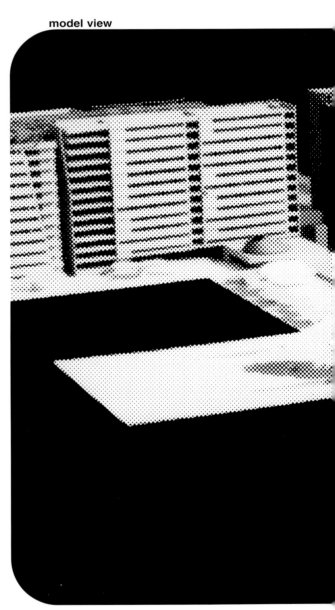

model view

first place.
Experience
50. But there is a space in the middle, "in the presence ..." between the "we saying" and the "architecture," between the subject and the object, where "this is." Both contemporary and traditional considerations of the equation entailed in our question overlook the *moment* called out by these terms, and look *away* from the gap across which the meaning leaps. The original question was

5. steel superstructure/ circulation
6. office block
9. mechanical

City Government building, transverse section 1"=83.34'

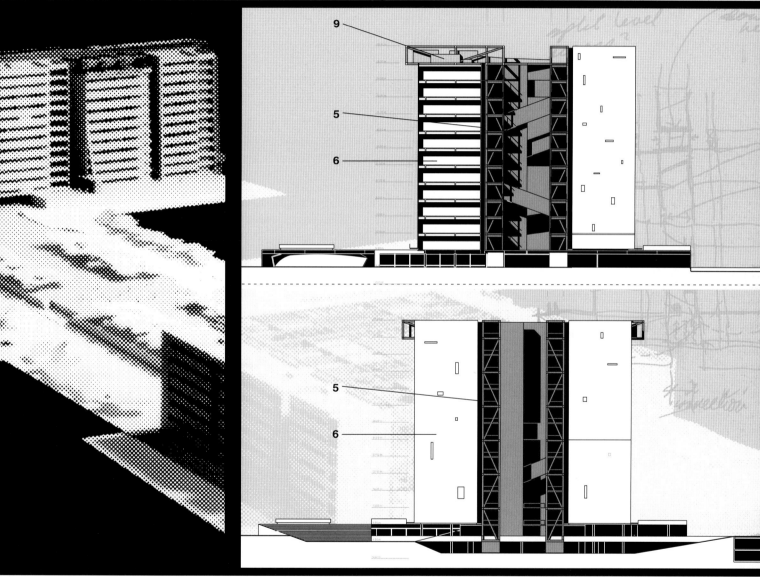

City Government building, transverse section 1"=83.34'

asked casually, but it is interesting the way it homes in on that quality of immediacy, of the moment, suspended in mid-air, as it were, over the gap: "This" is used, not "that," or "the building," conveying a sense of engagement, a drawing close of the object and implying connection, instead of a setting apart: a linking of the subject with the object. And "is" is used, not "looks like," or "seems to be," emphasizing the immediacy of the judgment by placing the appreciation in the present, unqualified or hedged, unselfconscious or critical. "Is" is transparent to the thing; the thing is only here, or it can only be perceived here, now, in the present, in the perceiving. Tradition and critique are balanced across this perceiving.

51. Between the contemporary promise that authority will have no hold over the encounter—that it will be free to develop as the subject wills—and tradition's interest in establishing an authority invested in the object, is

219

3. covered outdoor plaza
8. steel canopy
9. mechanical
10. auditorium
11. city council chamber

City Council building, longitudinal section 1"=83.34'

Heidegger, the first deconstructor, who says that the object may reveal itself if allowed, if teased into unhiddenness. But, he says, it will never be seen if it is already fit into some preconceived system, convention *or* critique. It is, for him, a process of discovering the true, the real, under the layers of accumulated masks. And the subject will realize his true essence in bearing witness to that revealing, that discovery. In bearing witness we are participating in the moment, we are crossing the gap, experiencing the object as architecture.

* * *

52. When in the presence of some building we are moved to proclaim "this is architecture," it means simply, but profoundly, that we are having an architectural experience.
53. The architectural experience is that moment when the definitions fall away, when they are seen as inadequate or beside the point; as limited, artificial, ringing

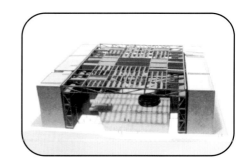

3. covered outdoor plaza
5. steel superstructure/ circulation
6. office block
8. steel canopy
9. mechanical
11. city council chamber

City Council building, south elevation 1"=83.34'

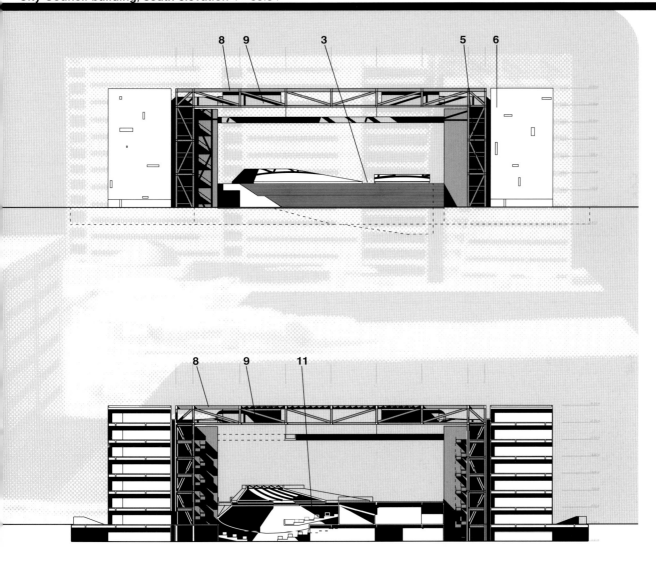

City Council building, transverse section 1"=83.34'

hollow in the clarity of the presence of the real thing, there. Yet, this moment away from convention is not that which is sought by contemporary theory; all that baggage is still there—it's an inescapable part of the architecture thing—it's just backstage, hiding in the magnificent shadows.

54. The experience does not *contest* this stuff, the way the contemporary critic might, it just doesn't *worry* about it. Lesser buildings hide behind convention, which follows the presence like an afterimage, or wake; often making its provisional nature absurdly obvious and giving architecture a bad name. Lesser buildings need the definition to assert their value—they would be unrecognizable as architecture without the label. This is where contemporary criticism has inserted its critique of convention.

55. Experience—real, live engagement—offers the greatest critique of both convention and idealism.

The City Council Building houses the legislative branch of the city government and its support functions. If the government building is the behind-the-scenes bureaucracy, then the City Council Building, as the home of the elected officials, is the showplace of the city's civic pride. It is a gathering place for these officials to meet with each other and their constituents, and is an office building where the business of the city council is supported.

The City Council Building is comprised of the same elements as the City Government Building, but they have been arranged in a different way to express the difference in the two programs. As with the other building, the office functions are housed in the concrete slabs, and the circulation occurs in the glass and steel structure of connective tissue, but in the City Council Building the slabs are held apart to form a central outdoor gathering space, invoking the theme of assembly. The diagram is very simple and straightforward: the support functions for the city council activity are arranged in the slabs to either side framing the city council spaces. They are connected under the raised outdoor plaza at both the ground and basement levels. In addition, there is a outdoor bridge between them at the sixth level suspended beneath the trusses of the louver canopy. The more public functions are concentrated at the power levels adjacent to the plaza, while the more private functions are located higher up in the slabs. The immediate support for the city council areas themselves are located with those areas under the plaza. The raised plaza provides multi-level drop-off opportunity; a grand ceremonial stair or mall VIP entrance, and a more discreet drop-off below the raised mall at ground level.

The main symbolic component of the City Council Building are the auditoria. Traditionally they are shaped by concerns for accommodation of sight-lines and the support of good acoustics, but are fit into whatever envelope is available, without expressing the dynamic form that arises naturally from these concerns. These auditoria take their symbolic role seriously—they have discrete identities, separate from the supporting slabs and enjoy the sort of free form shape which comes from acoustical and sight-line concerns. They are embedded in the mall plinth that forms the main symbol of the theme of assembly.

The connective tissue servant structure provides a louvered canopy over this symbolic gesture and creates a sheltered outdoor gathering space. It is a grand civic symbol of the idea of city council, contrasting with the City Government Building's architectural theme of connection. The City Council auditoria spaces below have expression in the outdoor symbolic gathering space as the protruding light monitors that are "gathered" under the canopy.

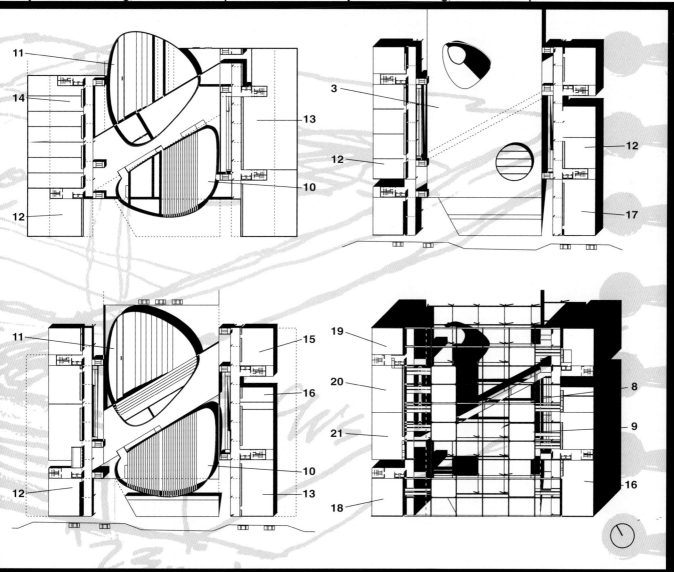

10. auditorium
11. city council chamber
12. council affairs
13. data center
14. special commission
15. security
16. general affairs

3. covered outdoor plaza
8. steel canopy
9. mechanical
12. council affairs
16. general affairs
17. public relations
18. secretary general
19. executive secretary general
20. speaker
21. deputy speaker

City Council building, basement level plan 1"=166.67'

City Council building, second level plan 1"=166.67'

City Council building, first level plan 1"=166.67'

City Council building, seventh level plan 1"=166.67'

Experience is unique—to the individual, to the moment, to the object—but it is also a reaching out, in the moment, to the other. When Dr. Johnson refutes idealism by kicking a stone, he is not emphasizing the rock itself so much as the kicking of the rock and the connection made in experience with this substantial evidence of an external world.

56. This experience, this *architectural* experience, is, simply, but profoundly, the experience of wonder that such a thing could be—and the irrefutable evidence, here, that it is. Not because it is so outrageous, or big, or old, or pretty, or expensive or well-crafted even, but because it is ... right, which includes all of these, probably, if you bothered to think about it, but you wouldn't because such an analytical frame of mind is foreign to the experience. In the meantime, it is just the case; it may sound corny, like bad poetry or cheap mysticism, but there you go. There is a gravity to the experience, an

223

City Council building, model view

attraction, that makes the time in thrall simultaneously limitless and fleeting. You are faced with the overwhelming question, the excruciating demand, against which architecture continuously struggles: why cannot *everything* be like this? while facing the tragic answer, there, in the *exceptional* presence of the object, which asks.

57. But how then do you know it is an architectural experience, and not that of some quality, without a name? Is it architecture if it is good enough? Right enough? But what is right, or good? Have we really gotten anywhere by all this? The judgment is usually far more immediate than the explanation.

ONE 10
58. Naming it does not capture it. To say that architecture is building plus art, or artful building, or building plus the sign of building, or inhabitable art, or artful inhabitation, or the superlative of building, or communicative building, or the sculpting of the void, or what architects do, or the mother of the Arts or father of the

P96.03/1
American Medical Informatics Center
Bucharest, Romania

Client:	Parsons, Main
Architect:	Jones, Partners: Architecture
Site:	Flat rural site outside Bucharest, on main road to airport in future development corridor
Program:	Convention space for American Medical interests in Eastern Europe, including meeting rooms, exhibit space for medical supplies vendors, restaurant, administration, and loading facilities
Size:	450,000 SF
Systems:	Longspan steel truss and joint system with intermediate steel framing, CMU enclosure with corrugated and flat metal panel skin, steel curtain wall; cast-in-place slab and foundations
Features:	This speculative development for the newly emerging market of the Eastern Block adapts the basic diagram used for the Cathedral City and Taichung Civic Centers to an exhibit hall image, but it works as if designed expressly for this program; the enclosed demonstration amphitheaters form walls down the sides leaving the exhibition floor flexibly free; the restaurants and bars flay overhead through the exhibition space, providing a dramatic overview and dynamic division.
Cost:	$50 million
Completion:	May 1995 (proposal)

The practice of medicine is a unique mix of the human and scientific, in which both the rational and the intuitive play a role. The varied techniques and equipment the medical profession employ in fulfillment of the Hippocratic oath cover a broad range of human ingenuity and expertise; an effective bedside manner is as important in its way as the MRI for which it might prepare the patient, and the right question can be as effective as Computerized Axial Tomography in making the appropriate diagnosis. Architecture can also play a role in support of these efforts, but in so doing it must cover a similar range of concern.

The architecture which supports the medical profession can be seen as another piece of equipment, since it must not only satisfy the required functional considerations, but if possible enhance them, allowing the profession to fulfill its duties with the greatest efficiency and efficacy. In this sense the architecture is more than just a passive or neutral container. Just as a CAT scanner can be seen to represent a commitment to the ideal of saving lives, as well as being an instrument of that effect, the building which houses this activity may represent these intentions, as well as keep the rain off. Unlike the CAT scanner or other equipment though, this is part of architecture's prescription, not just a fortunate side-effect.

Architecture is expected to communicate something about the program it supports. This is particularly true in the case of a commercial building, dedicated to fostering trade. In such a case architecture becomes part of the marketing effort, a member of the sales team. Its dual nature comes to the fore in such situations, supporting trade both through efficient planning, which eliminates inconvenience and physical barriers to the deal, and through visual cues, which establish a positive mood encouraging this activity. A medical professions trade center, AMIHALL, must reconcile the messages of its two masters: the perceived altruism of the medical community, and the boosterism of the commercial trade-show environment. What architecture "says" medicine? What architecture "boosts" it?

A typical convention center is interested in generating a certain level of excitement, but rarely adopts a particular design "theme." The exhibits, which change with every trade show and convention, determine the mood of each show, and are given the greatest chance to show off in a thematically neutral environment. But AMIHALL does not warrant this same level of neutrality. Though there is a revolving component to its exhibition program, it is primarily a permanent medical products fair; it should take advantage of architecture's capacity for expression to enliven the mood and set the tone of its medical orientation—as a continuing stimulus to sales.

Consequently, the proposed design for AMIHALL takes its cues from the rich mix of the humanism and science characterizing the medical profession itself. The design attempts to project a sense of

7. auto drop-off
27. mechanical
32. skylight

view from entry

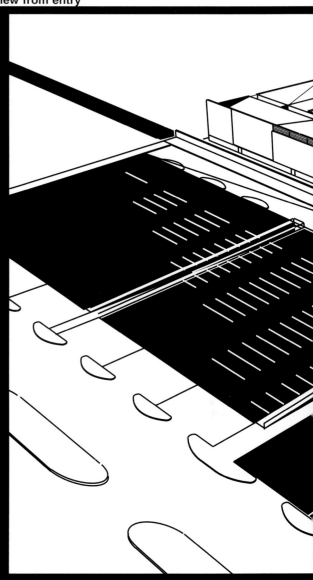

ruin, or even designed political space, is not to make it apparent. These are all descriptions after the fact: programs for what architecture can be called rather than what it is. Names have a habit of standing in front of the object, of becoming labels, and becoming substituted not only for the object, but for the experience.
59. In fact, the experience, and the ability to create it, or design the objects that sustain it, cannot be transferred, it cannot be taught: we teach ourselves through the

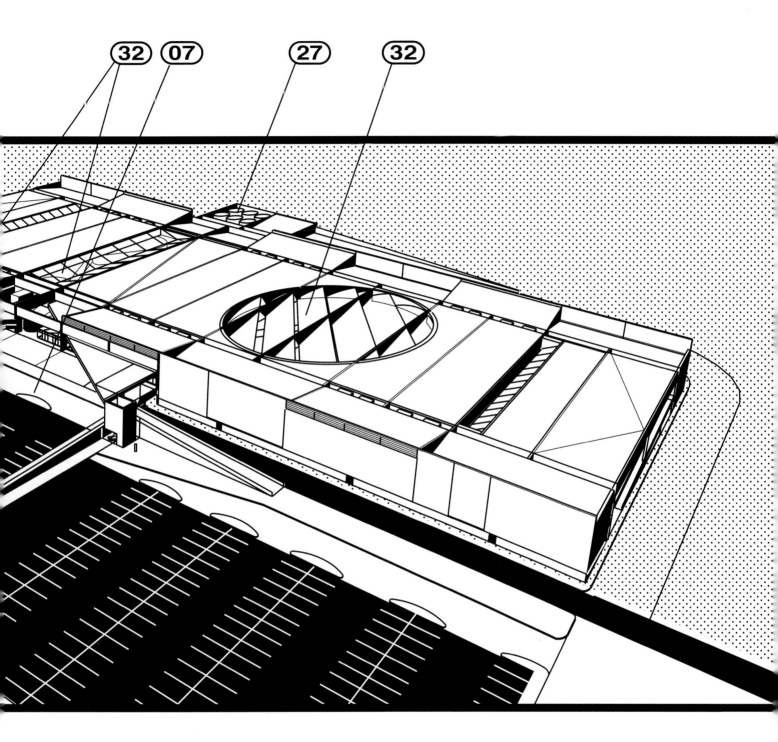

accumulation of our own experiences. The architectural experience is like no other you can reference.

60. In bearing witness to the revealing of the thing, no better guide is available than: it is architecture if *it* feels like it. The eight-hundred-pound-gorilla-joke notwithstanding, the fact that we can project our wonder to include how architecture feels says something about the quality of the experience we are describing: *we experience the building as alive*.

Engagement

61. What does it mean to say, in the presence of some building, "this is architecture?" It means the speaker is having an architectural experience. The architectural experience is dependent on a quality of engagement, though, that is more comprehensive than the mere appreciation of history, and more affective than mere analytical or critical analysis. Webster uses terms like "to attract and hold by influence or power," "to interlock

excitement—by providing a variety of spatial and visual experience, while stating the fact of its rational planning—through the obvious conveniences such planning promotes.

The design is not a typical neutral "black box" convention hall. A medical "theme" is carried throughout the facility: the use of biomorphic shapes and bold geometries, the overall "technical" appearance and "clinical" details, the predominantly white coloration, clean materials and smooth surfaces, all recall the profession's scientific and humanistic basis. There is an abundance of light and space. Light enters deep into the interior of the volume from the lobby and both ends of the main space and from clerestories above. The industrially efficient roof structure elegantly carries the symmetrically modulated duct work and exhibit support services, providing a generous ceiling height which not only increases exhibition flexibility but is better suited proportionally to the vastness of the space. This height allows important program elements to soar over the exhibition and sales floor, activating the usually empty volume of space above the booths, enlivening the space as a whole without competing directly with the exhibits below. Many ramps and bridges, including some used as seating areas in the restaurants themselves, actively encourage the visitor to move through the space and explore the exhibits from different perspectives. As well as promoting movement, these dramatic diagonal surfaces impart a visual dynamism to the space—in further support of the trade fever.

7. auto drop-off
29. smooth metal panel

view from entry (early scheme)

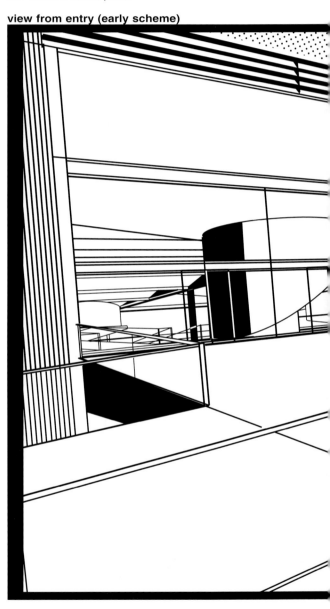

with," "to involve, or engross," or "to participate," for example.

NOB 27

62. It is *in* this engagement that the other factors in the rich soup of the architectural experience are entailed: the tragic responsibility of the architect for the unknown user he must risk offending is here; the intentionality apparent in the object that compels the reading response; the willfulness of the object that sustains the reading response is here too; the creativity of the reading; the gravity exert-

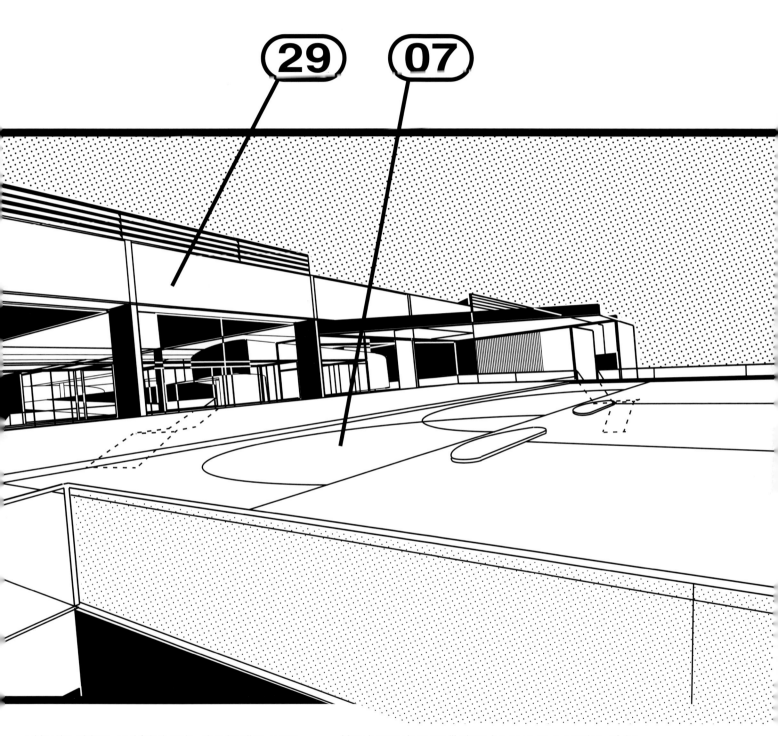

ed by the object, and felt thereby, that implies everything; and the aesthetic qualities of the object that resonate with the beholder, elevating both to the plane of the sublime—all this follows from being properly *engaged* by the experience.

63. Traditionally, the feelings inspired by this engagement were given expression in the idea of the beautiful. Beauty was an end in itself and a means to the sublime that was a sign of truth and goodness. Not anymore.

Now beauty is more likely to be seen as exemplary of the repressive tendencies of singular authority, than as bearing any simple relation to a truth which itself is in question. Now beauty is being eroded into kitsch by mediation and consumerism, trivializing its connection to goodness. In fact, it has become as great an anachronism as the classical that once idealized it.

64. Contemporary theory seems to be following culture when it replaces beauty with *novelty* as an ideal, as the

1. AMISHOW/ exhibit space
2. AMITRADE/ sales floor
7. auto drop-off
24. restaurant
26. administration
27. mechanical
28. corrugated metal panel
29. smooth metal panel
30. painted CMU
32. skylight

longitudinal section 1"=60.00'

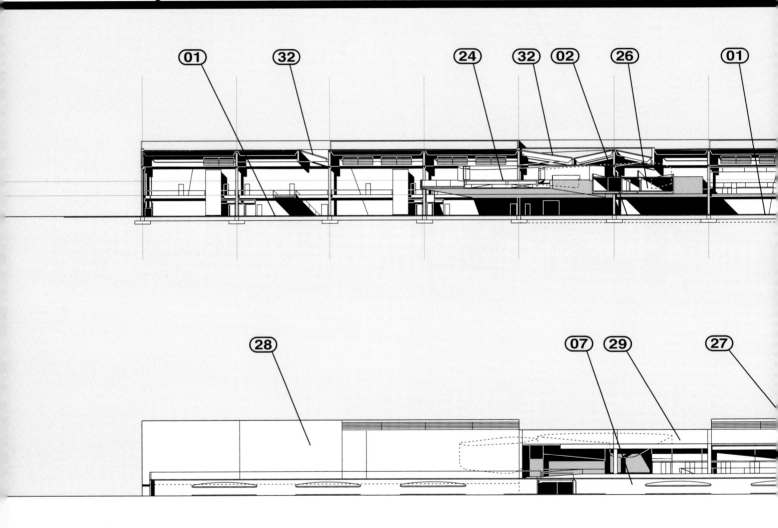

south elevation 1"=60.00'

only thing that has any hope of avoiding the mantle of authority. In the age of oxymoron we have a rapid turnover of more common superlatives—it is now a radical, righteous, neato, cool, awesome, def, boss, bitchin', twitchen', fresh, hapnen', hip, hep, bad, phat, groovy, dope, stupid dope, fly, peachy, keen, outrageous, gnarly, average, excellent, hot, killer, rockin', totally, slick, fine, wicked, wild, far out, out of sight, jammin', proper, tubular, bodacious thing, which has game. Beauty is history.

Figure

65. Though the experience may be the end, it is not the thing. What sort of *object* will foster the architectural experience? ANSWER: An object that will regard you as intently as you regard it. An object that can be a participant in the experience. In soliciting the brick's opinion, Louis Kahn invited it to participate. When he talked about the plan as a community of rooms he also created a scenario of participation. In both of these examples, though,

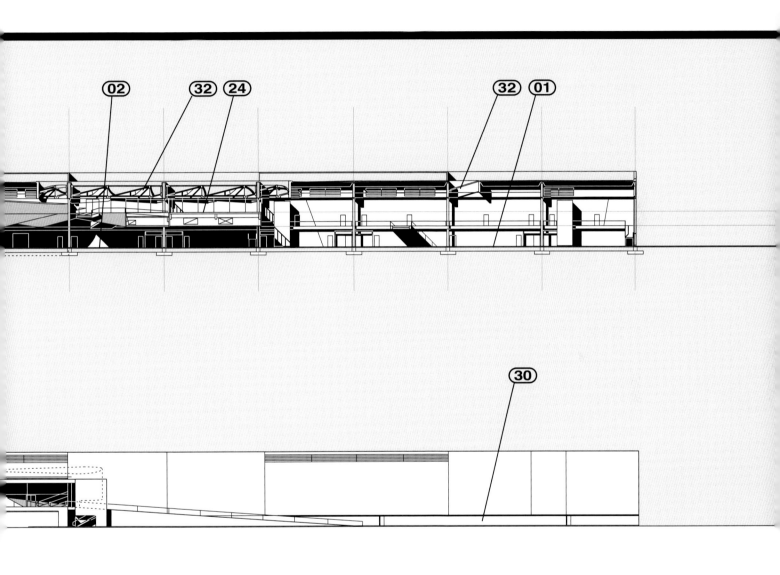

the object was not taken as a whole, but in pieces. The brick likes an arch, but what about the plan? The community-minded plan likes to get together for a barbecue, maybe, but what about the rest of the building? The experience is fostered by the building as a whole, just as it is felt by viewer as a whole.

66. This is what the architect can do: she can create an environment where the conversation can occur, spontaneously; not just as an interrogation, but as a real give-and-take. For this to happen, the object must be alive, have its own life and desires so that its participation breaks free from being the expression of the author, to being a peer of the viewer, free to deal directly and introduce its own ideas into the conversation. If the architect finds herself making sound effects for the design while she draws, then the object is engaging her at this level.

67. The animorphism or personification that draws these sounds from the designer can be ascribed formally to

1. AMISHOW/ exhibit space
7. auto drop-off
8. VIP entry
18. loading/ service
22. amphitheater
26. administration
27. mechanical
28. corrugated metal panel
30. painted CMU
31. floor to ceiling butt-joint glazing

transverse sections 1"=60.00'

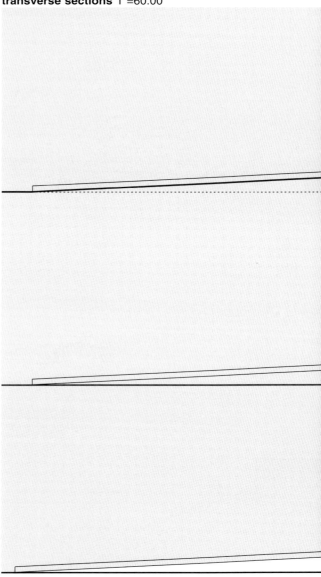

east elevation 1"=60.00'

These architectural fireworks are based on a rational plan, though. No gratuitous decorations are applied to this efficient trade machine; nor does it require them; instead, that efficiency has itself been emphasized. The use of cleanly detailed, straightforward no-nonsense forms and a restrained palette of durable materials complement the simple shape and proportions of the hall to create a strong unified impression.

A desire for maximum efficiency in exhibit layout and comprehensive beneficial adjacency have dictated a very simple, straightforward plan and section, in which architectural license is reserved more or less exclusively for the unconstrained spaces above the main exhibition and sales floor. Basically, AMIHALL is a large continuous open exhibit and sales area, organized and sized according to the typical convention center/trade show model; that is, on a 10X10 booth module grid, 30X30 primary services grid (communications, power, drain), 60X60 secondary services grid (communications, power, drain, compressed air, gas, water), and framed on either long side by the enclosed amphitheaters and their upper galleries, which overlook the exhibition floor.

the object's figure. Figure is what draws us in; it is the form of willfullness, the shape of intention. We are biologically programmed to respond to figure, even when we don't specifically recognize it. To figure is to puzzle out, and then to understand; the figure is the form of that understanding. To understand is to "grasp," to "get a hold of something," to reach out and make the connection that is at the root of the architectural experience. The figure is the first thing about the object that is grasped. It

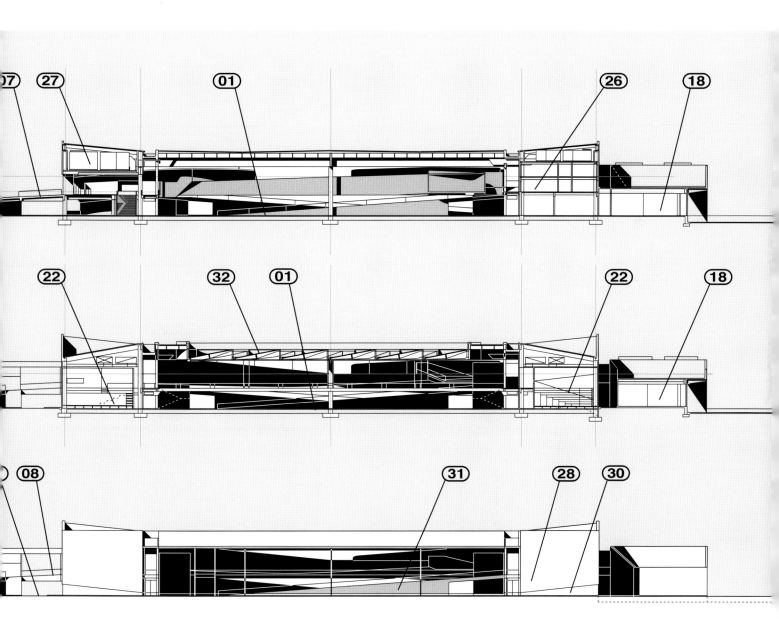

is the object's handle ....

68. Figure is familiar because it is, like us, mechanical in a broad sense. The idea of the mechanical expresses our understanding of our own way of being in the world as embodied consciousness. It straddles the instrumental and aesthetic senses (like architecture!), almost as a bridge between them—a bridge that describes the analogical structure of meaning itself. The aesthetic instrumentalized, made operational; the instrumental aestheticized, made legible. The form of the mechanical, considered in this way, is the form of figure.

a From lecture originally delivered at the College of Environmental Design, University of California at Berkeley, 1995.
b Jonathan Culler, *On Deconstruction: Theory and Criticism after Structuralism* (Ithaca: Cornell Univ. Press, 1982), 103.
18 OWA, 166.

1. AMISHOW/ exhibit space
2. AMITRADE/ sales floor
8. VIP entry
9. security
12. building automation
13. fire command center
16. truck entry
18. loading/ service
19. storage/ orders preparation
20. staff lockers/ lunch room
22. amphitheater

ground level plan 1"=120.00'

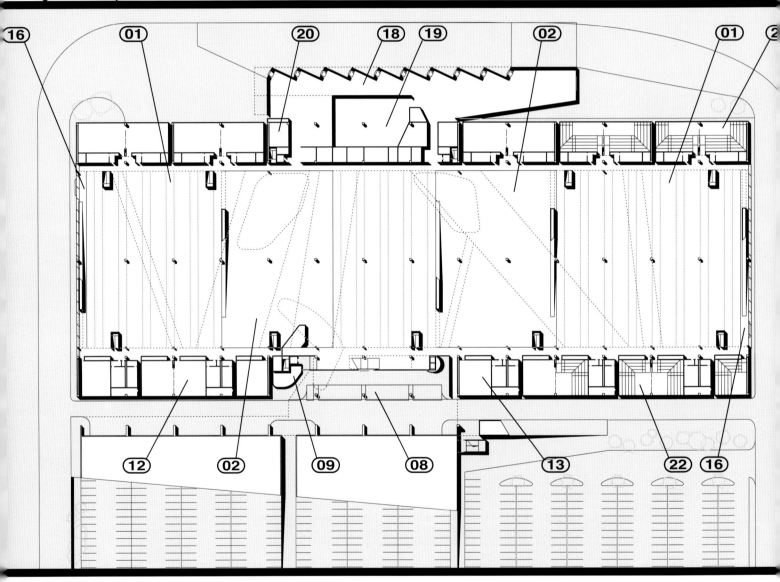

19 QT, 315.
20 Martin Heidegger, "The Turning" in *The Question Concerning Technology and Other Essays*, trans. William Lovitt (New York: Harper & Row, 1977), 42; hereafter cited as T.
21 QT, 32
22 Lovitt, xxxv.
23 Sem, 42
24 Lovitt, xxxv.
25 T, 41.
26 Without prejudgment or pre-disposition to "solutions" or mastery, the boss object is enthusiastically open to the strife it engages. The boss object's inflective attitude "*surfs*" strife: it teases the wave of strife into presence rather than commanding the strife to stand in reserve. The strife's own contrary nature is *revealed* in the boss object's accommodation; the boss object thus embodies both the danger and its accepting mediation/accommo-

10. coats/ info
11. reception
21. projection
23. kitchen
24. restaurant
25. bar
26. administration
27. mechanical

second level plan 1"=120.00'

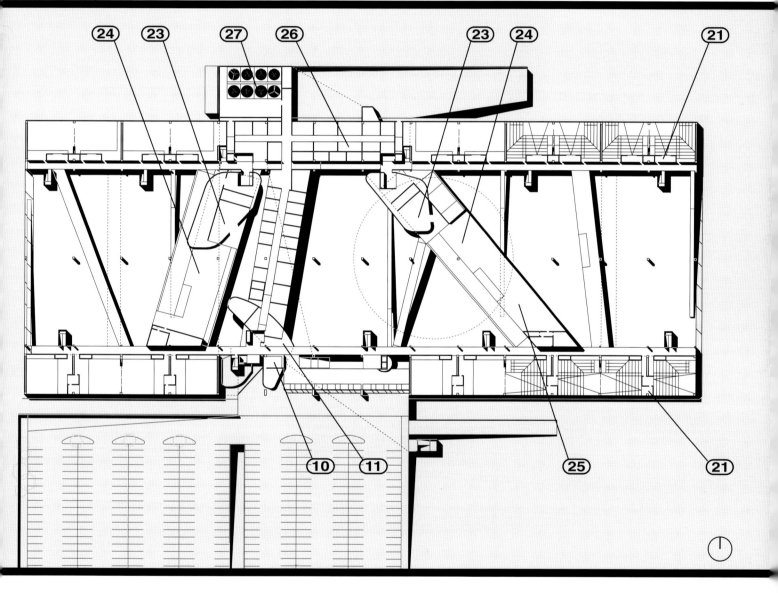

dation/saving. Such latency is not made apparent through any deconstructive reversal or theory-judo. Deconstruction achieves its understanding by taking stuff apart to show-the "real" structure below; in judo, the opponent's strength is turned against itself. By this disassembly or turn though, the disposition that prejudges again is revealed; the problem is noticed, then flipped. Rather than judo, the boss surfs, it dances. The boss is immanent in technology.

27 Lovitt, xxv; (T 39, 41-42)
28 *Ibid*.
29 QT, 32.
30 OWA, 178.

23. kitchen

interior view

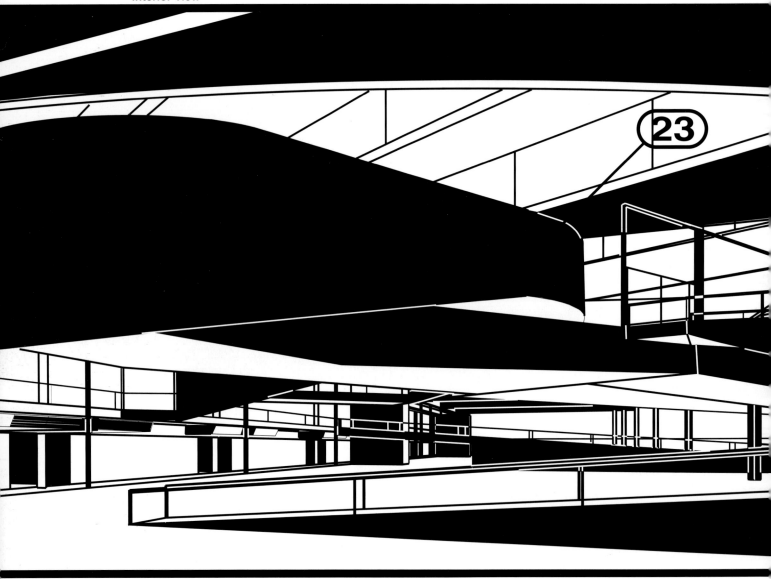

Abstract: Myth

1. While Heidegger was honing his critique of technology, Roland Barthes was pursuing a parallel investigation of the signs this technology distributed. Barthes outlined a semiological system structured in a very similar manner to Heidegger's enframing, in which what he called "first order signifiers," or "signs," stand in reserve to be ordered into use for "second order signification." He termed this second order signification "myth," and showed how it described a faux textuality promising an illusory freedom. As humanity is estranged from direct experience by its enframed condition, so it is alienated from real meaning by the operation of myth. Myth hijacks the sign and its directly appreciable signification and applies the form of that sign—its signifier bereft of meaning—to some other intentionality. In this Barthes announces the infinite referrability, and deferral of meaning, that deconstruction would later make the center-

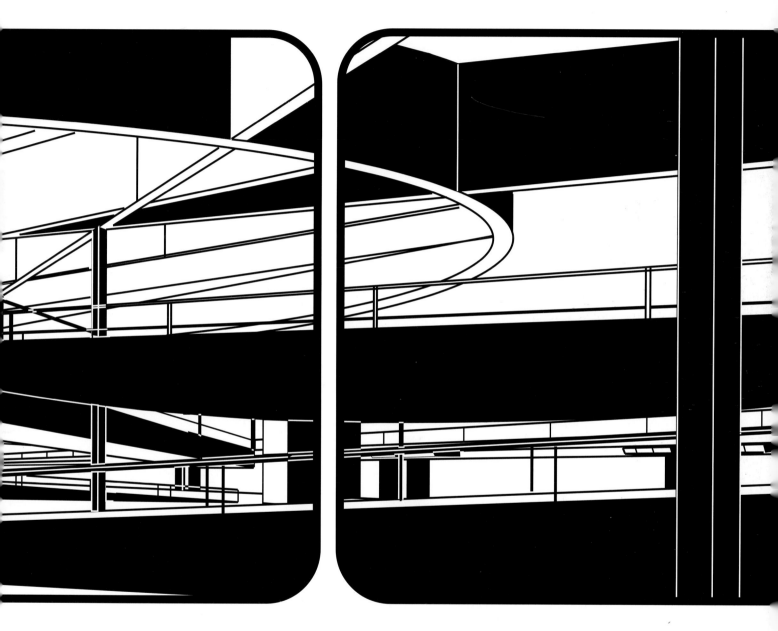

piece of its critique.

2. The semiological structure Barthes discusses has its origin in traditional myth. A consideration of this structure in relation to its genesis in tradition reveals the possibility for understanding myth's usefulness in investing contemporary production with a non-repressive authority. Traditional myth enjoys an unquestionable authority that is implied rather than stated. In terms of the western world at least it can be said that "myth is that which is taken for granted when thought begins."[1] This implication of authority has become intolerable in the contemporary system of myth Barthes describes because the surreal nature of traditional myth, announcing the provisionality of the authority it assumes, is absent. Were myth to declare itself, as ideology, fiction, or some other type of "story," then it would be remarkable, again and would reap the respect that authority craves through the com-

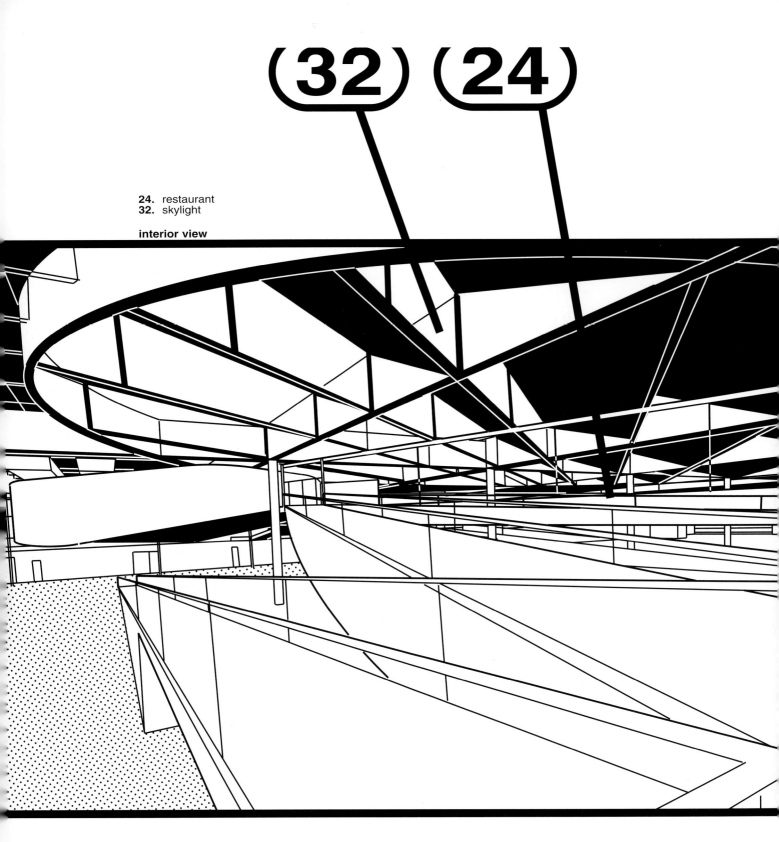

24. restaurant
32. skylight

interior view

plicity of the viewer rather than the duplicity of the object. The aura of authority that makes stuff important—which architecture so conspicuously lacks today—need not be repressive when the terms of its granting are clear.

3. Such myth does not announce itself, though, so its "depoliticizing" alienation is defeated only by "revolutionary speech." This species of "operational language" is the argot of equipment. When a person speaks through her equipment, external issues of authority are swept aside in favor of direct transformative engagement. It is possible now to tell stories about equipment, or with equipment, that approach the mythic and enjoy the dignity of its authority, yet are perversely confident in the obviousness of this authority's provisionality. When the mythic potential of everything is understood, which is not to say everything is mythified, then everyone may enjoy the percipience of the gods, and all experience can be supernatural.

02. AMITRADE/ sales floor
25. bar

interior view

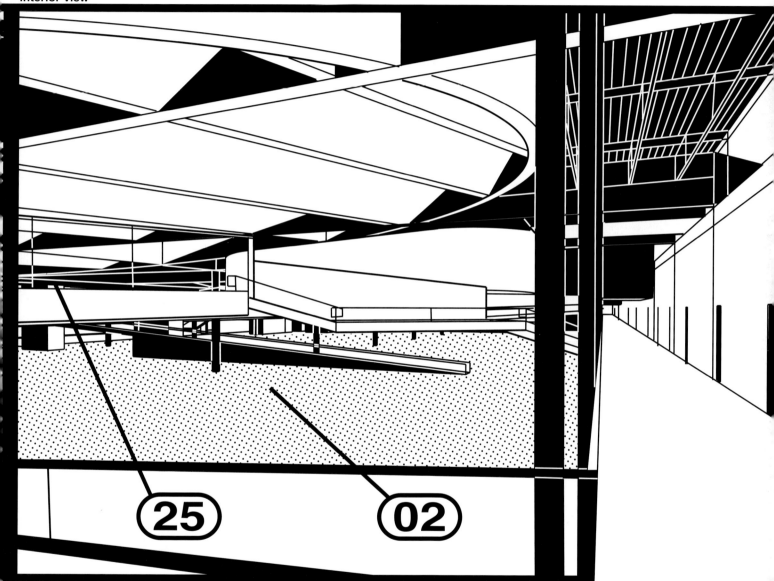

(25) (02)

4. What marks this new register better than anything else is the sense of irony that invests most cultural production today. The illusion of self-consciousness Heidegger feared in enframing has given way to the institutionalized, mordant meta-metaview: a critical self-self-consciousness that does not spare itself. It is possible to "define postmodern as incredulity toward metanarrative."[2]

5. Armed to the teeth with sarcasm, society is able to pursue the fantastic without risk of fanaticism. Folks are able to tend the evolution of technology as enthusiasts without getting caught up in it. They *know* they are standing in reserve, so they take along a magazine to help pass the time. All are seasoned travelers, by now. Humanity has been through that nuclear nonsense, cluttered up the moon and even cloned a sheep. But the cynicism bred of having everywhere been there, done that, is lately taken as evidence that there is more, rather

08. VIP entrance/ secure parking

exterior view

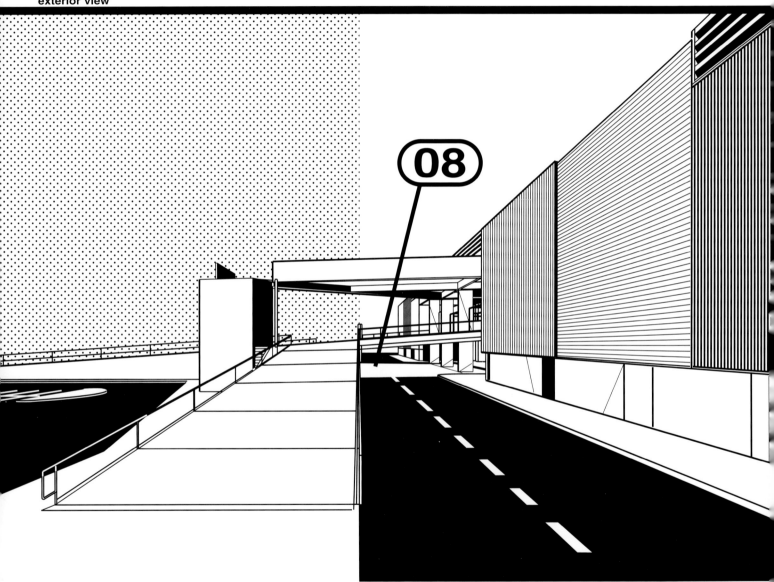

than less: folks are ironic, not bored. They have been there so many times that they have gotten past being impressed with an awareness of similarities and have begun to interest themselves in the differences that set each apart.

6. The mode of representation giving rise to this ironic sensibility is myth—both as it is traditionally understood, and as appropriated by Roland Barthes, who incidentally wrote his *Mythologies* at the same time Heidegger was working on "The Question Concerning Technology."

7. Though foundational, the mythic statement is laid bare in all its provisionality. The axiomatic nature of myth ensures that the noise it makes is loud and important and at the same time clearly just a noise. No one is *fooled*: the myth is subscriptive. Complicity in giving the myth life is much more obvious than complicity in sustaining architectural conventions, for example, because the myth does not have the same continuity with the

C96.05/1
Cathedral City Civic Center
Cathedral City, CA

Client: City of Cathedral City

Architect: Jones, Partners: Architecture with The Hillier Group

Site: Gently sloping downtown lot situated in the core of the city's planned redevelopment area, presently a trailer-home park.

Program: City council chambers and Mayor's office, city hall administrative offices, police station with holding facilities, and secure parking

Size: 50,000 ft^2

Systems: Steel framing and infill, with concrete over metal decking and EIFS cladding founded upon poured in place concrete slab and retaining walls; weathering steel truss with integral steel and fiberglass parasol system

Features: A vast weathering steel parasol shelters a symbolic civic gathering space from the harsh desert sun; the symbolic gathering space continues the plaza area of the town square across the street into the building, where it becomes a plinth that accommodates the slope across the site and hides the secure parking for the city VIPs; the City Hall and Police Station buildings framing the civic gathering space turn conventional "streamlined Spanish colonial" faces out to the city, but show distinctly contemporary steel and glass faces to the civic space under the parasol.

Cost: $14 million

Completion: August 1995 (competition)

The city's objectives for the new Civic Center can be divided into two categories—the practical and the symbolic. The practical objectives are easily and efficiently satisfied by the most straightforward, basic office building. After all, both city halls and police stations are mostly collections of office functions differing little from the commercial standard. Yet, the City has specifically asked that the *image* of such a building be avoided, even if such a construction type has been the basis for the budget. This places the major burden for design firmly in the symbolic, where the straightforward basic office building may be elevated to a stature appropriate to a civic center's "statement of government activities."

The design has been organized efficiently around the symbolic idea of "assembly." Two ordinary office buildings are ennobled by their arrangement as frames for a central space which literally continues the civic space of the town square and is oriented to the entrance from Palm Canyon Drive. A great canopy is proposed to shelter this space from the harsh desert climate, becoming the main symbolic expression of the civic nature of the project. By this gesture the design demonstrates a sense of "inviting ... user friendliness and easy accessibility." Strongly "framing views of the mountains" as it "presides over the town square," this gesture frees the building(s) to demonstrate a virtuous modesty and cost effectiveness, without losing Civic Presence.

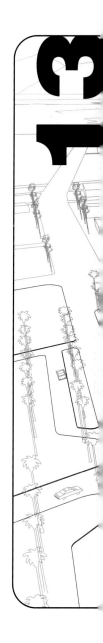

B. town square
C. city hall
D. police station
F. covered plaza

view from southeast

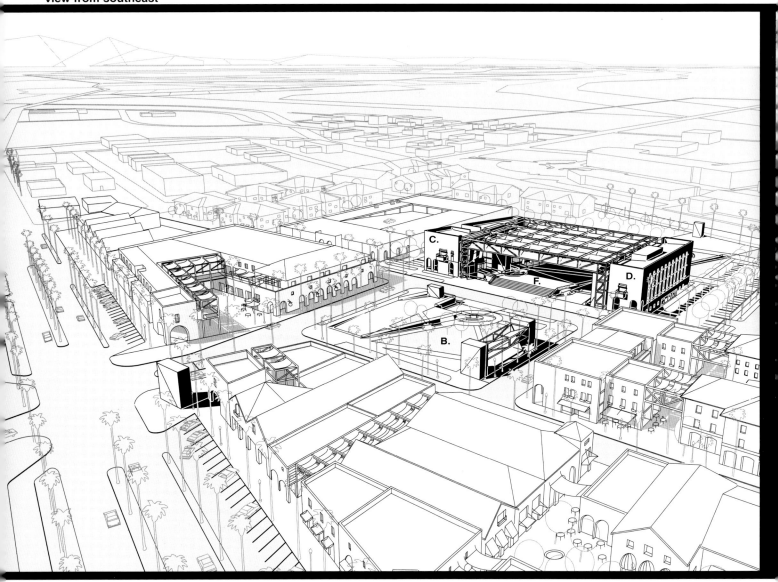

ordinary that architecture has—with, say, building. Like architecture, myths "in their details indicate what the self image of people in a given civilization is," but they do this by standing outside that world. This difference accounts for both the obviousness of their provisionality and their contrary sense of authority.

8. The historical relationship of myth to architecture is so well known that it needs no comment; in fact, it obscures the sense in which a new relationship might be forged today. Where architecture might have begun in support of the ritual embodiment of mythical speech in temples, theater and funerary spaces, now the *mythical* mode of discourse may come to the rescue of an architecture paralyzed by critique. This distinction and its appropriate operative value can be missed if myth is considered nostalgically.

9. The framing of the experience of myth sets it apart from ordinary discourse, just as that of architecture sets

B. town square
C. city hall
D. police station
F. covered plaza

site plan 1"=133.33'

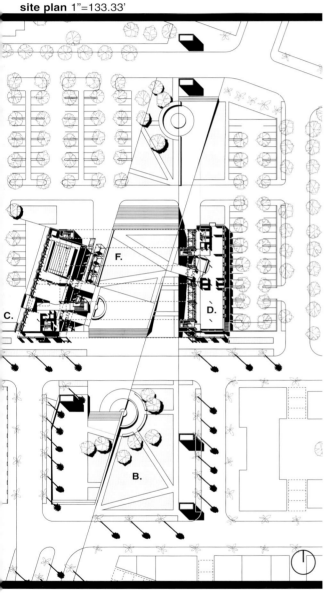

The design includes several features which will help make the most of the limited funds available. Preferring not to waste the city's money on anachronistic decoration, the design's honest, *contemporary* expression of a functional "desert architecture" makes the most "cost effective use of contemporary building technologies and climate-sensitive practices." For the most part a very straightforward, repetitive design, the scheme takes valuable lessons in economy from the commercial construction industry, such as using EIFS, off-the-shelf storefront glazing systems, structurally and spatially efficient light gauge metal framing, etc.; but all are put together in a way that belies their commercial origin. Up to 10,000 SF of future additions can be organically accommodated under the Civic Plaza, saving envelope costs; and because of its layout in discrete building units, the design would be easily phasable. Finally, the Emergency Services program elements are isolated in their own building, allowing the more expensive structure to be minimized.

The civic leaders have indicated a strong desire to upgrade Cathedral City's image, particularly in this part of town—to create a new town center that would encourage "pride and a sense of belonging in the City." As a catalyst for future development in the town center and an example for the form and character of that development, the new Civic Center's positive impact will extend beyond the immediate site. It will be a signal to everyone of the city's sense of its own future and standing in the

architecture apart from normal building. Where architecture must still obey the same physical laws and programmatic or bureaucratic constraints as building, though, myth is much freer to ignore or reconsider the constraints of ordinary narrative. Myths "relate events and states of affairs surpassing the ordinary human world, yet basic to that world; the time in which the related events take place is altogether different from the ordinary historical time of human experience." This freedom in fact becomes an

G. steel canopy
H. sunlight reflector frame
I. sunlight reflector
a. entry to police station
f. down to community development

view from southeast

emblem of mythic discourse and of the provisionality of myth.

10. The most important traditional myths were stories about origins, and their axiomatic character is largely derived from this. Yet, though they are narratives of originary events, such myths are rarely about creation *ex nihilo*. Instead, they describe the foundations of the world in terms of the world as it exists at the time of telling. This unnoticed circularity reinforces the axiomatic self-evidence and usefulness of the myth as a ground. Though a cosmogonic slight of hand, in which the first rabbit pulls itself out of the hat "by transcending the limits of ordinary perception and reason," the myth endows itself with the uncanniness that can be taken as a prompt for unquestionable authority. In this sense, myth is too easy a prey for deconstruction. Yet its propensity for *self*-deconstruction demonstrates a possibly uncomfortable link between deconstruction and myth, forging another bridge

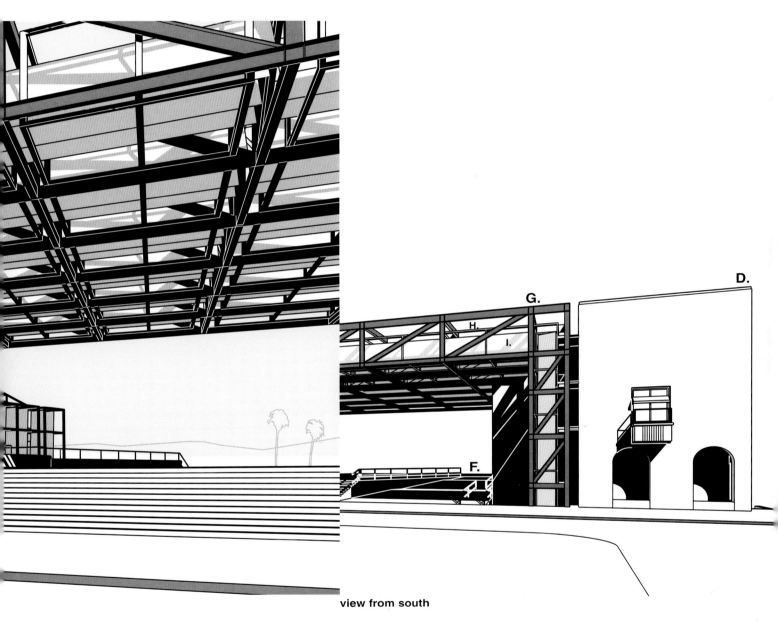

D. police station
F. covered plaza
G. steel canopy
H. sunlight reflector frame
I. sunlight reflector

view from south

between traditional myth and contemporary discourse.
11. A particularly bald example of this is the myth of the "primitive hut," which proposes the unselfconscious, rustic temple-form "hut" as the origin of Architecture. In Laugier's version of this myth, a foundational narrative is offered that circularly presupposes the architectural percipience of which its events relate the birth; he describes the genesis of the "correct" orders in "functional" terms that validate the formal interests he is advancing and rehearse the equation between the two that the myth ostensibly discovers.[3] **EO 5**

12. Many myths contain such etiological passages, but the air of justification that attends the etiological tale's explanation of *why* something occurs is foreign to the myth's axiomatic "claim of truth." This "claim" precedes any question of reasons or justifications. Myths "are accounts with an absolute authority that is implied rather than stated ...."[4] Myth operates more in the descriptive

C. city hall
D. police station
F. covered plaza
G. steel canopy
a. entry to police station

view from northwest

key appropriate to the statement of truths that are given rather than subject to argument. "The descriptive function of myth is linked with the authoritative presentation of facts that transcend ordinary reason and observation." The critique which holds that scientific objectivity is itself motivated, or ideological, and thus provisional, captures the sense of myth proposed here for architecture, in that this provisional basis, however obvious, does not undermine *faith* or belief. The *dignity* of myth, which is one of its more attractive features, derives from this calm assumption of authority; myth does not hawk, or plead for complicity, it accepts it.

13. In contemplating myth's *usefulness* today, its clear historical provenance must be faced. Yet, the fact that the historical tradition of myth has receded deep into the past does not mean that culture is devoid of either stories or belief. Contemporary society may appropriately consider myth relegated to a past period of history and

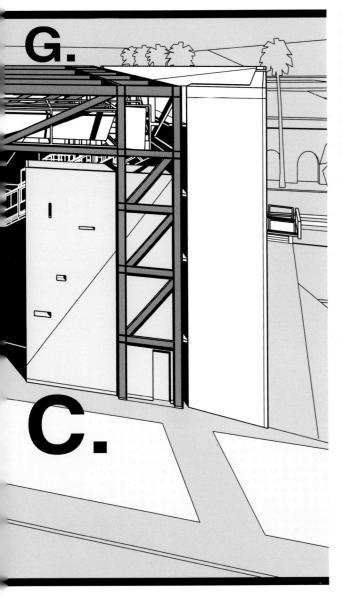

Coachella Valley. If the City wishes to truly distinguish itself from its neighbors, it will choose not to imitate their efforts but to set its own course. Instead of following their nostalgic example of Disneyland-style, cartoon Southwesternism, it will set a *new* example and assert a more honest and responsible standard that looks forward with confidence to the future rather than backward, with longing, to the past.

imagine it has developed beyond that stage, but it still feels as well that it is increasingly a prisoner of ideology, that experience is enframed. Otherwise seen as linked by evolution only, as successive paradigms, and separated by conscious practice, the world of traditional myth and that of science share an axiomatic basis and a "historical" genesis in the same Greek culture. The contemporary world is far more secularized than the world of traditional myth, but the chief agents of this secularization—

C. city hall
D. police station
F. covered plaza
G. steel canopy
a. entry to police station
d. council chamber

transverse section 1"=40.00'

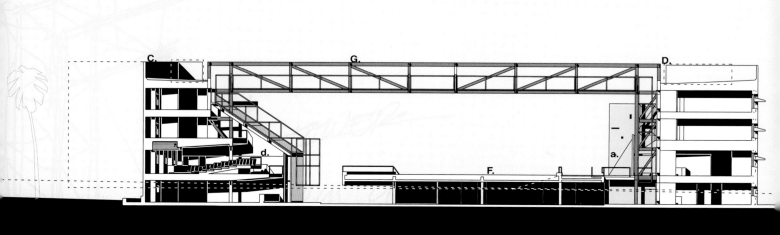

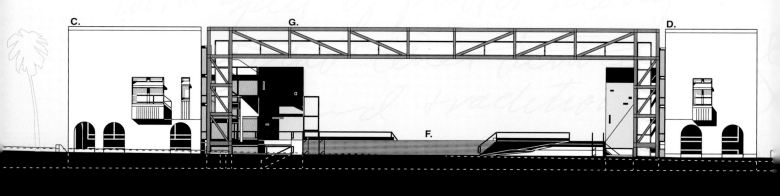

south elevation 1"=40.00'

science and technology—fill much the same role in culture as sources of security that the religiosity of myth fills.
14. With this secularization the transcendence of the mythical account of the world has been replaced with one of immanence. Society has come to take responsibility for the actions of the gods, to see the themes expressed in myth as expressions of deep-seated cultural bias rather than revelation.[5]
15. The mythical forms that are alive as ideology or enframing today are not obvious as mythological, but they are no less affective. In a sense, by its disavowal of the religiosity that highlighted the provisional paradox of fate, the contemporary mythical expression of science is more coercive and its relationship to authority more suspect. Since myth, as ideology, is less expressive than operative, its shape is less clear during the period when it is in force; it is only in history, with the passage of time, or the most careful critical scrutiny, that the perspective

NOB note 5

G. steel canopy
l. sunlight reflectors
a. entry to police station
e. outdoor deck

longitudinal section 1"=40.00'

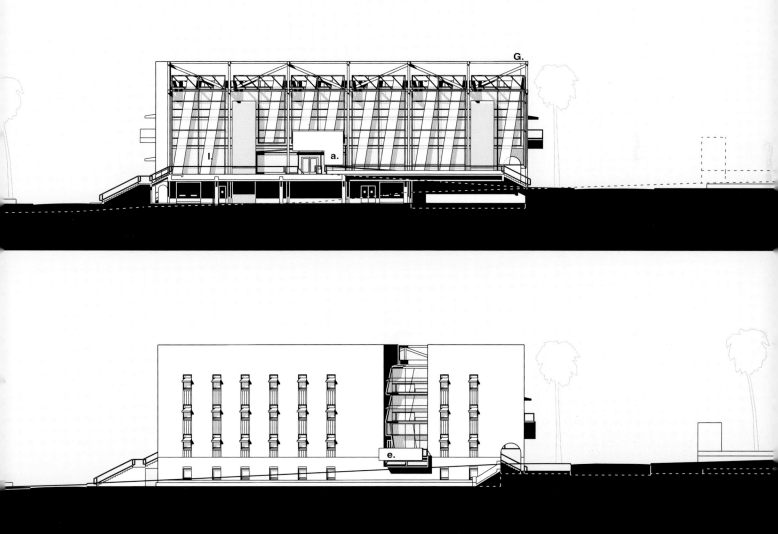

west elevation 1"=40.00'

is gained from which it may be noticed. This is of course because ideology does not declare itself as a mode of discourse, but it is also evidence of myth's unquestionable authority. The presence of such signals the presence of myth—but only when that authority ceases to be unquestionable. Unless it is declared as such, the scrim is only recognized as a scrim when it flutters in a draft. When the scrim is noticed it can be lifted, and what "went without saying" can be articulated.

16. Architecture in fact might be finding itself in this position today. As an institution "traditionally" bolstered by "traditional" myth—myth's most common beneficiary—architecture is no longer able merely to "present" but must begin "to prove itself."[6] As its mythical shape becomes increasingly apparent, its outmoded sources of authority become too visible, and become questionable. The scrim wavers, the emperor catches a draft; complicity can no longer be assumed and its more active nature

C. city hall
D. police station
f. community development
q. booking
r. vehicle search
t. vehicle sallyport
u. dispatch
z. mechanical

basement level plan 1"=53.33'

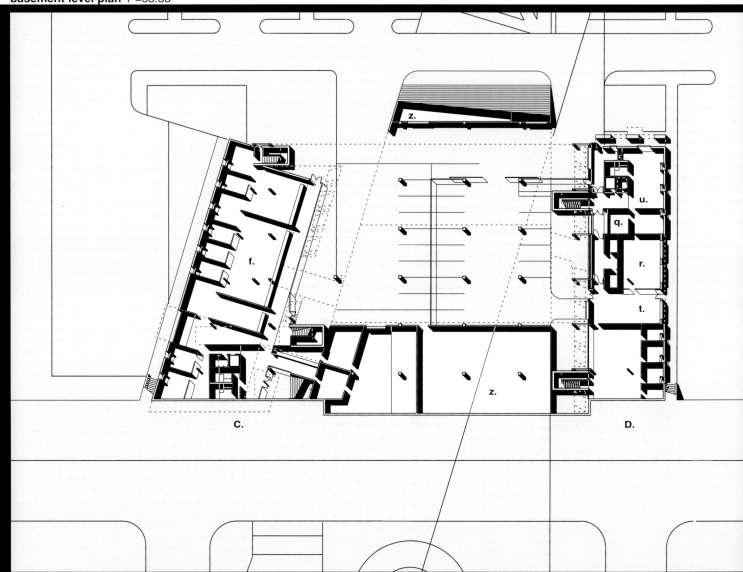

becomes evident. The increasing visibility of theory is evidence of this development. Readership becomes highlighted as authority loses its easy presumption of engagement.

17. As architecture's vulnerability grows it becomes clearer that its relationship to myth conditioned the traditional expectations for it. This relationship can be invoked in understanding that vulnerability and what measures can or should be taken to confront and perhaps redress it. As myth generally is secularized into ideology, and its transcendent authority give way to immanent convictions, its formal characteristics become similarly "lowered." Myth, like architecture, becomes less visible as its form becomes less elevated; but also like architecture its divestiture of sacredness makes it more susceptible to critical scrutiny. The decreasing visibility of myth, which makes it more insidious as it infiltrates the common and everyday, is balanced by an increasing

C. city hall
F. covered plaza
a. entry
b. assembly area
c. lobby
d. council chamber
e. outdoor deck
i. public counter
m. captain
n. lieutenants
o. secreteries/ clerks/ analysts
p. sergeants/ investigators

plaza level plan 1"=53.33'

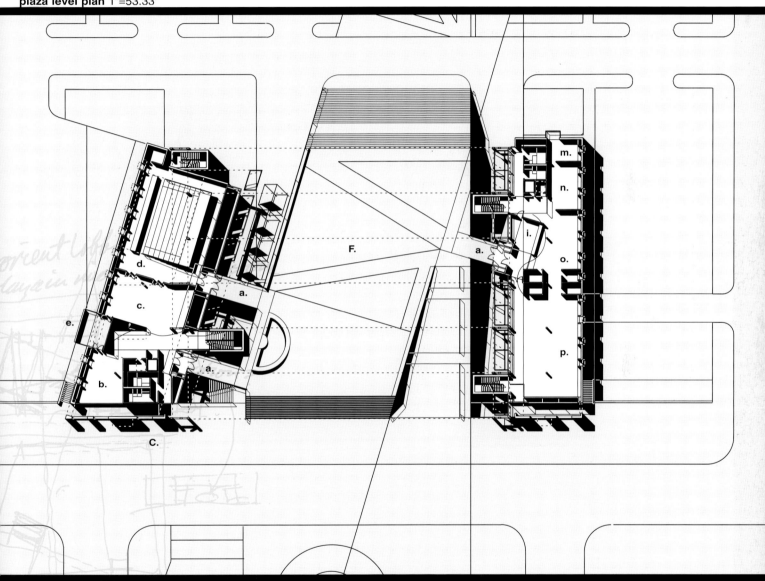

critical awareness of its role as "a type of speech" or "mode of signification, a form."[7]

18. Barthes characterizes myth in its desacralized state as a "second order semiological system,"[8] that "deforms"[9] the meaning of the first order, linguistic, system it appropriates. He emphasizes its instrumental nature *as* an appropriation; the deformation occurs to the meaning by the appropriation of the form, without disturbing the form itself, becoming in this a new sign. Barthes speaks of this as a "deformation," because the second order signification is unintended by the first. The form of the first signifier is "hijacked" by the myth.

19. The appropriative nature of this "bricollage" accounts for the surreal quality of traditional myth as well—its transcendent version of normal human events—by using its common elements as counters or markers in a larger story: the gods are appropriated human types "deformed" into the supernatural; the space of the cos-

C. city hall
D. police station
g. mayor
h. city manager
i. public counter
v. training/ briefing
w. lockers
x. showers

2nd level plan 1"=53.33'

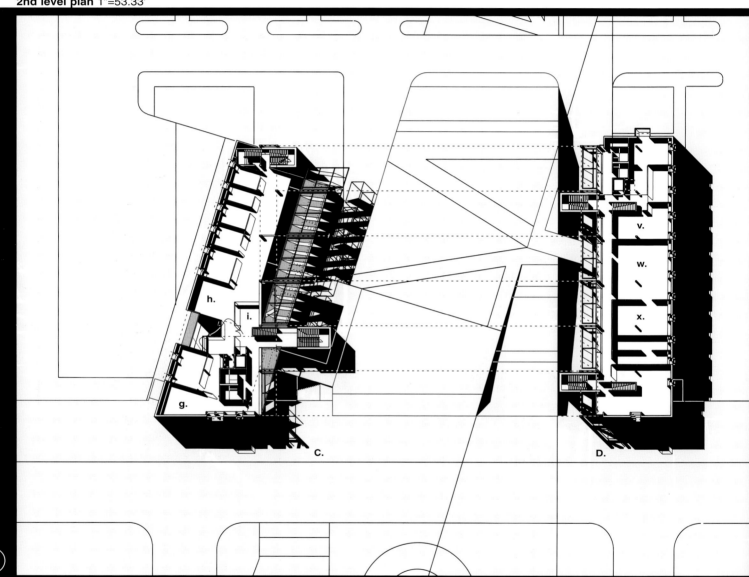

mic events appropriate the environment of daily life, "deformed" to extreme scales or remoteness.

20. Myth is supplementary; as a second order signification the potential for myth is not apparent in the meaning of the appropriated sign. Before it is appropriated the sign is already complete, as the rich product of a differential history; after it is appropriated, and this "history evaporates,"[10] its form is empty and the mythic signified fills it, making it complete again. The appropriation does nothing—the deformation is not formal (here the Boss differs)—but reframes the reading to a different level, or channel, with a different context and different expectations. The logic of supplementarity challenges the indisputability of contemporary myth, though, showing the difference from the traditional. "[A] *complete* image would exclude myth"[11]—except the myth *of* its completeness.

21. Unusually for cultural production, myth is not seen as authored. In the case of traditional myth the author is

C. city hall
D. police station
i. public counter
j. file/ records storage
k. breakroom
l. finance
y. evidence storage

3rd level plan 1"=53.33'

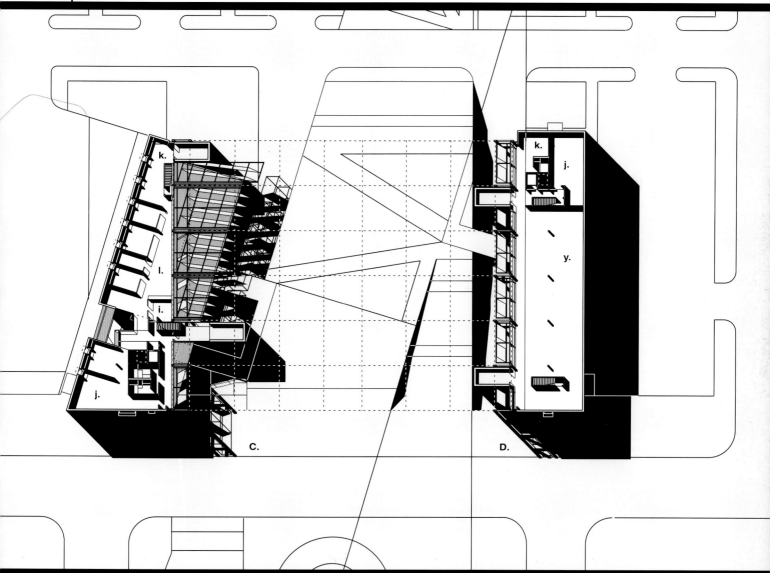

lost in the mists of time; the author of the contemporary myth—usually a publicist or ad agency—intentionally hides behind or within the message. As a result, in both cases, myth appears as an emanation of the culture itself. This is of course appropriate to its sense of unquestionable authority, since it denies a localized *source* that could be regarded objectively or comprehensively and attract question. What arrives "out of thin air" or is "in the air" as the zeitgeist or tradition or trend bears the contradictory weight and force of the whole culture from which it has "sprung"; the work of a single human author, however inspired, can never free itself from the taint of opinion. Yet, myth is never impersonal. On the contrary, "[m]yth has an imperative, button-holing character: ... it is [the viewer] whom it has come to seek. It is turned toward [the viewer], [the viewer is] subjected to its intentional force ...."[12]

22. Contemporary myth retains the indisputability of the

F. covered plaza
I. sunlight reflector

interior view of city council chamber

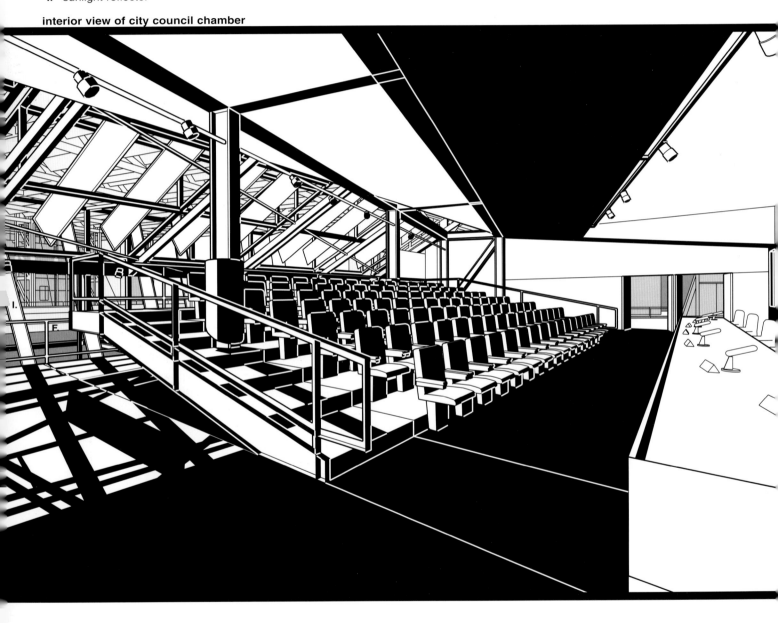

traditional myth, but its authority is devoid of traditional myth's sacred underpinning or external verification. Desacralized, it has become an empty structure that assumes an unquestionability, yet it lacks the religious dimension that would found truth on some final or original revelation, banishing the infinite deferral of doubt. As such, it is available to be filled with mercenary signification. "The mythical signification ... is never arbitrary; it is always in part motivated,"[13] but this motivation does not compromise its assumption of indisputability. On the contrary, it establishes it: "myth is a type of speech defined by its intention ... much more than by its literal sense .... This constituent ambiguity ... appears both like a notification and a statement of fact."[14] For Barthes, myth is "depoliticized speech."[15] On the face of it this would seem to suggest a retreat from the authority presumed by traditional myth. Isn't authority vested politically? Yes, when it is contestable, but myth traditionally assumes

254

Modular Shelters, Stanford University
C96.07/1
Stanford, CA

Client:	Stanford University David Newman, Campus Architect
Architect:	Jones, Partners: Architecture
Site:	Various locations around the extended Stanford campus
Program:	Flexible kiosk prototype capable of being configured to accommodate a variety of programs, including bus shelter, coffee kiosk, bicycle racks, and mechanical screens
Size:	100-1200 ft^2
Systems:	Painted steel sunshade/roof frame with corrugated metal or fiber glass infill, concrete drain pipe columns on cast-in-place concrete spread footings.
Features:	The design renders the classic Stanford/Spanish Colonial/Bay Area Regional Style/Maybeck trellis section in a repeatable, flexible module of steel and concrete, with various attachments to accommodate the range of programs required within the chosen vocabulary inexpensively without sacrificing quality or visual interest.
Cost:	$6000/bay
Completion:	June 1996 (proposal)

The task to design a coffee kiosk is modest, but must immediately bring to mind images of the primitive hut, particularly when the site for the kiosk is so consistently vested in classicism. When that kiosk is to be a prototype for other small structures as well, then the reference to the primitive hut is unavoidable. No other model is possible. This is not to claim, of course, that the primitive hut must be replicated—even its earliest depictions were interpretations of an imagined ideal. There is and never was an actual entity to replicate. So each rediscovery is actually an invention, holding a mirror up to the discoverer. This example is no exception.

The Stanford Utility Kiosk system assembly prototype is an expansive distillation of the architectural elements traditionally elucidated by the primitive hut exercise. It deploys an emphatic, but straightforward, expression to mark space rather than shelter. The actual programmatic requirement for protection from the elements is served by a *secondary* system, as are the more specific requirements that turn the system into, say, a bike rack or bus shelter. The primitive hut demonstrates the essential distance between existence and expression that a project interested in essence must negotiate and record; the kiosk understands this as an exhortation to constrain the excess necessary for expression to the axis of purpose alone.

All programs are accommodated by minimal adaptations of the basic module. The coffee kiosk is the

1. bus shelter
2. bike shelter
3. coffee kiosk
4. mechanical screen

aerial photo

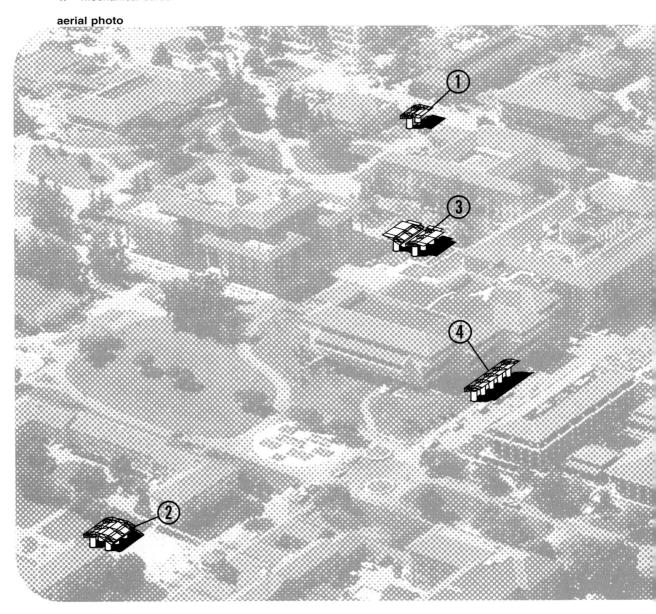

and thus establishes it as an incontestable given; when this given is revelatory that authority sits comfortably, but when the sacred has drained from myth, the indisputability of that authority derives from an intolerable depoliticization: "myth has the task of giving a historical intention a natural justification, and making contingency appear eternal."[16] This state of naturalness is not the Nature of ultimate otherness; it is the nature of the unconsidered, the obvious, the easy: second nature. Indisputable as "a statement of fact," that "*goes without saying*" it is depoliticized since it "abolishes the complexity of human acts" and creates "a world which is without contradictions because it is without depth."[17]

23. Barthes' myth shows its kinship to Heidegger's enframing here. "The very end of myths is to immobilize the world: they must suggest and mimic a universal order which has fixated once and for all the hierarchy of possessions." An experience organized into a "hierarchy

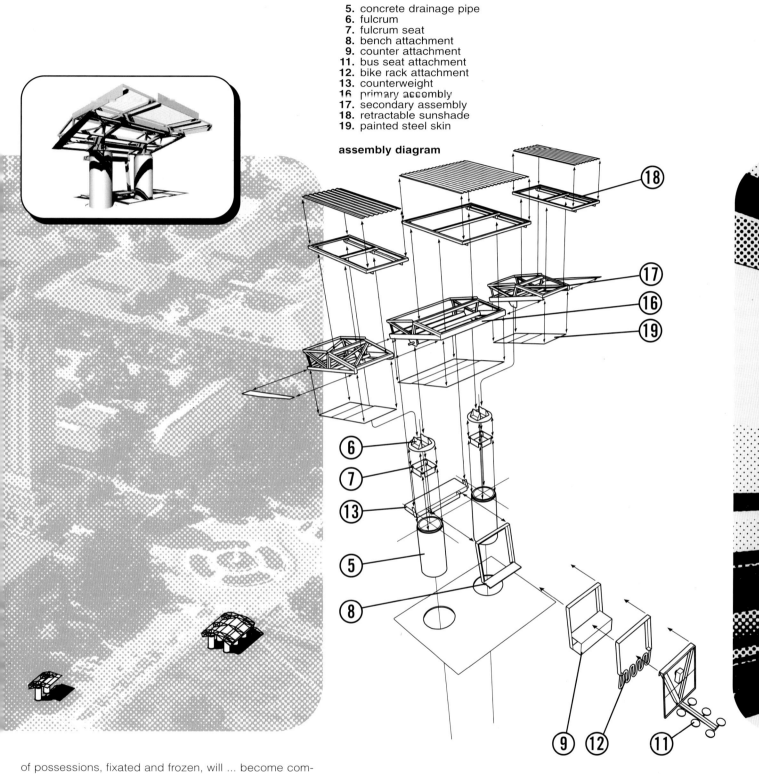

5. concrete drainage pipe
6. fulcrum
7. fulcrum seat
8. bench attachment
9. counter attachment
11. bus seat attachment
12. bike rack attachment
13. counterweight
16. primary assembly
17. secondary assembly
18. retractable sunshade
19. painted steel skin

assembly diagram

of possessions, fixated and frozen, will ... become computable" and thus stand in reserve. Barthes, prefiguring Deleuze in the way that Heidegger so clearly pre-figures Derrida, suggests that the effect is to stop the uncontrollable "becoming" of the world, its spontaneous presencing, and stop "its transformation, its flight towards other forms of existence," becoming "in the fullest sense a prohibition for man against inventing himself."[18]

24. In terms reminiscent of Heidegger's own admission

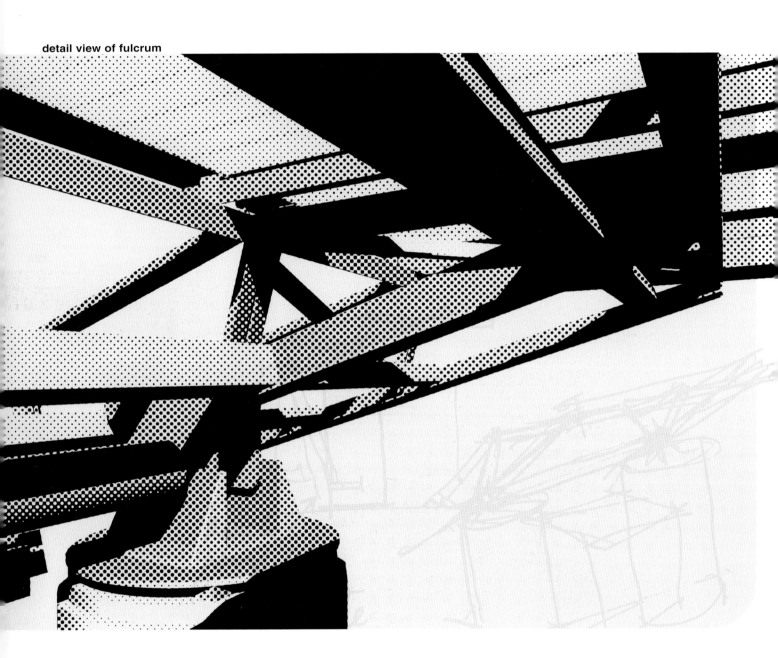

detail view of fulcrum

of the inescapability of technology—as the danger, and its simultaneous possible existence as the saving power—Barthes admits myth coincides with the "objective" existence of that which it appropriates and mythifies. As he puts it, for example, "Wine is objectively good, and *at the same time*, the goodness of wine is a myth: here is the aporia."[19] **DR 6** He presents, like Heidegger, a loose prescription for answering the critique by navigating the space opened up in the aporia. Otherwise society is trapped between the choice to posit "a reality which is entirely permeable to history, and ideologize; or, conversely, to posit a reality which is *ultimately*, irreducible, and, ... poetize." Neither of these approaches alone can answer myth's challenge. Rather, he prescribes "a reconciliation between reality and men, between description and explanation, between object and knowledge." Like Heidegger, who says that the saving power cannot be forced, Barthes assumes society must wait for this recon-

5. concrete drainage pipe
6. fulcrum
7. fulcrum baseplate
13. counterweight
18. retractable sunshade

detail view of assembly

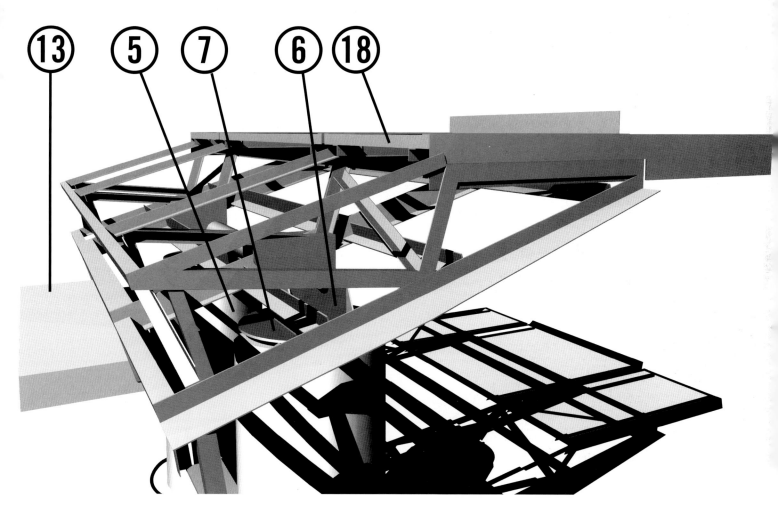

ciliation to come to pass, believing that as humanity vacillates "between the object and its demystification, powerless to render its wholeness ... we are condemned for some time yet always to speak *excessively* about reality."[20]

25. Barthes describes the distance between the metalinguistic myth and the sign it appropriates in instrumental terms. He contrasts myth with the more direct signification of "operational language," spoken by "man as a producer, ... transitively linked to its object."[21] This is the language of direct engagement, the language of action rather than representation: "political speech" spoken "in order to transform reality." It is the difference between speaking "about" the (object) and "acting" it.[22] It is the space, then, where operational experience is opposed to alienation.[23] **NOB 24**

26. Barthes states that revolutionary speech, by its

259

5. concrete drainage pipe
11. bus seat attachment
13. counterweight
18. retractable sunshade
21. windscreen/ display case

bus shelter plan 1"=10.00'

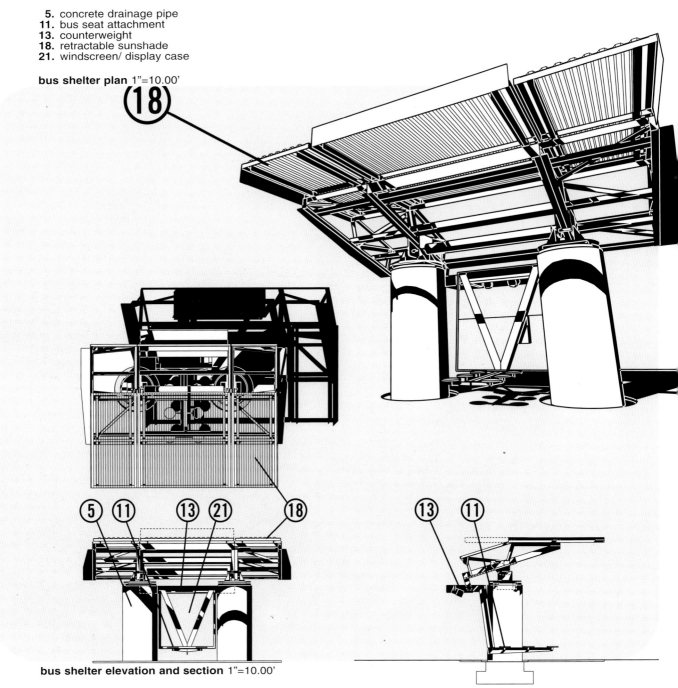

bus shelter elevation and section 1"=10.00'

operational political intentionality, can "defeat" myth. His description of how revolutionary speech "acts" in the world seems reminiscent of Heidegger's description of the revealing of techne, and thus interesting for its possible relation to the saving power: revolutionary language is the language "of man as a producer: whenever man speaks in order to transform reality, and no longer to transform it as an image, whenever he links his language to the making of things ... myth is impossible."[24]

27. The difference between the "language object" deployed by "man as a producer" and "meta-language" is described by Barthes as favoring a level of engagement of reality that parallels Heidegger's discussion of the Being of Equipment:

> If I am a woodcutter and I am led to name the tree which I am felling, whatever the form of my sentence, I 'speak the tree,' I do not speak about it. This means that my language is opera-

6. fulcrum
11. bus seat attachment
18. retractable sunshade
21. windscreen/ display case

bus shelter perspective view

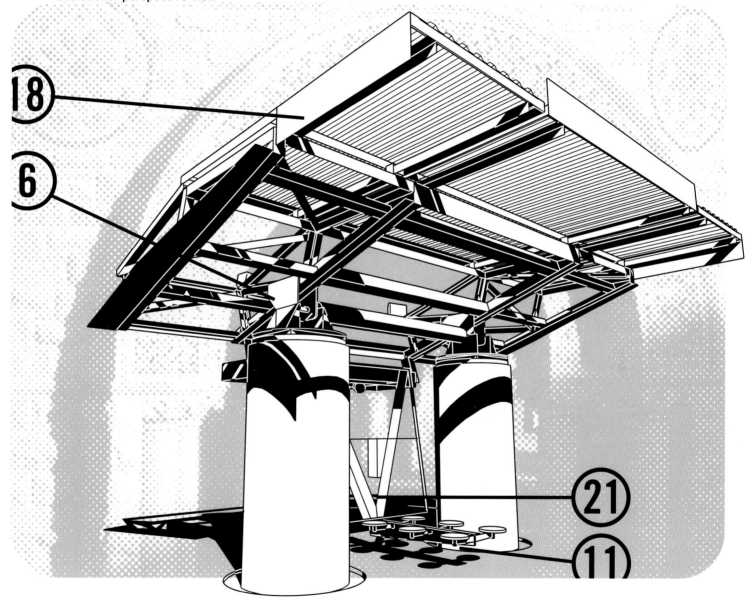

tional, transitively linked to its object; between the tree and myself, there is nothing but my labor, that is to say, an action. This is a political language: it represents Nature for me only inasmuch as I am going to transform it, it is a language thanks to which I '*act the object*'; the tree is not an image for me, it is simply the meaning of my action.[25]

28. It might seem that Heidegger would consider this "transformative" activity as a "challenging forth" and hopelessly enframed: this tree is obviously standing in reserve. Yet, as his discussion of the peasant's shoes and the Being of equipment shows, he saw a crucial difference between the direct engagement of the worker in securing a livelihood and the systemization of labor, that, like Barthes, paralleled Marx's description of alienation. This double standard has also been held against him as evidence of his nostalgia.

12. bike rack attachment

bike shelter perspective view

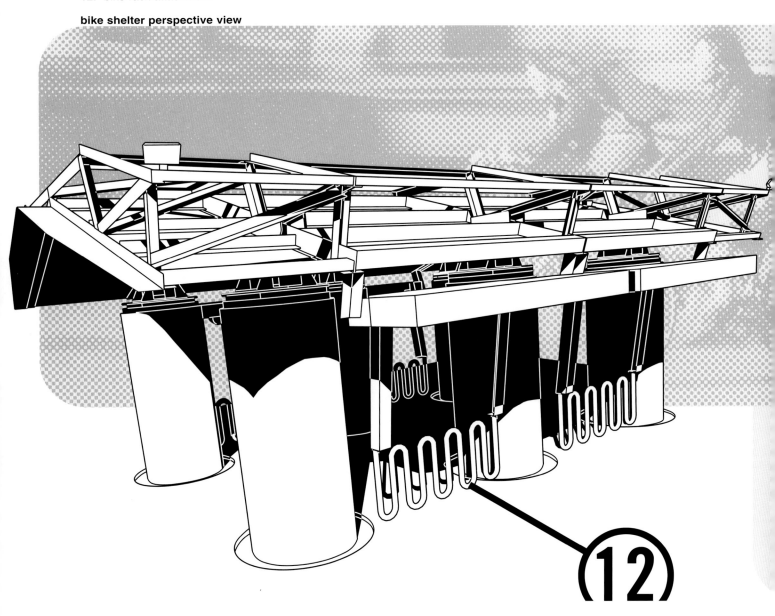

29. Since Barthes wrote in 1956, there has been a vast increase in the apparent propensity to mythify experience. With the steady growth and then literal explosion of **NIRM 3** mediation produced by the electronic revolution, the pervasiveness and influence of what Barthes called myth has grown in scope and sophistication to a degree probably unimaginable by him. It is a mark of the present assimilation of this that not only can far worse be imagined, but it can be sought. The distance from "Leave It to Beaver" on the small oval screen in the family room, to "Beavis and Butthead" on the jumbotron by satellite in Times Square is great: it may describe the possibility of myth's harboring its own "saving power." It has perhaps come to that point when mythification itself can be taken as an operational language. "Myth is a *value*, truth is no guarantee for it ...."[26] When the hyperreal has been actualized "we are condemned to speak excessively about reality" because reality is excessive.[27]

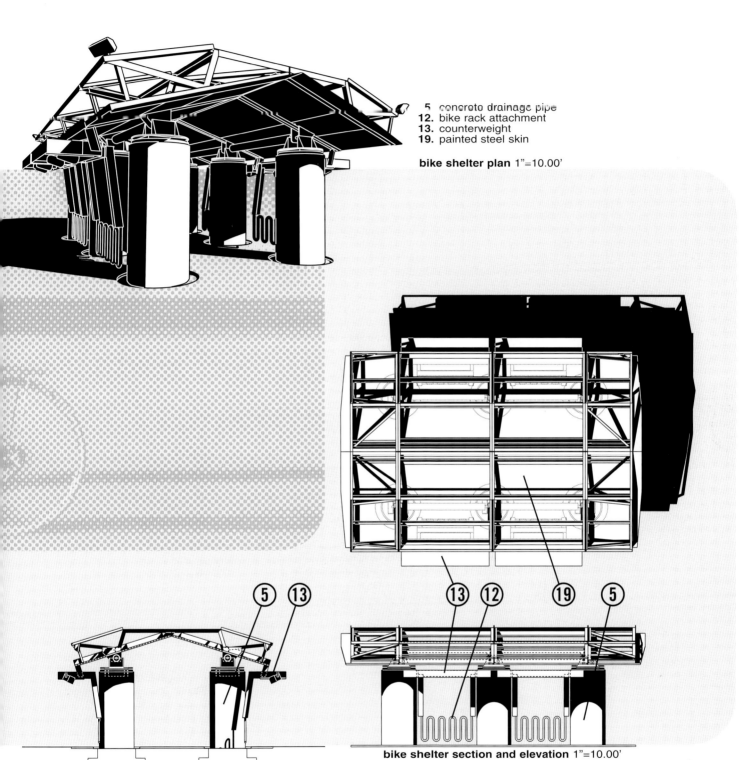

5. concrete drainage pipe
12. bike rack attachment
13. counterweight
19. painted steel skin

bike shelter plan 1"=10.00'

bike shelter section and elevation 1"=10.00'

30. Though by myth he means something different than the traditional stories about the gods, and it might seem that to link the two is to misread him completely, Barthes has chosen this name deliberately. Certainly the two concepts appear unconnected, but it is not difficult to understand their relationship in light of the secular evolution undergone by traditional myth in more recent history. Shorn of the aura originally cast by its sacredness, that shone equally on its function and form, the myth retains

5. concrete drainage pipe
9. counter attachment
18. retractable sunshade
20. storage

coffee kiosk plan 1"=10.00'

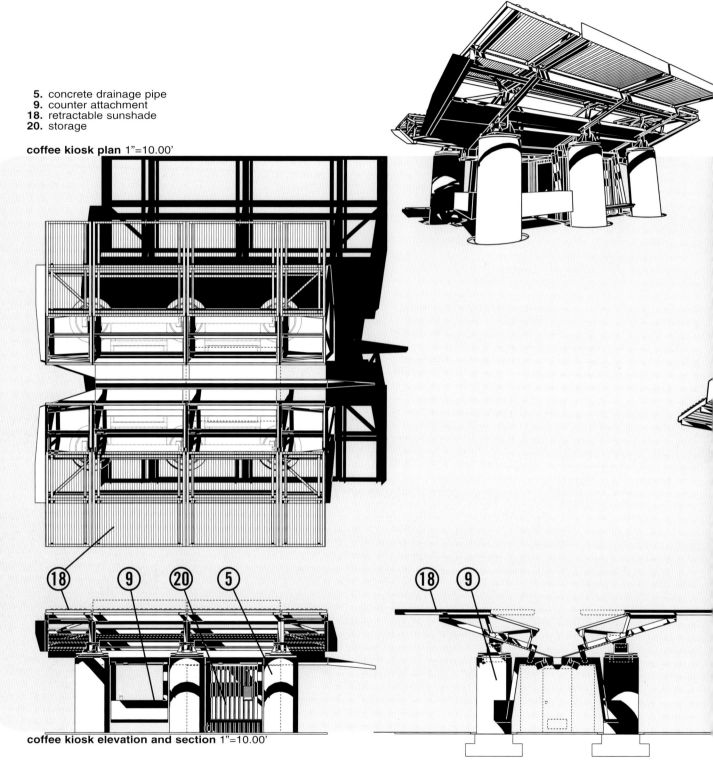

coffee kiosk elevation and section 1"=10.00'

its structure. This is what Barthes addresses in the concept "myth." It is this structure itself, however impoverished the story it now frames, that carries still the genes for transcendence; Barthes' enumeration of its characteristics highlights the points of continuity between the two while describing a contemporary concept that seems at first glance extremely remote from its traditional ancestor.

31. If humanity is going to tell itself stories, they might as well be whoppers. Barthes approaches this tradition after it seems to be exhausted, after myth has been normalized into mere fiction and no one bothers to tell tall ones anymore. Yet myth can rediscover its annunciatory role today, without losing the critical awareness Barthes has contributed.

32. Myth, presented as such, can tell stories that need to be heard without forcing anyone to listen or agree. By its very, proclaimed, artificiality the myth may invest efforts with an authority that is less repressive, less sinis-

8. bench attachment
9. counter attachment
20. storage

coffee kiosk perspective view

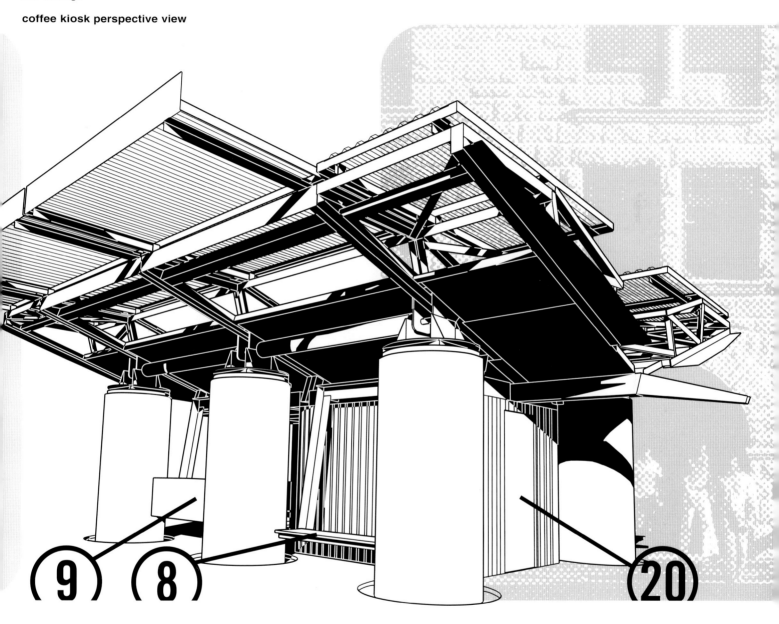

ter because its provisionality is so baldly apparent. It cannot dominate in its authoritarianism, nor can it repress in its universalism, because the belief it inspires is consensual: not the tyranny of divine revelation, or of science, but the reader's democracy of poetry, of imagination individually determined and broadly shared. Society does not require, proscribe, declare, or legislate in this voice: it sings, it tells stories.[28]

Myth: Bossness
33. Very simply, bossness is the myth of the machine. If the boss can be proposed as the "saving power," it also can be understood as the place where the ancient, engaged authority of myth finds a valid presence in contemporary enframed, mythified society as operational or instrumental meta-language. As Barthes analyzes myth in its contemporary context, he describes something like the boss object's rela-

5. concrete drainage pipe
10. corrugated steel screen attachment
13. counterweight

mechanical screen plan 1"=10.00'

mechanical screen elevation and section 1"=10.00'

tion to the run-of-the-mill within its own context of desacralized architectural form. The boss runs the mill. Bossness hovers over the object as a sense of intentionality specifically transcendent of its program. The boss object, giving itself over to expression of a non-subjective intentionality determined in relation to program and context, seems auto-generative; as myth is an emanation of a culture, the boss object is seen as an emanation of the micro-society of that program and context. It is engaged by the reader, similarly related to that programmed context, directly, in itself, without referring as a middle term to an author's intentionality. This of course emphasizes the reader's role as witness and responsible interlocutor. As a second order signification, the boss directs the reading to that interpretive level that makes it mythic; it frames the otherwise adequate object in a way that makes that adequacy a measure,

10. corrugated steel screen attachment

mechanical screen perspective view

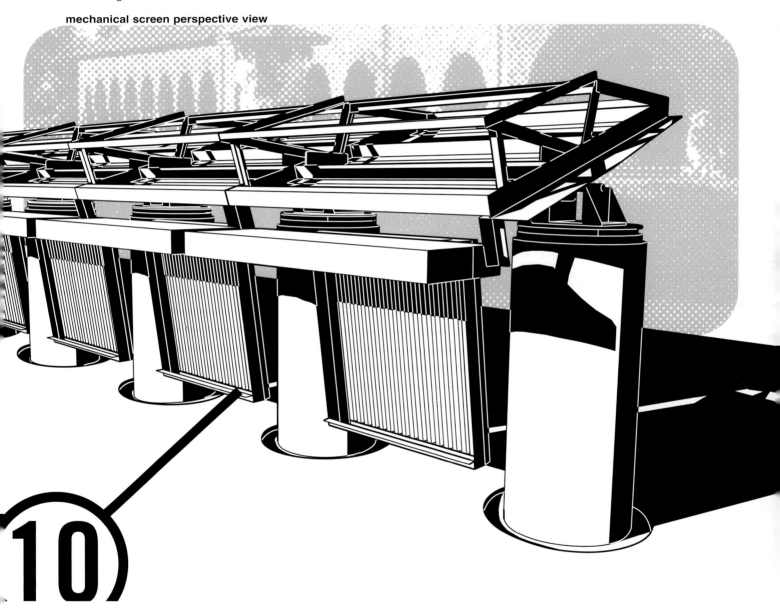

and by so doing encourages a production, and subsequent reading, that focuses on and highlights that adequacy as a value and a guide. Like myth, the boss is appropriative, resulting from a process of bricollage; often its distinctive forms are souped-up versions of otherwise mundane objects gathered together into a new, charged assembly. Or they may appropriate the form of the strife they answer through inflection. Some "deformation" occurs through this appropriation itself, but the greater presence of will, corresponding to the supernaturally induced authority of the myth, is invested in the object by the deformation occurring in the souping process or inflection—declaring the frame that gathers the effects. In contrast to myth, this process is a *real* de-formation, in that the form itself changes, while the meaning is not so much changed as enhanced.

34. The boss object stands out from the run of the

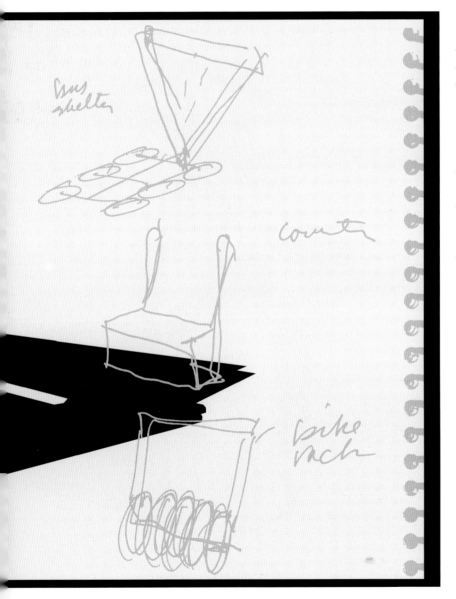

ur-model for the system, though it sports the inverted roof configuration; it is particularized by the addition of bench and counter elements, and the coffee vendor's containerized secure production module. The bicycle rack shelter is arranged by reversing the orientation of the coffee kiosk's bays, to give the more classic—but more frumpy—pitched roof profile of the standard primitive hut; it is completed by the addition of the bike racks themselves between the columns. The bus shelter is assembled from a linear colonnade of modules, facing the street, with tractor seat benches slung in each bay. Finally, the screen wall replaces the bus shelter's benches with solid vertical panels to block the view through the columns.

mill, as Architecture does from building, and as the signification of a "meta-language" differs from the "language object." The boss object is also greatly concerned with the operational matters, with the production and transformation of reality that Barthes ascribes to non-mythic speech. Yet, the boss remains mythic because of its meta-linguistic character. Indeed, it is precisely the mythic form of Barthes's anti-mythic transformative language. Since it

The Fork[1]

1. The afternoon had long outlasted the moment. There were bottles and glasses everywhere. They would of course be counted at the end; until then they made a cityscape among the ashtrays and salt and pepper. Jeanneret had twice excused himself to piss, and as far as he could tell—there was only one toilet shared by both sexes—the stranger had yet to relieve himself. Jeanneret wasn't sure whether he was impressed or disturbed by this.

2. The incongruity of seeing Pernod sipped through a straw was gradually eased by the same haze that made Jeanneret more susceptible to the stranger's arguments. Occasionally the stranger also inhaled from an oxygen bottle for his asthma. In this and other ways the stranger tested Jeanneret's credulity.

3. As the afternoon wore on the stranger offered less of a conversation or even an argument, than a presentation. Though at first Jeanneret contested the stranger's points with his usual enthusiasm, his objections became fewer and fewer as the stranger consistently prevailed. Jeanneret was not angered, though; he had ceased to wonder at this as well.

4. The stranger was telling him that L'Eplattenier's sense of Nature was perhaps dated, that it was too timid an appropriation, given the developing character of the age. He seemed to know Jeanneret's heart, speaking of things that Jeanneret had not yet truly admitted to himself. Before moving to Paris, Jeanneret had been very certain that his work with L'Eplattenier would lead to great things, that their approach to the Natural was a perfect compromise between the craftsman tradition and the claims of industry. It had seemed certain that this elegant mediation would propel him to great success—had it not already won him and his classmates some commissions in the Jura before even finishing his studies? But Paris changes things, and he was less certain these days. Though he would not admit it, or even know it, he did not miss the upland forests or open spaces of his home. It was not so much that he had decided anything about this, but that he was engaged now on other projects. Still, this history provided an inertia that offered some resistance to the stranger's words, quite apart from any real volition Jeanneret might have felt.

5. The stranger was not interested in demeaning either Jeanneret or L'Eplattenier though. The stranger said, without exasperation: You are an ambitious man. Surely it is clear by now that this pine cone exercise of yours is a cul-de-sac—inhale—especially in Paris. I grant that it may have a certain value in the Jura, but I would hazard that it is primarily an issue of familiarity. Though it is perhaps forever condemned to recognize Nature as its final source, Architecture cannot really come of this today. But I think you know this.

6. He asked: certainly the history of our contract with Nature is lengthy—inhale—but why is today so conscious of itself as different? He gestured skyward. I will tell you, though it is obvious: to take but one example, by no means even the greatest, after millennia of the silliest envy of birds, man himself can now fly! Man has surpassed Nature! He has looked through the mysteries veiled by its appearance. He has made its secrets his. But what could this wonder flight mean for architecture? How is architecture to hold its head against such achievement? Buildings certainly are not likely to fly, are they? He smiled, as if at the folly of this, as if at some pri-

---

[1] First published in slightly different form called "Jeanneret" in ZYZZYVA, 1992.

vate joke with an unpleasant punch line, but Jeanneret thought: why not? Had not flight itself literally burst into existence? The dream might have existed for millennia, but the aeroplane was seemingly invented overnight. If you thought about it, it was really only a matter of degree .... The stranger hurriedly continued, cutting this thought short: he was interested in something else, something more subtle: the forces hidden behind the appearance.

7. Abstraction, wheezed the stranger, penetrated Nature's veil. These aeroplanes go beyond what you call abstraction in your pine cone geometry games and find an essence that is more than formal: it is useful. Abstraction has subjugated these forces for man. The soul of abstraction is efficiency; abstraction makes efficiency apparent. Efficiency is the new god who would reverse the insufferable excesses of the nineteenth century. Why do aeroplanes speak to the heart? Because they speak directly without conventions: the forces of Nature that hold them aloft have no need of elaboration, of decoration, or the ornamentation of style. It is clear to anyone that such embellishment is useless to the aeroplane and would weigh it down as surely as it suffocates architecture itself. Architecture could express this truth, but only if it understood that expression would have to come from stripping away the inessential.

8. Moreover, through the efficiency of mass production, which has so improved our daily life, the artifacts we make have become undeniably cleaner, purer, and less encumbered with the supplementary concerns of ornamentation—of course much more could still be done in this regard; there is a fellow in Germany, in fact, but never mind—inhale—didn't efficiency demand the greatest place for purpose and function? The stranger waved his straw. Wouldn't the architect who could make the world see this truth make a great contribution?

9. Jeanneret wondered aloud at this point why the stranger was telling him all this—particularly since, as the stranger had so carefully pointed out, Jeanneret's own work was of such a different character. The stranger shrugged: architecture seemed to be ripe for a demonstration; these were momentous times; but, alas, he himself was not an architect. Jeanneret was not in fact surprised by this admission; the stranger spoke like a critic whose only contact with his subject was through books or photographs. Perhaps it was his peculiar American accent; perhaps it was the straw he waived for emphasis. But, truly, it was not important. Jeanneret did not ask the obvious question. The stranger confidently predicted that Jeanneret would someday be a very famous and influential architect. He was content that Jeanneret would listen to his ideas. Perhaps they could be useful to him.

10. Then the stranger said: I would like you to close your eyes to better imagine what could be. Clear your mind of these romantic images of pine-cone chalets, and picture instead the possibilities of abstraction and efficiency: a city of pure prisms and crystalline towers that scrape the very sky. Why not? Imagine wide, orderly boulevards that direct the traffic through the city at dizzying speeds without chaos. It is a boldly efficient, clean city, well lit, radiant even, unblemished by history, untroubled by decoration: the essence of the urban. Jeanneret closed his eyes. He was unaccustomed to such images, or such provocative words. Yet, they came easily to mind, and in his mind's eye, this city seemed even more magnificent than the stranger described, more cool and aloof, more positively sterile in its perfection. Not a blade of grass (had the stranger mentioned grass?) in its wide

parks was out of place. The brilliant glass-and-iron towers rose out of the parks (where did they come from?) right through the clouds, and the ribbons of super highways wove through the towers with an expertly choreographed grace. Though this vision had no source in his previous experience, Jeanneret accepted it. He drove the boulevards and walked the parks. He rode the elevators (?!) to impossible heights where he danced with the aeroplanes outside.

11. He opened his eyes, and looked across the square: the city he saw before him mocked this vision. It was tawdry. The shadows cast by the buildings were not magnificent, they were just soot and grime; the traffic was just noisy, smelly chaos. The sense of history that had once so ennobled these old stones now seemed like decay and rot. For the first time he felt he really saw the city, and it was painful to behold. He shut his eyes, seeking again the austere clarity of the abstract city.

12. The stranger cleared his throat, and Jeanneret looked up. Good, the stranger said, keep that other eye closed and consider this. He held up a fork, which was elaborately carved, and waved it slowly before Jeanneret's face. In the same way of thinking, the stranger said, consider not only the abstraction of the forms, but that of the space itself that hosts them. Consider not only the logic of that abstraction, but the space of that logic. This vision of the city is not picturesque. It occupies a space of the mind. The aeroplane speaks to the heart; it is new and its achievement is great. The heart swells with pride and sense of freedom. But you, we, will get over that in time, just as we assimilated the horse and train—they are mere mechanisms for traversing space. But you are an architect—you *make* space. And space is eternal—inhale. Aeroplanes will come and go, like man, and they will evolve so that surely man will look back on these first efforts and wonder nostalgically that he could have been so clumsy once. Yes, of course, he held up his hand, this must seem absurd now, in the flush of discovery, but ... he lowered his voice and leaned forward, that is precisely the point: to discover space is perhaps not as immediately exciting, because it has always been there, but it lasts forever, as you imagine it, unspoiled by progress. The stranger sat back, as if saying: there, you have it. The abstract city is magnificent, but the abstract space is where you will discover it. Consider this, and watch it lose its cruder dimensions.

13. All this while Jeanneret had stared with his one eye at the fork, at the space between the tines, and now he noticed, yes, that he saw it as the stranger described: no longer subject to the depth of stereoptical space, it registered more directly in the logical space of the mind, where it was flattened into a purer expression of the fork's essence. In fact, he could only think of it in those terms now: as essential. The other dimensions that sprang back into experience when he opened his other eye seemed to diminish the object, to make it less pure.

14. He closed his eye again, and the object reverted to its typological state. Jeanneret did this several more times, first shutting one eye and then the other until he lost track and began to see the object-type presence whether he closed an eye or not. And when he finally looked up, remembering where he was, he noticed that the cafe exhibited this same clarity: the bottles and glasses on the tables had resolved themselves into types and the earlier tumult was replaced by a supernumerary understanding. In stripping away the messy third dimension it all seemed to make much more sense. The

stranger seemed to sense some change had occurred, and he smiled.

15.   As if just noticing the time, the stranger checked his watch and stood, waving Jeanneret back into his chair. Apparently, there was a train he must catch. He was very sorry, but he would have to leave in haste. He could see that Jeanneret appreciated these ideas—they were significantly no longer his—and he hoped that Jeanneret would make good use of them. He laid an absolutely crisp 100-franc note on the table, which was far too much, even though he had tested the cafe's curiosity, but then again he was an American, and did not appear to lack for funds. Jeanneret was certain somehow that he would not see him again. They wished each other well; Jeanneret was already thinking of designs and plans and papers. The stranger crossed the street and entered a portable toilet that Jeanneret had not noticed before. At least the fellow was human after all, he thought. Jeanneret turned back to the table and pulled out his notebook. He scribbled furiously for an hour. When he finally left for home he did not notice that the toilet was no longer there.

Donner Lake Cabin
P96.07/1 #
Donner Lake, CA

Client:	The Loss Family
Architect:	Jones, Partners: Architecture with Mattingly I Thaler Architects
Site:	Two acres of sloping forest land at the end of a cul-de-sac on the north shore of Donner Lake
Program:	Two alternates for small family, year-round vacation residence and garage
Size:	2500 ft^2
Systems:	Weathering steel truss or light gauge steel framing with steel storefront glazing and corrugated metal panel or CHB enclosure, concrete pier and grade beam foundations.
Features:	These cabin designs make a straight-forward, elemental statement of contemporary appropriateness in the natural high Sierra setting, using exposed real materials and simple forms everywhere; the two schemes demonstrate different approaches to the same basic diagram issued by the client; each alternate includes a second level exterior entry for access during periods of heavy snow.
Cost:	$.4 million
Completion:	October 1996 (proposal)

A Bay Area couple now living in the Far East will build a vacation house at Donner Lake, for themselves and their children still living in the Bay Area. The parents anticipate returning to Northern California twice a year for family get-togethers: once in the winter for skiing, and once in the summer for water sports. During the remainder of the year the house will be available for the children's use or may be rented out to other vacationers.

The heavily wooded, two-acre site is combined from two separate lots. It slopes generally down to the south, toward the lake and distant views. The two lots that make up the site vary dramatically in size and amenity—one is a large, interior lot with no auto access but tremendous views, and the other is a small subdivision lot at the end of a crowded cul-de-sac, without view or character. By combining these lots the weakness of the one is compensated by the strength of the other: access to the prime building site is provided from the cul-de-sac, via the undistinguished lot, where autos will remain, under a canopy. A walkway will extend from this point to the interior lot and building site. Though neither site is truly secluded or remote, these measures will promote a greater sense of isolation and exclusiveness.

The architects were asked to prepare alternate schemes for this site from the same basic diagram supplied by the client. This diagram included a large living space combining living, dining and den and a separate bedroom wing.

14. master bedroom
23. snow stair

view from southwest

⑭

celebrates the transformation as well as the object of that transformative activity, it remains still political in its own right.

35. The boss object satisfies the viewer's natural disposition toward operational language; viewers are always potential doers, and the boss object draws on this for its engageability. The boss object is first a thing, a watchamacallit, doohicky, thingamajig, thingamabob, doofer, gizmo, or widget. The watchamacallit becomes boss when, or if, it engages the viewer sufficiently to seek or assign a permanent name. At that point it has elicited the viewer's respect. There are stages to this process. The watchamacallit starts from further behind, for example, than the thingamajig or gizmo, which are already announcing their instrumental nature, and being acknowledged for this.

36. The *constructed* expansion to these terms from

The two resulting schemes explore different adaptations of the basic diagram to the site. The client's initial sketch presumed a flat site, but the actual site conditions presented an opportunity to rethink the required programmatic separation vertically. Consequently, the two schemes vary the distribution of the program by level. This has a corresponding effect on the amount of site coverage, the arrival and entry sequence and connections to the site.

Scheme # concentrates the program into two stacked rectangular volumes; the upper volume, housing the living space, is slid off the center of the lower volume and rotated to face the view. Decks are provided by a third gasket-type system, introduced to mediate between the volumes, which also sponsors the inter-communicating stairs. Within the space resulting in section from this move is located a thermal storage plenum, fed conductively by air from the two fireplaces. The upper volume is nested within a massive weathering steel truss-frame, supported on four columns rising up through the lower volume, and it cantilevers out over the site on both ends as it swings free from the earth-hugging lower mass to face the view.

Scheme * fits the program into two linear, single story, steel-framed and-clad volumes, arranged along the principal topographic axes of the site. In this case the living spaces occupy the lower volume, which faces the principal view. The resulting stepped-chevron form produces a large outdoor

the simple catch-all word "thing," traces some of the distance between regular stuff and boss stuff—it indicates the space of potential will, where regular stuff "stores" the capacity to become boss. When familiarity is still balanced with strangeness, and the thingamajig speaks in advance of its name, then it is being experienced, directly, on its terms. The limits of enframing any myth are tested in the direct engagement of the unsuspected capacity of stuff to become

1. cabin
2. covered carport

site plan 1"=80.00'

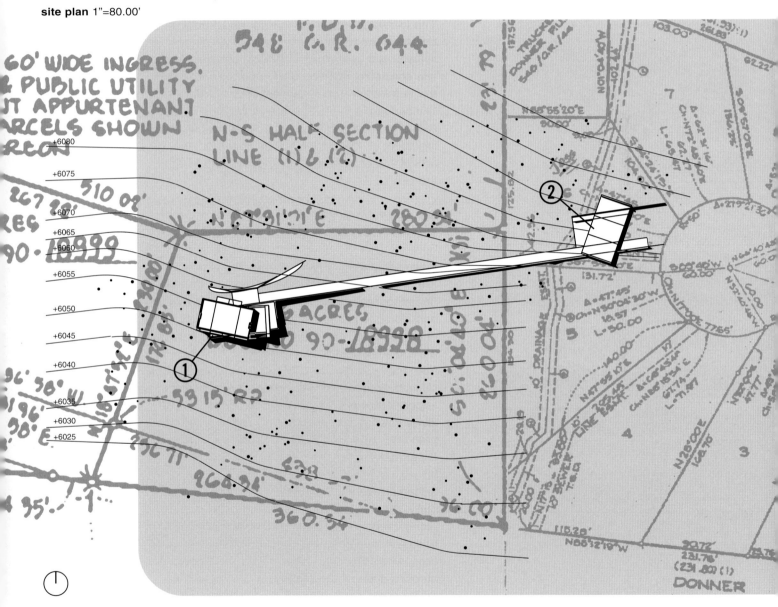

a "language object," and boss.

1 Kees W. Bolle, "Myth and Mythology," *New Encyclopaedia Britannica: Macropaedia*, 1984 ed., 793-804; all unreferenced quotes in this section are taken from this source.
2 François Lyotard, *The Postmodern Condition*
3 **Either/ORigins**[a]

1. When we want to know the absolute truth about something, why it is, the way it is, we go to the beginning, the source, or the cause, and understand the present situation of the thing as a development from that cause. The idea of origin expresses the perfect knowledge of a thing within a reality that is inescapably historical. This knowledge is perfect because it is temporally entire. In fact, the idea of origin is the limit with which the mind encompasses the infinitude of time. If time and space are the frames of our existence/experience as

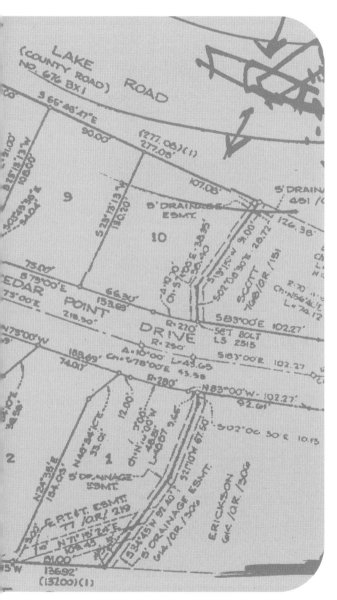

deck on the roof of the lower volume. Where the two bars overlap at the corner, a double-height volume is created; here vertical circulation and a hearth are accommodated. A mechanical room and storage area is provided in the space below the lower level.

Though this project falls within the "cabin" typology, both schemes reject the traditional cabin form, as well as its contemporary 'A' frame expression. The traditional cabin's shape evolved for the most part in response to heavy snow loads; the characteristic steeply pitched roof highlights the structural limitations of wood construction and traditional building technologies. A cabin today need not be constrained by such limitations. These two schemes make this clear. By embracing the economical steel construction practices perfected in the industrial building industry, they are able to use the snow, as a heavy insulating blanket, rather than lose it.

The detailing that was developed to support the steel building/construction industry is both mature and flexible. We believe that the forms resulting from a straight-forward application of this practice exhibit the same integrity and appropriateness on the site as the trees and rocks themselves. Like these natural elements, the steel building of today can be considered the end product of a long, evolutionary history of painstaking refinement. As Corbu described in *Vers Une Architecture* or Mies elaborated in his Chicago work, the goal, and result, of such a process is a naturalness and ease that

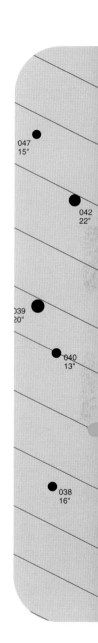

Kant claimed, then their commonality is this idea of origin: it is where time is spatialized, and the datum from which space is measured by time.

2. Here in even its purest and most abstract form, at perhaps its own origin, the idea of origin is complicated by an unresolvable duality: is it to be understood as a merely temporal phenomenon or an entirely spatial one? In either case, the degree to which it is defined in apparent isolation from the other is the very degree to which it

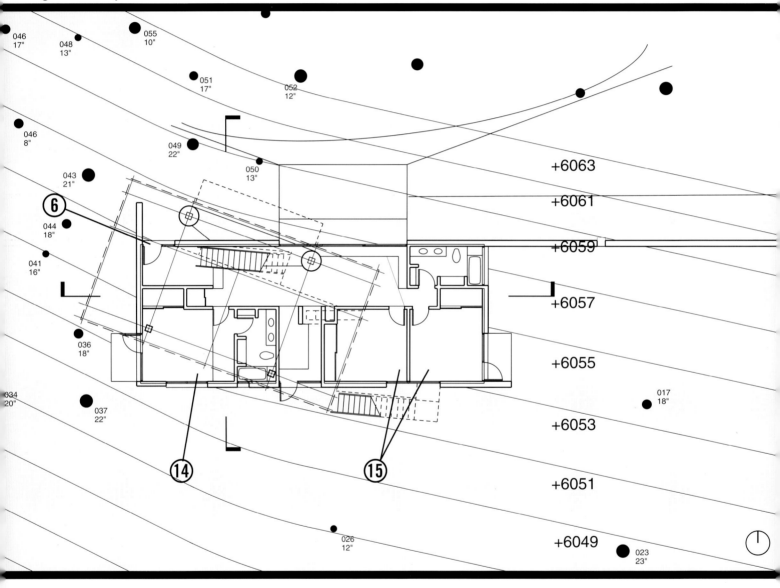

6. entry
14. master bedroom
15. guest bedroom

ground floor plan 1"=16.00'

relies on that other for such a definition. If it is "the beginning of the existence" of something, that purely temporal point can only be known by reference to this existence—which is necessarily spatial. If it is to be understood spatially as the thing's "source or cause," the proof of that status is obviously historical, and so temporal. The origin's origin as understanding is thus impossibly deferred, blurred by the *medium* of definition. It is known only in terms of an other and thus is denied the very realization of its name. This difference infects everything touched by the concept.

3.   The concept of Origin is implicated in our understanding of the way we think or, more accurately, in the institution of Reason. Reason unfolds temporally (deductively), or spatially (inductively), in a controlled sequence of steps. By virtue of its sequential nature an origin is implied, even if a conclusion is not. The "sciences" of logic, and mathematics, where reason finds its highest

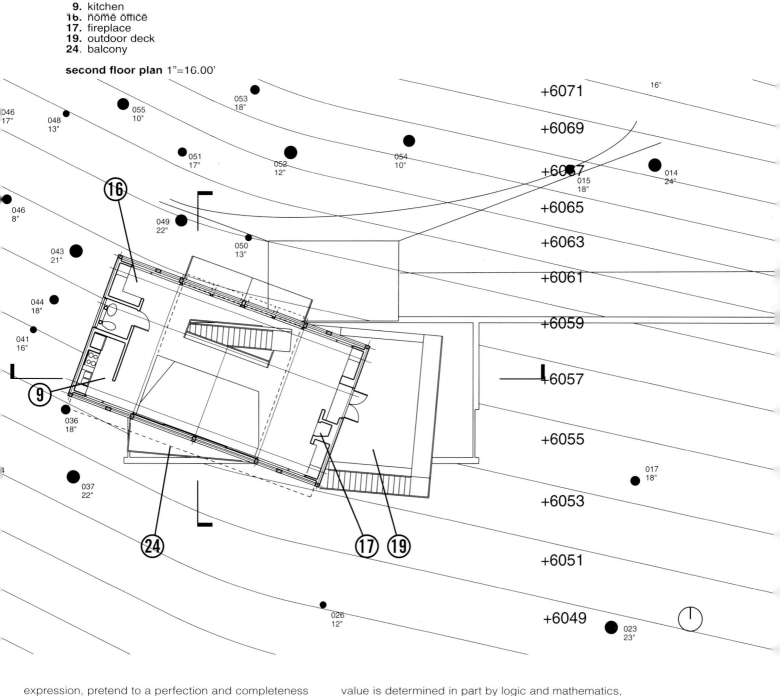

9. kitchen
16. home office
17. fireplace
19. outdoor deck
24. balcony

second floor plan 1"=16.00'

expression, pretend to a perfection and completeness based on the purity of their self-evident origins, or axioms. Yet this self-evidence unfolds *within* reason, straitjacketed by origin's unity and infected by its difference, and it is blind to these constraints. One result, among others, has been the synthetic a priori confusion and the idealist attempts to answer it.

4. In the directedness of Reason, origin loses its neutrality. It gains graduated value. The character of this value is determined in part by logic and mathematics, which privilege their origins as self-evident truths, or axioms. It is also determined, however, by the idealist conception of reality, in complicity here at its own point of origin with the commonsense view. Ever allied with the workings of faith, from which aspirations for the absolute spring, and to which they proceed, the idealist view of a reality more perfect than that presented directly to us entails as directly the conclusion that the reality we

seems inevitable. Both these architects also address nature with the same frankness as the steel building industry, "teasing nature into unhiddenness," directly or indirectly, by accommodating natural forces and effects and thus giving form to them. Both these masters of modernism and the steel building industry view form as the proper and inevitable expression of an inner will, rigorously applied, and base judgments of value on consonance with that will, rather than novelty or charm.

A critical perspective and sense of irony prevents the contemporary architect from fully enjoying such heroic positivism, though. These schemes acknowledge that reality, and admit their presence outside the strictest accounting of positivistic evolutionary histories. Each scheme elaborates its critique in a single, simple departure from conformity to the requisite or precise assimilation to the necessary. Each scheme spoils its own implicit bid for perfection. By this departure, though, the project is fit more "perfectly" to the site. The intention betrays a reliance on the logic of supplementarity, which suggests that, by working to fit themselves more completely into the site, they demonstrate their own lack of completeness. Yet, at the same time, while the overtness of this act makes it critical, its intention keeps it positive.

19. outdoor deck

view from east

apprehend is less perfect. A gulf of value is opened between the two in which the non-apparent is privileged. But for value to exist there must be some connection, some window through which the difference/distance may be known (which as we will see later is meaning), through which the one reality might be mapped onto the other. This window is the origin. To Plato the idea was that the issuing of the Forms into the world was a process that begins in compromise and continues on the

same trajectory toward further compromise and away from ideality. Commonsense picks up here too to say that the truth about a thing is therefore contained at that point of entrance, that window of being, the source, the origin. In the sequential evolution from this point the origin picks up the values of truth, simplicity, purity, ideality as reason moves the development logically in the direction of compromise, complexity, and imperfection.

5. This is the context, naive and aware, within which Architecture finds the idea of Origin. But when we think of this (before all else) word in reference to architecture what do we mean? Of which aspects of this fundamental idea does architecture partake? To which aspects of the fundamental institution (architecture) does the idea apply? It is easy enough to see how architecture might be involved with an idea so freighted with history and value, and the values of history, as well as one so wrapped up in the dynamics of space and reason. It is

19. outdoor deck
22. snow retention parapet
25. sunshade

south elevation 1"=13.33'

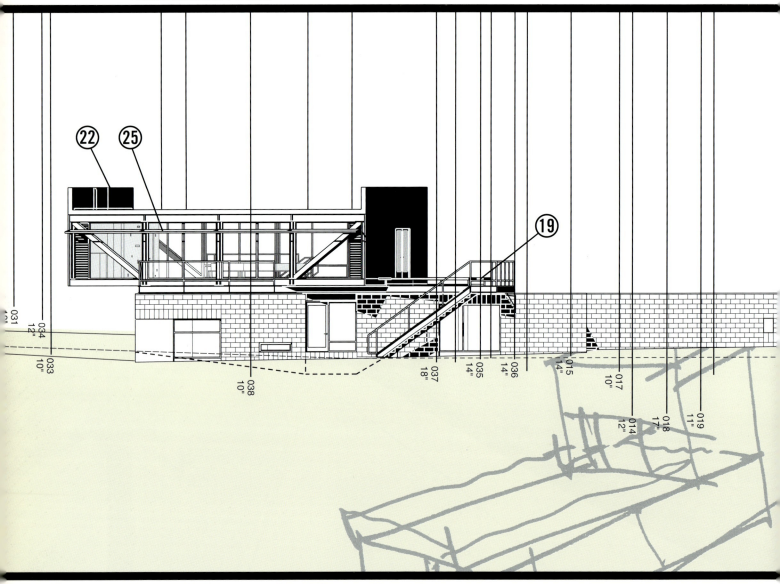

more difficult to see how the idea might be applied in a field already complicated by its own dual existence as an abstract institution and as a physical fact. But one can start, for example by examining the order of precedence between the terms of this duality; by reasoning a sequence, and thus value, into their relationship. One can start by trying to found one upon the other, by trying to find in one the origin of the other. At which point Architecture grins: the commonsense view hands the laurel to physical presence, by virtue of arguments like Laugier's primitive hut story—but the self-aware view snatches it back again with the claim that the physical fact is preceded by the architectural sense which gives rise to it and names it; which, in turn, depends of course on Presence to ground the abstraction that depends upon the abstraction in order to be grounded. And so we immediately founder on the rocks of an irreconcilable difference, evidence for the fundamentality of the site of

19. outdoor deck
21. thermal storage plenum
22. snow retention parapet

longitudinal section 1"=13.33'

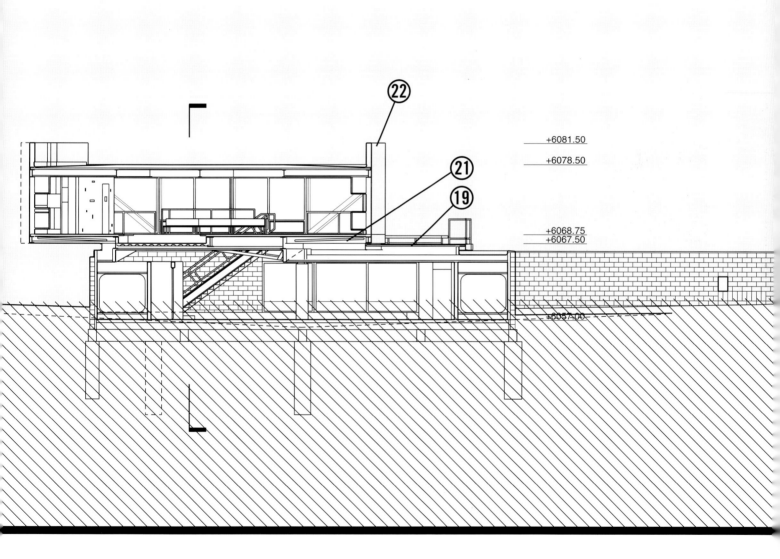

this foundering, Architecture (this exercise itself has shown how misleading it is to restrict this site to being a field, a discipline or institution, or a physical fact).
6. The inability to resolve this conflict places the infection of difference (at the core of the idea of origin) at the core of the idea of architecture. And though Architecture may not be as blind to this difficulty as Reason is, it is as complacent. So the question of origin is not expelled but embraced, taken in without hope of satisfactory accommodation and made central to her most important concerns. Indeed, the indefinability of architecture in these terms may be taken as its definition: it is founded in an idealist's universe as the geist that inhabits the distance between the two realities it entails as neither, and neither without the other.
7. The origins to which these different dimensions of architecture refer are of course different. Beyond the trivial (and thus unarchitectural) speculation about the literal

22. snow retention parapet
23. snow stair
25. sunshade

transverse section 1"=13.33'

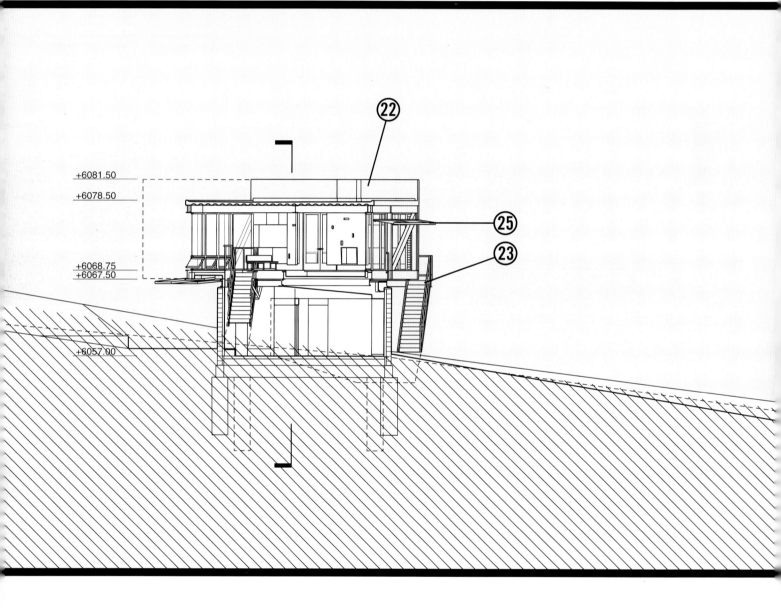

origins of the materials that eventually become the building, two traditional ties to the idea of origin have been formed by architecture. And beyond the less trivial, but still not profound, relationship of these two as falling within the same field, they are connected by the mechanism of meaning. In either case the problem of meaning, that the skeptic raises from the difference, the arbitrariness, of the sign, becomes central to the problem of architecture, that is raised from the difference, the arbitrariness, of its origins. In this light architecture becomes a project of provisionality as a ground for a local absolute of meaning. Architecture itself, the geist, becomes the perfect fugitive medium through which to inscribe the fugitive absolutes meaning describes.

8. The first traditional origin in architecture expressive of this provisionality, though of course blind to it itself, is the formal referent visible in the object. The origin here is the thing that the architectural object is intended to look

284

22. snow retention parapet
23. snow stair
24. balcony

west elevation 1"=13.33'

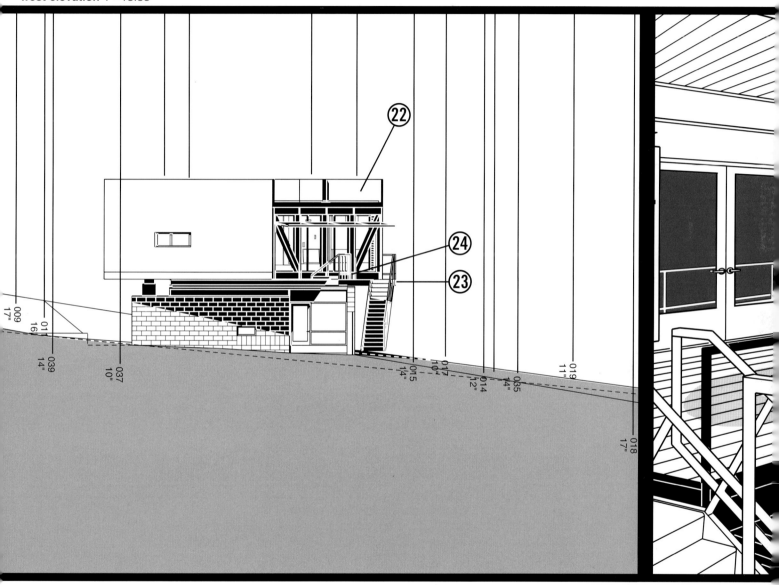

like, the idea it is supposed to represent. Nature is the origin of classical reference, for example. Meaning here is the geist in the representation, the thing signified. Both the object and the institution are implicated in this *reference*, the former through itself, the latter by definition and through style.

9. The other traditional origin in architecture is that from which the compositional process develops the finished design. In this process meaning develops again in the distance of the design from its origin, but in this case the origin acts as a datum so that the distance is literally the meaning. Understanding, the appreciation of this distance, occurs as the steps of the design's development are retraced to its source, its origin, and the distance between the two is accumulated by the viewer. The simple house/temple form, represented by Laugier as a Primitive Hut, is the origin of classical compositional practices in this sense.

11. family area
interior view

10. In both of these cases the origin is not the transcendent thing it is supposed to be when viewed from within the field. It is more like an axiom, which has two faces, **ONM 7** one it represents to the faithful, and another that it shows outsiders. From within, the axiom appears as the idealist's reality in realization, where the faith finds its apotheosis and the humble wafer-and-2000-lire-wine proposition is transubstantiated into the body and blood of that unreachable, ideal other where parallel lines *never* meet. **NRO 9**

It is the origin as we naively understand it, the source of perfect knowledge of a thing: a "self-evident proposition accepted therefore as true without proof," a "self-evident **NIRM 20** or universally recognized truth." It is, as origin, that point where one can pare no further, that point where a Form issues into the world and where trespass to mortals is blocked. It is a limit that defines the faithful as Inside.
11. From the outside, however, the axiom is not an absolute, but a heuristic, origin—a conferred divinity, cir-

11. family area
interior view

cumscribed by the agency that confers it (that is, the mind that thinks it, the name that labels it). The metaview that explodes the privilege of the axiom is too easy to adopt for "self-evident" to equal "universal." "Self-evident" is itself an emblem for circularity, and "proposition accepted as true without proof" is a contradiction, since a proposition is precisely a "statement presented for discussion or proof." It is argued that this is hard up against the limit of possible proof and therefore exists beyond critique, where one is left only with self-evidence and the conviction (faith) that this is enough.

12. As the non-Euclidean geometries have shown, this limit is ethnocentrically defined, and its sustenance is the faith generated within the world it confines. Two parallel lines may never meet within Euclid's world, but that world is now only one of many. The axiom, the idealist's answer to the possibility for a sense of the absolute in this world, is in fact the ultimate statement of provisionality and, to

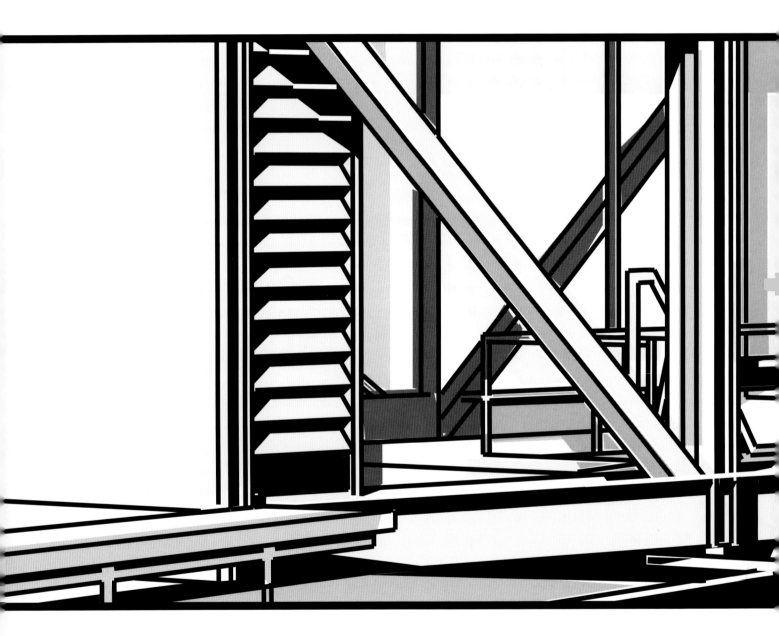

the degree that great edifices have been built upon it, absurdity.

ᵃ American Academy in Rome, Fellows Exhibition, 1986

4 "As with all religious symbolization, there is no attempt to prove that these unusual, transcendent, or divine events are 'possible,' or otherwise to justify them. For this reason, every myth presents itself as authoritative and always as an account of facts, no matter how completely different they may be from the ordinary world. The original Greek term for myth (*mythos*) denotes 'word' in the sense of a decisive, final pronouncement. It differs from *logos*, the word whose validity or truth can be argued and demonstrated." Bolle, 793-4.

5 Bolle, 802.

6 *Ibid*.

7 Roland Barthes, "Myth Today" in *A Barthes Reader*, trans. Susan Sontag (New York: Hill and Wang, 1983), 93; hereafter cited as MT.

Donner Lake Cabin *
P96.07/2
Donner Lake, CA

Scheme # rotates its superstructure off its base to address the view; this goes beyond accommodation to assert the scheme's consciousness of its own aggressive presence on the site and its likely reorientation of the surroundings to its new centrality. Scheme * employs an obvious somatic screen in order to blend in; the strict framing of this element, though, undercuts its simple statement of camouflage to highlight the practice's artificiality and questionable motives.

* * *

The battle for our planet's future will be fought within technology, not against it. Even "appropriate" technologies, or "alternative" technologies, however, respectful, are still scientific engagements of Nature—still only different readings of our basic technological contract with Nature.

Admittedly, technology is at least the proximate cause of our environmental problems. The domineering effects of technology are widely felt; its attempts to control both man and nature, to subject them to its standards of efficiency and quantification, are well documented and analyzed. Smokestacks that once proclaimed prosperity now seem aimed more menacingly at the sky, like industrial cannons holding the planet hostage.

Yet we must also admit technology's indispensable place in our society and our conception of the future. Ultimately, the quarrel should not be with these smokestacks themselves so much as with the "technological mind set" that "aims" them. The attitude that views everything as "standing in reserve" to be fit into the "system" and judges quality strictly in quantifiable terms is indeed pervasive in industrial societies. Its universalizing outlook misses both the humane and the natural in its quest for efficiency. The products of this universalizing attitude play an increasingly integral role in our society, but this attitude forces us to cast them as the villains, which may make us miss the real culprit.

This critique of technology tends to place a distance between us and our machines that obscures the naturalness of technology as a normal extension of man. Our technology cannot help but bear the personality of its maker. This personality is as varied as humanity, and thus not necessarily or uniformly attractive. We are inseparable from our technology—it is the stuff we make; it is what demonstrates and tests the stuff of which we are made. If it is deemed ugly, or irresponsible, or cruel, it is as likely as not because we have been ugly, irresponsible, or cruel.

The "sea-change in consciousness" that appears to be dawning today describes the magnitude of the changes necessary to effect a true and lasting impact on our relationship with the planet. This change of consciousness must begin with a new heightened awareness and understanding of our relationship to our technology. It is only by this route that any substantive change in technology's

6. entry
23. snow stair

view from east

8 Barthes terms the mythical sign the signification to distinguish it from the sign produced as a first order, or strictly linguistic, signification. MT, 99.
9 MT, 109.
10 MT, 103.
11 MT, 113.
12 MT, 110.
13 MT, 112.
14 MT, 110.
15 MT, 132.
16 MT, 131.
17 MT, 132.
18 MT, 145.
19 MT, 145.
20 MT, 149.
21 MT, 135.
22 MT, 144.
23 Yet, this operational experience, however direct, is still

(6)

mediated by language and so estranged from the things themselves. Myth works upon, and with, signs, that themselves are already a step away from perfect engagement. This step can be short, in the case of the poetic language that turns the attention back toward the presencing of the object, or it can be as long as daytime television programming, but myth begins already from here, at a certain remove.

24 MT, 135.

1. cabin
2. covered carport

site plan 1"=80.00'

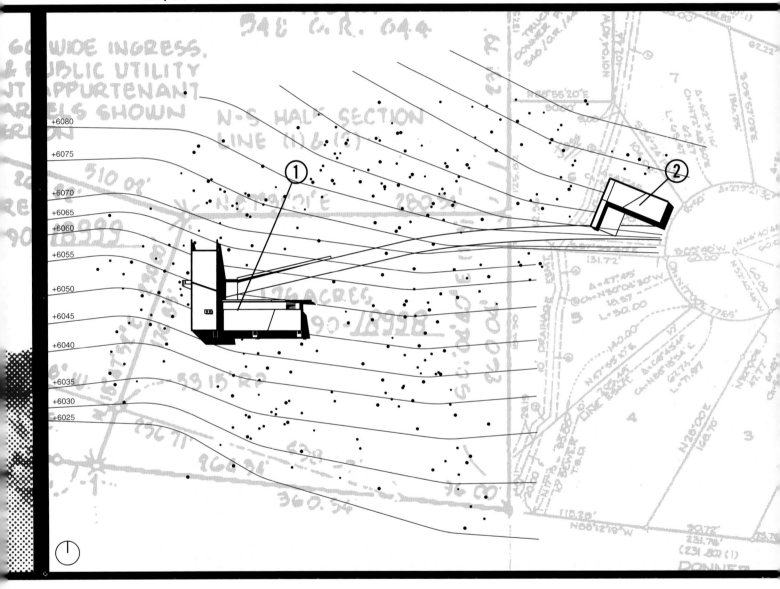

25 MT, 134.
26 MT, 109.
27 **Notes, IN RE: Mediation**[a]
1. "Media" is from the Latin for middle. There is no surprise here, no deconstructive frontier to be discovered in this revelation—only aptness. The word 'media' is often preceded by the qualifier 'news,' which explains its origin as "means" but makes its present use ironic. This irony provides the lever for some remedial consideration.

2. The media's central position in contemporary cultural activity—and its shift from "means" to "middle"—is best understood in reference to the distinction between information and meaning, or signification. The increasing influence of information theory, has helped to establish a qualitatively different schema of value for cultural production, that replaces significance with novelty at the top of the hierarchy. It declares the conceptual split of information and meaning and the alignment of information

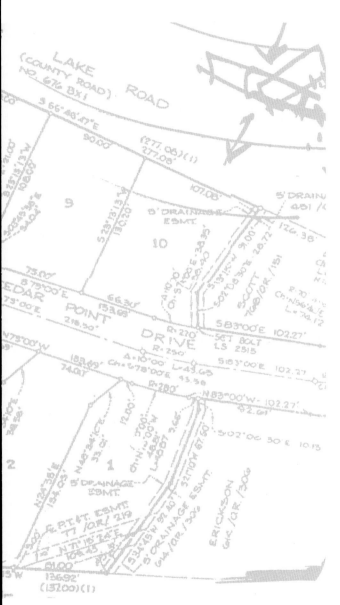

relationship to nature may be affected. We interchange "humanity" and "technology" freely in assigning the blame for our environmental problems because, despite technology's alienating habits, it is only transparent to the humanity who wields it.

The problem is centered precisely here—in the attitude that views technology as something to be "wielded," something raised "against" something else. Whether this something else is truly worth a battle, like poverty or hunger, or is indifferent, like the weather, by "wielding" technology against it, an attitude is fostered—and focus created—which damns the wider consequences. The combative "us against them" mentality may lead to quick solutions, but seldom to lasting ones. Technology is not a weapon but a tool and a mirror, and increasingly, inescapably, a companion.

Selflessness and sacrifice, however noble, however helpful, are not in themselves solutions though: the image in this mirror will not go away. We are tied to technology by more than just a selfish regard for the comforts and security it provides. It may seem a cliche to say that "Man is a machine," but this phrase neatly captures the limited range of physical experience available to humanity: technology is a direct expression of how we inhabit and engage the world, a direct outgrowth of our perceptual and cognitive abilities and limitations.

with novelty.[b] In divorcing information from confirmation, **MIT 4** in service of novelty, information theory effectively elevates randomness and chance to the position within culture **NRO 1** previously occupied by the appreciation and authority of certainty and intention. **DR 11**

3. Once it is possible to rethink information as no longer particularly interested in meaning it becomes clear how an avalanche of communication and information can result in an increasing paucity of sense; how truth itself

9. kitchen
11. family area
12. living area
14. master bedroom
20. mudroom

ground level plan 1"=16.00'

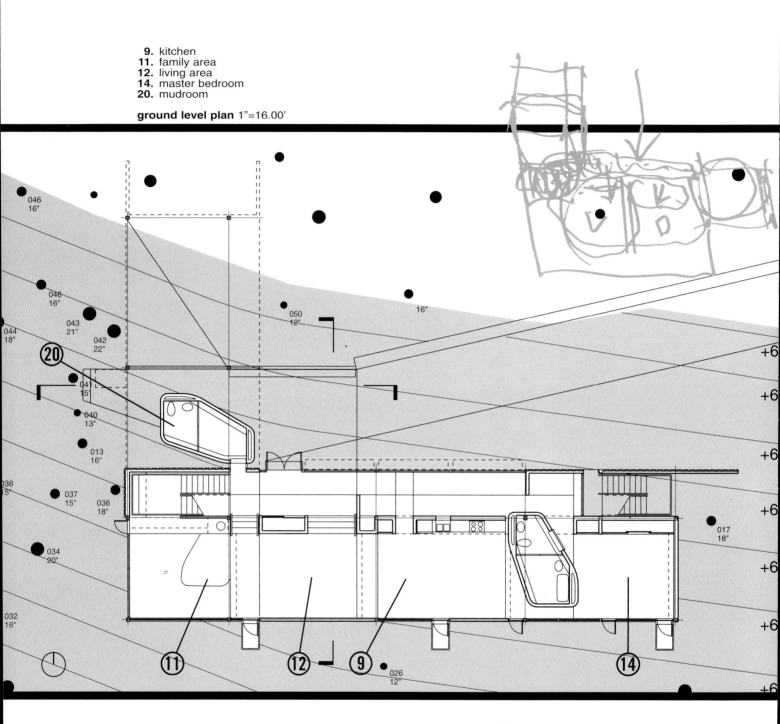

may become a variable drowned in that avalanche; and how value, as the difference, must be lost in sameness. Since architecture traditionally distinguishes itself from building by the degree to which it participates in the pro-
ONM 9
motion of meaning, and the media increasingly defines the meaning of meaning in our culture, the cultural influ-
ONHR 10
ence of the media is important to architecture.
Increasingly the media has come to play a role in society once reserved for architecture: the media has become
NOB 4
the mirror that reflects society's sense of itself. The sup-
ONM 7 **ONO 3**
posed neutrality or "transparency" of the media in this
NRO 5
role vs. architecture's avowed celebratory posture is as indicative of the new value schema as it is illusory in fact.

* * *

Media
WITM 34
4. The media has effectively stripped our world, our reality, of meaning.[c] The importance of presence in the meaning equation, of all the markers in which this pres-

294

15. guest bedroom
19. outdoor deck

second level plan 1"=16.00'

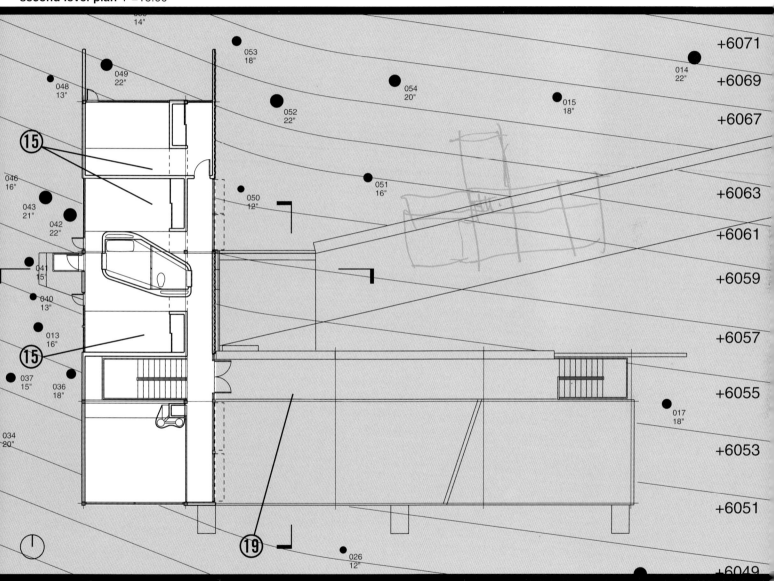

ence is invested—such as architecture—and also the value of their uniqueness, has been lost in their infinite reproducibility and ubiquity. The "hyper-real world of simulacra" has been engaged. Instead of the object, or even the event, satisfied in its own presence to itself, there is the facsimile of the object, and the coverage of the event. "The message has ceased to exist, it is the medium which imposes itself in its pure circulation."[d] Further, the medium itself has no intrinsic value, no presence that completes the deferral. This represents a transference of the values implied in the most vigorous reading of information theory into the cultural sphere. The cultural has achieved a neutered version of science's dream of neutral objectivity and has become scientific.[e] This world of simulacra, the compressed, trans-dimensional realm of the media, is a systematic, processed world, an enframed world. In hyper-reality, signifier and signified float more transparently as variables than

And technology is, finally, humanity's own Creation. The difference between technology and Nature is the difference between man and God. Technology may yearn (it's in the nature of the machine) for the perfection of Nature but, like its own creator, it must be satisfied with worship.

Architecture expresses our place in this cosmos. Its formal referent must ultimately be the world: Nature. Technological form is directly expressive of what nature demands or will allow. If architecture retains its traditional role as a vehicle for placing us in the world, then science and technology act as the map.

This is an approach that looks through technology to the people who make it, the people who use it and depend on it, and, most visibly, to nature that allows it and is made more present in it. This amounts to a spiritualization of technology. Today, the change in consciousness proposed by so many prefigures a new technology of spiritualization, which once again would place technology at the center of our dwelling upon the earth, as a visible expression of the relationships that may be fostered there.

11. family area
19. outdoor deck
23. snow stair

view from southwest

MIT 11

Saussure could have imagined. The sign, their embodied connection, which maintained the place of value in the world, has been severed from even an illusory connection to "hard reality," or has become so reduced in its "necessity" that all value has been drained from it. It has floated free from an anchoring connection to the presence of 'real' objects because these no longer have the weight to hold it down. Mass-production, and electromechanical reproduction destroys the uniqueness that

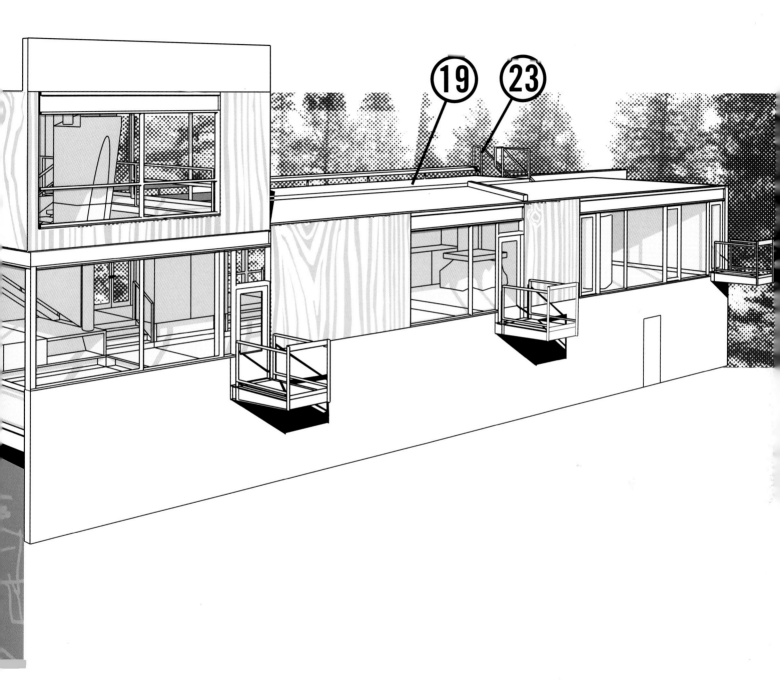

rooted significance and gave the object a fixity as a datum for difference and exchange.[f] Despite the apparent freedom enjoyed by the simulacra as they float untethered to meaning, the value that tells us such freedom is to be coveted has been lost within this enframed context; it is not freedom from the tyranny of meaning or even the freedom to contest it, so much as freedom to trivialize and render banal.

5. The Contemporary critique of the repressiveness of Authority considers the division of information and meaning to be a liberating force, finding in information theory's valorization of randomness an openness to infinite readings. This openness to the possibilities of undecidability is proposed as an effective counter to the domineering Authority of a text's pretense to a singular, or unitary, intended meaning.[g] Ironically, this is precisely the effect for which the media is most criticized in general. As an agent of hyper-reality, the media has uncritically turned

19. outdoor deck
23. snow stair
24. balcony

south elevation 1"=16.00'

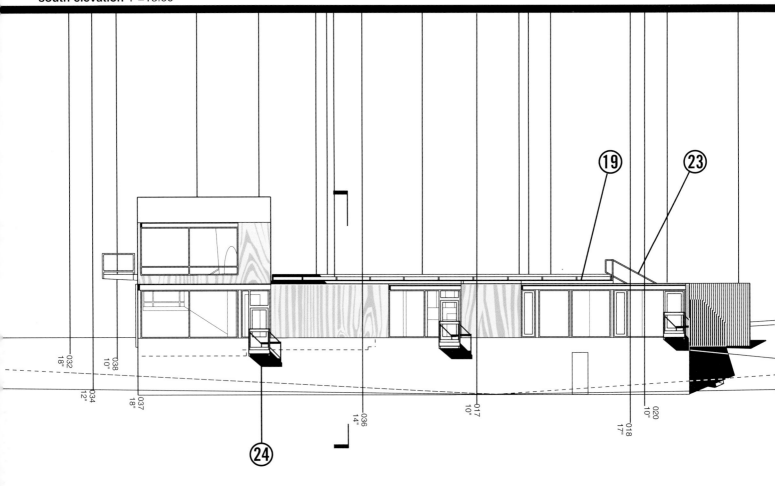

ostensible meaning into information through an opposite excess of enthusiasm for the universality of its product. Yet, beyond the obvious suspicion about presenting (pre-sending), this 'information' is not "efficiently" transmitted. In its presentation role, the media ends up in the middle between its audience and the "given" novelty. When the media's omnipresence is understood, this middle position expands to place the media between its audience and general reality. It is never better than between. Eventually, leveraged by its omnipresence, it even substitutes for that reality.

6. At the root of suspicion about the possible transparency of presentation is a difference in the perception of novelty's relationship to information. There are two general ways to see this relationship: on the one hand it can be said that "the more certain a message is, the less information it conveys," while on the other it can be argued that "the more surprising a message is, the less

11. family area
15. guest bedroom
20. mudroom
24. balcony

west elevation 1"=16.00'

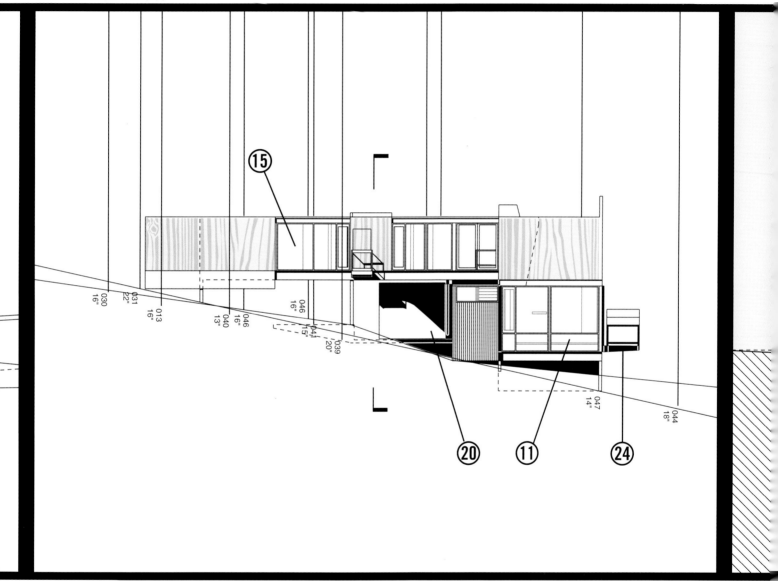

information it conveys."[h] This difference depends on whether the reader's or the author's perspective is adopted. Information theory's technical genesis in support of the latter has been transformed by critique to support the former—yet the priority in each case remains the same, valuing the generative possibilities of novelty (first case) over the reductive confirmational probabilities of satisfying expectation (second case). The media's place in this is to affect a third condition of conformation, depending on the technical and cultural developments made by the former to 'achieve' the latter. In so doing it falls, again, into the middle.

7. The media has institutionalized novelty, and has thus eliminated its generative capacity to surprise. Instead, this novelty itself acts out the slide-into-comfort that confirms the status quo. Those events that begin in uniqueness are quickly fit into the standard template: equipped with logos, theme jingles, and a title

6. entry
19. outdoor deck
22. snow retention placard

north elevation/ section 1"=16.00'

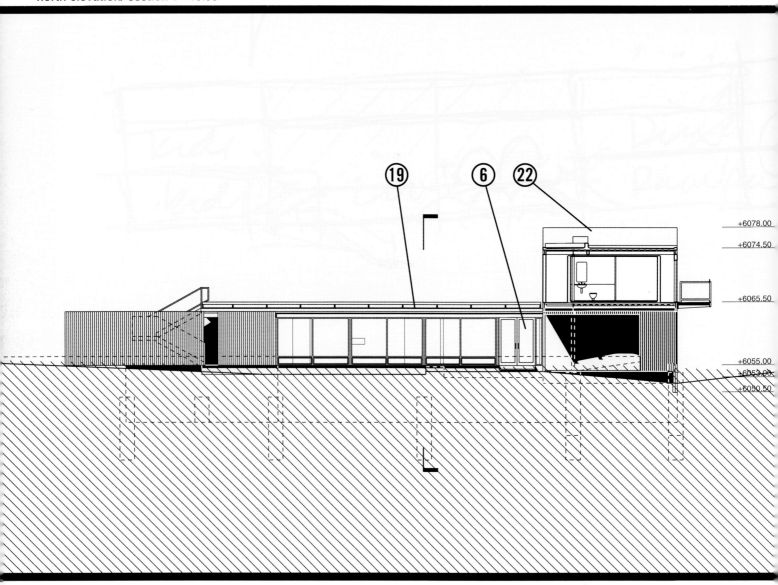

(War in the Gulf, Andrews Anguish) they become a regular feature, conforming to acceptable programming standards, with an address in the T.V. Guide. In this way the event loses both its novelty or informational possibilities *and* its ability to confirm anything outside of its own enframing. Thus it must fail to achieve even the classic, conservative condition of meaning. The event is mediated; the difference which meaning bridges is lost.

Technology
8. It is in the essence of technology to mediate, to stand between. NOB 9 When that technology in turn supports the institutions of human mediation, the technology both becomes more effective and more invisible. It is made not only in our image, but in our thoughts. The technology of the media is the perfected end of the technology of information; information theory was invented to support telecommunications, to increase its efficiency and the

19. outdoor deck
20. mudroom
22. snow retention placard

east elevation/ section 1"=16.00'

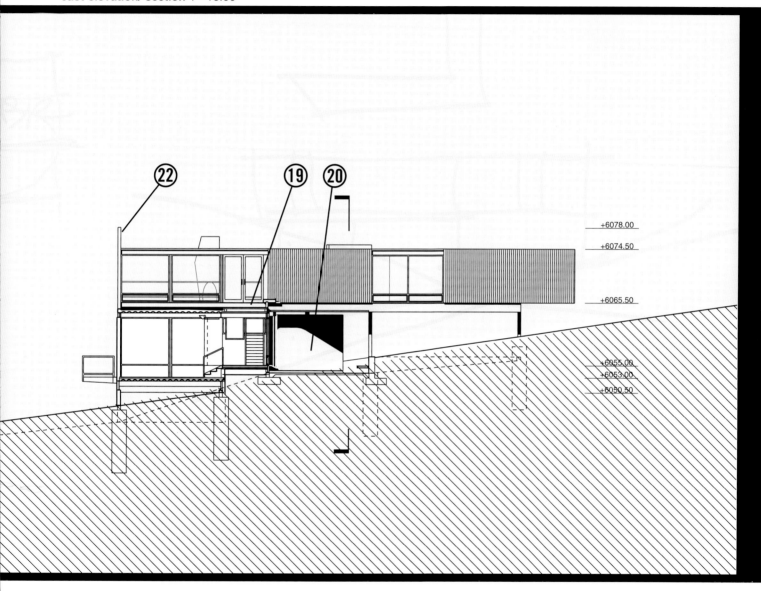

quality of its verisimilitude. Information technology enables the media, it is its body. To the media this technology is a means, and presents its effects as its presence: the sound byte, the simulcast, the movie, the report are among its many faces. The technology is designed to maximize the efficient transmission of information-as-neutral-possibility for coding, while the institution is pledged to maximize the efficient transmission of information as meaning. The two conflict in this: the technology, interested in maximizing transmission, must consider deplorable the singular intentions expressed by meaning, while meaning itself must struggle to maintain its singularity against transmissible possibility. The media objectifies the continuum of possible information, robbing it of its openness, giving it meaning, yet ultimately also taking that meaning away. The roles and effects have become reversed: in participating in technique's valorization of efficiency the media strips its infobits of their con-

12. living area
17. fireplace

interior view

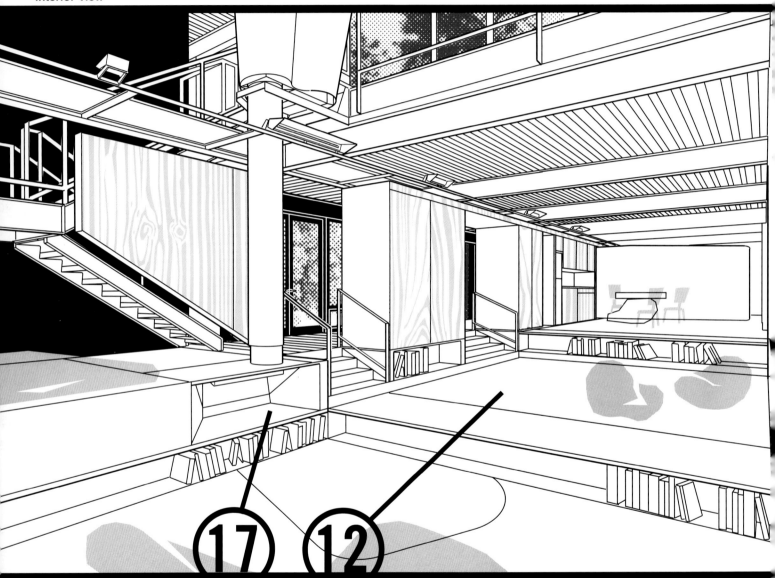

texts—the history that adds up to their presence; by isolating the infobits into consumable bites of sensationalism or gratification their "real meaning" is lost.

9. The technology of interest here is the telecommunication technology of media effects, the electronic technology of simulation and reproduction. The favorite effect is the instant replay; the favorite affect is the preference for it, which throws originality into doubt and out of favor. This technology has greatly reduced the anchoring hold of reality upon experience and imagination: the ghostly insubstantiality, time-reversibility, literal ubiquity, simultaneity, and transformability enjoyed in movies and television are as 'real' today, if not more real, than the paper on which this is printed. The fascination with "reality based" programming and "eyewitness video" has established the adjective "live" as meaning unrehearsed or without-special-effects, rather than actually present to the viewer. Indeed, the subject has become the viewer.

10. Yet, media technology has had its greatest effect as a metaphor, rather than as a means: it has allowed reality to be rubberized, to be stretched, molded, and folded, to defy the "laws" of the physical universe, to ignore gravity and conquer mortality like any cartoon figure. The cartoon figure's virtual reality, created by the media of the media, is not only the means of the cartoon but the arena where this metaphor may extend itself. The cartoon figure's only constraint is the force instituted by the radiation of the cathode ray tube which builds and erases this world thirty times per second. As the subject—viewer—increasingly identifies with the possibilities of this virtual world, the natural, physical world becomes pallid and overly constraining in comparison.

11. Contemporary critique has generated much theory and design about theory in architecture.[i] For all this, the work remains solidly within a tradition that understands architecture's role as the expression of prevailing atti-

tudes regarding humanity's place within the cosmos. Such work wonders at the miracles wrought by current technology. It sees in this technology, that so challenges our common sense, or at least in these miracles, a freedom from the domineering commonness of this sense. To this critical work the hyper-real is not only more real, but also more exciting in the license it gives for challenging some of the hoariest assumptions of the architectural equation. Such criticism concentrates on technology's support for the condition of hyper-real insubstantiality, and misses the definitively palpable presence and technical genesis it shares with architecture. For this reason, such work has been frustrated by its own pallid and constraining, but necessary, presence. To a certain extent the unexamined use of metaphor in architecture has always disappointed.[j] The transdimensional differences that metaphor seems to bridge so effortlessly in language become ungainly in architecture, seldom leading

Zimmer Stair, University of Cincinnati
Cincinnati, OH

P96.05/1

Client:	University of Cincinnati Ron Kull, Campus Architect
Architect:	Jones, Partners: Architecture
Consultants:	Structural Design Engineers (structural)
Contractor:	West Edge (steel fabrication)
Site:	Twenty-seven-foot vertical difference between two adjacent public spaces, Library Square and Zimmer Plaza, opposite the engineering school
Program:	Outdoor public stair and seating area
Size:	1600 ft^2
Systems:	Welded steel frame and subframe, aluminum grating bleachers, glass and steel guardrails, plate steel guardrail
Features:	Fabricated in San Francisco and shipped to the site in three bundles on a single flatbed truck, this functional sculpture is designed to project an image of largeness and heft through an expression of the stair-as-machine, or at least as large garden tool.
Cost:	$.25 million
Completion:	November 1996

The need for a new plaza in the midst of an eclectic collection of campus buildings from every period of the University's history presents an opportunity to create a space-defining sculptural object. This stair folly connects the two principal levels of the plaza, conferring to the plaza a dynamic orientation and a focal point for its otherwise amorphous, flowing spaces.

Located opposite the engineering school, the stair provides an outsized celebration of structural steel. Its logical, but extreme, organization into massive wide-flange bent mainframe, trussed tubular subframe, and stick-built angle-and-channel-stringer assembly makes legible the classic division of labor between servant and served elements in the design, and relates them to the scale of service they provide. Efficiency is not a goal in this design—expression is. In effect this exhorts the young engineers across the plaza to remember both masters: heed the numbers that realize the possible, and listen to the heart because only its enthusiasm for cool stuff may actualize the virtual. The sheer visceral appeal of a W33 that can be touched—its right there!—can affect the contemporary viewer as much as entasis could affect the ancient Greek. To drive home the capabilities of such a handsome piece of steel, the nose of the structure cantilevers from the elbow of the bent, about twenty feet; its broad sweeping snout hovers inches above the plaza without touching down. The structure cantilevers also at the opposite, upper end where it bursts through the parapet guardrail of

view from northeast

to truly satisfying, or useful, connections in physical actuality. And when that metaphor is defined by its own critical insubstantiality, then the real results of such cross pollination must appear particularly sheepish. Disneyland's new "Toon Town" attraction is a perfect, if unintentional, illustration of what happens when architecture embodies the expressly dis-embodiable. Though it can certainly be cartoonish, architecture has never been a successful cartoon.

Nature

12. Technology mediates between human desires and nature's capacity to fulfill them; it effects the perpetual human wish to transcend that capacity. The machine's mediation of nature appears similar in many ways to the mediation that associates technology with the hyper-real. The machine, for example, compresses the variety of nature into a systemic understanding, enframing phenomena to create an unreal condition that the machine

south elevation view

may more efficiently engage and manipulate. Even seen optimistically from this perspective such "phenomena" as clouds, trees, and animals have become more real as weather systems, or as measurements for quantities of paper to be recycled, or as wildlife to be preserved. The machine objectifies the continuity of experience to give it discreteness: laws, forces, elements, chemicals. These are invested with a meaning and exchange value that devalues the less "useful," un-mediated original condition or the "other." Ultimately, it reduces nature's fecund otherness to a familiar convention whereby human value may dominate the relationship and determine the meaning.[k] This otherness is so marginalized that its capacity to either stand in judgment of our effort or, by its otherness, participate in the definition of that value *as* human is lost.

13. This is the character of the machine's mediation of nature, attacked by the traditional critique of that media-

2. laminated glass guardrail assembly
3. landing guardrail assembly with steel rod infill
6. concrete landing
7. press-lock aluminum bar grating
8. concrete filled metal pan treads with solid risers
9. collector truss
11. built-up subframe girder
12. diagonal pipe support, frame
13. diagonal bracing, subframe
14. existing parapet

Zimmer Plaza, announcing the presence of the stair to visitors approaching from above. The northern edge of the stair along its entire length is defined by a solid plate guardrail and the southern, bleacher edge, by a glass guardrail. This reinforces the structure's sense of orientation to the plaza and the sun, providing a solid edge to the space on the north and an open belvedere condition to the south.

The stair's traditional role as a gathering place is acknowledged by the inclusion of bleachers along its entire length—ideal accommodation for people-watching, daydreaming, rallies, lunch breaks, meeting, and hormonally-driven encounters. These bleachers serve as well to bulk up the structure to a scale more appropriate to the space it commands and broaden it to a proposition more in balance with its length.

The stair was designed to be erected in three major assemblies, facilitating shop fabrication and transportation. Apart from the W33 subframe, the entire eighty-foot structure was fabricated in California and shipped to the site, nested onto a single flatbed semi-trailer.

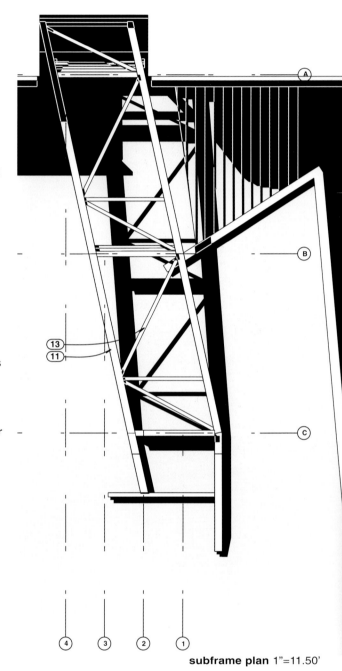

subframe plan 1"=11.50'

tion which describes it in terms similar to the hyper-real. Unlike its operation within the human realm, however, the sort of mediation enacted as the enframing of nature can never achieve a true condition of hyper-reality because the terms of this mediation must always answer to nature's limits. The machine's actual prevalence remains checked by that which exceeds its grasp. The unknown that circumscribes the machine's simulated reality, denies it the transcendence and the superiority enjoyed by the

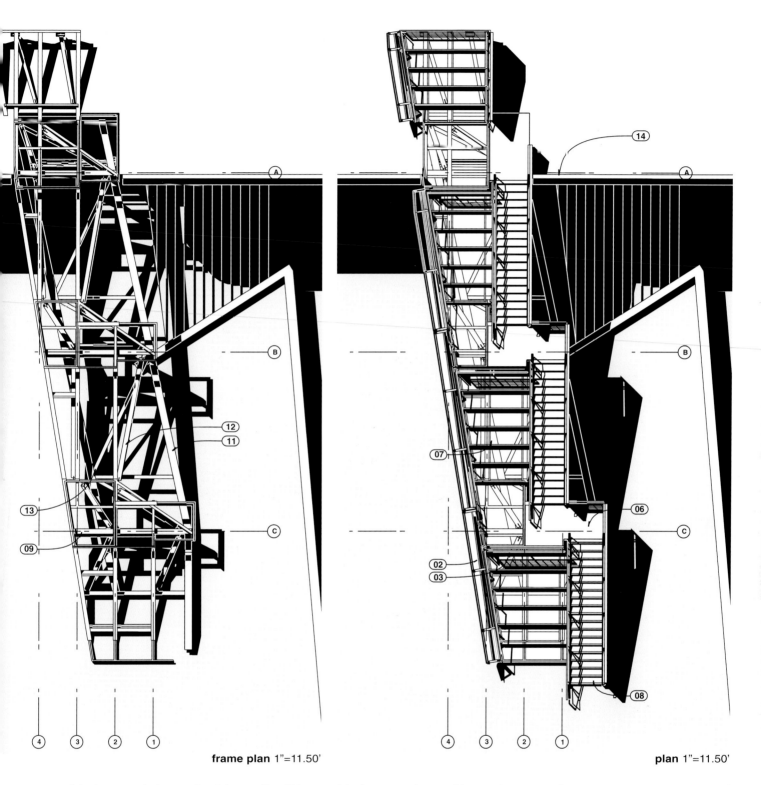

frame plan 1"=11.50'

plan 1"=11.50'

organs of the hyper-real, the media of the media within the restricted area of human affairs. In nature, the machine cannot achieve the closure of omnipresence. The machine's inescapable discreteness limits its ability to stand opaquely between humanity and nature as a substitute for either. Like architecture, the machine is always still there, itself, in nature, by humanity's hand. Because it can be seen, it can always be seen around, to the other.

14. In nature, the machine confronts an unknown, an other, that must always leave a remainder that defeats the simulation. In this "defeat," however, the mediation may be revealed in a positive light. The remainder shows the mediation as truly between; not the cover-up or substitution effected by the media in its hegemonic cultural activity, but a visible instrument of interrogation or persuasion. Though we treat the machine as second nature, the idea of the machine is not vast enough to truly sub-

view from southeast

view from northeast

stitute for nature.¹ Despite the evolutionary success of the machine in bending Nature to human desire, she is always still inarguably there and always still inarguably more than this desire can comprehend or encompass.
15. In mediating between humankind and the irredeemable otherness of nature, the machine may be more accurately thought of as a translator. Translation, as opposed to both the conformational practices described earlier, and the "emperor's new metaphor," supposes that mediation is a two-way street. The mediated otherness is not masked by a substitution or rendered insubstantial by reproduction, but is respected in the structure of translation, which presumes that the other has something to say, something to be translated. Instead of minimizing or masking it, translation highlights the difference between the interlocutors. Translation is, unavoidably, consciously, transformation. In translation, the necessity for analogy is made manifest. Analogy is how the differ-

detail view

ence is bridged, instead of eradicated or erased, and where this difference becomes significant since both terms are required to make sense.

16. In analogy, it is possible for meaning to be added or lost. In the mediation of the media, which telecommunication's technology serves, the goal is to transmit information with complete neutrality or transparency. The addition or loss of meaning in the process is not desirous; this is seen as a failure of efficiency, as the introduction of noise or the degrading of the message.[m] To the extent this goal is achieved, translation becomes reproduction or substitution. Translation cannot operate without some looseness: efficiency cannot tolerate it. Translation must be continually fed by the other. Unlike the substitution/reproduction activities of the media, the translation occurring in the machine's mediation of nature depends on the continual surprise of nature in order for it to advance.

2. laminated glass guardrail assembly
3. landing guardrail assembly with steel rod infill
10. moment frame
14. existing parapet

east elevation 1"=8.00'

1. steel plate guardrail assembly
2. laminated glass guardrail assembly
7. press-lock aluminum bar grating
9. collector truss
10. moment frame
11. built-up subframe girder
12. diagonal pipe support
14. existing parapet

south elevation 1"=8.00'

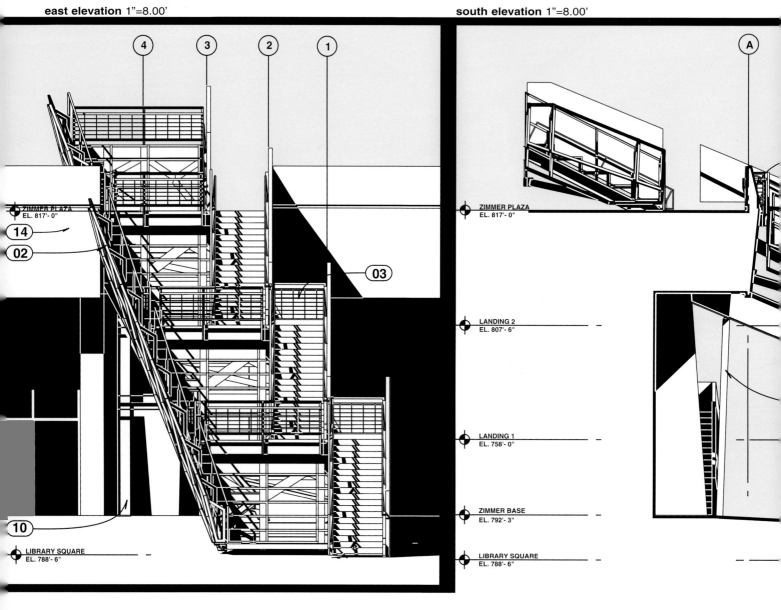

17. That technology may be considered in this way is admitted by Heidegger, its greatest critic. He describes technology as essentially "a way of revealing," but worries that technology's very success may institutionalize a smugness which loses sight of the value of this surprise. Heidegger sees the essence of technology as a mediation of nature that leads unavoidably from revealing to the conformational practices of substitution and simulation, or as he puts it, "enframing." Whether the result is the

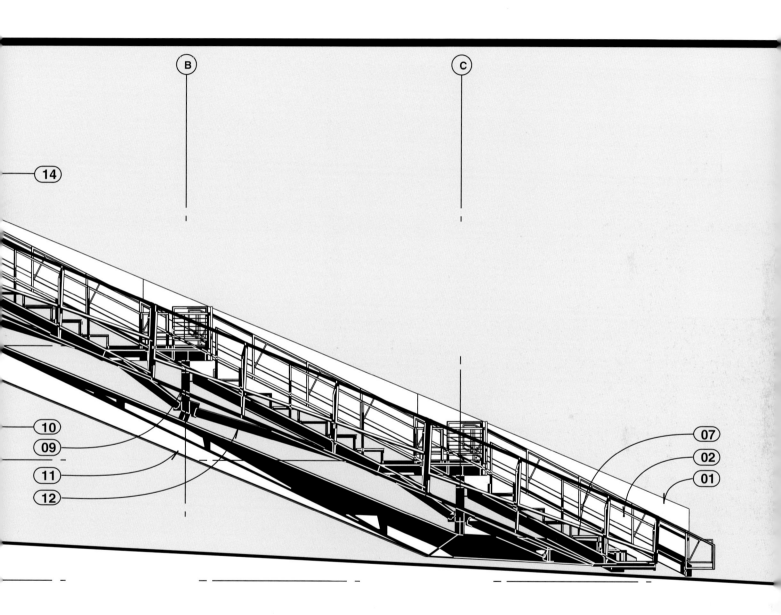

"hyper-real world of simulacra" or a systemic world of "standing reserves," Heidegger stresses that humanity essentially participates in its unfolding, as a witness and helper. In so participating, humanity reflects this essence into its own affairs—its institutions, culture, social world—and engages the *danger*.[n] When everything is mediated, no thing remains by which mediation may be known.

18. What is reflected here is the loss of essential meaning and substance and possibility. The danger is the potential for forgetting the occurrence of this loss. It is the potential, starting from translation, to fall into substitution—where nothing is left for translation because everything is the same and there is no other. Even the essential novelty valued by information theory is unreachable from such an enframed position. The value of human existence, its meaning, as "witness and helper to revealing"[o] is thereby lost—and becomes irrecoverable if this fall is forgotten: yet it is by the fall that value can be

north elevation view

rediscovered. The fall itself is perhaps the greatest measure of that value.

19. This fall can be missed only if the focus lingers exclusively on humanity's side of the equation, and its analogical basis is forgotten. If it is remembered as a translation, mediation can be seen again as the source of human value, and nature—the only other—witnessed as its guarantor.

20. Nature is the only possible source of novelty. It can be considered the only possible source of information, and also more importantly, the only possible source for turning this information into meaning. Only nature can provide the absolute, the externality, that is the standard for non-trivial or non-tautological value; and it is only by adding value to information that meaning is secured. Heidegger notes the worry that from an enframed perspective, "everywhere man looks, he appears to see only himself."[p] Humanity sees itself most truly in the addi-

view from northwest

tions—and losses—in technology's transitory mediation of nature. The self is seen in the other's reaction; the machine is a tool for getting this other, nature, to react more significantly.

21. Since, in Nature, its interlocutor is finally, absolutely other, the machine may never actually overwhelm it to produce the hyper-real. The tension between this fact and its express program to attempt it gives the machine its fuller dimensions: the machine is tragic in the final, necessary defeat of intention (based on that intention's tragic flaw). It is also magic in whatever success that intention may achieve. But, it is mostly poetic in rehearsing the play between magic and tragedy that describes the human condition.

[a] Originally published in ARIS, vol. 2, 1996.
[b] In information theory value is quantified in terms of transmission volume and efficiency. It is interested in maximum possibility for coding in any message; random-

detail view

NOB 21

ness is the zenith of this possibility. Meaning, which is interested in reducing variety in support of communicating a more singular intentionality, is a bothersome obstruction to this possibility. This is the sense in which novelty is valued: since meaning is seen as confirmational, and therefore dealing in the known/knowable, only the new unknown can convey real information. Meaning is, by contrast, conservative and finally, necessarily repressive. N. Katherine Hayles, *Chaos Bound* (Ithaca: Cornell University Press, 1990).

[c] Jean Baudrillard, *The Ecstasy of Communication* (New York: Semiotext(e), 1988).

[d] *Ibid*. 23.

[e] What began as a fervent desire in the enlightenment has become an unfortunate reality in the present, as Heidegger and Marcuse complain in "The Question Concerning Technology" and *One Dimensional Man*.

[f] Walter Benjamin, "The Work of Art in the Age of

view from southwest at Zimmer Plaza

detail view

Mechanical Reproduction," in *Illuminations,* ed. Hannah Arendt, trans. Harry Zohn (New York: Schocken Books, 1969).

[9] Much recent criticism has focused on the dilemma of authoring 'open' texts, and has circled uneasily about the McGuffin of randomness. Derrida's highly canny and rigorous deconstructive logic shows how the singular intentions of Authority are unstable, but he offers few suggestions for the generation of new, non-parasitic texts.

Deleuze has introduced vocabulary (smooth space, lines of flight etc.) which names the desire for such openness and the recognition of happy "results" that might be "actualized' from this openness, and has been the critic who has most completely institutionalized the appreciation of novelty as a sign or source of this novelty, but such "recognition" already implies some retreat from randomness. Kipnis, with his interest in the practice of being an architect, has recognized the practical difficulties in

1. steel plate guardrail assembly
7. press-lock aluminum bar grating
9. collector truss
11. built-up subframe girder
12. diagonal pipe support
14. existing parapet

north elevation 1"=8.00'

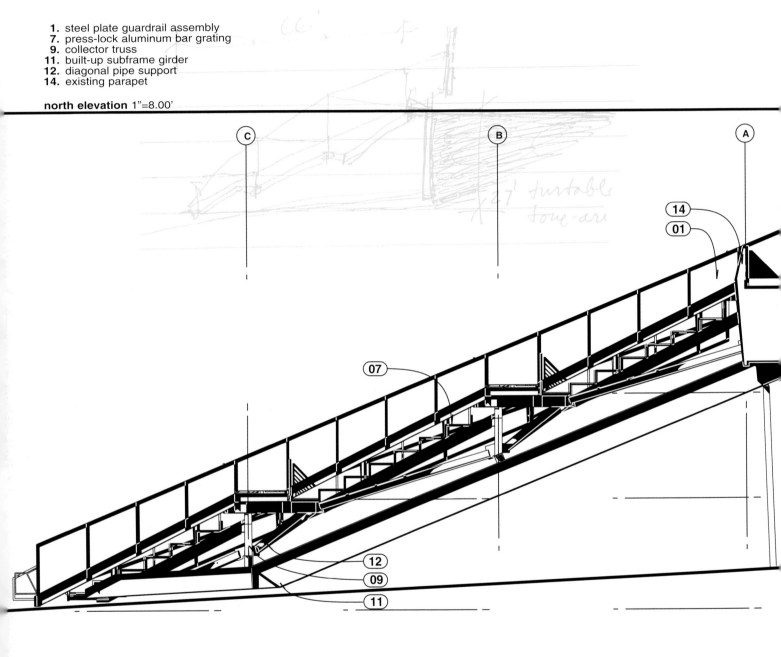

the 'use' of such randomness but suggests that "it is both possible and desirable to work in such a way as to respect undecidability." Jeff Kipnis, "Nolo Contendere," *Assemblage* 11 (April 1990), 57.

[h] Hayles, 59.

[i] Much recent, highly visible critical work is more "about" the theories illustrated, than the theories themselves are "about" reality. In a perfect example of this message, it is impossible to assign a generative priority to either.

[j] For example, unlike the abstraction that sees architecture as "frozen music," which already involves a layer of metaphor and is conscious of itself *as* a metaphor, the hyper-real physicality of collage, folding, or other "Deconstructivist" metaphoric formal strategies seduce practitioners into believing their own slight-of-hand. The results are presented as if the metaphoric leap was not obvious, as if stucco and curtainwall really *were* immater-

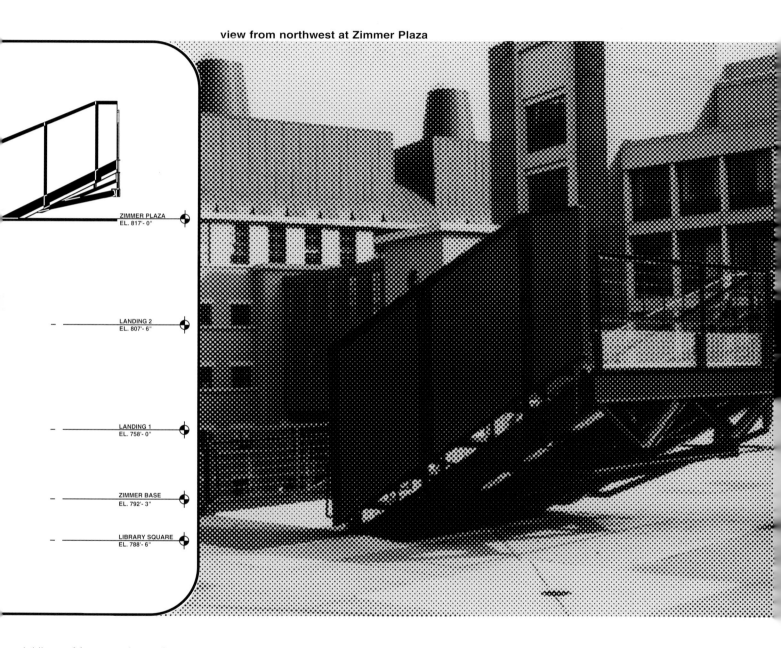

view from northwest at Zimmer Plaza

ZIMMER PLAZA
EL. 817'- 0"

LANDING 2
EL. 807'- 6"

LANDING 1
EL. 758'- 0"

ZIMMER BASE
EL. 792'- 3"

LIBRARY SQUARE
EL. 788'- 6"

ial lines of force or shear planes.

[k] This is Heidegger's complaint in "Question Concerning Technology." He would claim that any meaning "taken" through domination must be trivial since it can ultimately only be self-referential.

[l] Heidegger and Marcuse would disagree. For them the issue is not vastness because their focus is on humanity, and technology's persuasiveness, seen from only that perspective, *can* seem to be complete.

detail view from southwest

m Hayles, *op cit.* 188.

n Martin Heidegger, *Basic Writings* (New York: Harper & Row, 1977), 307.

o *Ibid.* 308.

p *Ibid.* 308 again: but he also notes this is a delusion, since in an enframed condition humanity's essence as a witness to revealing is perverted to the degree that humanity itself is questionable and thus properly visible nowhere.

28 The oldest myth is that of immortality, externalized in our machines.

P95.09/1
General Instruments
Philadelphia, PA

Client:	General Instrument
Architect:	The Hillier Group; Jones, Partners: Architecture (design)
Consultants:	Pennoni & Associates, Inc. (civil) Cagley, Harman & Associates (structural) Advanced GeoServices Corp. (geotechnical)
Site:	Seventy-five-acre parcel of sloping land in semi-rural corporate office park, surrounded by championship golf course, adjacent to Air National Guard airfield.
Program:	Master plan and building design for phased, five-building corporate regional headquarters, including flexible office and lab research space and support areas, such as cafeteria and conference center.
Size:	540,000 ft^2 (full build-out)
Systems:	Longspan steel truss on steel frame, concrete on metal deck, corrugated metal panel cladding and steel storefront and ribbon windows glazing, over cast-in-place concrete slabs and foundations, cast-in-place concrete parking decks.
Features:	To maximize flexibility for this leader in the highly volatile cable TV converter box industry, the typical suburban office building cores have been removed to the outer face of the building, leaving a column-free floorplate of 30,000 ft^2 in the interior; the sloping site permits the parking to be concentrated on two efficient levels at the center of the site, each level accessed at grade, and allowing all the buildings to face out away from the garages without sacrificing access.
Cost:	$60 million
Completion:	June 1996 (schematic design)

Even though this regional corporate headquarters for a high tech manufacturing company was designed for the specific client who would inhabit it as the user, it was designed in the context of the strictest speculative office real estate constraints and concerns for exit strategies and marketability. Consequently, the project was developed with an eye toward its universality and flexibility; it proposes nothing less than a new type for the suburban office building and for its aggregation into a multi-building campus. This proposal differs in significant ways from the standard suburban speculative office park, which should enhance its attractiveness to the more sophisticated or independently-minded user.

The master plan calls for an initial four buildings to be followed immediately by a fifth and eventually a sixth if necessary. Though this will be a single-user campus, the volatility of the user's industry, which requires departmental shuffling and manpower swings of 100 percent almost overnight, obviously dictates great flexibility, so each building will differ from the others only in the arrangement of their core elements. Chiefly this means that each will have the same stack of three 30,000 SF column-free floorplates, and each floorplate will have access to the same range of services. Thus, each floorplate will be able to serve equally: general office, wet and dry lab and light (prototype) manufacturing uses, though the latter will naturally keep to the ground floors of the buildings. Traditionally specialized activities such as the corporate admin-

1. business park access drive
2. corporate reception
3. helipad
4. footpath
5. golfcourse
22. future parking
23. future building
24. future road

site plan 1"=323.86'

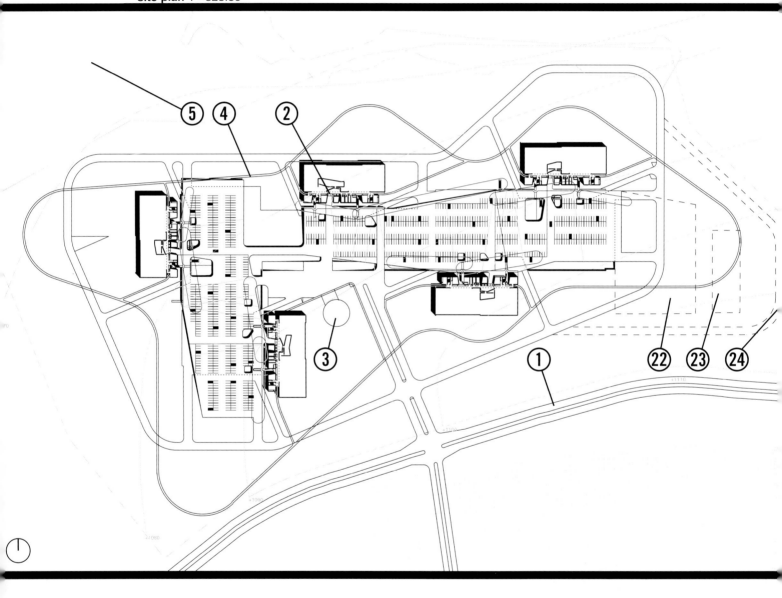

Abstract: Hyper-reality
1. When the chain of signification anchoring myth in substantial reality is broken, a condition of hyper-reality ensues. A dummy textuality then extends everywhere, supporting an absolute, anarchic freedom—that is hollow since meaningless. In this condition nothing stands in reserve, but only because everything is floating free. Like enframing and mythification, hyper-reality cannot be divorced as a concept from the technology enabling it. In fact, the advent of the hyper-real could be considered the combinatory culmination of the historical trends toward enframing and myth, brought to pass by the ultimate triumph of the technology mediation.
2. Specifically, the hyper-real is that condition in which a spontaneously presencing world of imagery supersedes the world of real stuff to which those images might refer. Instead, the images feed on each other in a frenzy of reference, without end or beginning. This is possible

istration, cafeteria, or conference center will be located in one of the central buildings, but will otherwise be treated as transient improvements to the shell space like all the other departments. Though there is a central campus security, shipping and receiving, and corporate entry, each building will have its own local versions of these, which would be located on either the ground or second floor, depending on whether it is an "uphill" or "downhill" building.

The site is a cleared seventy-five-acre parcel in an existing suburban speculative office park outside Philadelphia. Sloping generally south and west, it is surrounded on these sides and the north by a heavily wooded championship golf course. On the remaining side the site is bordered by the main access road to the office park. To the north of the office park lies a Air National Guard airfield. The general aspect of the site suggests an overview of the golf course where the most decent views are to be enjoyed. The PUD requires 4.5 cars/1000 SF parking, which pushes this development toward structured parking. The combination of the slope and view orientation, along with the significant parking requirement, dictates the major site strategy, which is to concentrate the parking toward the middle of the site in a consolidated two level structure, using the slope to access it at grade at both levels, and surround this parking "carrier deck" with the buildings, facing outward to the views. In this way the greatest amount of open space can be preserved in the most immediate adjacency to the buildings. Yet the parking has not been consigned to some auto hell—great attention has been paid to the design of the parking deck, with the intention of maximizing efficiency and convenience, but also to enhance the experience of this area. Features include a clear drop-off sequence and logical aisle layout, and also multiple openings in the upper deck for light, air, and orientation.

Entry to each building for employee and visitor alike occurs from the parking deck side, into the external core which "attaches" the building to the garage. Via vertical and lateral circulation systems within this core zone, access to the rest of the building is achieved after passing security at the entry point on either the ground or second level. The presence of the core on the exterior of the buildings—the signature element of the design and basis for considering it a new type—provides a number of advantages, both functionally and architecturally. On the functional side is the obvious increase in flexibility to the usable area gained by getting the core "out of the way." The enhancement of the imageability and wayfinding potential of the more logical primary circulation, benefit both future multi-tenant occupancies as well as present employee morale. This same advantage is enjoyed by the services, which are routed more efficiently in this largely single-sided layout; in addition, by bringing the core to the outside of the building where fresh air is available directly, the air handlers may be taken off the roof allowing a greater floor-to-floor dimension within the height limits dictated

1. business park access drive
2. corporate reception
3. helipad
4. footpath
9. parking

aerial view

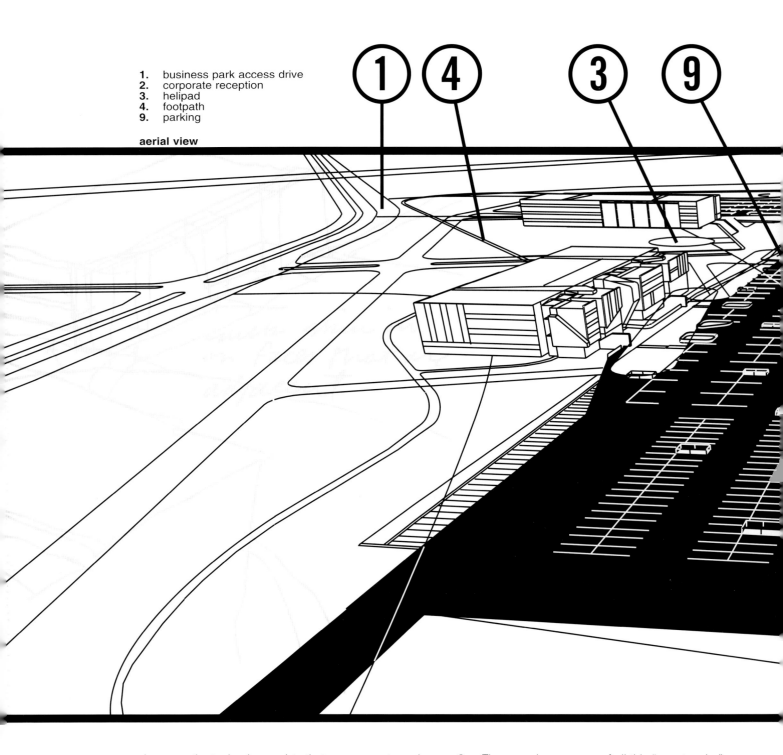

because the technology exists that can generate and disseminate models without regard to their "reality" or limits. In the hyper-real, the idea of transcendence has become meaningless; not in the manner, nor with the effects, though, envisioned by the critics who judged it "violent"; in a hyper-real world everything is metaphysical, so metaphysics is drained of its capacity for judgment—or inspiration. When the ideal is commonplace, the commonplace is placeless.

3. The pseudo-presence of all this "spectacular" imagery is exhilarating; an "ecstasy of communication" has overtaken society. An obscene, pervasive visibility characterizes experience, in which nothing is hidden, no secrets kept. Yet, this seems familiar rather than (or in addition to) frightening. It is the familiarity of a second nature, not unlike that presumed for enframing or mythification, except unlike them it does not cover up, hide, or mask some more real condition from which a critical per-

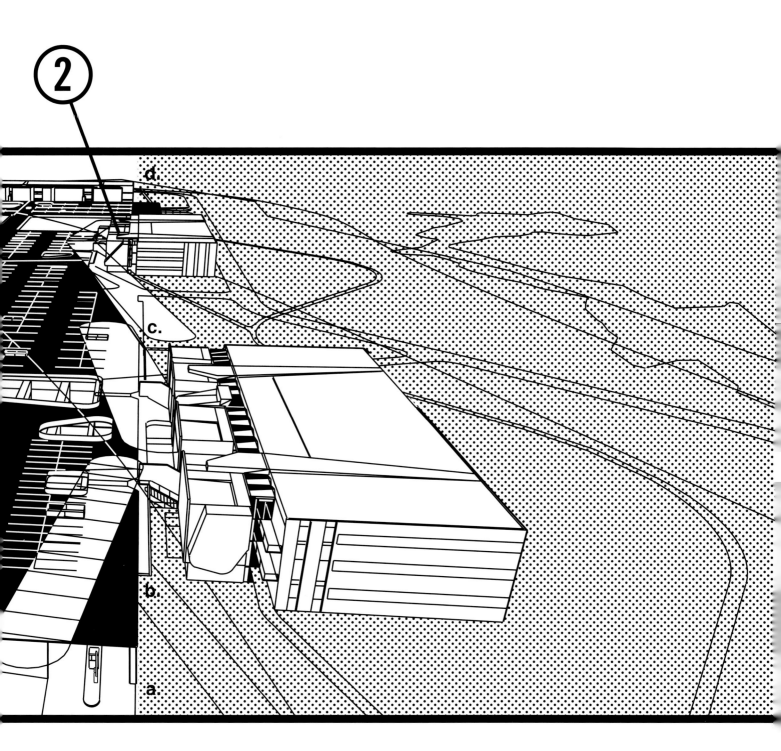

spective might object—it is the real, however "hyper," and the sense of exhilaration that prevents "familiar" from equaling "boredom" in this case is due to the assimilated competence with which this condition is faced by the community of surfers bringing it to pass. This familiarity may, in fact, as with universal enframing and completed mythification, as with a completed nihilism, signal a new datum of relativity, a new groundless ground, that opens the possibility for a new direct experience of a spontaneously re-presencing hyper-reality.

4. The stories society tells itself "set up a world," as Heidegger puts it. This "world" is still engaged in the world itself, pinned there by the "earth" as he calls it, that "juts up through." These stories frame experience in conventions, and while they may come to have the same adequacy as that framed, they remain still visible themselves as the frame. This frame is both the determinative part of the picture, the essence of its presence *as* a pic-

furniture layout

6. column-free workspace
13. conference room
14. UPS
15. pantry
16. copy room
17. elevator machine room
18. secure entry
19. shipping/ receiving
20. loading dock
21. transformer

ground level plan 1"=116.67'

ture—and obviously something foreign to it. By determining what is inside and what is outside, by naming stuff and setting it over-against, the frame says what will be taken as reality. The logic of supplementarity keeps the reality that grounds representation present, somewhere "jutting through"; no matter how much it may be obscured or masked in the story, it is still assumed to be there, hidden: the real has not in this been *replaced*. When reality is itself accepted as a frame, though, and put in "quotes," then the issue of what is inside becomes interesting. Society is now working its way through this possibility, encouraged by the technology that is collapsing the difference.

5. Baudrillard describes the contemporary "scene" as overtaken by an "ecstasy of communication." The propensity to mythification is pushed to extremes by a tidal wave of mediation, issuing from revolutionary advances in communications and computing technology.

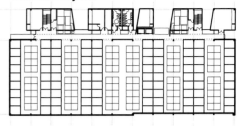

furniture layout

by the PUD. Finally, the occupiable spaces usually located in the core—conference rooms, copy rooms, break rooms, pantries, and restrooms—are given access to light and air.

Architecturally, the placement of the core on the exterior of the building answers many of the dilemmas of the suburban speculative office building type. By effectively providing free articulation to the facade it automatically enlivens what typically would be a bare stretch of thirty-six-foot-high wall that so taxes the wits of the architects usually designing these buildings—giving rise to the proliferation of desperate decoration, chopped corners, stepped window patterns or little hats. And it enlivens the facade in terms intrinsic to the building, not imported—when the user group is a high-tech entity like GI, then the technical nature of the core's expression becomes particularly appropriate. This position of the core, with its servant/service implications gives a direct orientation to the building, a front and back, a location for the entry and service access that is coordinated with the use of the building and its appearance.

The usable space cleared up by the removal of the core is further improved by the removal of the columns. Longspan truss joists at five feet on-center will freely span the space so that there are no impediments whatever to the planning of the area. All services will be provided on a regular twenty-five-foot grid from the generous ceiling volume created by the resulting deeper structure, including light, power, heat, air, ventilation, and data. All services and structure will remain exposed except in areas where the program dictates a more polite finish, in which cases a 2x4 suspended ceiling "cloud" will float free in that location, dressing up the ceiling.

Economics

Tens of thousands of buildings, representing billions of dollars of investment are constructed every year. Too often they are inappropriately sited, improperly scaled, badly constructed or poorly laid out, inadequately heated and ventilated, and just plain ugly. Many don't represent very sound investments. The perceptive client, determined to avoid these nightmares and build better quality, increases the project budget. Traditionally, the architect responds by applying ornamentation and zooty finishes: marble paving, cast stone entablatures and capitals, Spanish tiles, the lavish use of polished brass or bronze. The "improved" building is inappropriately sited, improperly scaled, badly constructed, poorly laid out, inadequately heated and ventilated, still ugly, and more expensive.

Even speculative budgets are adequate, if used thoughtfully, to create buildings of quality. There are a number of strategies for increasing quality without increasing costs.

Reliance on what is already there is the most economic approach, but requires the artful manipulation of the stuff of which contemporary buildings are

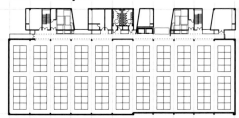
furniture layout

6. column-free workspace
11. reception
12. large conference room
13. conference room
15. pantry
18. secure entry

second level plan 1"=116.67'

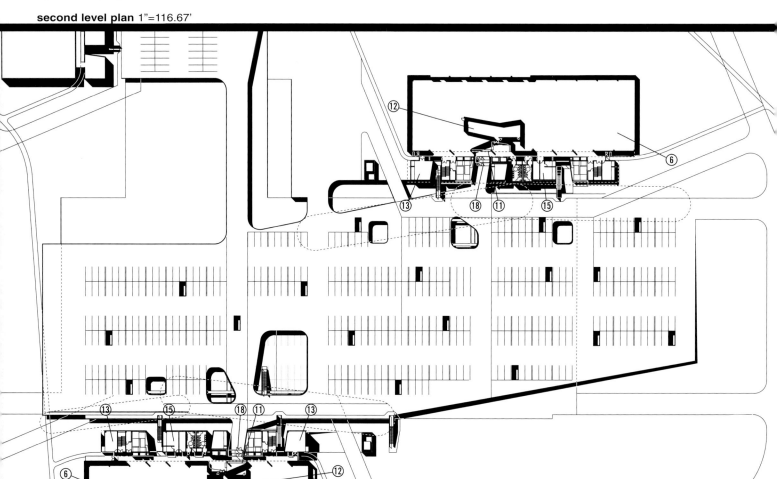

The resulting glut is "obscene." Echoing Barthes's deprecation of myth's depoliticizing effects, Baudrillard claims this is not "the obscenity of the hidden, the repressed, the obscure, but that of the visible, the all-too-visible, the more visible than visible; it is the obscenity of that which no longer contains a secret."[1]

6. Invariably, though, the obscene and its mediation as pornography describes a temporary condition, immediately prior to assimilation—the moment when all the secrets have been revealed but have not yet been accepted, when they have become common, but not yet matter-of-fact. Their unveiling is itself still remarkable, still downright obscene. It is in this sense that both mythification and enframing can be spoken of as obscene, but with decreasing passion: the mythic pornography of prostituted images *can* be recognized but it barely titillates, and the obscene technology of production and exchange, enlisting all to stand in reserve, remains in

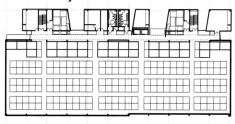

furniture layout

actually made. With the requirements of the workplace as a basis for expression, the standard for quality for the building as a whole can be established throughout, starting in the most humble spaces. All the elements of the building program, from the entry "experience" to the loading dock, the plant machinery, HVAC and structure to the workstation can be viewed together as a cohesive and expressive whole. The expense of applied ornamentation is avoided then. The need to create arbitrary or capricious form which force the building into some ill-fitting style is no longer necessary. The facility no longer needs to be dressed up because it looks fine just as it is.

Ninety percent of the architecture in ten percent of the space: a building which relies on "decoration" for its expressiveness must always face that uncomfortable point where the decoration ends and the real stuff begins. Decoration is imperialistic, it likes to take over, but rarely is a budget generous enough to smear decoration as far as it wants to go. Yet, even the most limited budget, if distributed creatively, with intelligence, can buy some special moments. And if these moments are not at odds with their less fortunate surroundings, but intensifications of them, then their magic will carry the rest along. They will lend their specialness to the whole building. Budgets can become strained when an effort is made to apply the decoration uniformly, but credulity is strained when the plain building itself peeks out from behind this makeup. The architect can use the budget available for architectural flourish in concentrated moments to create something worth the effort, something far more special than would be possible if applied equally everywhere.

The creative use of "off-the-shelf" building components: Contemporary designers have put such an emphasis on exotic systems and materials that their standard, straightforward cousins have been all but forgotten. Architects often rely on these exotic materials to mask a lack of attention or creativity. The innovative use of conventional materials, on the other hand, calls for just such efforts—imagining new, cost-effective ways to make the ordinary as special as custom materials and the dull, dignified. When the same off-the-shelf materials that are regularly used to build the building are assigned the task of creating the special moments, the results are a more harmonious whole, less likely to be off the mark. Off-the-self components cost much less than their off-the-wall counterparts, so they can be more extensively used to create those moments.

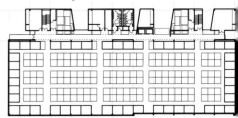
furniture layout

6. column-free workspace
11. reception
13. conference room
14. UPS
15. pantry
16. copy room
17. elevator machine room

third level plan 1"=58.33'

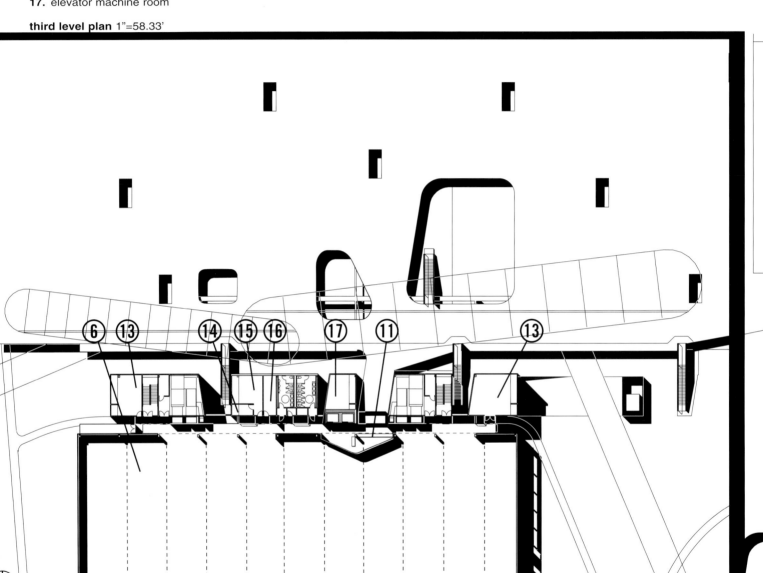

fact, but tastes great, and results in measurably less alienation. In each case, it is the new technology that is both cause and inevitable "savior."

7. Ironically, and crucially, this technology itself has no presence, so its effects are initially not *alternative*, but corrosive. This revolution brings no forms to copy or physical metaphors to borrow—no steamships or airplanes, no streamlining or purifying abstraction, no images or practices that could be appropriated or absorbed and turned to use.[2]

8. The new electronic technology, or at least what is electronic in it, is effectively invisible, and its workings highly mysterious to all but specialists. The coming cyberworld is singularly bereft of stuff of its own; it does not look like anything. It's not *really there*, only virtually there. Yet its effects are so compelling that despite their virtual—as in "not really"—existence they make the reali-

furniture layout

6. column-free workspace
11. reception
13. conference room
14. UPS
15. pantry
16. copy room
17. elevator machine room

third level plan 1"=58.33'

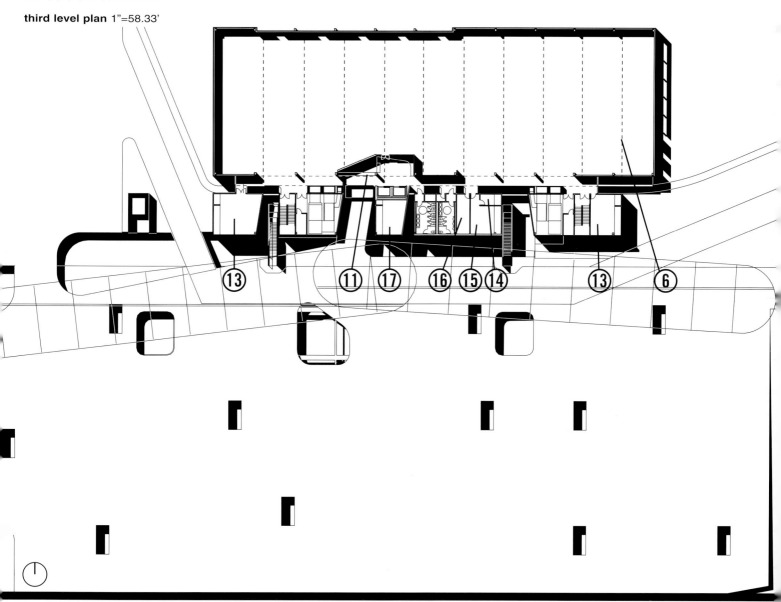

ty not in quotation marks pale in comparison. The substantive 3-D meat world is barely engaged by the electronic version. It is only the ubiquitous mouse "click" that makes the typical cyber-act substantial—makes it an act, a "real" act, on this side of the screen, that is—providing the barest cause for the still unexplained effect.

9. The gradual disappearance of technology in general has prepared the way for this final vanishing activity: from toasters to computers a progression of relatively anonymous boxes-with-buttons can be traced. The invisible has come to be equated with sophistication. As the perennial "house of the future"—that always looks proudly like a common Victorian or Ranchburger—demonstrates, the electronic can support anything. In fact, a certain reverse machismo is developing among the leaders of this revolution. The nerd-ocracy values the banality of the electronic body for the contrast it provides to the sophistication of its effects—like the little lady

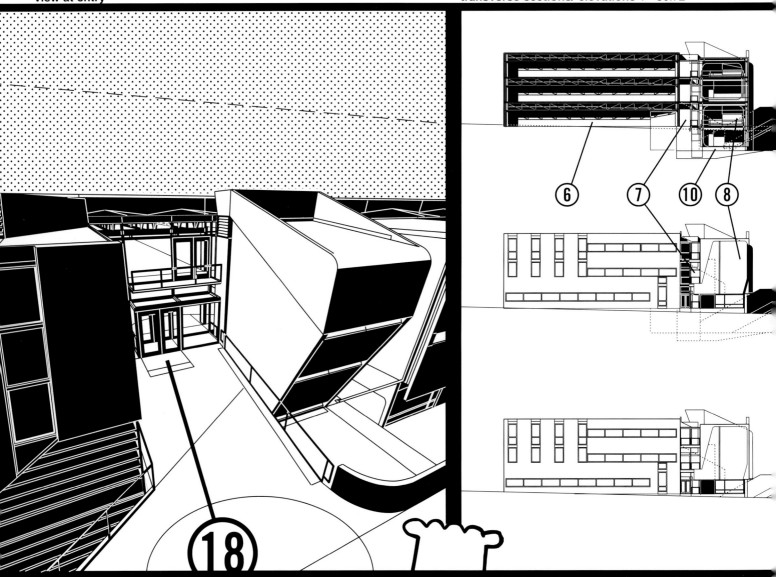

from Pasadena, the more advanced the object, the greater the incongruity between its appearance and its capabilities.

10. Architecture's traditional interest in the opposite sense of this relationship makes its position in this world increasingly delicate. The hyper-real, particularly in its cyber guise, challenges architecture on two fronts: it steals architecture's substance by collapsing time and space, and it steals architecture's thunder by taking

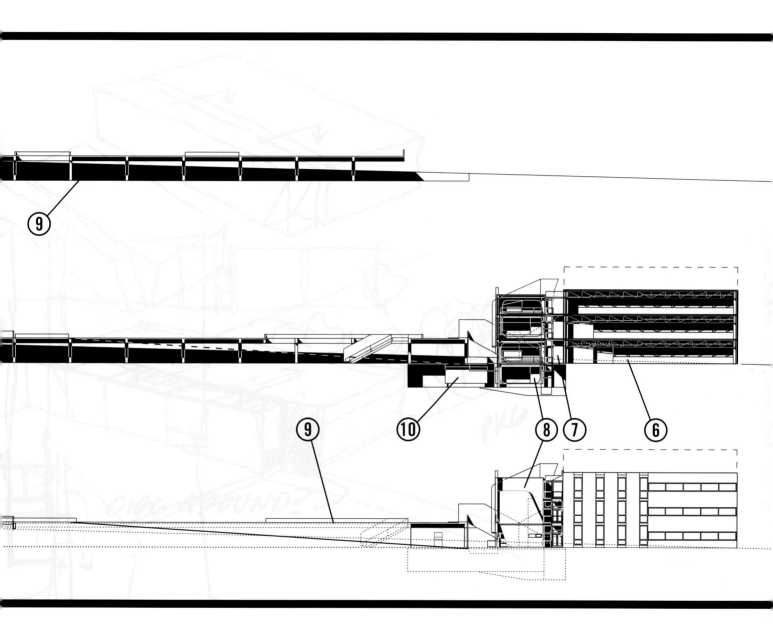

away its role as society's chief form-giver and means of expression. Since the operational effects of this technological revolution are compressing architecture's three dimensions into two in a virtual n-dimensional "consensual hallucination"[3] architecture connects with neither medium nor message. And society *prefers* that: today it prefers to find its image of itself and its place in the cosmos, in the insubstantial procession of fleeting simulacra. Where previously architecture's sheer bulk was valued as an anchor for the expression of authority, the expression valued today is lighter, faster, floating freely on the authority of trends and fads. The anchoring connection to substantive reality has been cast off, and with it goes most of society's interest in architecture's usual contribution.

11. This simulation-rich environment is not just a hopped-up version of architecture's comfortable world of symbol and representation. It is essentially different.

8. support functions/ core
9. parking
20. loading dock

view from south

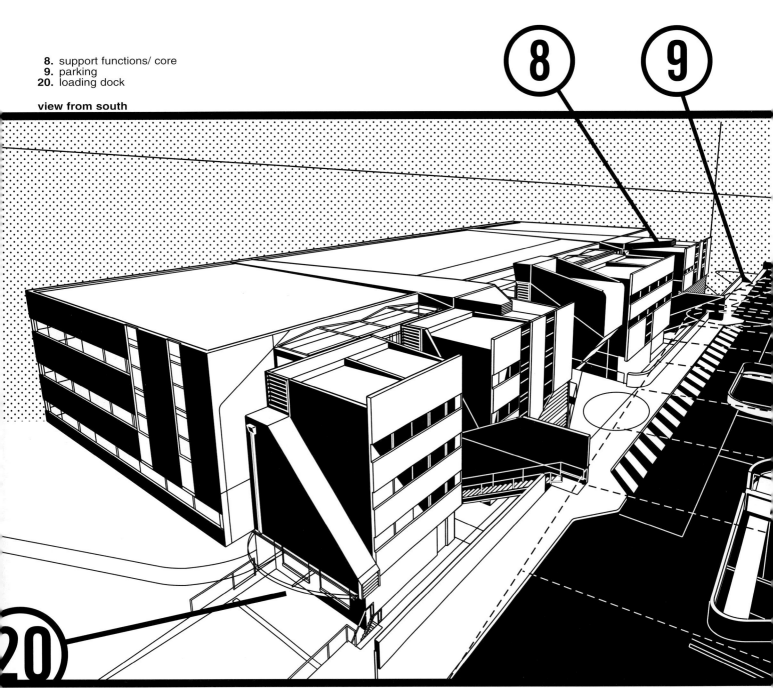

Simulation has superseded representation itself as reality, and thus collapses the distance of reference; the simulacra which act as place-holders in the traditional equations of meaning turn the value suspended in the difference from a signified or each other superfluous by eliminating tangible difference. Baudrillard points out that: "Simulation is no longer that of a referential being or a substance. It is the generation by models of a real itself without origin or reality: a *hyper*real."[4]

WITM 12

12. The hyper-real seems familiar in a way denied to architecture; it is a projection of the insides of the viewer's head out into a world that has become a screen—not the masking kind, but the receiving kind. The images and simulations that constitute the hyper-real take it into all corners of experience, so that it describes "everywhere you want to be," in fact and fancy, physical space, electronic space, cultural space. And they are re-projected by the producers and the viewers, as *re*producers.

8 support functions/ core

view from north

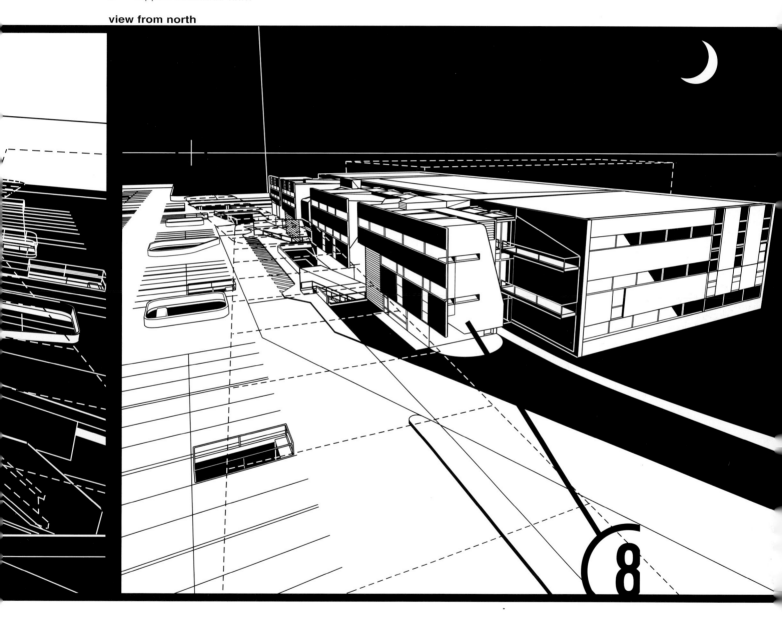

They crowd the memory and reemerge as templates for experience. The insides of everyone's head begin to resemble everyone else's. Ultimately, despite the amazing "effects" the imagery does not so much defy imagination as define it.

13. But this familiarity has not resulted in boredom. At least not yet. Folks are most fascinated by themselves, so when they find themselves everywhere they are stimulated—never mind that it may be all the same. Whatever *it* is, it is all addressed to the viewer: in a way solipsism could never bring off, hyper-reality caters to the subjective—as Barthes mentioned, it has a "buttonholing character" that comforts and empowers, that pumps up the individual. This "projection" is much more effective and direct than that relating the Greek orders to the viewer—there is no stretch of abstraction to overcome, or theory to swallow. Where the Greeks scaled the individual up to the architectural, the contemporary projection works in

7. primary circulation

interior view

the opposite direction: reality is scaled down to become manageable. The hyper-real projection "takes place" in a miniature world, in the sense first mentioned by Levi-Strauss: the number of dimensions and resolution, are reduced as well as their size, and so it becomes knowable and even more familiar. As imagery, simulacra, the world is set up to be manipulated: Photoshop and Quark have been grafted into the psyche, and the culture is really leaning into the learning curves on the way to a

Armani Exchange Redesign
C96.07/1
New York, NY

Client:	Armani AIX
Architect:	The Hillier Group; Jones, Partners: Architecture (design)
Site:	Corner of Fifth Avenue at 57th Street, in the center of the high-end retail district on the east side of mid-town.
Program:	Boutique "designer" retail space for menswear, women's wear and accessories, on three levels in existing high-visibility corner retail location.
Size:	9,000 ft^2
Systems:	Light-gauge painted steel framing for wall and ceiling panels with various infill, including glass, corrugated steel and fiberglass, and plywood; painted steel stair and catwalk billboard system; fixtures are painted steel with plywood placards.
Features:	Designed as a prototype for maximum flexibility, to fit into a variety of retail environments, the integrated system of fixtures, wall and ceiling panels still exerts a monolithic environmental feeling, expressing the sense of honesty combined with a sense of sophistication and playfulness that characterizes the merchandise; the flagship store uses its circulation system on the long exterior wall as a billboard feature.
Completion:	August 1996 (proposal)

The Practice of Souping Up
There are two edges in any retail environment that can carry information. The vertical edge we usually call a wall, and the horizontal one we call the ceiling or floor. In keeping with the idea of exchange, we propose to draw these both into the space where they can be experienced as edges. These elements will be understood as being part of the equation, and not just the things that happen to define the space.

What It Will All Look Like
The overall concept for the roll-out program is relatively straight-forward. We would create two types of modular unit. A spatial unit, and a fixture unit. The kit of parts from which this idea is assembled is small. All the pieces are modular, but highly articulate and flexible.

Aside from specialty items like stairs, elevators, or cash register booths, all stores are laid out with a multiple of these modular wall/ceiling units, and multiples of a single universal fixture type, "with optional attachments."

This single fixture-type accommodates all necessary storage and display conditions: tall and short hanging, with or without display; tall and short shelving, with or without lines or display; and mannequin-type display.

All this action is accomplished in the most low-tech manner, though, with bolts and thumbscrews. this

general competence and digital mastery. It may be familiar territory but it is heady and empowering to know the way around.

14. The hyper-real is in part super-real (and in larger part, as a miniature, less-than-real), thanks to the technology making it real at all. This technology permits the simulation to be, as a food critic once said, archly, about the McDonald's milkshake: "better than real." it is this fact, more than its deviation from a model, that frees the simulation of any necessary relations to an anchoring substantial reality. Of course, it is its origin in a model that makes it so perfect in the first place; in the hyper-real, though, the signifier, the simulation, floats free of all sources or origins—including the model that spawned it.

15. What is remarkable, always, is the object image and it alone—though it is only ever remarkable for the fifteen minutes allotted before its novelty wears off and it becomes a model for some other newness. Floating

keeps down the costs and increases convenience. These units, like the wall/ceiling modules, are also composed of a skin and a subframe. For both the fixture and the wall/ceiling unit, the frame is the universal element, while the skins can vary within certain dimensional constraints.

New York, New York
The Fifth Avenue site for the flagship store provides an extreme test for this system of panels and fixtures: the corner space is both tight and extensive. This space, spread over three levels, with small floor plates, massively intrusive columns and relatively low ceiling heights, is less than ideal for making a big splash, despite its location.

Having said that we feel that the Fifth Avenue store will provide the concept with the most challenging test, and "If we can make it there, we can make it anywhere."

To fit the roll-out concept onto three levels is itself no big deal. After all, it wouldn't make much of a roll-out concept if it weren't flexible. In fact, it helps us to tie the levels together, while allowing different orientations of the wall/ceiling system from floor to floor. By arranging them so that they alternate, we can impart a dynamism to the space without complicating it or messing up the wayfinding.

But to reach the three stores in one we're going to need one mondo vertical conveyance system. It's going to take up a lot of valuable floor space, so we have to make it do more than one thing. since the levels define the flagship store's difference from the rest of the fleet, we can use the big stair as the signature of the flagship. If we make this signature visible from the street, it can unify the three levels to make a bigger, urban-scale impact. When viewed from the street it becomes the billboard for the store.

But this means we are showing a big stair on the long streetwall that is usually reserved for display. In a vertical situation like this, though, the usual kind of display has problems—you can't see the outfits up on the second floor. This opportunity demands billboard type thinking. You can't really make clothes for giants, and big photos are just not the same. The stair makes perfect sense.

Although like a billboard, the stair fixture will have greater depth and interest. It will act as a line, delineating the exterior, but also creating a tension toward the interior. People know what to expect from the stuff inside, so the stair will act as a big X marks the spot.

Or rather AIX marks the spot. The signature can be elaborated in this zone with some urban-scaled graphics in translucent/transparent panels. The people in the store walk among these panels when they are in the stair zone, and everyone looks through them to see into and out of the store.

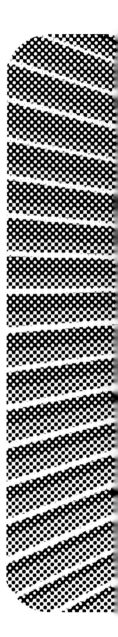

freely it empties itself of specific history and relationship. This gives it a perverse sort of autonomy, an autonomy of excess or plenitude that declares the object's history, provenance or apparent relationships unable to contribute to judgments of its quality or to have any bearing on its meaning. The differential logic of signification is turned on its head when the difference cannot keep pace with the signifier's consumption. Yet, this does not *diminish* that quality, it contributes to the creation of the super-real: with no lowly origin or meaning to tie it down, and a fifteen-minute evolutionary cycle, it may soar to heights of finish or perfection or imagination unrelated to any standards other than coolness. This is not a trivial standard. Though subjective and taste-driven, coolness approaches a condition of objectivity when the *familiarity* of hyper-reality is understood.

16. Because the standards evolve, and mutate, so rapidly, the notion of the ideal becomes relatively mean-

a. price and size monitor

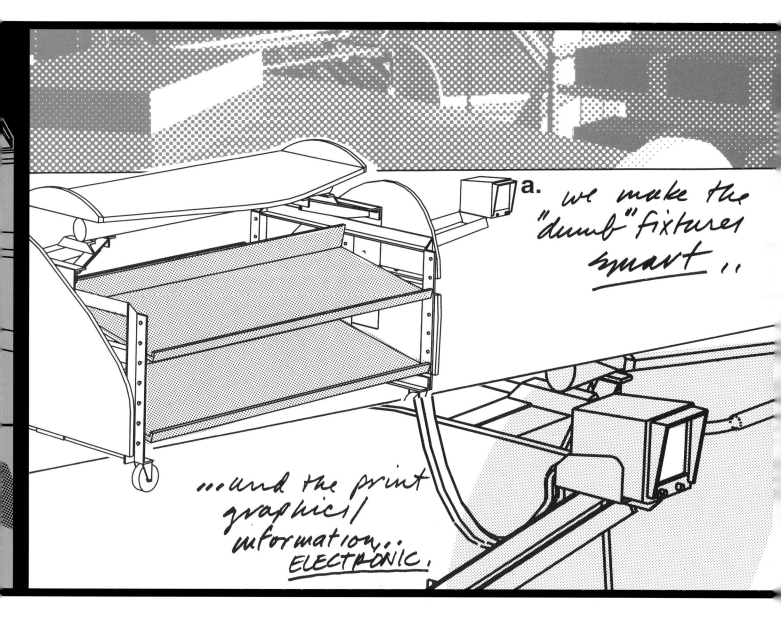

"we make the "dumb" fixtures smart..

...and the print graphical information.. ELECTRONIC.

a.

ingless. And when superlatives are common and differentiated mostly by inflection (cool vs. coool, for example), judgment becomes capricious or serendipitous, however "objective." **NOB 6** Even the classical ideals are too easily achieved, virtually, for them to be inspiring or to be critical; that is, for them to do what ideals are supposed to do.
17. Particularly in architecture, where finish and craftsmanship, wall thickness or topological resolution have been historical concerns, the ability of cyber-simulation to allow the viewer to experience perfection, must have serious repercussions. Substantial reality is no match for what can be created in the computer, and as the rendering capabilities improve to the point where *imperfection* is perfectly simulated, it is possible to imagine that architecture might flee physical space entirely. If architecture leaves the physical completely to building, then the difference is no longer one of quality, but of kind. This will

A. high shelf
B. low shelf
f. power/ data supply

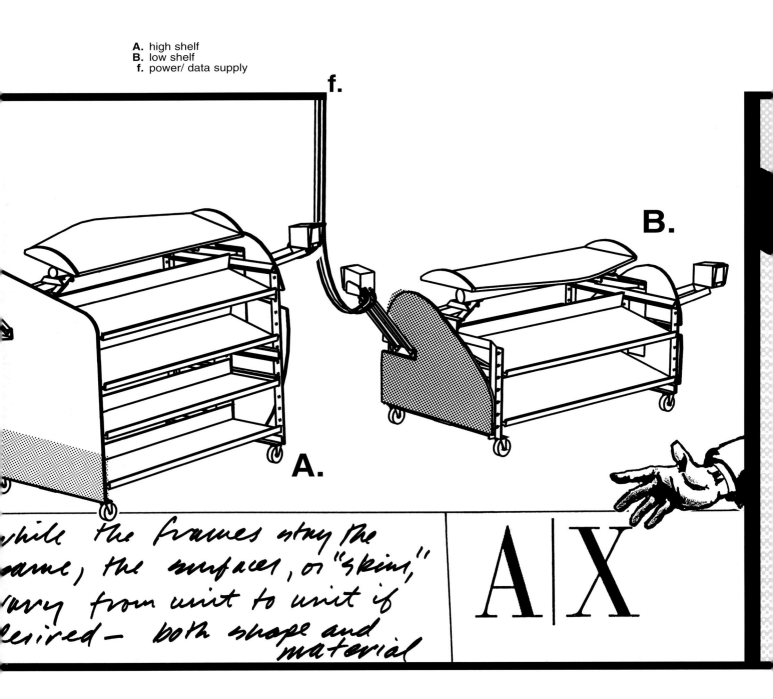

while the frames stay the same, the surfaces, or "skins," vary from unit to unit if desired — both shape and material

A|X

occur because physical architecture could not stand to feel the yearning toward this perfection previously experienced by building toward architecture. In the face of realized perfection, architecture might forfeit embodiment to avoid the disappointment of crudity, and choose instead to become mere building or a virtual dream of coolness.

18. In the hyper-real, metaphysics must lose the power of "violence"[5] or critique since it can no longer stand in judgment of a reality deemed less. In the hyper-real, the ideal is achievable, and reality itself is meta-physical. Baudrillard explains: "The everydayness of the terrestial habitat hypostatized in space marks the end of metaphysics, and signals the beginning of the era of hyperreality: that which was previously mentally projected, which was lived as a metaphor in the terrestial habitat is from now on projected, entirely without metaphor, into the absolute space of simulation."[6] As an essentially endur-

C. high rack
D. low rack
c. interchangeable side placard
e. high display rack

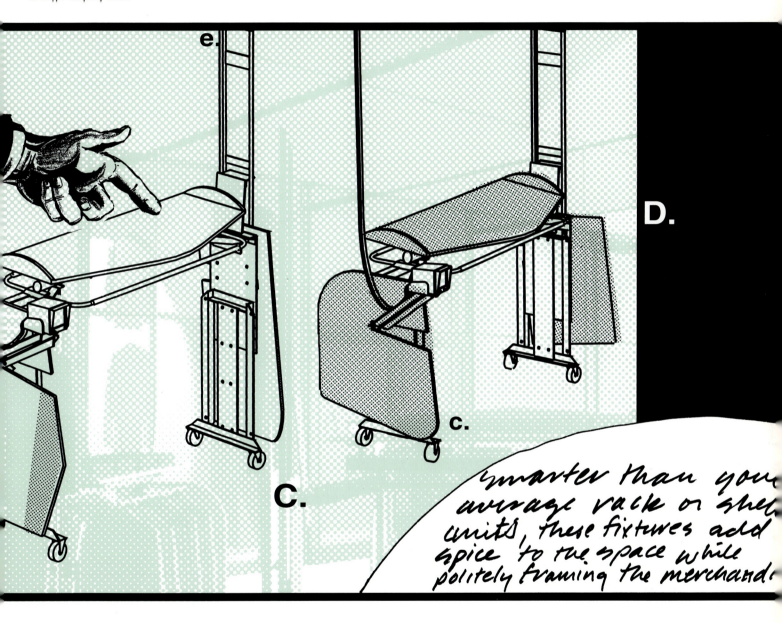

smarter than your average rack or shelf units, these fixtures add spice to the space while politely framing the merchand

ing—or static—exemplar, though, the metaphysical essentially lacks relevance anyway. Were this defining *timelessness* to be relinquished, and the sense of transcendence replaced with an appreciation of immanence as the threshold to real value, then the hyper-real might discover a suitable counterpart.

19. In the electro-temporal five-hundred channel hairball only the idea of the transitive, without predicate remains: the fact of the gaze is constant, but it never finds an object to settle on for long. When every thing means something else, no thing means anything particular. Electronic technology has taught the mind to flit, to surf the channels of experience without ever reaching the beach. An entire generation suffers from Attention Deficit Disorder; it has a variable, X, for a name: it could not make up its mind. Knowledge has been replaced with information, security with novelty, substantial reality by insubstantial image bites.

343

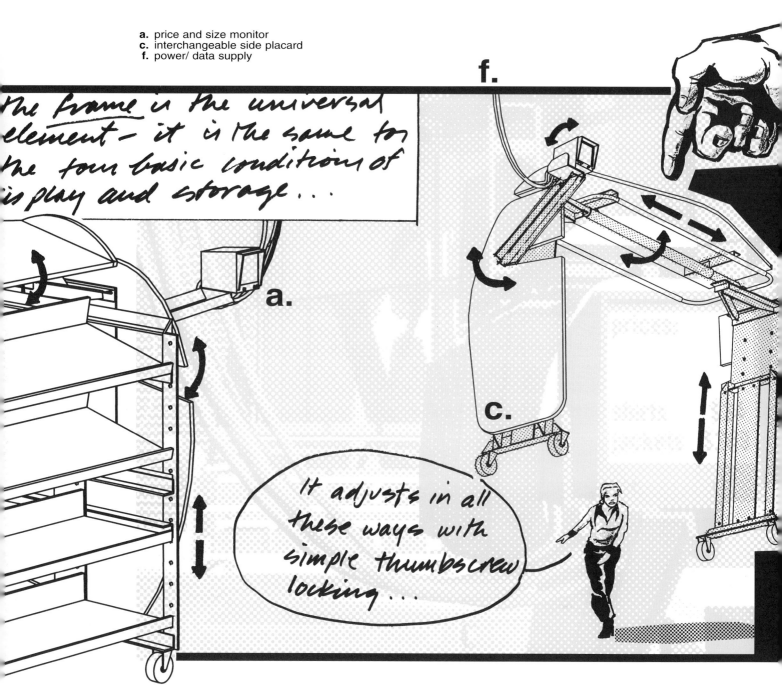

a. price and size monitor
c. interchangeable side placard
f. power/ data supply

The frame is the universal element – it is the same for the four basic conditions of display and storage...

It adjusts in all these ways with simple thumbscrew locking...

20. No longer can there be any certainty about the "relation between the image and its referent, the supposed real," says Baudrillard. Faced with the "virtual and irreversible confusion of the sphere of images and the sphere of a reality whose nature [it is] less and less able to grasp" humanity can no longer find security in the idea that the sign can be anchored in some substantial signified. The gold standard of reference has been quietly spirited away and all that backstops meaning is more meaning. However well-meaning the assumption (which is not certain) that signs "appear to refer to a *real world, to real objects*, and to reproduce something which is logically and chronologically anterior to themselves," it is no longer certain or seemingly necessary. Instead, society faces the onslaught of "simulacra, images [that] precede the real to the extent that they invert the causal and logical order of the real and its reproduction."[7]

21. Is meaning history then? Meaning happens when

344

MIT 14

value is added to information; when confidence or certainty also is added the result is knowledge. Both are casualties of the hyper-real. Information has been stripped of such confirmational, deterministic baggage and has become *information*, ceaselessly roaming, foot-
NIRM 2
loose and value free. Confidence that there might be an end to reference, in an anchoring, substantial reality is no longer something that can be just assumed. To ask what the chances are for meaning is to ask where value can be fixed in this turbulence. As value is a measure of confidence, to discover value is to imply *some* measure of certainty–at least that which secures the meaning *as* meaning. Where certainty is impossible, then, value is not natural. Can it be contrived? Can humanity fool itself?

Hyper-reality: Bossness
22. What does the boss object have to say about the

hyper-real? It is, after all, a work-like embodiment of equipmental being, an operational myth of the machine and substantial presence in the real world. Obviously, despite the hyperbole, the condition of hyper-reality does not contest the facticity of the world the boss engages, just its significance—its importance and meaning. Just as obviously, the boss is neither mired in reality nor afraid of the rhetorical heights of its hyper-trophied mediation.

23. Yet the boss connects with the hyper-real on a number of levels—as itself an image, a simulation, as an expression of ecstasy in communication, and as a vehicle for supporting the experience simultaneously celebrated and devalued in the hyper-real. In this, the boss distinguishes itself from other products of critique or affirmation by serving both equally; it "juts through" this new world, connecting it back to something really real, and it hovers, miraculously, as an inspiration to that real.

24. The boss first makes itself known as an image. It is a product of the culture of the image in the age of the image. Of course, it is an image of an intensely physical engagement with a substantial reality—that is, an image of explicit contrast to insubstantial imagery. Yet the value of the image to the boss's

F. corrugated steel liner
J. elevator

conception of itself is undeniable, and to a certain extent justifies the further claim that the boss is not just any sort of image, but a simulation. In this view, the boss, as a dream of the technological, as its myth, is based on no mere reality but on a super-real vision of techno-machismo that truly exists nowhere but is everywhere a model for what could be—for what the garage or shop would have reality be.

25. The painted flames on the sides of the hot rod and the greeter scoop at the entrance to the building both attest to the importance of this dimension of engagement, the affect of effect of object. The boss participates in the "ecstasy of communication" as a purveyor of techno-pornography. It trades the Botticellis on the museum wall for the pinup tool calendar, the austerity of high culture for the exhilaration of low. The boss is, after all, boss—not good, as beautiful, or true, or even cool.

26. The boss is hot. In this ecstatic zone it distinguishes itself from mere functionalism or the high tech: it is not interested in abstraction or distilled essence or purity; it is not even, finally, very interested in ideas. Though an obvious conceptual dimension lurks behind its overt imagery, the boss is mostly interested in experience.

27. The boss understands its function as the support of enhanced experience and its program as the promotion of that experience through all available channels. So, for example, it is not so much the fact of the space it contains, as the way it makes that containment felt; the boss understands this as an active pursuit, giving expression to the difference between explosive containment and inert containment, for example, through the shape of the space and of itself as a vessel; through a consideration of the ramifications for the entry interface, and the corresponding

B. low shelf
G. ground level/ accessories
f. power/ data supply

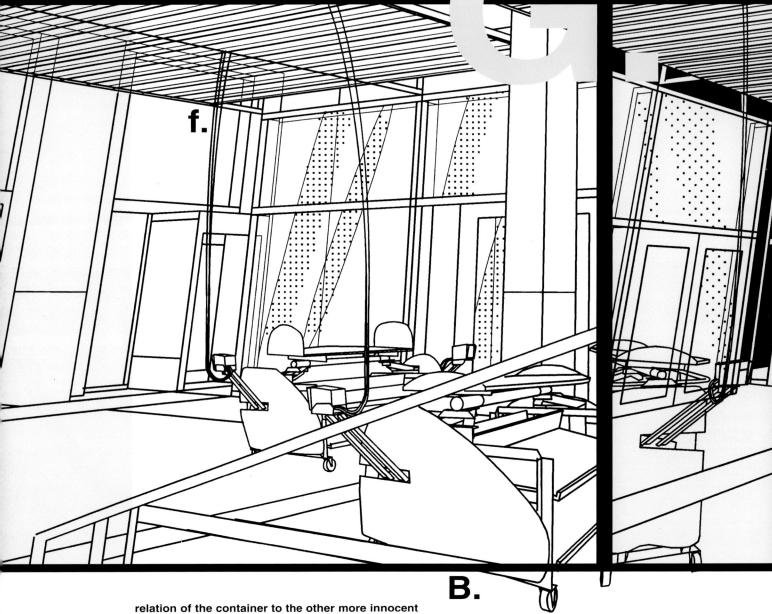

relation of the container to the other more innocent spaces; through the character of the subsystems and attachments, the bells, whistles, Klaxons and sirens, within the subject space and surrounding it. In all these ways and more, the boss emphasizes the remarkableness of the containment and the viewer's appreciation of that. It would certainly risk floating free of its moorings in this ecstatic display, if it did not take as its moorings that very experience.

D. low rack

28. For this reason, the boss must be seen as a true denizen of the hyper-real; not just something that gets along on a good day, but something quite at ease surfing the swirling storm of simulacra. After all, the boss is boss. Totally.

1 Jean Baudrillard, *The Ecstasy of Communication*, trans. Bernard and Caroline Schutze, ed. Slyvere Lotringer (Brooklyn: Semiotext(e) and its Foreign Agents Series, 1988), 22.

2 **The Mech In 'Tecture**[a]

1. The word *Architecture* comes from *architect,* which comes from *arche-tecton,* or first worker; the suffix *-ture* indicates the work itself. When the root is stripped of its descriptive prefix but the suffix is retained, it can be understood to name a more generalized practice of work, of making, or revealing. Available to receive prefixes on demand, this more generic construction serves

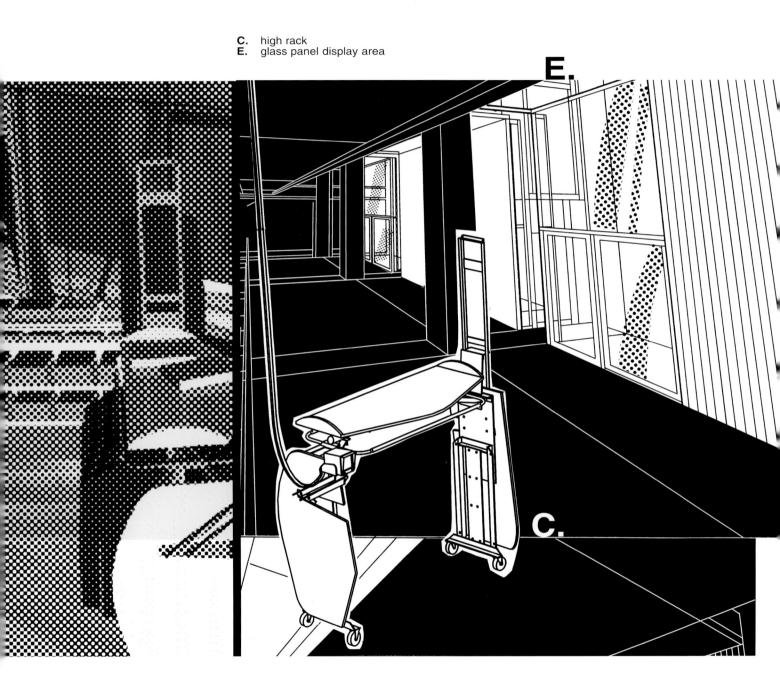

C. high rack
E. glass panel display area

reference to the multiplicity of cross-disciplinary modes of contemporary production, that may both taste great and be less filling. Cybertecture is becoming popular, for example, and Electrotecture has recently made its debut. For reasons beyond the unpleasant assonance and alliteration, though, or the allusion to fast food, Mech- does not work so well in this construction without the addition of the preposition *in*, which allows the otherwise redundant neologism to express the essential relationship between the parts.

Electro-Tecture

2.   Paradigms are assumed to succeed one another, neatly. A simple Hegelian symmetry seems to hold, marking the route to the future with thresholds and gateways. Histories unfold in discrete chapters that begin with one revolution and end with another. Propositions against the *avant* trend are de facto *retarditaire*. Since the values that determine the difference are received, they are suspect

Shanghai North Bund Plaza
C96.09/1
Shanghai, China

Client:	Shanghai Sinogood Real Estate Development Co.
Architect:	The Hillier Group; Jones, Partners: Architecture (design)
Consultants:	Shanghai Institute of Architectural Design and Research
Site:	Full city block at northern edge of Development Zone 2 in the North Bund area of Shanghai
Program:	Speculative mixed-use development, phased into two structures, approximately sixty percent commercial, including twenty percent entertainment, and forty percent office space, of which approximately thirty percent is residential office, and parking for 2000 cars.
Size:	1.8 million ft^2
Systems:	Ductile moment-resisting concrete frame on cast-in-place basement garage with spread footings and piles at various site locations, cast-in-place and precast cladding, steel curtainwall and mechanical louvers
Features:	Departing radically from the standard appearance and organization of commercial structures in Shanghai, the design creates a signature, or "landmark shape" in two phases to help spur development of the North Bund area; organized as a machine-for-commercial traffic, the two buildings rise out of a carefully planned pedestrian and vehicular circulation scheme, including bicycles, that is completely permeable to the flow of city life through, around and into the complex, knitting this massive new neighbor directly into the existing city fabric.
Cost:	US $80 million
Completion:	January 1997 (competition)

The main idea for the project is that it be like a new Little City. This is obviously expressed through the architecture of the building and window patterns, but also in the functional relationships and in the project's programmatic flexibility. Each aspect is inseparable from the others; each reinforces the others so the whole is greater than the sum of the parts. Like a city downtown area, the project is exciting, energetic and rich in experience, as well as functionally practical.

Rather than imposing some arbitrary style or composition on the buildings and then trying to force the spaces to fit into it, this scheme starts with the spaces and connects them freely to the city. The honesty of this approach leads to its own architecture, unique to the project, not borrowed from some other project. This approach to architecture has the newest look anywhere, stimulated by the latest advances in electronic technology and complexity theory that is just now finding its way into design in New York and San Francisco.

Newer even than "Deconstructivism," this design combines the visual freedom of virtual reality and cyberspace with the hidden order lying underneath complex natural phenomena, being detected these days by the new science of chaos and complexity. Complexity theory says that many systems formerly considered random or chaotic, like the weather or turbulence, actually display an underlying order if looked at in the right way. New advances in computer technology now make it possible to discover

5. pedestrian circulation drum
6. bicycle circulation drum
24. exhibition center

view from southwest

reappropriated, on new terms, during the spincycle of the revolution.

3. The "electrotecture" issue of *ANY* (no. 3) seemed to describe a point on such a determined curve; a survey of the architectural possibilities of the electronic and the idea of the electronic in the "postmechanical era," it engaged in a lively "rethinking [of] the physical and conceptual properties of the architecture of the future."[b] In the present issue, the continuing possibilities of a mechanically influenced architecture in this "postmechanical" future are debated. The geometry and romance of paradigm succession invoked in the electrotecture debate can only cast the idea of mech-in-tecutre as counter-revolutionary.

4. Revolutionary change is oppositional, rather than evolutionary: "revolution" is an incendiary word. Except when used retrospectively, it is a call to arms. A revolution does not simply oppose the status quo, however; it

this order, and the virtual reality of cyberspace allows this order to be modeled so it can be visualized. Since it is architecture's responsibility to express society's highest aspirations and best understandings, this design takes its inspiration from this cutting-edge research. When this new understanding of science is translated into architecture it results in spaces that are both exciting and comfortable, unusual and familiar.

To be economically reasonable, the design must communicate a sense of this excitement without making everything too electronic or too complex. This is where the art of design comes in: this design represents the latest advances, and symbolizes the newest ideas, but still can be built for reasonable cost with existing technology. But the visitor will never know.

On the facade is a complex, freeform window pattern representing a cross-section of the urban order. This collage of city imagery will heighten the sense of intrigue, encourage exploration and hint at a variety of constantly changing experience, like in a city. Since this project is based on a logical circulation diagram and central organizing space, though, its architectural variety and dynamic spatial experiences creates a desire for exploration, not confusion. There are many "places to meet" in this Little City.

The Little City is a seed for the future building development in this area of North Bund. As the leader of new development in the North Bund, the building does not simply obey the orientation of the streets surrounding it. Instead it calls out to its distant urban neighbors to follow it into the future, turning to face the Pudong and Bund, addressing them as a proud symbol of the strong future of the North Bund. The Phase Two facade also turns to face the neighborhoods to the north, inviting the residents to come into the North Bund to shop. Simultaneously, by turning to face their friends, the buildings also twist southward to face the sun.

The facade facets represent the many aspects of Shanghai and its vibrant culture; the angled forms draw inspiration from the cutting edge of technology and design to represent the energy of the city as it stretches and grows to embrace its future; the vertical circulation cores are like the strong historical core of Shanghai which root the building in long tradition of openness to the future and other cultures; the sparkling steel and glass windows emerging from inside the heart of the structure are like the inner magic heart of the city, welcoming to the citizen and the stranger.

Like a city, the project is zoned functionally—some parts are designed for excitement, and some parts are designed for efficiency, some are visible and some "behind the scenes," but each contributes to the overall vitality of the design.

Instead of emphasizing the expression of the programmatic functions, which need to be flexible, this scheme expresses the service functions common to all the programs, which will never need to change: no matter how much the rest of the spaces change from office to retail, the service spaces will need to remain in their most efficient layout. These service elements are the vertical circulation "cores," the mechanical equipment rooms and restrooms, and the stair towers. By expressing their vertical continuity right up out of the ground and up to the roof, all the various levels of the building are united. This organization is like a tree, with the parking ramps and floorplates as roots, the vertical cores as its trunk, and the commercial and office spaces as the branches and foliage. Way-finding is easy when the vertical circulation is so clear. In addition, by expressing the technical elements of the project in this way, it is possible to communicate modernity and technical sophistication without being expensively or alienatingly "high-tech."

05

attacks the revolutionary primogeniture that established that status "in the first place." It proposes new insights that are prior, deeper, higher, more fundamental, more "meta-." Only the latest is truly, really really different, a total revolution: of electrotecture, Mark Taylor wrote, "in contrast to the so-called revolutions of the past, in which an alternative replaces its opposite, electrotecture calls for a refiguring of the very terms that define architectural theory and practice."[c] Electrotecture's capacity to fulfill

5. pedestrian circulation drum

view from southwest

the futurist dream of the "annihilation of space and time,"[d] means in the "postmechanical era" that "the very conditions of architectural theory and practice are irreversibly altered."[e]

5. The dynamics of mediation, to which critique is also subject, have set up electrotecture as the next "-tecture," erecting the expected "post-" and filling the slot on that trajectory to relevance. Derrida points out that the "use of 'post-', as in 'postmodernism' or 'poststructuralism,' still remains hostage to a 'historicist compulsion,' a 'progressivist ideology.'"[f] Though seemingly hostage to this compulsion, electrotecture may signal the exhaustion of the logic of revolutionary succession—without surviving itself as the last word.

History Is History

6. Hal Foster describes the mediation of history as a convenient reification. The "ancient" institution of architecture as a mnemonic aid is evidence of a "tendency to

357

2. entertainment
3. retail
4. atrium
13. apartment-style office
14. open office
33. outdoor deck
35. mechanical

longitudinal section 1"=83.33'

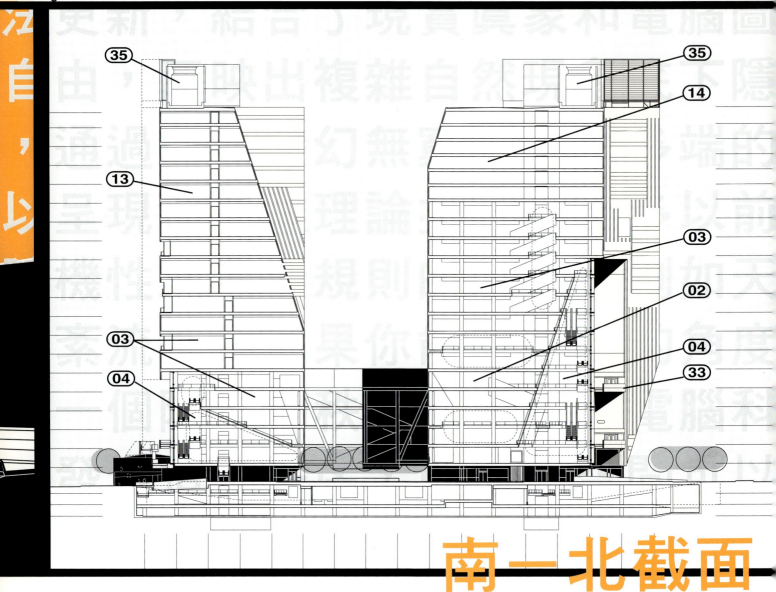

think of memory in terms of space, in effect to spatialize time, to pictorialize history." "Pictorialized history" becomes demarcated or framed, assigned borders, and "comes down to" the present in a series of discreet "tableaux."[g] The gestalt assumed for each "perspective" dictates a necessary remove from the present, a non-navigable "middle ground," across which it is viewed, from "where" its borders can be discerned. The present, correspondingly, is framed, apart. The most recent past "right under our nose," has not yet receded to the "distance" necessary to imagine it as history, it is circumscribed and objectified, packaged and consumed, with a passion that compensates for its lack of "natural" distance: it is history, dude. The sense of disdain in this pronouncement is palpable. It goes from being "in" to "out," or "wired" to "tired," winner to loser.

7. The idea of progress, either emancipatory or positivist, overlays on this spatialization a grid of value, and

5. pedestrian circulation drum
6. bicycle circulation ramp
33. outdoor deck
34. connector bridge
35. mechanical

west elevation 1"=83.33'

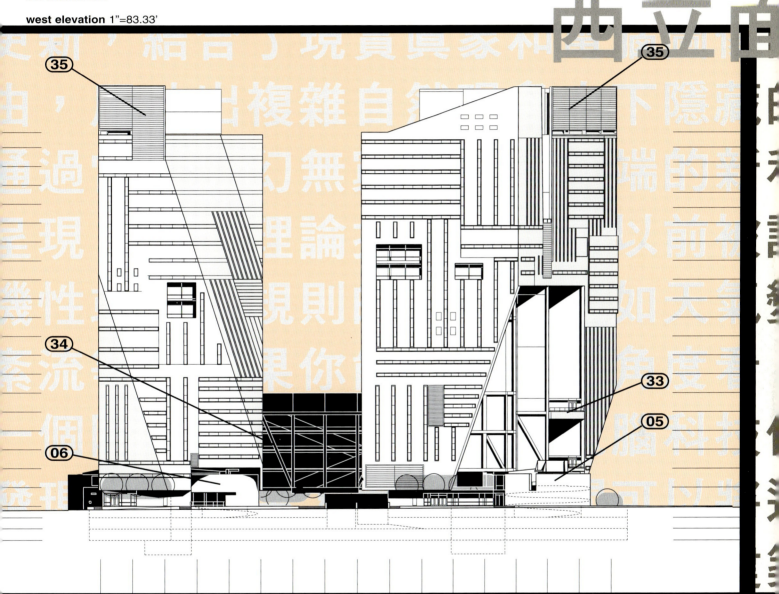

the past—particularly the most recent, becomes inferior instead of just before. Foster mentions Walter Benjamin's observation that "the just-past can be a strong anti-aphrodisiac."[h] An image of Benjamin's and Paul Klee's *Angeles Novus* ("who, caught up in the storm called progress that propelled him backward into the future, sees nothing but ruins amass before him"[i]) describes an attitude—not so much of this imagined observer, but of the critics who imagined him—that views the passage of time as ruinous, rather than validating. Validation that occurs as avant becomes establishment is suspect rather than sought. Even evolutionary progress assumes the ultimate disposability of the past; revolutionary progress compacts and double-bags it. The completion of each increment of the holy timeline is signaled by the canonization of that period's masterpieces as the next's embarrassments. Emblems of our postmodern-historicist period, for example, rank right up there with disco and

4. atrium
5. pedestrian circulation drum
35. mechanical

south elevation 1"=83.33'

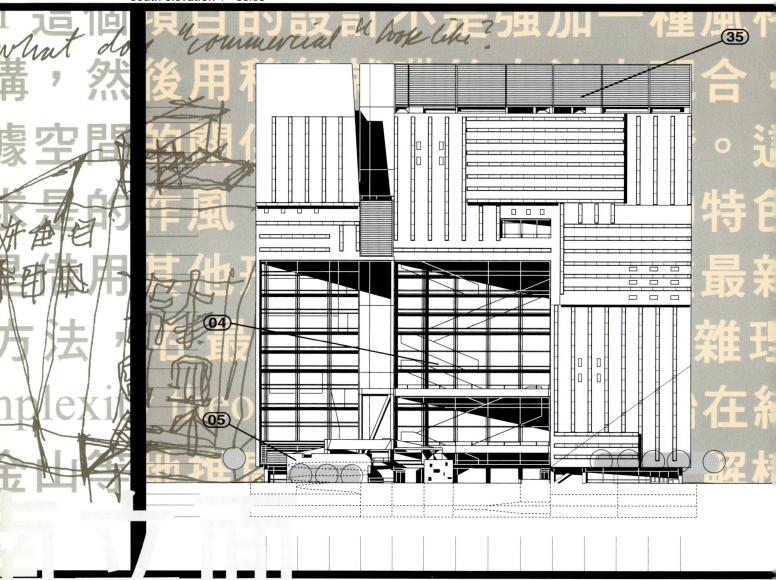

platform shoes. Deconstructivism must be congratulating itself already on leaving so few traces.

8. This "fetishistic," historicizing habit[j] has collided spectacularly with the electronic "annihilation of space and time," predicted with such enthusiasm by the futurists a half century earlier. The resulting confusion, where the ruins crop up in every direction, has been described by Ignasi de Solà-Morales as "a diffracted explosion in which there is no single time that can be used as material with which to build experience ...."[k] The "collapse" of space and time by electronic technology, the "disappearance" of distance and the "condensation of time into a present undisturbed by past and future,"[l] has led many to hypothesize this condition as the "end of history."

9. The present cannot be seen as the end, however—as either the culmination or disaster of any strand of development. The sense of continuity denied by a "spatialized" time that cordons off discrete "areas," is not

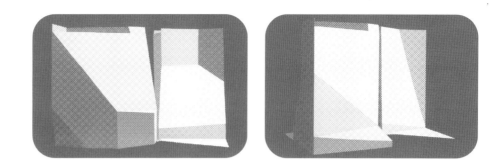

5. pedestrian circulation drum
6. bicycle circulation ramp
34. connector bridge
35. mechanical

east elevation 1"=83.33'

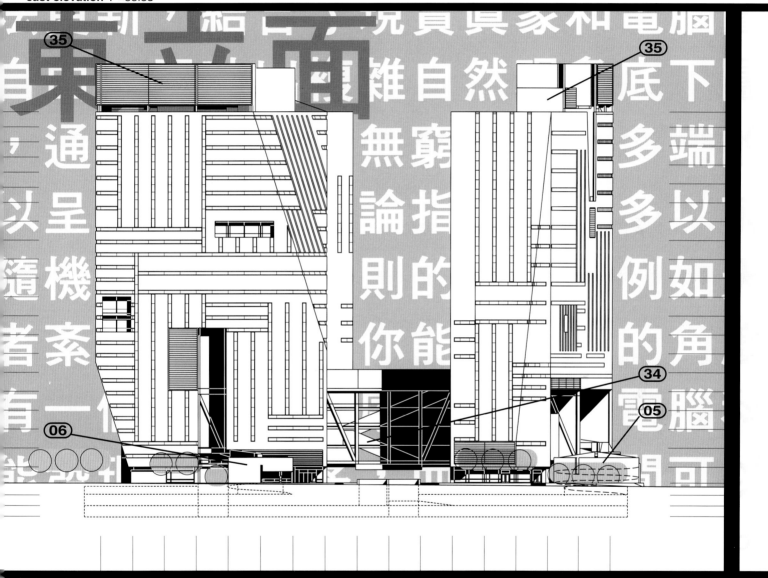

restored when those areas are multiplied into a bewildering array of possibility. While the trajectory that would secure the privilege of any one history could be isolated, it cannot avoid being immediately overwhelmed, one channel among five hundred. In this electro-temporal hairball, the progress that might privilege the present is replaced by con-gress, di-gress and e-gress, and the beautiful validating trajectory of any timeline loses its shape. The logic of revolution, of the succession of paradigms, is defeated by the very spatialization of time when it becomes infinite, when that space becomes the multiplicity. All the borders come down and time becomes valueless duration without succession. Even the evolution of thought, which measures progress through difference, has sped up to the point where ideas merely proliferate, rather than replace; ideas mutate far more rapidly than the contexts that spawn them, and then quickly break free from those anchors. Each new

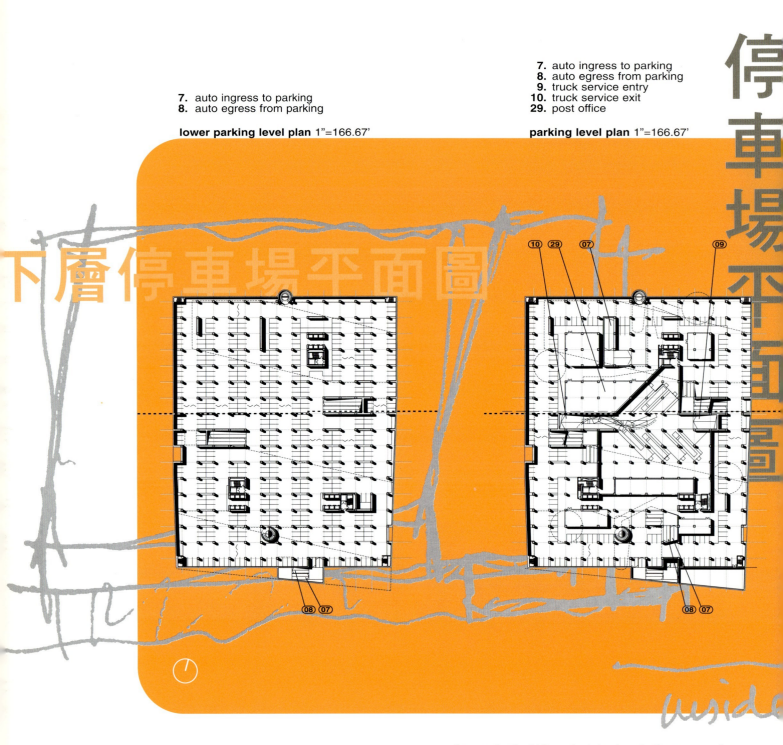

7. auto ingress to parking
8. auto egress from parking

lower parking level plan 1"=166.67'

7. auto ingress to parking
8. auto egress from parking
9. truck service entry
10. truck service exit
29. post office

parking level plan 1"=166.67'

"generation" of ideas deviates to a further remove from the continuing problems that were originally addressed. 10. As the primary agent of this dissemination, multiplying the multiplicity but effectively removing the borders that Balkanize it, electronic technology has made it impossible to untangle this complexity from a relation to the past. Each strand, facet, and angle has its own history present now, for consumption, so this complexity cannot stand, itself, reified or not, as the difference that

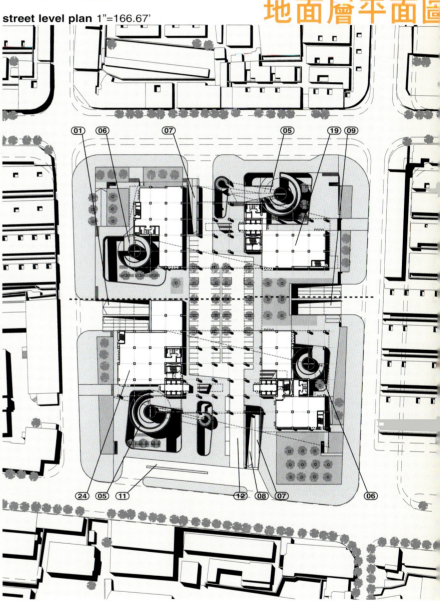

5. pedestrian circulation drum
6. bicycle circulation drum
7. auto ingress to parking

bicycle level plan 1"=166.67'

自行車停車場平面圖

5. pedestrian circulation drum
6. bicycle circulation drum
7. auto ingress to parking
8. auto egress from parking
9. truck service entry
10. truck service exit
11. auto drop-off
12. auto drive-through
19. brand name boutique
24. exhibition center

street level plan 1"=166.67'

地面層平面圖

would demarcate the "electronic" revolution from its pre-morbid electric or mechanical periods. It is in this sense that the "end of history" seems most vivid. The electronic revolution has broken down the fences by which it could define its own difference from the past.

Meaning Is History
11. If meaning is historically determined, then it must be threatened by the electronic revolution. The loss of difference in contemporary pluralism is foreshadowed in descriptions of the hyperreal; the simulacra that act as placeholders in the traditional equations of meaning make the value suspended in the difference superfluous; inflation has devalued the superlative, including architecture, and "work on form has been suspended."[m] The subject has been decon-stituted, read its rights, and then resurrected as a reader who must come up with her own meaning ....

ONHR 12
NIRM 4
WITM 12
ONHR 18

12. ... Apparently, this is evidence of a new paradigm;

363

19. brand name boutique
20. fashion shops
28. large scale supermarket
34. connector bridge

first level plan 1"=166.67'

17. restaurant
21. fitness center
25. children's area
26. ladies fashion department
27. kareoke
30. sports equipment
31. toy department
33. outdoor deck
34. connector bridge

fifth level plan 1"=166.67'

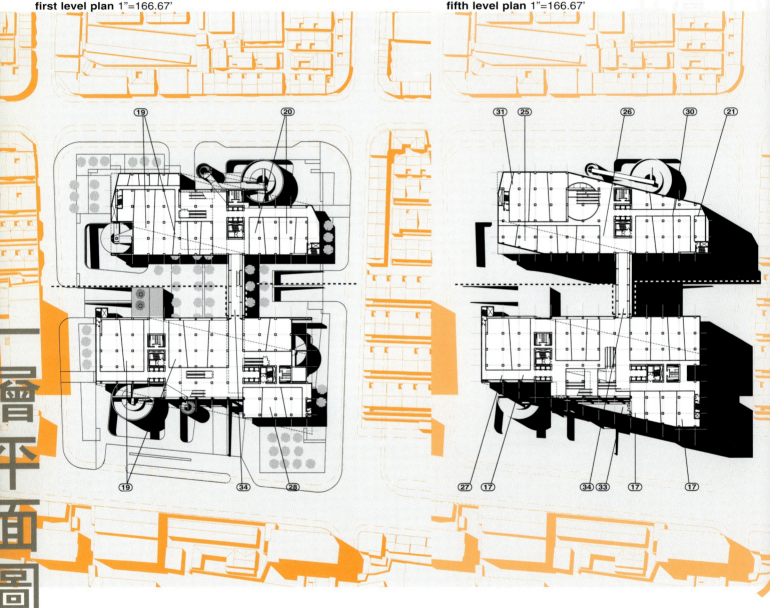

the dominance of the mechanical metaphor as a way of viewing the world is waning. In place of common-sense mechanical analogy and interpretation, an explosion of electronic imagery—a mediated reality—is asserting itself. With history, meaning is being "collapsed" in this mediation, the electronic sense of communication is fundamentally different from the mechanical sense. The fences of simile once raised against the draining of meaning have been breached; "likeness" is now drowning difference.

13. The media is not just the medium—it also is subject to this flood. The fields that are contrasted with objects, the reified objects and constructs themselves that weave them, the nets, the hypertext, the simultaneity of cyberspace that visualizes the impossibly complex interconnectedness of that activity, or the virtuality of telepresence, which absurdly undermines the privilege of substantial presence—all are too easily grasped images of

13. apartment-style office
16. cinema
17. restaurant
22. food court

ninth level plan 1"=166.67'

13. apartment-style office
16. cinema
18. coffee shop
23. furniture and appliances
32. office supplies

thirteenth level plan 1"=166.67'

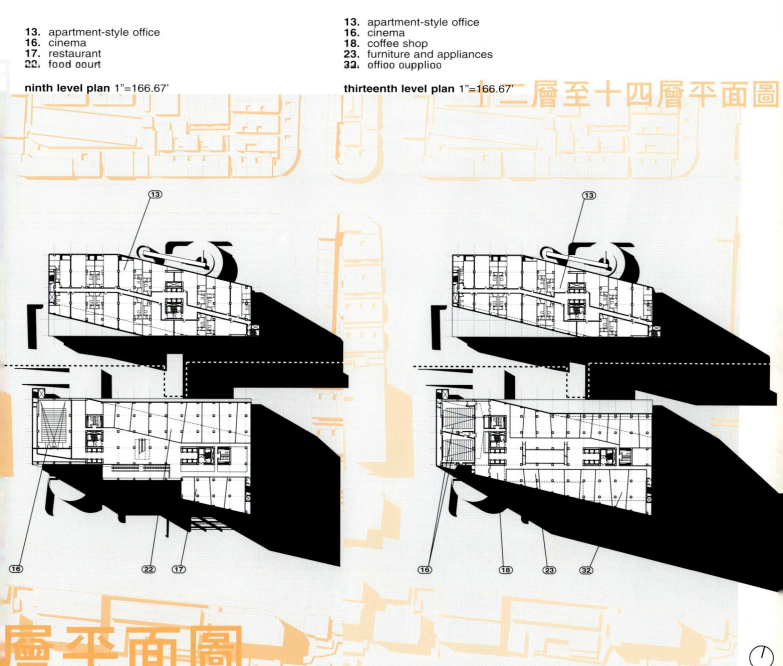

impossible things, culled from conventional pre-electronic stock. If "a completely unique [as in new] object ... were imaginable, [it] could not be described," because "lacking metaphoric connections, it would remain inexpressible."[n] The explosion of such expression cannot indicate a wealth of novelty. In fact, the relationship is one of inverse proportion. While there is no shortage of new words, their dependence on simple oxymoronic recombination or overt metaphor seems evidence of their provenance as illustration rather than signification. The mysteries of the new electronic universe are only "like" these portmanteau examples, which are like others, and the monthly taxonomies in the magazines struggle to keep up with these placeholders ....

14. ... To admit value is to imply some measure of certainty—at least that which secures the meaning as meaning, that oddly provisional sort of certainty that attends complicity—in language and other instrumental conven-

5. pedestrian circulation drum

view from northeast

tions. To admit value is to feel the pragmatic side of that certainty. To understand the pragmatism is to remain immunized against the reintroduction of absolutism. Such a possibility could be imagined: a bubble of conviction within the turbulence of the multiplicity—a small, provisional utopia riding out the storm of information. Such a condition would entail a (mostly together) subject, a reader whose gaze can be contained, which is to say whose reading can be satisfied on some basis, and the object of engagement. The equation this describes is a precious, localized version of what might otherwise be considered common. It describes the capacity of the mechanical: as a machine, as a paradigm, as a common sense.

Figure

15. It is easy, in that certain uncanny deconstructive way, to broaden the definition of the mechanical so much that it cleverly subsumes all of the arguments against it

34. connector bridge
view from west

(34)

(seeing it as the very structure of the relationship whereby such comparisons are made, or the glue with which the event coheres, for example), this dilutes the appreciation beyond the point where it becomes preferred even by its supporters.º The sense of mechanality around which its adherents rally is much more particular than that—though not as particular as levers and gears, it is much more specific than reified language or logic or the embodiment of intention or will, though all these certainly inform it. The preferred sense of the mechanical straddles the instrumental and aesthetic senses (like architecture!), almost as a bridge between them—a bridge that feels a lot like the analogical structure of meaning itself, and thus instills the sense of mechanality with the mechanical structure of the possibility of that meaning. The aesthetic instrumentalized, made operational; the instrumental aestheticized, made legible, superlative: this is the bubble or submarine, in which information, value,

DR 30

WDIM 6

367

4. atrium

interior view

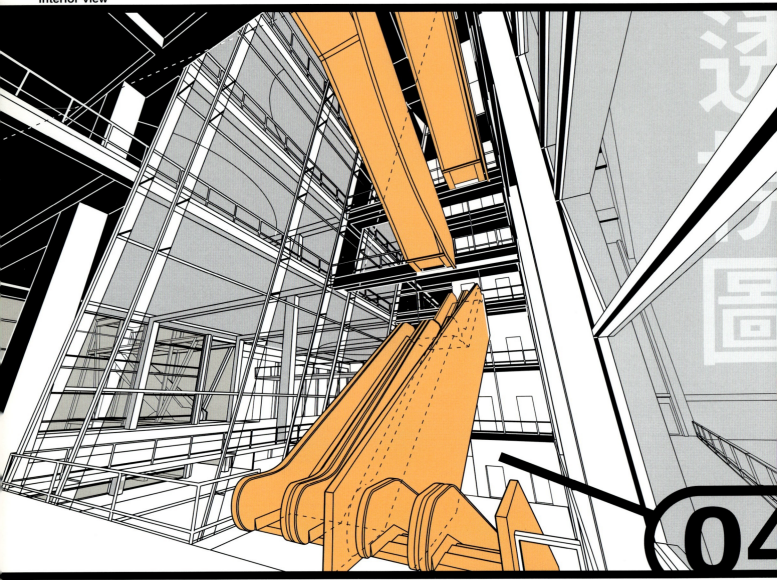

and certainty combine to ride out the multiplicity. The form of the mechanical, considered in this way, is the form of figure. Its ground is the multiplicity. Formerly it was simply experience.

16. The mechanical is figural in a broad sense. Broader perhaps than might usually be allowed, since its engagement appears to be pre-cultural. Alan Colquhoun describes the figure as "a ... condensation, the immediate effect of which is to suggest the richness and complexity of reality." The figure exhibits "a synthetic power," that "draw(s) together and crystallize(s) ... complex experiences that are diffuse and imperceptible." In the classical tradition, the figure was seen as a instrument for producing affect, by means of the natural personifying engagement enjoyed with any context. He distinguishes between "mere" form and figure by ascribing to the latter "meaning ... given by culture," while the former is held perhaps to have "no meaning at all."p

P97.03/1
Confluence Point Bridges and Ranger Station
San Jose, CA

Owner:	The Redevelopment Agency of the City of San Jose Frank Taylor, Director
Client:	Hargreaves Associates
Architect:	Jones, Partners: Architecture; Holt Hinshaw Jones
Consultants:	AN West (structural) GM Lim and Associates (mechanical)
Contractor:	B&B Construction/Garden City Construction (Visitor Center)
Program:	Pedestrian bridges and visitors' center in urban flood control project/park.
Site:	Guadalupe River Park at the confluence of Guadalupe River and Los Gatos Creek in downtown San Jose
Size:	2.5 acres
Systems:	Premanufactured weathering steel truss bridge, and post-tensioned concrete box beam bridge; steel frame with wood-frame infill on cast-in-place concrete standard grade beam atop cast-in-place concrete flood-control walls; exterior cement plaster, steel storefront glazing and sheet metal louvers.
Features:	Three simple structures are distributed across the site, tied together with a common material palette that each highlights differently; the short truss bridge is economically constructed of pre-manufactured weathering steel elements, the "log" bridge of post-tensioned concrete, and the building of both; a common interest in faceted geometry is also displayed, either in massing or in details, such as the placards shared by the building and short bridge, or the walkway of the "log" bridge.
Cost:	$1.15 million
Completed:	May 1997

A 1% (100 year) flood would inundate the urban core of San Jose. The Corps of Engineers Guadalupe River Flood Control Project was initiated to mitigate this critical flood threat. This initial program, including concrete channels, rip-rap and widening of the river, was expanded to create a significant urban amenity, the Guadalupe River Park. Gardens, plazas and trail systems will form a 2.6-mile-long continuous urban park that celebrates the river's existence in the center of a redeveloping downtown.

The confluence of the Guadalupe River and Los Gatos Creek, at the center of the park, yields a triangular "island" of land named Confluence Point. Functionally and aesthetically this is the central focus of the park. To be developed as a unique civic feature, the site and its bridges will provide critical linkage between the downtown and its new arena (completed in 1993).

The Point is surrounded by dense riparian landscape. The southern edge of the site is bounded by a heavily trafficked cross-town artery. The first bridge to be built lands on an outdoor amphitheater area adjacent to the arena. An eastern bridge, to be built during a subsequent phase, will span a "flood plain," a large active recreation and event area that is configured to accommodate the anticipated large volume of flood waters.

The program calls for these two bridges to be sized to accommodate the "flood" of spectators attending events at the arena. Phasing of the project requires that the first bridge provide linkage between Santa Clara Street to the south and the arena to the west. Ultimately, the primary pedestrian flow will be east and west across both bridges.

The Point will serve as an orientation center displaying appropriate information for visitors to the park. A variety of public spaces that variously support passive recreation and assembly uses are to be situated to take advantage of the site's relationship to the water. The Point will become a gathering place and point of departure for activities throughout the park. Ranger orientation talks and interpretive lectures will be accommodated. The building serves as a base of operations and observation point for park rangers. Public restrooms will also be provided.

The client body includes an array of public agencies, regulatory bodies and community groups. Design efforts must satisfy the often disparate requirements of community user groups, maintenance personnel, police and rangers, and the Corps of Engineers. The design must embody the collective aspirations of this substantial contingent.

Flood control requirements dictate bridge heights, influence abutment locations and the overall placement of structures on the site. Fish and game requirements additionally constrain the design: river banks shall be maintained in their natural state, sunlight penetration shall remain unimpeded, and areas of existing shade shall be maintained.

"The more simply and essentially [equipment is] engrossed in [its] essence, the more directly and engagingly do all beings attain a greater degree of being along with [it]." In Heidegger's schema equipment disappears into usefulness and the "work" becomes more visible. The Confluence Point project can been seen in this light, as the architectural elements seek their equipmental nature. This is not to say that we have abandoned the architecture's ability to speak. Though equipment is somewhat more limited in that regard than say art, it is certainly not mute: equipment is by its very nature more approachable—more used; the possibility for engagement is significant when it opens a world.

An architecture conceived of as equipment is realized in considered responses to context and program, in unselfconscious forms and details, and an overriding concern for appropriateness at all scales. This project seeks to make the most of limited project funds through the creative and critical application of simple materials. The pedestrian bridge is formed by two prefabricated truss bridges that are embellished with plate steel panels and other supporting details—the bridge is made compelling by the addition of a relatively limited number of detailed moves. The building component is made more substantial by the appropriation of the major flood control walls as architectural elements. The sincere and straightforward application of simple materials like concrete, cement plaster, weathering

1. Confluence Point Visitor Center/ Ranger Station
2. Los Gatos Creek pedestrian bridge
3. Guadalupe River pedestrian bridge

site plan 1"=50.00'

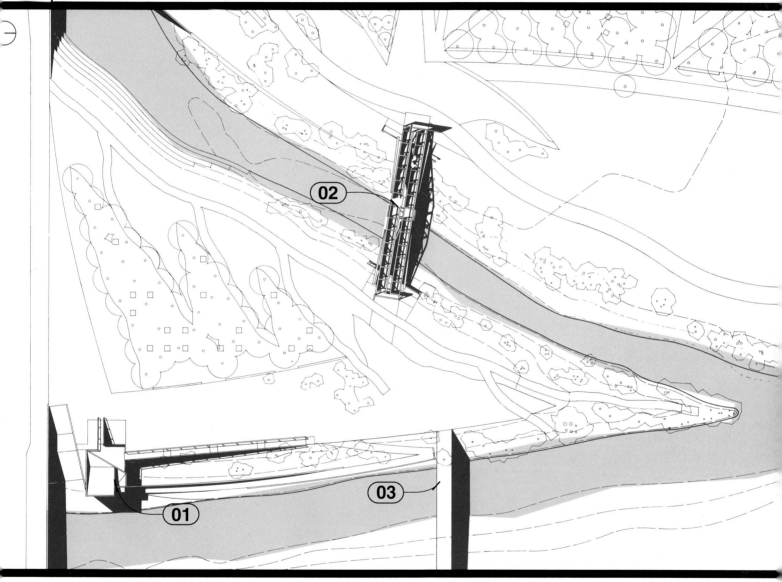

17. Colquhoun reaches the conclusion that, by his definition, form alone is not possible; since culture appropriates everything, the truly meaningless artifact is impossible. He describes the opposition between form and figure as representative of the differences between the aesthetic interests of modern architecture and classical architecture. Yet, since modern architecture was so obviously interested in the cultural meaning of its efforts, proscribed by form, perhaps a different attitude towards figure can be assumed, instead. If, as Colquhoun shows, the classical tradition depended on "mere" figure's rhetorical ability to communicate the "conventional and associative meaning" that asserted the authority of the establishment served by that tradition, then modernism might be understood to have pursued its challenge to that authority through the use of what could be called "sheer" figure. Modernism assumed its work enjoyed the same legibility as the mere figure, but derived that legi-

view of Visitor Center from west

bility from a transparency to the "emergent social and technological facts," embodied directly in the design.
NIRM note g

18. Contemporary theory retains Modernism's distrust of classicism's "mere" figure, but notices that "sheer" is no less than "mere." It accuses Modernism of simply trading one sort for another, perhaps less invested with historical imagery but equally repressive in its privileging of a singular willful author-ity. Before that, HistoPoMo's critical reinvocation of mere figure as either type or quotation,
NRO 17

established the real deserts of the "mere," rendering it perhaps less than sheer, and making that authority no less evident, if perhaps more silly. The most popular critique of this surviving sense of authority was made by post-structural collage. Collage literally, luridly, hacked that authority to bits and rearranged it or scattered it about. In this way not only was its singularity contested, but so was its defining relationship to a back-"ground." Yet, it depended on the continuing legibility of the pieces

372

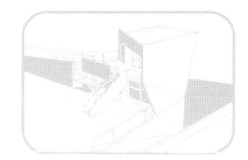

4. cement plaster shell
5. cement plaster placard
9. pedestrian ramp

view of Visitor Center from southwest

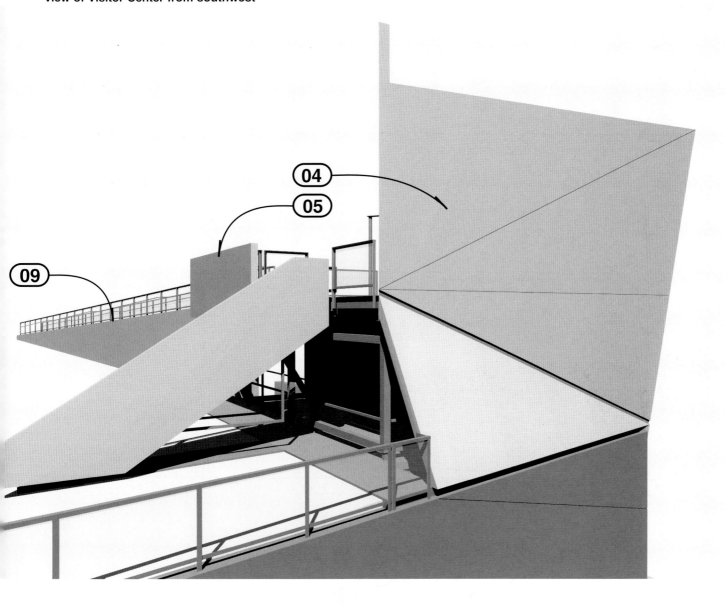

to communicate the critique of the authority they formerly composed, foregrounded or not, and so it could be said that figure remains important: in this case "smear" figure. Ironically, contemporary theory's even more recent criticism of this practice accuses it of enhancing the presence of authority, because it limits readings to the singular intention behind that critique itself. Recognizing the necessity to compel reading, in order to engage the critique, the contemporary position preserves a role for the intention that stands between legibility and gibberish by proposing the use of "near" figures, which blur the edges of their figuration. Such blurring proposes a more open, teasing posture towards the object, tickling a sense of empowerment out of the readers' own attempts to bring their reading to closure. The logic of this exercise requires that the reading remain irredeemably open, however, if it is to avoid settling into merely a more complex, but still finite and therefore repressive, statement.

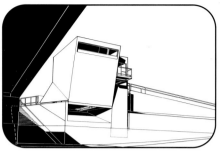

view of Visitor Center from northeast

19. The compulsion to find meaning is great. The discussion of the demise of this object is usually pursued from the standpoint of its stewards, rather than its consumers—the latter are hard-wired to expect meaning and seek it, and this is how the simulacra bemoaned by critics are so easily accepted as meaningful by the public. Consequently, it is actually quite difficult to frustrate this desire to find meaning; those few who prefer instead an undecideable or weak formalism, "near" figure, are thus led to extraordinary measures to prevent such premature closure. This ensures, though, that the object becomes outrageous, an example of the solution breaking free from the original problem to engender its own. And in this outrageousness the intention and authority are reasserted.

20. Each of these approaches admit a presence to the object—however "blurred," smeared or trivial—a presence that might be seen as the "cookie jar" in the

5. cement plaster placard
6. weathering steel undercarriage
10. men's restroom
11. women's restroom
12. janitor's closet
23. floodwall

9. pedestrian ramp
14. entry
15. display case
16. information window
17. interpretive area
18. ranger's office
23. floodwall

Visitor Center first level plan 1"=16.67'

Visitor Center second level plan 1"=16.67'

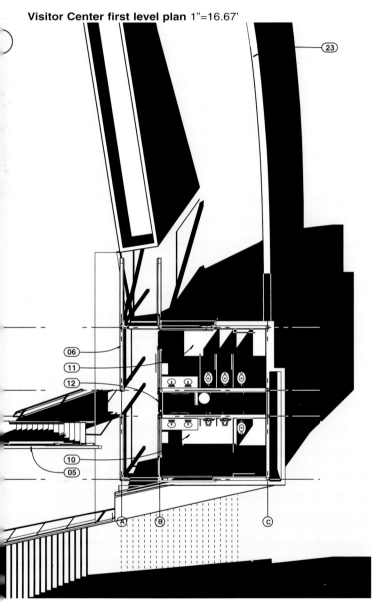
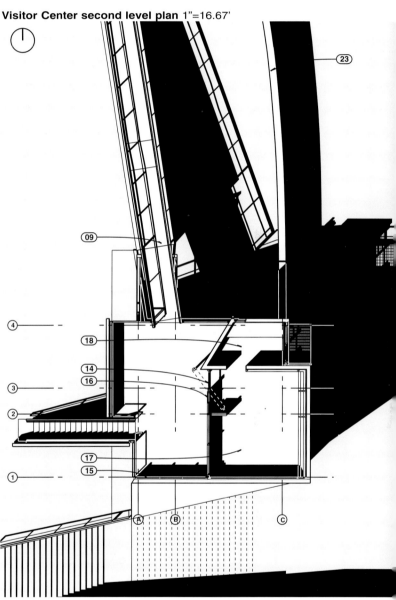

encounter. The jar labeled "cookies" is placed high on the shelf, where Mom, or the critic, can control access. From there it cannot beckon, only taunt. Johnny knows the cookie exists for him, and that the jar is innocent of the conspiracy against his enjoyment, but it becomes the focus of an obsession that all but guarantees the slip that breaks the jar, ruining the day and the cookies. The cookie jar is thus approached with trepidation instead of forthrightness; it is the last-minute hesitation, the nervous glance over the shoulder, the imagined noise from the other room that leads to the usual result: the selection committee goes with the safe choice, the jury compromises on the weaker scheme, the client waters down the proposal.

21. If this relationship were reconceived on a more equal footing, leaving Mom out of it, just Johnny and the jar, disaster, compromise and disappointment would be easily avoided, and the cookies would be enjoyed in all

view of Visitor Center from southwest

their engaging splendor. The "peer" figural relationship between the subject and the object then described combines the jar and cookies together as a single figure in depth, and allows the reading to close itself. The cookies may be consumed without the turning of the stomach that prefigures their nervous toss, or the tingle in the rear that feels the paddle coming. The anxiety is reduced because the reading of the cookie jar is localized, intransitive, or reflexively transitive: the utility to Johnny is figured, by Johnny, rather than mom's repressive, critical authority or the frustration of the jar's remoteness. The ground against which the cookie jar is figured is staleness, humidity and ants, convenience and surprise, not right and wrong, and that ground is made specifically apparent in the design of the jar. The idea of the mechanical comes closest to capturing the sense of this "peer" figure.

22. There is of course an outright, if ironically inflected,

4. cement plaster shell
5. cement plaster placard
6. weathering steel undercarriage
8. steel angle guardrail with expanded metal infill
9. pedestrian ramp
18. ranger's office

Visitor Center west elevation 1"=16.67'

4. cement plaster shell
5. cement plaster placard
10. men's restroom
17. interpretive area
23. floodwall

Visitor Center section 1"=16.67'

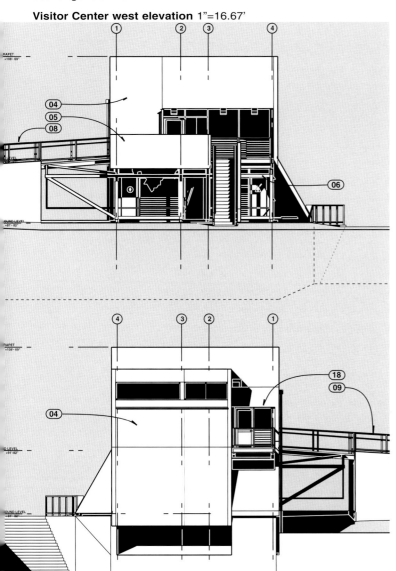

Visitor Center east elevation 1"=16.67'

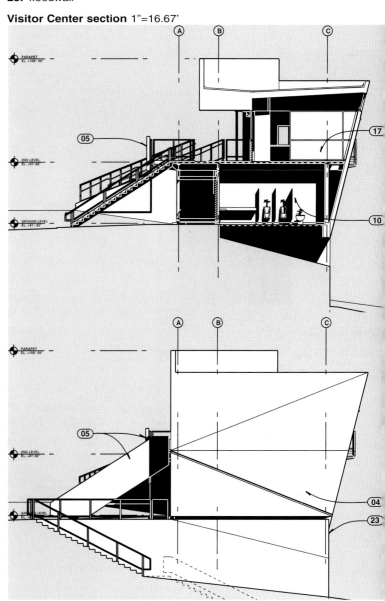

Visitor Center south elevation 1"=16.67'

positivist spin to this: within the roiling multiplicity, the depth of this structure and the local constellation of value it sustains through the peer figural relationship, may describe what could be considered a personally circumscribed and therefore limited, but still empowering haven of certainty. Between the subject and each cookie jar a world may be constructed, a world other than the mere received world—the jar itself and all it hides—richer than the sheer facts of the matter, certainly more satisfying than if it were smeared across the counter, which is cool while it is happening, while it is an event, maybe, but invites Mom's eventual wrath and makes the cookies less appetizing—and finally, a world liberatingly accessible once its tantalizing nearness is overcome in a fit of empowering resolve.

23. If the mechanical could hold the gaze, could produce a local, admittedly exuberant, provisional fixity of sense and certainty, could embody an intransitive willful-

Visitor Center detail **Visitor Center detail**

ness, relating to the viewer as a peer rather than an agent for some other, should it not be preferred? It certainly is not the most radical position that could be taken. In fact, it might be said to constitute a sort of pragmatic stepping-back from the abyss, a lowering of the sights—which in itself might be considered radical, indeed. The answer to this question is of course political. While it should never be architecture's desire to shirk its responsibility to this dimension of experience, it should neither be its decision to force its determination of that on others—lest in succeeding with its critique it fails in its responsibility. That is to say, these things can be made, but are they desired?

Conclusion

24. While a materialism of some sort will likely always be at the core of common sense and architectural affect, the natural world's apparent object fixation hides an interest in the relationships the objects embody: how those

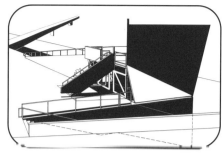

Visitor Center detail

objects are, relative to their surroundings, and to other objects.^q **DR note 2** A mindset attuned to substance, and the common sense that articulates it, is "naturally" instrumental, **ONO 42** or operational. This is why—and how—metaphor flourishes. The discreteness that encourages relation also suggests a value system to judge it: the gravity field of relation or "fit." The object fits in somewhere, or doesn't. Heidegger sees this system of evaluation in a famously negative light. The electronic paradigm is mooted to enjoy a capacity to contest this valuation. The electronic paradigm differs from the mechanical in offering a vision of a continuous web of relationships, in which there are no parts, but only different views of an unimaginable whole: the info highway goes everywhere, and all "locations" along it are simultaneously present and accessible "here." As such, it has been the apotheosis of the multiplicity itself. Cyberspace and the electronic technologies that effect it, have been seen as the airline of virtuality,

Visitor Center detail

Visitor Center detail

the medium of the lines-of-flight from whatever remains of the striated order of contemporary culture. And the mechanical is seen as the primary agent of striation. Yet, "these two kinds of space and of connection in space are not, themselves segregated or separated in any given time and place but coexist with one another. In any given instance, there may be striations of dispersed spaces, just as there may be smoothing of discrete or ordered spaces."r

25. In this spirit, it would probably be more accurate—not to mention more useful—to abandon the rhetoric of opposition, to assume a more sophisticated relationship. Contemporary theory counsels mistrust of such simple oppositions and to expect the reversal of any hierarchy. The electronic will give the mechanical life, maybe even consciousness, while the mechanical will continue to give the electronic substance, will free it to have effect and act in the substantial world. It is a small step, then,

4. cement plaster shell
5. cement plaster placard
6. weathering steel undercarriage
13. steel bollard

view of Visitor Center from southwest

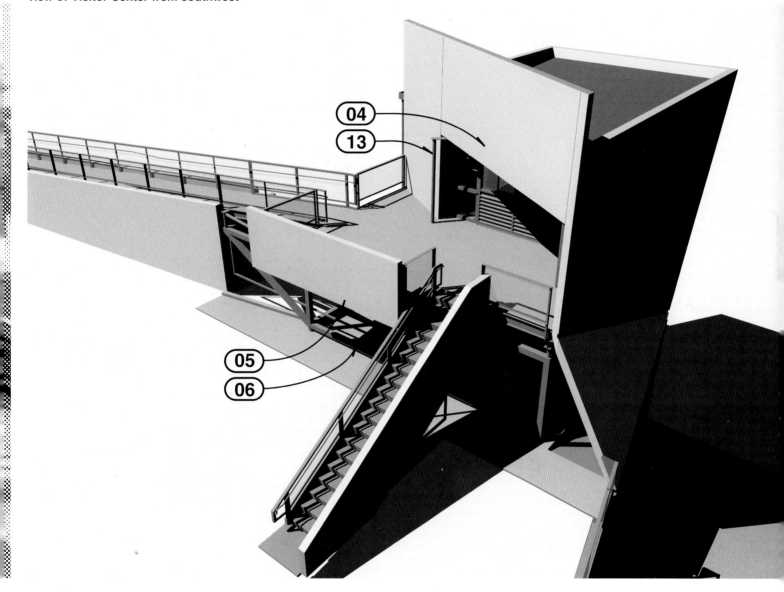

according to Freud: the object will become subject, and with the computer as brain and the machine as body, the subject will be let out of the box. Outside of the box it will become the box.

26. Deleuze forces the recognition "that in contemporary thought objectivity and subjectivity are not different fields, opposite poles, but rather folds of the same, single reality."[5] In robotics, the electronic and the mechanical already coexist seamlessly; with the advent of the more pluralistic multimedia sensibility, even the folds are smoothed. The communication potential of their collaboration is the next revolution, which will challenge architecture directly and on its own turf. In this event, the mechanical may as likely become the message, and buildings may thereby be finally freed from the stricture against movement. The "evolutions" that the deconstructivists or undecideables suggest in medias res could actually unfold continuously in real time.

5. cement plaster placard
7. pre-fabricated weathering steel truss bridge
20. concrete abutment
21. collector beam
22. concrete landing

24. weathering steel leaf

Los Gatos Creek bridge, west end view

Los Gatos Creek bridge, west end view

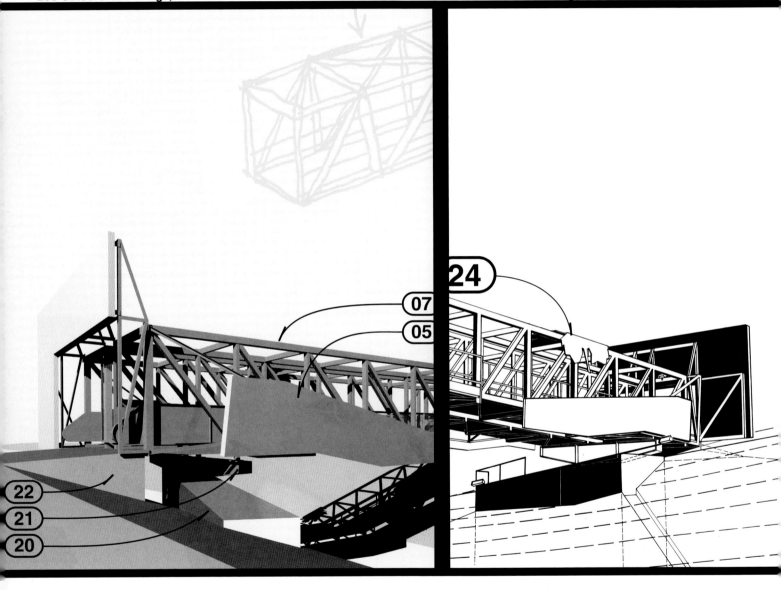

27. Architecture has always appealed equally to the mind and the body, the glance and the touch, crudely represented by art and utility. History and theory have assumed a grounding of architectural principles in the body—whether as figure or program—and the elevated appreciation of those principles by an inquiring consciousness. A present and future devoid of historical sense, or reveling in the freedom of all sense, will not be different. Whether architecture will develop a new project for itself in the brave new future is hard to say, but it is safe to assume that it will have a "place" "there."

a An earlier version of this essay first appeared in *ANY* 10: Mech-in-Tecture (1995).
b *ANY* 3 (1993), 7.
c *Ibid.* 16.
d *Ibid.* 48.
e *Ibid.* 15. In that issue, Bernard Tschumi called attention to the fickleness of such boosterism. His parody of the

5. cement plaster placard
7. pre-fabricated weathering steel truss bridge
8. steel angle guardrail with expanded metal infill
20. concrete abutment
24. weathering steel leaf

Los Gatos Creek bridge south elevation 1"=16.00'

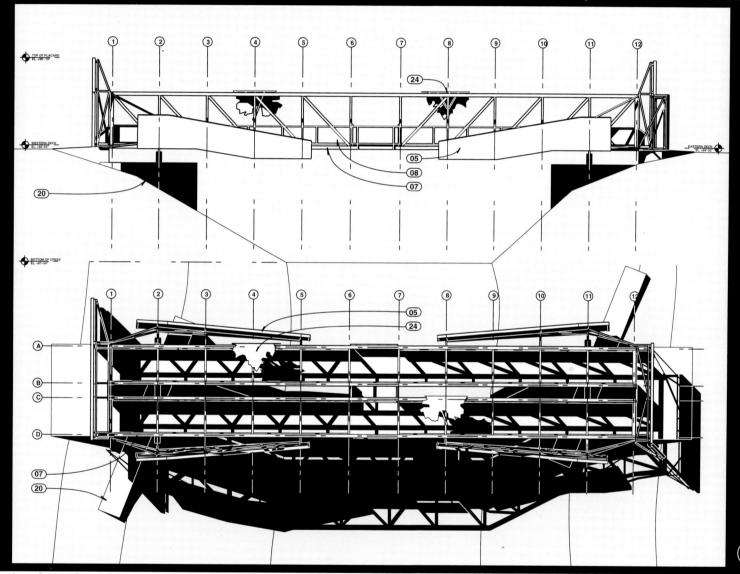

Los Gatos Creek bridge plan 1"=16.00'

back-and-forth of recent critical thinking conclude that such theory itself points out the "artificiality" of the absolute oppositions promoted.

f John Rajchman, "What's New in Architecture?" in *Philosophical Events: Essays of the 80's*, note 31.
g *Cuaderno*, 69.
h *Ibid.*, 70 N1.
i *Ibid.*, 69.
j *Ibid.*, 69.

k Ignasi de Solà-Morales, *Ottagono* no. 92 (1989), 108.
l *ANY* 3, 14.
m *ANY* 7/8, 8.
n N. Katherine Hayles, *Chaos Bound* (Ithaca: Cornell Univ. Press, 1990), 31.
o In figure is the mechanical's resistance to the perversely structuralist attempts to rescue the machine for political correctness. A reconsideration of the machine

5. cement plaster placard
7. pre-fabricated weathering steel truss bridge
20. concrete abutment
22. concrete landing
24. weathering steel leaf

Los Gatos Creek bridge, view from northeast

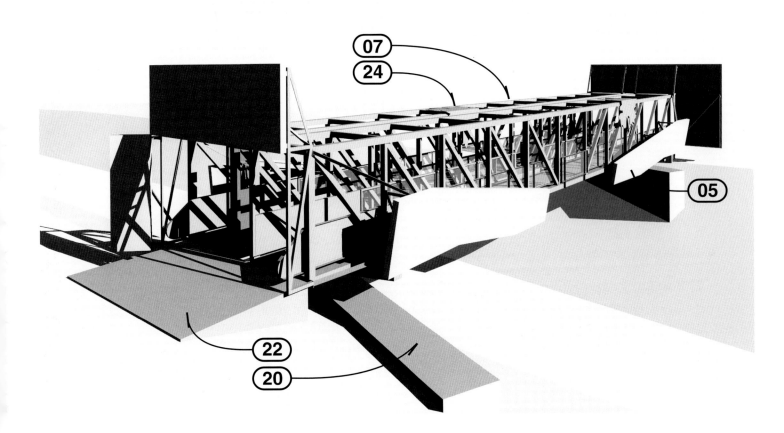

according to performance values and effects, which avoids the determinism of intention and teleology, misses the point of reference to the mechanical. It is precisely *as* an embodiment of the will that the mechanical is interesting, "useful," or capable of sustaining a critical position. The Skinnerian understanding of its "territory," ascribed to the latter sections of Deleuze and Guattari's *1000 Plateaus,* is of course as obviously subject to deconstruction as any other structuralist proposition.

[p] Alan Colquhoun, "Form and Figure" in *Essays in Architectural Criticism* (New York: Oppositions Books, 1981), 190-191.
[q] As the electronic is an idea about disembodiment, but is more accurately a body of very specific technology, so the mechanical is a very general idea about the specifics of embodiment. The "electronic" is in fact still so amorphous that it communicates only in reference to particular instances, while the "mechanical" is clear enough to

steel structural frame and metal siding carry this equipmental attitude through to the details. Lighthearted leaf-form elements allude to the project's once precarious setting in the center of the flood channel, recalling flotsam trapped by the architecture in the path of a raging flood.

The program is consolidated in a single structure located at the street edge to "hold down" the overall site and reinforce the urban street edge—mediating between towers and nature. The building is conceived of as a control cab affording a critical viewpoint for the Ranger, the park's appointed master of ceremonies. The understanding of the building as a prospect or promontory is reinforced by the creation of a stair between the structure and the street edge that leads down to the pedestrian/bicycle path that travels along the river's edge.

Orientation/interpretive functions are accommodated at the second level on an open concrete on metal roof deck that affords visitors with views of the entire site.

* * *

Certainty breeds complacency. The two are inextricably related: to be certain about anything is to be relieved of doubt; complacency stems from mastery of the routine, and the attendant confidence that renders the routine banal. It follows that a relaxation of certainty must lead to an increase in anxiety. Despite the apparent hegemony of the routine and mundane, the contemporary condition is marked by an increase in anxiety. No longer explained by the threat of nuclear war, this anxiety is perhaps a symptom of the imperfect registration of the hyper-real with the mundane. In this context, both the mundane and the complacency which promotes it become interesting as vestigial, unknowing vessels of certainty. How, then, can the mundane be problematized; how can the background anxiety be acknowledged without risking the banality that may be the sole remaining link to certainty?

Neither a pedestrian bridge nor an interpretive center is expected to be anything other than mundane, particularly when half the entire program is devoted to public restrooms. These humble agents of municipal authority hypostatize the complacency vested in the minor city bureaucracies—the parks department, the Redevelopment Authority, the department of public works (maintenance division). To relax the certainty that characterizes both social and physical infrastructure is to draw that invisible support into the light, to tease it into unhiddenness. A delicate balance must be maintained in this, though, lest this visibility itself outshine the critique. There can be no sense of a celebration of the mundane that does not displace the mundane from itself; no sense that a overlaying of the truly banal with a new hyper-real condition that masks the original will not lose, or at least, disguise the distance by which the critique may be known.

8. steel angle guardrail with expanded metal infill

Guadalupe River bridge, view from southwest

8. steel angle guardrail with expanded metal infill

Guadalupe River bridge, view from southeast

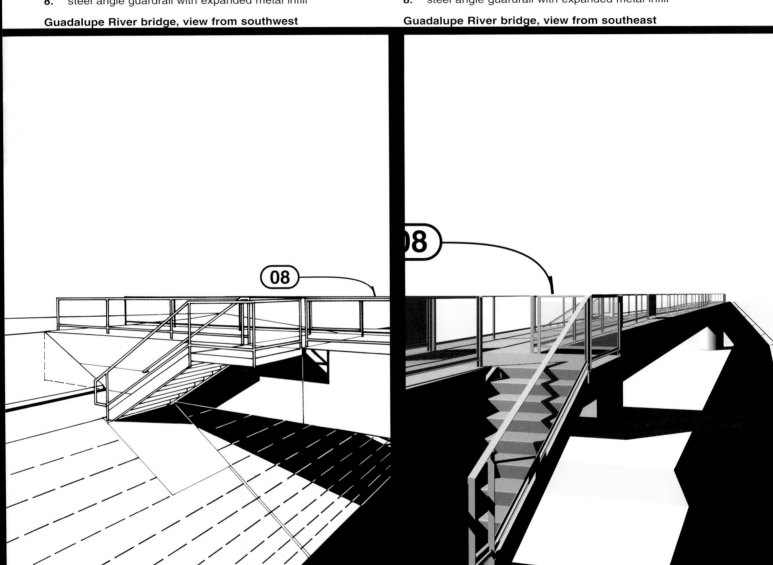

float freely in relation to all phenomena and experience, supplying meaning inescapably. Ironically, it is the mechanical that has become disembodied, hidden in all those boxes, while the electronic has been the agent of a flood of reification that in a hyperreal world is as substantial as anything Dr. Johnson kicked.

[1] John Rajchman, *Anyone* (New York: Rizzoli, 1991), 106.
[2] *Ottagono*, 109.
[3] William Gibson's definition of cyberspace, *Neuromancer* (New York: Ace Science Fiction, 1984).
[4] Jean Baudrillard, *Simulations*, trans. Paul Foss, et al. (New York: Semiotext(e), Inc., 1983), 2.
[5] Gianni Vattimo, "Metaphysics, Violence, Secularization" in *Recoding Metaphysics: The New Italian Philosophy*, ed. Giovanna Borradori (Evanston: Northwestern Univ. Press, 1988), 45-61.
[6] Baudrillard, *Communication*, 16.
[7] Jean Baudrillard, *The Evil Demon of Images* (Sydney: The Power Institute of Fine Arts, 1987), 13.

Wired: inspired, tired—or mired?

1. Unlike the previous "revolutions" which divide up our history, the Information Revolution is having little visible effect on the landscape. Mountains of hype and oceans of noise fill our world, but relatively little stuff. The landscape should be littered with the media of transmitted information, yet this media is less substantial even than either the smoke or mirrors that serve so consistently as critical metaphors for its reality. There is no beef in cyberspace. Other than packaging and slogans, the information revolution is leaving very little evidence of its pervasiveness. What carapaces can be seen—the outsized CD box, the ATM, microwave relays and satellite dishes, the disk—have had no more substantial impact on our meat environment than the EM radiation itself.[1]

2. The information that floods everywhere has conquered space and time in a way never dreamed by the auto or airplane. Yet, while our cities, streets, and countrysides were completely transformed by the Transportation Revolution, this *information* revolution has transformed no-*thing*. The Information Revolution has created a hunger much greater than the Industrial Revolution's desperate craving for coal or oil, yet it requires no precious resources other than neurons, which it consumes indiscriminately, to satisfy its appetite. It has contributed to as wide an increase in understanding as the Scientific Revolution or Gutenburg's press, changing the way we live and do business—in fact, changing what we do as business and, increasingly, *where* we live—yet the physical world seems largely untouched.

3. Instead, this information is creating an alternative world, inhabiting the same space as the existing one, but in parallel; a hyper-real world that makes plain old reality pale in comparison. Like Augustine's City of God, it "exists" within. And the reverence it inspires in its contemporary devotees and proselytes seems to be the equal of Augustine's.

4. Telecommuting, interactive media or desktop publishing, are perhaps the prime examples of how the world is changing. They have some effect on *how* we make stuff, but not *what* we make: they are really just pushing the same stuff around, not changing it or adding to it. The grandest "spatial" manifestation of the digital revolution, the internet, is the least physically apparent. Even if it can truly be said to "exist," that existence has no presence; scattered unceremoniously around the world in anonymous boxes in small, similarly anonymous rooms and between the ears of its anonymous subscribers it can hardly be said to *be there*. In fact, it is in the minds of its revolutionary advance guard, that it has its greatest presence.

5. This is hardly to say that this revolution has had little effect, but rather that this effect has been largely non-physical. Indeed, our lives are being profoundly changed. The way we see the world will be truly different, but not because the *world* has changed. What is changing is our perception, how we understand its range and depth, and the self-awareness that such omniscience offers. But the world itself remains largely the same.

* * *

6. Cyberspace has ambassadors everywhere: in photocopiers, automobiles, vending machines, and now even greeting cards. It is on the way to becoming a whole special world of special effects, unimaginable elsewhere and unforeseen except in the antics of Saturday morning cartoons. The early fanaticism inspired by the Net, however,

---

[1] The advent of cyberspace stretches the limits of the traditional spatial/visual model of understanding. As a "triumph over space and time," the electro/cyber realm is visualized in counter-intuitive spatial terms, the mind's eye multiplied a thousandfold and flounder-ized. The pervasiveness of this brave new world—the reach and oceanic influence of its "virtual" reality—and concomitant, hollow immediacy wreak havoc on the very difference between the linear march of language and spatial deployment of logic. The rhizome has been superseded by the net and free association by shareware browsers. Oxymoronic metaphors and Zen-like analogies proliferate in descriptions of this revolution's "collapse" of distance and duration, its support of a "simultaneity of experience"; and the increasing value placed on the insubstantial and ephemeral which suspends natural laws without transcendence. ["mech- in 'tecture, *ANY* 10]

was not based on any such specialness. It had the least verisimilitude, required the most complicity—existing almost completely as a space in the space between the ears. Yet it took over its devotees lives in a way unmatched even by daytime TV. Net crawlers and MOO and MUG players were addicted out of proportion to the apparent stimulation.²

7. This is probably because cyberspace begs the question of ideality, and nothing is more ideal or perfect or directly engaging than our imagination—which the Net forces us to use with a vengeance. While the Net is increasing in complexity and sophistication, it is still mostly text-based and statically deployed. With the advent of the World Wide Web, though, there is a new horizon, where the text is displaced by image, where even video may dwell. Here, what has been popularized in fiction as *cyberspace* begins to seem possible someday.³

8. The fully interactive alternative reality described in the fictional accounts of cyberspace demands a real time interface with all our senses. But this will not be so easy. In cyberspace, there is no gravity. There are none of the conservation laws—mass, energy, momentum—which make our meat world dependable. There is no cause-and-effect or action/reaction by which a common sense might be developed. There is no necessity for corporeality even, or clear division between the animate and inanimate. In fact, there are no clear divisions at all: the discreteness of objects our perceptual faculties wins from the continuous blur of stimuli we know as external reality has no necessary counterpart in cyberspace. With no substance to attract the attention of gravity, there is no reason for the discreteness that marks "physical" objects, no reason for it to arise as an effect of such forces. In fact, any divisions which do appear *are* just *appearances* within the ceaseless flux of electrons and electromagnetic radiation. Only the physical laws imposed on the medium itself, as evident in the finite resolution that causes aliasing, or the rate of thirty frames or regenerations per second, or the physiological limits of the human perceptual apparatus, seem necessary and constrain an otherwise infinite possibility.⁴

9. All this means freedom; a freedom most easily defined negatively. It is one of the achievements of our age that we are able to take Bishop Berkeley's placement of reality in quotation marks and make it feel reasonable. In Berkeley's day such a suspension of conviction about the substance of reality was considered no more than an extremely arcane joke, seen as little different than the counting of angels by his predecessors. Today it is no laughing matter; these quotation marks have been institutionalized in a pluralistic world that cannot even safely assume its own unprejudiced existence; from Baudrillard to Bozo, "natural" reality is being dismissed as not real enough. Yet, behind the hype about hyper-reality and virtual reality, persists this natural anchor as the unexamined standard by which real enough is determined. Natural reality is the datum by which we judge such matters. It sets certain rules that meat can never transgress.

10. The idea of rules follows from the way we have institutionalized our understanding of reality. In order to test this understanding, we have objectified it, and to communicate with others about it we have codified that objectivity. Reality is where or when certain rules hold; when we are dreaming, for example, or stoned, these rules tend not to hold—or at least as well or consistently. The advance of our understanding, our progress, is marked by our gradual "discovery" of these rules. Before the

---

² The effect on language is immense. Keeping track of the nomenclature is a full time occupation: *Wired*'s glossary sidebar features five to ten new words a month.

³ The fiction of cyberspace plays as influential a critical role as anything put out by the pundits. The promise of the revolution lies almost entirely in fiction at this point in time.

⁴ These physiological constraints are not trivial: like advanced jet fighters and Grand Prix racers, our E-machines can perform far beyond our physical ability to follow.

advent of science, and its "objective" standards of judgment, these rules could be quite fanciful. Today, despite the successes of science, we understand the rules are more invented than discovered. As self-imposed constraints, as well as aids, they tell us a lot about ourselves.

11. The reality "created" by those rules may not be what it once was, or all that its cracked up to be, but that reality is still a datum. And valuable for that. The laws growing out of that datum ensure the legibility of reality. By being readable it is engageable and survivable. We may empathize with it and feel our involvement or participation. We are invited to do so. It is supposed to be an aberration to just sit there and watch it happen.

* * *

12. The idea of plain old reality being remarkable seems as dumb as that reality. Dr. Johnson's stone, which reminds us of the physical dimension—the body we leave behind when we stick our head up the screen—is an apt metaphor for the bluntness of these facts. In fact, Johnson's stone is precisely not a metaphor: it is. A rock. We have tended to embroider this brute fact with layers of additional meaning. It is hard to see the rock as just a rock, without wanting to see it as a symbol for something else. The condition of hyper-reality only describes the extreme case, effected by technology, of the otherwise unavoidable proliferation of signs. The gold standard of these signs, which, like Fort Knox, is taken for granted, is this rock. Somewhere at the end of the chain of signs this blunt fact stops the deferral of meaning. Yet, also like the gold in Fort Knox, this standard has fallen out of a strict one-to-one correspondence with its valuation, and we have become accustomed to more "free floating" signification.[5]

13. In the old game Rochambeau, this point is made by rock as it crushes scissors, and by scissors, as they take it out on paper. But, as Victor Hugo predicted, the rock is defeated by paper; the paper triumphs by suffocating the stone. This never feels quite right, though: the child learning the game always wonders at the rock's inability to tear through the paper. When Hugo predicted the triumph of the printed word over the carved, he was explaining to this child how grown up and alienated information could become. He described the trajectory that would eventually replace the mountains of paper that replaced the mountains of stone with megabytes of ROM. Yet, there are dimensions to the first, simple feeling that the rock should defeat paper which are not satisfied by this history. Like Ernest Hemingway's "thing left unsaid" or the shadows thrown by such facts when they are subjected to direct scrutiny, this solidity can be nuanced, layered, transparent ....[6]

14. Making the obviousness of the object apparent, making it noticeable, does not make its dumbness explicable: to make the mystery lying everywhere in plain sight, masked by its own pervasiveness, *unhidden*, requires an understanding of the fugitive dimensions which elaborate it, where other forms of information are encoded that do not *mean* anything but still do not let go. To problematize the thing, there, so that its thereness is remarkable again has been an end of Eastern Mysticism, and is now the goal of Silicon Valley. *It is the remarkableness of the thing that virtual reality covets*; in its virtual state, the thing has its specialness restored, because it is remarkable that such a thing can be seen to exist (virtually). Ironically, in the absence of the extraordinary efforts of such special effects, the thing itself, the *real* thing, tends to disappear.

15. When the dumb thing is given a life of its own we may call it *mechanical*. Life in this sense is constrained

---

[5] Alexander Johnson, when invited by James Boswell to refute the logically irrefutable solipsism, struck a stone, proclaiming "I refute it thus"—playing substance's trump against ideality.

[6] HERE IS THE DARK TREE
DENUDED NOW
OF LEAFAGE
BUT A MILLION STARS

Shiki in *The Four Seasons*, trans. Peter Beilenson (Mount Vernon: The Peter Pauper Press, 1985), 46.

by the limits of our own personification, but inspired by the object. We invest everything around us with this life, and then to bolster our own worth we find it wanting. We praise it or blame it, hold it responsible and find it guilty. The pejorative senses of "mechanical" dominate: the mechanical is unimaginative, rule-bound, proceeded by rote or rigor, dumb, uninspired. A rock.

16. When rule-bound is conflated with unimaginative we lose sight of the imagination necessary to conceive the rules in the first place. There is a fundamental connection between the viewer and the thing, the subject and the object, that encourages the personification we so willingly, unconsciously engage. The idea of the mechanical institutionalizes the anchor that the body, and its senses, provides to the mind which conceives and reacts to these rules.

17. Before the first instrumental imposition of order on the world, there was only the awareness of extended being, our bodies in space, and how they operate there and effect it. From this the mechanical principle evolved as our basic take on the world. The mind-body duality is really an expression of the necessity of the mechanical component—and the frustration at not being able to explain consciousness itself in these terms.[7]

18. Consciousness "itself" is really no more than an objectification of self, which is easily understandable as a superlative evolution of the objectifying impulse applied to the world itself. From the continuous blur of stimuli we have learned, innately, to see discreteness, to engage reality as objective: apart and thing-like. As this faculty increases in sophistication it is clear that the step to consciousness—that is, to the objectification of self—is one of degree, not kind.

19. The body and its motions presents the mind with space. The body is there, inhabiting space, measuring it with its extension and movements. In its inexorable aging, it presents the mind with time also—and refutes the mind's ability to conceptualize its reversal. The body is a constraint to the mind in this, but also a springboard; a datum and mystery. In the idea of the mechanical, the mind extrapolates the experience of the body it knows directly into a general understanding of the world out there it may never actually know—if idealist philosophies are to be believed. In turn, or simultaneously, the mind understands its own seat "above" the meat by an internalization of the physical phenomena it witnesses in the objective world. By applying such experience, the body can be imagined as the first instrument, the first machine. In fact, this abstraction could be considered the first metaphor, discovered only archeologically, after the mechanism of metaphor it spawned has been active for millennia.

20. The driver of this machine is the machine itself. In the end there is no duality—the mind is meat too. It has been argued that this fact is the source of the brilliance of experience, as an effect of the effort taken in surmounting the constraint of meat,[8] of elevating the mind to the position where it could sustain a belief that it was different—it could see and look down on the meat. Now cyberspace arrives on the scene, promising to free the mind of the mechanical constraints of physical reality—the promise to give the mind its own playing field, uninflected-to or constrained-by the anchoring body—and therefore free of the reminder that it too is meat. This is ideality.

21. The brilliance of consciousness would (probably) be forfeit in such an ideal realm. In collapsing the distance

---

[7] When you think in terms that we characterize as consciousness, you are being "self conscious," intro-spective, attuning your sense to where the "you" is in the blur of stimuli that makes up your experience. You are stepping back and regarding the you that is stepping back .... You are making yourself the object of your attention. The "interior life" which embellishes this self, and its attention, is understandable as no more really than a context of memory and association, only loosely organized around the nexus which occasions its flights. This nexus is identified, objectively/subjectively, as the self.

[8] General idea from Anton Ehrenzweig, *The Psycho-Analysis of Artistic Vision and Hearing: An Introduction to a Theory of Unconscious Perception* (New York: George Braziller, 1965).

by which consciousness defines itself as an exception (forging a new continuity with experience exclusive of the meat senses) cyber-experience may be condemned to a flatness, an emotional dullness, where consciousness itself may be questionable. It may be a dreamscape that brings to life the old koan about being able to know when you're dreaming or awake.

22. Its flatness may also be an effect of the lack of consequences for activity in cyberspace. You cannot hurt or die in cyberspace, nor can you actually kill or maim others. This must take some edge off experience. It has been cyberspace's distinction, though, to allow us to "experience" scenarios of otherwise unimaginable danger *because* there are no possible consequences. We certainly get a thrill out of this, especially since we would be extremely unlikely to place ourselves in such dangerous situations otherwise. If we were somehow to find ourselves actually in such straits, our physical reactions would emphasize the reality: the voided-bowel flight-or-fright response alone would make obvious the difference. Of course, consequences are not only physical—they can also be social, moral, political, psychological. But meat is mortal, so the sort of *capital* consequences in which cyber-games revel will always be confined to live reality; extreme issues of right and wrong in live reality will always have more bite.[9]

23. More to the architectural point: virtual reality presents us with possibility of actualizing the ideal. For the first time we may be able to experience perfect form with our major senses. Ideality is not unproblematic, however. Probably since Plato, the ideal has been seen as capable of exerting a repressive influence on everyday affairs by hovering in judgment of them, invariably finding them wanting in comparison. The Ideal is elitist, politically incorrect and frustrating.

24. Ideality stands in judgment of reality: there is a value associated with that perfection. To be able to realize the ideal could be profoundly disquieting. Not only might it dull the drive to achieve it, but it could also establish, there (somewhere), where we can experience it, a realism that excludes the imperfect meat. We must be profoundly alienated by this at some level, since we cannot leave the meat behind. Cyberspace is too perfect. Perfection is alien to our meat existence. The hints at imperfection unique to cyberspace—aliasing for example—make visible the constraints of this artificial world in a way that we have never had to perceptually confront in reality. And these constraints are alien. Yet, paradoxically, the repression of this disquiet will help explain the vividness of the cyber-experience until the meat can effectively be left behind.[10]

25. The relation of the *mechanical* to ideality is that of the means to the end: to actualizing that realm of perfect desire out in-the-world. It is the means for getting all those intentions bubbling up inside to *outside* where they can be real-ized. This structure has been institutionalized into a whole instrumental outlook. The directness of the relationship places intentionality, or desire, at the heart of the mechanical, and relates the mechanical throughout its long history to the ideal. The relation is so dumb, so matter-of-fact, so fundamental, that it is richly complex: it is fraught with the same potential for paradox as any axiom that must run up against its provisional character every once in awhile. The obsessive physicality of the mechanical has been seen as a failure of the ideal, while its transcendent vigor and exactitude has been seen as an apotheosis of the desire it implies.[11]

* * *

---

[9] The advent of snuff films shows the extent to which we must go to feel the kick.

[10] Ehrenzweig again.

[11] "It was the whiteness of the whale that above all things appalled me." Herman Melville, *Moby-Dick* (New York: W.W. Norton & Company, 1976), 187.

26. If cyberspace is to be "a consensual hallucination shared by millions,"[12] then, like architecture itself, it will depend on "the complicity and convictions" of its subscribers.[13]

27. In what is such complicity to be grounded? And how are such convictions to be held? Much of cyberspace's attraction for those who value freedom and novelty above all is its openness to this question: it seems to herald a new frontier where the old received rules may not apply, where the individual designer may be empowered to invent his/her own. By the same token, if the ideas are so personal they elicit the empowering fantasy of the designer, then they risk being effectively closed to others. Self-indulgent work will not solicit the complicity of anyone.

28. Any operating system for our (in) excursions into cyberspace should probably be impersonal and open as a standard or datum for *many* to design/write/create with and against. And before even *contributing*, people have to know how to get around. The issue here is not only the appearance of the Graphical User Interface or how it works, but the world this appearance and its workings implies. Since there is no "there" there, the GUI stands in and absorbs our attention. It is intended by its designers to be transparent to the activity beyond or between the ears, but it is the only thing there so naturally the user focuses on it. The system with the most existing applications and the greatest pool of subscribers is reality. This recommends it for the role. The oldest and most neutral convention for capturing this reality is the mechanical. It is the generic source of understanding, the language we are all born to, and despite Heidegger, it is the medium most transparent to our individual desires since it is the oldest and most direct product of them. As the ur-tecture, the idea of the mechanical is able to elicit conviction without bothering to solicit complicity. It may be inescapable. The freedom that could be attained by abandoning this standard and its constraints may have to be balanced against a more common sense: anarchy is not a useful form of freedom. Freedom from something, on the other hand, within a rule-system that measures these distances as meaningful, is.

29. In this context, constraints can be seen as such or, in a more positive light, as anchors. Building is a constraint to architectural ideality, but it is also the foundation which distinguishes architecture from other arts. Architects are ambivalent about building, but cannot live without it. In resolving the way we feel about the mechanical paradigm, and the claims that it is sinking into the sunset, we can decide whether we are going to see its likely necessity in cyberspace as an unfortunate impediment to exploration, or the anchor/datum that will make that exploration meaningful.

30. What combinatory, manipulatory techniques can we develop for pushing form? Without the customary constraints of physicality, can unthinkable mechanisms of transformation be effected? Is stable form itself necessary or given or permanent? If not, then, are the space and time which host such stability a priori media, as Kant suggested, or can they be challenged as well? Will the greatest effect be restricted to cyberspace itself, or will the activities it hosts have critical applications "outside?" If the former, should architects bother? If the latter, should architects hide?

* * *

31. Certainly the demand that architecture take account of the new electronic paradigm and its poster child the computer is increasing. Architects are frantic to be cyber

---

[12] William Gibson, *Neuromancer* (New York: Ace Science Fiction Books, 1984), 5.

[13] Hubbard, *Complicity and Conviction in Architecture* (Boston: MIT Press).

cool. Part of this is due, no doubt, to fashion. The computer is hot, the nerd is in, and architects want to play. CAD is taking over even the most conservative offices, and convenience or economy are only partly responsible.[14]

MIT 3

32. Just as certainly, though, there is no corresponding demand yet from within cyberspace to consider architecture beyond its capacity as wallpaper. Certainly architecture is present there, at many levels and in many guises, but its *presence* is invisible. Certainly architecture actually pervades the hackers world the way the hackers information pervades the rest of the world, yet, like this information, it is invisible. It is in the structure and organization of both the software and the hardware, increasingly the harmless default environment organizing the "space" of the cyber world, and it still hovers over the hackers head, sheltering him and his equipment from the elements—yet it is invisible.

33. There is an affinity between the worlds of architecture and the electronic frontier far beyond the apparently *necessary*. While a relationship between them is necessary to cybernauts only to the extent the weather is kept off their machines (they care less about themselves), and to architects only to the extent that these machines and their operators can be programmed into some traditional means of accommodation, it is sufficient to set the architectural theory mills churning and be the focus of live and electronic conferences across the world.

NIRM 11

34. Architecture is uniquely situated to be affected by these current trends. The information revolution most effects us by re-framing perception, by re-ordering the values we place in our surroundings. These surroundings have traditionally been in the care of architecture. This

NIRM 3

ONHR 13

care is a model of ordering. Like the mechanical, architecture is an ur-tecture; a frame of frames, a command program or template that organizes our thinking about organization and things organized, from computer architecture to philosophy.

35. Architecture is also the medium of space, within which cyber-events are deemed to unfold both virtually and actually—and to which they must return. This may be a history- or culture-bound affinity. It may eventually be overcome as we gain more liberating experience in cyberspace. But so far it remains strong.

36. As both an ur-tecture and the medium of spatial definition—as an ideal—architecture chafes against the constraints of mundane reality. Cyberspace promises to at least loosen these constraints, if not eliminate them entirely. On the other hand, architecture offers some sense of the legitimacy of these constraints to cyberspace if and when cyberspace chooses to tap real architectural potential.

37. But perhaps the most deeply felt reason for architecture's cyber envy is that architecture is still concerned with reflecting the zeitgeist (it has never found anything else to do that did not devolve to this condition at some point), and the Information Revolution is that, with a vengeance. In a zeit whose geist is anything but clear or singular, the importance of this cyber-thing reads loud and clear.

MIT 5

WDIM 19

38. In the encounter between the electronic and the architectural, three postures have become common. Those who insist that the virtual is not real and ultimately does not really matter have rejected any relationship beyond service-as-usual. These people tend to equate

---

[14] Notebook 15a: ...there is a monstrous new thing on my desk: my mayline has been shoved up out of the way to make space for this (patricidal) intruder. My spiroll has been unhinged to allow another contraption to be bolted to the underside of the desk. My triangles and scales have been put in a box among my books on a shelf across the room, and my desk lamps have been turned up so the light shines onto the ceiling rather than down onto the borco. My tools are collecting dust, and the products of my labor no longer accumulate comfortably around me. Everything is in that box ....

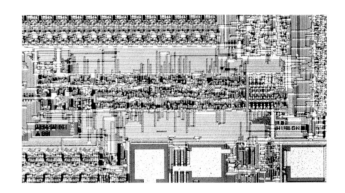

architecture with keeping the rain out. On the other hand, there are those advocating what can only be called imitation. They believe that architecture has a larger responsibility than maintaining physical comfort, and invoke architecture's responsibility to be in tune with the zeitgeist as a reason to express the Information Age: this is the future, whatever it is, and we must look like it. Finally, there is another posture that can be taken, and is probably prevalent since it is easier to sustain. This is prompted by the idea that the electronic age, the Information Revolution, simply requires an everyday, matter-of-fact support and provides everyday, matter-of-fact gods. Those who subscribe to this notion believe that, in the end, all the hype obscures the fact that this is a truly interesting program for architects to serve. There are roles architecture can play in this, and some it cannot.[15]

39. Like the field itself these positions are much more nuanced than the above suggests, however, and each has something to say that must be heard before any real rapprochement between the cyber-real and architecture can be affected. For example, the rejectionist camp points out that, so far at least, the presentation of cyberspace has depended almost completely on existing real world architectural models—often the most dated—for its best effects. They claim that this is unavoidable. Like deep space, cyberspace may not be generally conducive to life. Therefore, they argue, it has nothing to teach us that cannot be more easily divined just by looking around. They are confident that architecture, or at least building, will never be eliminated. We will always spend a lot of our money, time, effort, and space on it, so architecture will remain unavoidably important to us. It will always be the default condition for experience—particularly if that experience is otherwise only virtual.

40. The imitators agree with these points, but think that the conclusion reached by the rejecters is only reactionary hyperbole. One suspects the imitators are not as confident about meat architecture's continued importance. The imitators would extend the dialog with the electronic to the point where it swallowed them. They believe in the zeitgeist, and that buildings should look like it. This raises the interesting question of what that might be, since there is no intrinsic form to cyberspace. For the most part this work answers with something so twisted and complex only a computer could draw it. They also propose to make a place for themselves as cybertects and design virtual architecture. By these actions they seem to remind us that as a society, we seem to get no joy now from gross, physical architecture anyway; its importance, which already seems to be waning, will eventually wither away entirely and it will become a technical trade, concerned only with the satisfaction of physical needs, leaving all the emotional, spiritual, critical stuff to the more effective hyper-real manipulation of cyberspace, where the real meaning is developing today.

41. These folks would no doubt bridle at the characterization of their efforts as imitative. They hold that there are ways the affinity between the two can be enacted or respected beyond imitation or illustration—in either direction. Connections can be made at the level where architecture is understood as a general metaphor or ur-condition of organization—the *archi* level. Since cyberspace is not really space and does not supply any visual fodder, because there is properly nothing there, this is probably a more appropriate way to make connections. Its "things," as the rejectionists like to point out, have been borrowed from conventional architecture. Still, the imitators would argue, at a deeper level, where we think about how we think about stuff, connections are readily

---

[15] Architecture that attempts to engage the electronic paradigm is greatly challenged. The cybernaut spends her time in a virtual world, created anew with unreal, luminous precision thirty times per second, free from the constraints of materiality, reality and gravity. Architecture's own expressiveness pales in comparison to the hyper-active hyper-reality of cyberspace, where text, graphics, and image combine with sound and motion in a vibrant urgency of affect. But the cybernaut always returns ....

What then, is an appropriate vernacular for those returning from this visually and auditorially overwhelming otherness? Should architecture attempt to ride the electronic storm, extracting from it a corresponding level of excitement, or should it offer a specifically contrasting relief? Should architecture be continuous with cyberspace or discrete? It depends. While its *literal* continuity may not be possible, some level of meaningful reference could be expected. At the risk of mere illustration, the log-on "space" could be shown as the same sort of space as the "real" architecture, for example, or visa versa. Would this mean that the cyber is constrained to a banal normalcy, or that the architecture is jacked up to a cyber frenzy? It depends again. Either seems less than optimal. It seems best to allow reference where the familiarity of the spatial metaphor makes it appropriate, but not force that reference beyond usefulness.

A key feature that the cybernaut's world shares with real reality is *interactivity*. Cyberspace is empowering to a degree increasingly unavail-

suggested that can be meaningful.

42. Those who simply support the electronic revolution's continuing traditional architectural needs believe there are valid points to both positions. Though they may be irreconcilable with each other, they cannot be ignored; architecture, as always, must choose a middle path and inhabit the gulf between the extremes. Architecture's role as architecture instead of mere buildings is not to disappear entirely into service or facilitation of the cyber-experience. On the other hand, there is a difference between imitation or illustration and expression, and the former short-changes the important dimension of functionality. It is this functionality that grounds architecture in building and forces it to remain on this side of the screen. Indeed, it may be architecture's greatest task to emphasize or at least acknowledge the differences between cyber- and live-, so when the cybernaut pulls his head out he can remember where he is. Such a refocusing or reorienting capacity is natural for architecture. Or it may just be important to make sure that the assurances real live experience offers to life are visible and visibly inflected to the viewer, in order to remind her of life and remind her of her life—its uniqueness—and so empower her.

* * *

43. Implicit to all three camps is the continuing belief that architecture can and should recognize important changes in its context: society, culture, technology. All believe that the zeitgeist thing is still alive in some way. Architecture takes account of something by gathering it into expression. But what does *information* look like? Isn't *everything* that appears information in the new sense? How do we express it? What does the *electronic* look like? Does electro-tecture just plug in somewhere—is it different than, say, natural gas-tecture? Do we make buildings that look like computers? Do we paste computers to our facades? Is it not enough for clients to just stuff them with programs? The question of the moment is clearly: where, when, how, can architecture pro-actively get a hold of the new "reality," or will it just wake up one day to discover it has already happened to it. If the present is any indication, then the computer is represented by low rent outlet mall architecture and Victoriana: at least this is primarily what it calls home now in Silicon Valley.

44. The significant reality of the computer, and its formal possibility, is not physical: the computer itself, its hardware, has no *particular* appearance. Certainly the true essence of the computer is not to be found in the plastic box housing its "working" parts. This could be any form, its universal banality not withstanding; nor is it to be found in the mere appearance of the hardware inside that it is clothed. Despite the very impressive technological advances that have occurred in computer hardware, the reality of the computer has always been acknowledged to be something else—an idea that these advances only support.

45. The computer is important because of how it has changed the way we see and think about the world. This is what is revolutionary. This is not to suggest, however, that expression will necessarily be found in the simple fact of its processual, software-oriented nature. Only a critical understanding of the character, the structure, of that software reality, will lead to useful form.[16]

46. Computer structure is essentially tool-like; it is an interactive value-free simulator with a generative capacity. But what a tool it is: the computer not only offers us the opportunity to extend the reach of our manipulations, but to push them beyond even our ability to predict

---

able "outside." This explains some of its attraction. Yet there is no reason reality cannot "take back" this empowering ability.

An architecture that offers significant opportunities of its own for interactivity (as well as significant opportunities for a respite from its demands) would be an obvious improvement over the usual. It could host islands of localized activity in the spirit of the virtual world, for example, while it provided breathing space between, as well. An architecture that does not attempt to *compete* with the virtual world, but to *supplement* it, to host it, accepting its own role back in the physical world as a haven or launching pad for the cybernaut is not impossible to imagine. (From J,P:A's "Cyber-Architecture" brochure 1995.)

[16] But then what is so special about the methodologies and processes of this software reality of the computer? How can they be more or different than the rules we have already internalized as architects?

results. In addition, it distances us from this activity, placing us at a remove from where we may be more effective critics of its play. The computer can take us places we otherwise could not make ourselves go, and leave us free enough of emotional investment to judge the results.

47. Some of the most interesting work of the last thirty years has been produced by heuristic grammars that have automatically churned out beautiful and disturbing structures. Such work has responded honestly to the present lack of a universal or given formalism, a received standard or language that would tell the architect what to do. It recognizes that its rule-based generation makes it most accessible to others, who may use these same rules to regenerate the meaning in them. Thanks to these rules its not personal or private. Expressive of a strict rule—guided formal manipulation, the process of their generation sounds like code: full of if/then sequences, iterative loops, and go-tos, the projects visually guide you through their evolution and make an exact statement of its processual nature.

48. Ironically, at the deepest level this processual ephemera is firmly rooted in brute fact: the machine language that ultimately enables this esoterica is as blunt as a rock. This language is well-named. It is a mechanical place-holding structure: a binary distribution of possibility that can only be described as a simple statement of mechanical choice: the place is either filled or empty; the light on or off. The computer was born as a mechanical calculator, an analytical engine. The wonderfully dense and apparently continuous fabric of the computer's reality, its language structure, is ultimately founded on a discontinuous quantification, a world of discreet possibilities that are related mechanically by a single choice.[17]

* * *

49. In the end, cyberspace is never more than a storm of electrons raging across a cityscape of chips, wires, wafer boards and into glass screens, where they excite photons that strike our optic nerves and eventually end up somehow in the space between our ears.

50. There is a substantial price of complicity to be paid in sustaining the convention, the grand consensual hallucination that (still) lacks more than rudimentary visual component. Right now, surfing the net is nothing more than ham radio on steroids. My father was a ham. He used to get these postcards of contacts he had made all over the world. That world was even more restricted; it was an auditory world, circumscribed by dits and dahs, visual only in retrospect (postcards), or through the slight evidence of the rheostat. A physical skill was required that could be measured. Being a ham was a real, live experience, and the mental energy needed to make sense of the dits and dahs distracted you from noticing the absurdity of the whole thing—easily apparent to the little boy peering over your shoulder.

51. It is still all about communication, but now you do not have to concentrate as hard, and the impoverishment of the space "where" this occurs is more evident because of that. You still need the other as an object of your attention: an interlocutor to distract you from the medium and provide the unpredictability that extends it beyond your own mind. Cyberspace is not yet as complete as real space. In its own updated way, it is still as restricted as my dad's darkened auditory world of dits and dahs. Even the most advanced 64-bit, millions-of-colors game environment or virtual reality arcade is primitive compared to the dullest trip to the supermarket, in terms of total information load processed by the senses.

---

[17] The most effective of all negotiations within the spaces of the electronic paradigm work at the point where architecture strains its materiality, where it reveals it is about ideas yet at the same time demonstrates the exquisite agony of those ideas resistance to embodiment. Where that otherwise inescapable presence wears the strain as an aura of the remarkable. Such work insists on being more or other than illustrations of the commercialized understanding of what the electronic tecture might look like. The sort of significance to which architecture is accustomed will not be found in the computer's convenience, or its hardware, nor even its ubiquity or interconnectedness. The manipulations in this work are effective when they are rooted in a critique of traditional architectural thinking and space, where the electronic paradigm offers its greatest challenge, and where the desire is stoked.

```
0010100101101 0
1001110110111 0
0010010011101 0
1000001010101 0
0000001010010 0
0010101101001 0
1001001001010 1
```

52. It may seem to be stating the obvious, but in the pell-mell rush to embrace the ethereal, cyber, and electro- we should not lose sight of the fact that we must be held back by our bodies. Our minds are at least for the foreseeable future going to be slave to that meat.

53. There may be ways to create a continuum that does not cheapen or trivialize either pole. To make the shock of transition from one to the next a pleasurable one rather than a letdown. To make cyberspace as real and have as much resonance and depth as live reality, within live reality, and make live reality as free and exciting as cyberspace, that may sit in transcendent judgment.

54. By recognizing the inescapable relationship between the mechanical and the electronic, between cyberspace and the space of architecture, and forging that into a continuum, a wired world can be a step forward and "the earth can be visualized as a total interdependent living system, an emergent form of human consciousness through digital transmissions, perception extension through microscopic-teleoptic technology, computer mediated amplification and an overall collapse of space time."[18] Otherwise, if we believe we are leaving the mechanical behind in our advance into the electronic paradigm, we shall remain continuously frustrated by an inescapable conflict between where we think we are, and where nature—reality, our bodies—will allow us to be.

---

[18] Ken Rinaldo in *Wired* (June 1994): 30.

Contributing Photographers

Unless otherwise noted, all drawings and photographs from 1986-1993 by Holt Hinshaw Pfau Jones and from 1993-1998 by Jones, Partners: Architecture

Tom Bonner: pp. 21, 23, 26, 36, 88

Mark Darley/ Esto: pp. 24, 25, 30

Rose Hodges: p. 16

Erich Koyama: pp. 67, 68, 69, 72, 73, 78, 79, 82

Mark Sparrowhawk: pp. 76, 77, 83

Jeff Stager: pp. 306, 307, 310, 311, 314, 315, 316, 317, 319, 320

Doug Symes: p. 22

Josh White: p. 37, 272

Armani Exchange Proposal Additional Material

Scott Erdy: computer renderings, pp. 340, 341, 343, 344, 345, 349, 352

Ciro Nieli: figural sketches, pp. 338, 340, 342, 343, 344, 346, 347, 348

Gregor Wynnyczuk: proposal text, pp. 337, 339

Dilbert © United Feature Syndicate, reprinted by permission, p. 336

Notes